FRANZ LISZT

GARLAND COMPOSER
RESOURCE MANUALS
(VOL. 29)

GARLAND REFERENCE LIBRARY
OF THE HUMANITIES
(VOL. 754)

GARLAND COMPOSER RESOURCE MANUALS

General Editor Guy A. Marco

FRANZ LISZT
A Guide to Research

Michael Saffle

with discographical contributions by
Ben Arnold, Keith Fagan,
and Artis Wodehouse

GARLAND PUBLISHING, INC. • NEW YORK & LONDON
1991

Library of Congress Cataloging-in-Publication Data

Saffle, Michael Benton, 1946–
   Franz Liszt : a guide to research / Michael Saffle ; with
discographical contributions by Ben Arnold, Keith Fagan, and Artis
Wodehouse.
      p. cm. — (Garland composer resource manuals ; vol. 29)
(Garland reference library of the humanities ; vol. 754)
   Includes indexes.
   ISBN 0–8240–8382–2
   1. Liszt, Franz, 1811–1886—Bibliography. 2. Liszt, Franz,
1811–1886—Discography. I. Title. II. Series. III. Series.
Garland composer resource manuals ; v. 29.
ML134.L7S2 1991
016.78'092—dc20   91–11182
                                                             CIP
                                                              MN

Printed on acid-free, 250-year-life paper
Manufactured in the United States of America

for Sue, with love

GARLAND COMPOSER
RESOURCE MANUALS

In response to the growing need for bibliographic guidance to the vast literature on significant composers, Garland is publishing an extensive series of research guides. This ongoing series encompasses more than 50 composers; they represent Western musical tradition from the Renaissance to the present century.

Each research guide offers a selective, annotated list of writings, in all European languages, about one or more composers. There are also lists of works by the composers, unless these are available elsewhere. Biographical sketches and guides to library resources, organization, and specialists are presented. As appropriate to the individual composer, there are maps, photographs, or other illustrative matters, and glossaries and indexes.

CONTENTS

ILLUSTRATIONS
(following page 358)

TO READERS OF THIS RESEARCH GUIDE

Each of the annotated bibliographic citations in this volume is identified and cross-referenced by number. Thus Alan Walker's *Franz Liszt* is identified and cross-referenced as "item 1"; Peter Raabe's *Franz Liszt* is identified and cross-referenced as "item 2"; and so on. Each volume of multi-volume works is identified by number and letter. Thus *Franz Liszt: The Virtuoso Years, 1811-1847*, Volume I of Walker's study, is identified as "item 1a"; *Liszts Leben*, Volume I of Raabe's study, is identified as "item 2a"; and so on. In a few instances sections of larger works are also identified and cross-referenced separately. Thus the "Zeittafel" ("chronological table") from Raabe's *Liszts Leben* (item 2a) is identified and described separately as "item 373"; the catalog of compositions from *Liszts Schaffen*, Volume II of Raabe's study (item 2b), is identified as "item 48"; and so on. Discographical citations presented in the Appendix are identified and cross-referenced by numbers beginning with the letter "A." Thus the "Recorded Treasures" anthology of early Liszt recordings is identified as "item A101."

Throughout this guide the titles of books, periodicals, and non-generic compositions (whether or not they belong to larger works) are italicized; thus *Liszts Schaffen, Acta musicologica, Harmonies poétiques et religieuses*, and *Funérailles*. Quotation marks are used to indicate the titles of articles and informal compositional titles; thus *Etudes d'exécution transcendante*, but "Transcendental Etudes" or "Transcendentals." (Quotation marks are also used to set off foreign-language words and phrases as well as titles of phonorecords and compact disks in the Appendix.) Generic compositional titles, on the other hand, are not italicized; thus Sonata in b minor, Ballade No. 1, and so on.

Library and archival sigla follow *New Grove Dictionary* conventions. Russian transliterations follow Library of Congress conventions except that ligatures and other diacritical marks are omitted. The only abbreviations employed regularly are: "DAI" for *Dissertation Abstracts International*; "RILM" for *Répertoire International de Litterature Musicale*; and "ms." and "mss."—in lower case—for (respectively) "manuscript" and "manuscripts."

PREFACE

Four years ago, when I received an invitation from Marie Ellen Larcada to contribute a book-length Liszt bibliography to Garland's "Composers Resource Series," I accepted with alacrity. The previous summer I had completed for *Acta musicologica* a survey of Liszt studies published since 1936, and when Ms. Larcada's invitation arrived I was putting the finishing touches on a supplement to that survey dealing with 1986 'Liszt-Year' publications (both item 40).[1] Although generous to a fault, *Acta* editors Hellmut Federhofer and Lorenzo Bianconi were unable to give me enough space to deal adequately with the hundreds of Liszt publications that had appeared in the previous fifty-plus years. Writing a book about those publications, I decided, would enable me both to consolidate my previous bibliographic work and to discuss at greater length recent developments in the rapidly expanding field of Liszt studies.

Franz Liszt: A Guide to Research identifies and evaluates more than 1,200 books, monographs, articles, and sound recordings concerned with Liszt's activities and accomplishments. Insofar as possible I have refered in these pages to *every* significant Liszt study published between 1936 and late 1989. I have also described some of the most important studies published during the nineteenth and early twentieth centuries—among them, several monographs overlooked by Lajos Koch in his monumental 1936 bibliography (item 39). Finally, I have mentioned a few very recent studies as well as a few important projects still in preparation or in press. Ben Arnold, Keith Fagan, and Artis Wodehouse have been kind enough to identify and evaluate important Liszt recordings of various kinds; the choices are theirs, although I assume responsibility for the quality of their work as it appears at the end of this volume.

Yet it must be emphasized that the present guide is *not* comprehensive, even with regard to post-1936 Liszt publications. At least three categories of secondary sources have been deliberately excluded: summaries of Liszt's life and personality written from a popular perspective, publications intended exclusively or primarily for public-school and studio music teachers, and publications devoted primarily to non-Liszt topics. Thus Chapter IX ("Biographies and Character Studies") omits dozens of superficial Liszt "lives," while Chapter XX ("Pedagogy, Performance Practice, and Instruments") omits a considerable number of "classroom" and "studio" publications. Furthermore, only a handful of the pre-1936 publications identified by Koch and only a few of the Liszt-letters publications described by

---

[1] Item numbers that appear throughout this volume are explained in "To Readers of This Research Guide."

Charles Suttoni (item 41) are discussed below in any detail. A few editions of Liszt's compositions are described in Chapter V ("Musical Editions and Related Studies"); readers who wish to learn more about Liszt's published music should consult the catalogs prepared by Peter Raabe (item 48) and, more recently, by Humphrey Searle and Sharon Winklhofer (items 47, 54, and 57).[2] Ephemera like second-hand newspaper stories, advertisements for sound recordings, and so on are ignored for the most part, but a few important press clippings, book reviews, and discographies are described in Chapter IV ("Reference Works and Related Studies") and in other chapters. Finally, articles in semi-popular Czech, Polish, and Hungarian music magazines are omitted, and a number of Russian-language may have been overlooked because they were unavailable.

For the most part this guide is organized according to the general scheme adopted in item 40. Descriptions of general studies are followed by descriptions of reference works, editions, and documents of various kinds; biographical and musical studies are examined in chapters of their own. Many studies, of course, do not fit neatly into only one chapter; an article about the B-minor Sonata, for example, might also refer to Liszt's activities in Weimar during the 1850s or to the so-called "Lehman ms." held by the Pierpont Morgan Library of New York City. Such an article would be *described* in Chapter XIV ("Original Works for Piano") but *cross-referenced* in Chapter X ("Specialized Biographical Studies") or Chapter VIII ("Document and Source Studies"). Whenever possible, studies dealing with secondary topics (like these) are cross-referenced under appropriate headings. Studies devoted to single compositions or genres are described in Chapters XIV-XIX. Studies of musical processes and influences in more than one work or genre are described (respectively) in Chapters XII-XIII.

Each chapter of this guide is divided into several sections; in each section certain studies are described in greater detail than others. Reliable, detailed, and/or recent studies, for instance, are generally described ahead of unreliable, cursory, and/or outdated items and receive more attention. If a study has appeared in two or more editions, the more reliable and/or recent edition is mentioned first. If it has appeared in two or more languages, the English-language edition, most recent edition, and/or most reliable edition is cited. A few studies are identified only within annotations. Many of these are outdated, difficult to locate, or available only in languages like Czech, Slovak, Hungarian, Rumanian, or Polish; others are earlier versions or contain much of the same material as later publications; still others appeared too recently to be cited and described independently.

Generally speaking, better-researched and better-written books and articles deserve more attention than poorer ones. Exceptions exist, though, and a few inferior studies are mentioned primarily in order to describe their weaknesses. Consider Ernest Newman's *The Man Liszt* (item 376), which has adversely influenced

---

2 A comprehensive catalog of Liszt's compositions has been announced for publication by Mária Eckhardt, Direction of the Liszt Ferenc Memorial Museum and Research Centre, Budapest. See Eckhardt's report "A New Thematic Catalog of Liszt's Compositions" in the *Journal of the American Liszt Society* 27 (1990), pp. 53-57. NB: Like other recent Liszt studies, Eckhardt's appeared too late to be described independently in this guide.

generations of readers. Newman's book, like several other inferior studies, is also discussed in Chapter II ("Liszt Studies Past and Present"); so too, of course, are outstanding studies like Alan Walker's *Franz Liszt* volumes (items 1a-b).

Two special problems confront American Liszt researchers: locating Liszt studies and dealing with Eastern European Liszt publications. Many of the books and articles described in this guide are hard to find; consequently, archival sigla and shelf-numbers are provided whenever available for rare works owned by major collections like those of the Library of Congress in Washington, D.C. (US-Wc), the National Széchényi Library, Budapest (H-Bn), and the Goethe- und Schiller-Archiv, Weimar (D-WRgs). No one archive owns *every* published Liszt study, however, and even the recently established Liszt Ferenc Research Center (address: H-1064 Budapest, Vörösmarty u. 35, Hungary) has gaps in its collections. Typescript doctoral dissertations can be especially difficult to secure, and available archival information about them also appears below. It was impossible, however, to examine a few studies mentioned in important reference works or bibliographies. For these publications, only available bibliographic information is provided.

Books and articles about Liszt printed in Eastern European languages also pose special problems. Some are outdated, while others are full of Stalinist bombast. Many Hungarian-language studies published after the early 1960s are extremely important, however, even though they can be difficult to obtain. (Generally speaking, Liszt studies published in Polish, Czech, Rumanian, and other Eastern European languages are less important.) Fortunately for non-Hungarian readers, periodicals like *Studia musicologica* and the *New Hungarian Quarterly* regularly reprint in Western languages articles that appeared originally in *Magyar zene* and other "exotic" magazines. This does not mean that studies published *only* in Hungarian can be dismissed out of hand. What it does mean is that Hungarian is becoming somewhat less important to researchers interested in secondary source materials; for this reason, a few Hungarian studies have been omitted deliberately from this guide or identified only within annotations for other works. Furthermore, Hungarian-language studies translated into Western languages are identified primarily in terms of translations. It has been taken it for granted, by the way, that readers will recognize English, French, and German titles. Only studies published in other languages—Italian, Spanish, Danish, Russian, Polish, and so on—are identified by language.

§

Completing this research guide would have been difficult without the assistance of several individuals and organizations. I would like to thank Philippe Autexier, Jennifer Crewe, Mária Eckhardt, Joanne Eustis, Keith T. Johns, Dezső Legány, Johann Norstedt, Jon Polifrone, Lennart Rabes, Paul Sorrentino, Charles Suttoni, and Gerhard J. Winkler for the information they shared so generously with me. Ben Arnold, Keith Fagan, and Artis Wodehouse deserve special thanks for compiling the discographical entries that appear in the appendix.

The following libraries and archives allowed me to consult their collections of monographs and musical scores: The Library of Congress, Washington, D.C.; The New York Public Library; the libraries of the University of North Carolina,

Chapel Hill; the Music Library of the University of Virginia, Charlottesville; the British Library, London; the Bibliothèque Nationale, Paris; the libraries of the Universities of Frankfurt a.M. and Heidelberg; the Bibliothek Preußischer Kulturbesitz and the Deutsche Staatsbibliothek, both of Berlin; the Goethe- und Schiller-Archiv, Weimar; the Library of the University of Wrocław, Poland; and the National Széchényi Library and the Liszt Ferenc Memorial Museum and Research Centre, both of Budapest.

Although they did not intentionally subvent this guide, the Alexander von Humboldt-Stiftung and the Council for International Exchange of Scholars provided funding for other projects that also helped me finish this one. Virginia Polytechnic Institute and State University provided access to and funding for the use of its IBM computer facilities. Zsuzsa Domotos corrected the Hungarian-language citations in this volume, while Angelia Graf proofread the Russian-language citations and corrected the transliterations of their titles. Finally, the assistance, encouragement, and patience of Marie Ellen Larcada and the Garland Publishing staff made my task more pleasurable than I would have believed possible.

M.S.

22 October 1990

Liszt and Liszt Studies:
An Introduction

I: LISZT'S LIFE, PERSONALITY, AND WORKS

Franz Liszt was born on 22 October 1811 at Raiding, a village located today in the Austrian Burgenland. He received his first piano lessons from his father, Adam Liszt, a employee of the celebrated Eszterházy family and an amateur musician of some skill. Young Franz quickly won local fame as a budding concert artist, and in 1820 a group of Hungarian magnates offered to underwrite his future musical education. Shortly thereafter the Liszts moved to Vienna, where Franz studied piano and composition with Carl Czerny and Anton Salieri. (Liszt's earliest surviving work, a variation on Diabelli's famous waltz, dates from 1822 or 1823.) Performances in Vienna earned Liszt local fame, and even Beethoven expressed interest in his capabilities.

Seeking additional training for his son, Adam Liszt attempted to enroll him at the Paris Conservatory in 1823; young Franz was denied admission on grounds of nationality, however, and took private lessons in harmony and counterpoint from Ferdinando Paer and Anton Reicha. Just two years later the fourteen-year-old composer produced *Don Sanche*, his only opera, which was presented five times in Paris during the fall of 1825. Performances as a pianist in England and France were more successful, and by 1828 Liszt had published several piano pieces (including his first volume of keyboard etudes) and drafted at least one piano concerto. A few years later Liszt made the acquaintance of artists and intellectuals like Victor Hugo, Frédéric Chopin, Heinrich Heine, Hector Berlioz, and Felicité Lammenais. He also heard Paganini perform and—so the story goes—immediately resolved to master every aspect of keyboard technique. Six years of intense practice culminated in 1837 in a "duel" with the celebrated virtuoso Sigismund Thalberg which earned Liszt a place among the greatest performers of his age.

Liszt was almost entirely self-taught; reading stimulated him enormously, as did contacts with the literary and philosophical giants he met throughout his life. His childhood education was sacrificed to musical pursuits, but he soon discovered and devoured works by Homer, Plato, Locke, Byron, and Lamartine. Books accompanied him everywhere he went: he read assiduously during the innumerable coach and train trips he made during the 1830s and 1840s, discussed politics and philosophy with professors and princes wherever he went, and studied paintings and sculpture in major European collections. Letter-writing also occupied much of Liszt's time; he corresponded with a number of prominent public figures. His letters, most of them written in distinctive French, reveal a keen interest in the ideas and events of his time.

Sometime in the early 1830s Liszt met and fell in love with the Comtesse Marie d'Agoult, a married woman who later established a reputation for herself as an historian and novelist. In 1835 the couple fled from Paris (and the Comtesse's husband) to Switzerland, where for a while Liszt taught at the recently-established Geneva Conservatory. For several years the lovers lived comparatively secluded lives, interrupted by travels through the Alps and Italy. Liszt gave occasional concerts and devoted himself to composition. By 1838 he had published several important works, including the first version of *Harmonies poétiques et religieuses*, fantasies on themes from operas by Auber, Pacini, and Meyerbeer, and piano transcriptions of works by Rossini and Schubert. During those years the Comtesse gave birth to Liszt's only children: Blandine, Cosima, and Daniel. (Only Cosima, who became the wife first of Hans von Bülow, then of Richard Wagner, was destined to enter musical history. Blandine died in her twenties after marrying a diplomat; Daniel died in Berlin in 1859.)

Spurred by generosity and restlessness, Liszt offered in 1839 to raise money for a Beethoven memorial at Bonn. By that time his occasional appearances as a concert artist had grown into a full-fledged career. Between 1838-1847 he visited nearly every corner of Europe, dazzling audiences with his skill. His tours took him to England, Scotland, Ireland, France, Germany, the Lowlands, the Iberian peninsula and Gibralter, Denmark, Austro-Hungary, the Balkans, Russia, and even Turkey. Honors were showered upon him: he received decorations from a dozen European monarchs, the University of Königsberg made him an honorary Doctor of Music, and the citizens of Budapest presented him with a hero's sword. Meetings with artists like Schumann and Wagner stimulated his imagination, and he managed to complete dozens of new piano pieces (as well as his earliest songs and sacred compositions) and to draft his first mature works for piano and orchestra. Liszt was cut off from his family during his "years of transcendental execution," although he managed to spend three summers with the Comtesse on the island of Nonnenwerth, just south of Bonn. Unfortunately, Liszt and the Comtesse quarreled more and more frequently, and they separated permanently in 1844.

Weimar was only one of many towns Liszt visited in 1841, but he returned the following year to receive an appointment as "Kapellmeister extraordinary" to the local court. Already he had begun to tire of his nomadic activities; after meeting the Princess Caroline von Sayn-Wittgenstein during a tour of the Ukraine in 1847, he suddenly retired from the concert stage, spent some months in seclusion with her, then returned to Weimar to devote himself to composition and conducting. For more than a decade Liszt lived in a house known as the Altenburg (much of that time with the Princess); he gave recitals, taught himself orchestration, directed concerts of his own and other composers' works, and composed much of his most important piano pieces, almost all of his orchestral compositions (including twelve of his thirteen symphonic poems), and dozens of songs and choral works. He also revised a number of early keyboard pieces and completed two piano concertos he had drafted during the previous decade. Although his carefully staged and conducted productions of *Tannhäuser* and *Lohingrin* failed to impress Weimar's conservative citizens, Liszt became one of Wagner's most loyal admirers and apologists, Wagner (at least sometimes) one of Liszt's closest friends.

Weimar never entirely approved of Liszt's artistic activities or his alliance with the Sayn-Wittgenstein. As the 1850s drew to a close Liszt found himself subjected increasingly to criticism from local officials as well as the musical press. He became discouraged, and the disasterous Weimar reception of Peter Cornelius's *Barber of Baghdad* prompted him to resign his Court appointment in December 1858. Almost three years later he finally left Germany and settled in Rome. The Princess planned to join him after Pope Pius IX confirmed her petition for a divorce from her Russian husband, but Liszt did not marry her. Instead, he devoted himself to religion and composition. In 1865 he received minor orders in the Catholic church and began work on the *Missa choralis*, a liturgical composition so conservative in style it eventually won the support of the Cecilianist movement in Germany. Occasional trips outside Italy did little to interfere with his musical activities, and by the end of the 1860s he had completed his oratorio *Christus*, a second oratorio based on the life of St. Elisabeth, and the so-called "Gran" Mass (commissioned for the commemoration of the Cathedral at Esztergom in Hungary).

In 1869, Liszt accepted an invitation to return to Weimar and settle in the Hofgärtnerei, a small house on the city's outskirts. Liszt continued to pay regular visits to Rome, however; and when his appointment as a Royal Hungarian Counselor in 1871 required him to visit Budapest at least once a year, he began what he later called his "vie trifurquée" (or "three-cornered life"). Liszt had taken piano pupils as early as the 1820s, but during the 1870s and 1880s he gave more of himself to pedagogical activities. Hundreds of artists from Europe, Russia, and America flocked to study with him, first in German, then at the Academy of Music he helped establish in Budapest. And although he apparently devoted less time during his later years to composition, he nevertheless completed a number of important piano pieces, songs, and devotional works.

Old age brought Liszt increased respect from the Western musical world. He visited most of Europe's major cities to attend performances of his works, medals were cast in his honor, and in 1877 the Catholic church promoted him to the honorary rank of Canon. Liszt also kept in touch with contemporary musical affairs; Grieg showed him the score of his famous piano concerto in 1869, Borodin spent several months visiting him at Weimar during the early 1870s, and young Debussy met him and heard him play at a private recital in Rome several years later. Yet his last years were also unhappy: his children were dead or estranged from him, his health began to deteriorate, and he repeatedly fell prey to doubt and discouragement. Wagner's unexpected death in 1883 reminded him of his approaching end, and his last works include a series of dark, even morbid piano pieces written in memory of his former friend (as well as some lively keyboard transcriptions). Three years later, in 1886, he undertook a final and triumphant European tour, visiting England, Belgium, and France before arriving in July in Bayreuth to see his daughter Cosima and to attend performances of Wagner's works in the recently completed Festspielhaus. His health had been deteriorating for some time; by 30 July 1886 he had become very ill and, after a spell of delirium, he died just before midnight on the following day. The Princess Sayn-Wittgenstein, with whom he had corresponded almost to the day of his death, survived him by less than a year.

§

Liszt's personality, which fascinated his contemporaries as deeply as it does us, was an amalgam of conflicting attitudes and interests. Liszt himself once wryly claimed to be "half Franciscan and half Zigeuner" (item 186d; p. 316)—in other words, half saint and half sinner. His champions, of course, have emphasized the saintly side: his kindness, generosity, and religious devotion. Felix von Weingartner, for example, Liszt pupil and lifelong admirer of the man and his music, described his teacher in glowing terms:

> With Liszt, nobility was innate. To see him among princes was to recognize him as their king. . . . [Yet] he . . . paid no heed to caste. He could treat the simplest musician with warm cordiality, and the highest aristocrat with gentle disdain. He felt respect and veneration for any real artistic accomplishment, for the masters among his contemporaries no less than for those of the past. It seems to me superfluous today to point out again what he did for Wagner, for Berlioz, for Peter Cornelius, for Joachim Raff, and many others whom he thought deserving of his support. . . . He was an altruist of the purest water, always ready to make personal sacrifices or offer help. His innumerable benefactions, throughout his life, he tried to keep secret; it was only by accident that occasionally they came to light . . . He was the example of greatness and generosity.[1]

Other acquaintances of Liszt provided more balanced accounts of his character. Amy Fay, an American pianist who studied with Liszt at Weimar during the 1870s, wrote a series of delightful letters describing him in considerable detail:

> Liszt is the most interesting . . . man imaginable. . . . All Weimar adores him, and people say that women still go perfectly crazy over him. . . . Nothing could exceed [his] amiability, or the trouble he gave himself [with my lessons], and instead of frightening me, he inspired me. Never was there such a delightful teacher! You feel so *free* with him . . . he doesn't keep nagging at you all the time [and] he has the power of turning the best side of everyone outward, and also the most marvellous and instant apreciation of what that side is. . . . I shall miss going to him inespressibly [sic]. (Item 236; pp. 205-206, 212-213, 231, and 269.)

But Fay also commented on Liszt's occasional snobbishness, superciliousness, and capacity for calculated cruelty:

> Liszt is just like a monarch, and no one dares speak to him unless he addresses one first, which I think no fun. . . . He must be among *artists* to

---

[1] Felix von Weingartner, "Franz Liszt, as Man and Artist," *Musical Quarterly* 22 (1936), pp. 255-256. Like many Liszt reminiscences, Weingartner's was not included in Chapter VIII of this research guide.

unsheathe his sword. . . . He rarely mortifies any [of his students] by an open snub, but what is perhaps worse, he manages to let the rest of the class know what he is thinking while the poor victim remains quite in the dark about it! . . . [His expression on one occasion] reminded me of the expression of a big tabby-cat as it sits and purrs away, blinking its eyes and seemingly half asleep, when suddenly—!—! out it strikes with both its claws [sic], and woe be to whatever is within its reach! (Item 236; pp. 209, 233, 242, and 259.)

Some of Liszt's friends believed his virtues outweighted his vices. (As Alfred Brendel puts it, Liszt's vanity "was counterbalanced by his selflessness, his urge to dominate held in check by his humility" [item 281; p. 8].) Others thought less of him; they claimed he wasted his time flattering admirers and overindulged his fondness for good foods, strong liquors and cigars, attractive women, wealthy surroundings, and pride in worldly glory.

Liszt occasionally courted favors, and he often ate and drank to excess. But he also grew more honest with age, more willing to admit his limitations. In 1863, for example, he confessed to Alfred Brendel that he had struggled with himself for decades:

[In your last letter] I was especially pleased with the axiom: "the artistic temperament, when genuine, corrects itself in consequence of the change of contrasts." May it prove to be so in my case, for it is certain that few have had to labor at the tiresome business of self-correction as I have. . . . A clever man, some twenty years ago, made the not inapplicable remark to me: "You have in reality three personalities to deal with in yourself: the socialite, the virtuoso, and the thoughtful and creative composer. If you manage to control even one of them properly, you can congratulate yourself." We shall see! (Item 186b; pp. 50-51.)

But Liszt was also taken advantage of by many people, as he himself came to realize. In an undated letter to the Hungarian composer Ödön Mihalovich he wrote:

Everyone is against me. Catholics, because they find my church music profane, Protestants because to them my music is Catholic, Freemasons because they think my music too clerical; to conservatives I am a revolutionary, to the 'Futurists' an old Jacobin. As of the Italians . . . if they support Garibaldi they detest me as a hypocrite; if they are on the Vatican side, I am accused of bringing Venus's grotto into the Church. To Bayreuth I am not a composer but a publicity agent. Germans reject my music as French, the French as German, to the Austrians I write Gypsy music, to the Hungarians foreign music. And the Jews loathe me, my music and myself, for no reason at all. (Item 377; p. 92.)[2]

---

[2] Also quoted in item 21. (With regard to Liszt's observations on the Jews, see item 598.)

It may be that Liszt's conflicting interests drove him alternately toward limelight and cloister, wealth and simplicity, a worldly life and inner peace. His friends and enemies alike made use of those inconsistences, capitalizing on whatever attributes Liszt possessed and might be praised or blamed for. All this is true. Yet Liszt's generosity and capacity for work helped make him one of the most deeply loved and respected men of his age. It is especially unfortunate, therefore, that so little seems to have brought him lasting happiness. He apparently died a deeply disappointed man.

§

As an artist Liszt was undeniably prolific: he saw hundreds of compositions through press during his lifetime and left a substantial number of unfinished works behind him when he died.[3] Liszt divided his compositions between two categories: instrumental and vocal works (see items 49-50). Scholars like Peter Raabe and Humphrey Searle, on the other hand, have divided his music between "original" compositions and arrangements, paraphrases, and transcriptions of other composers' works (see items 47-48, 54, and 57). As an "original" composer (i.e., one who drew exclusively upon his own motivic and melodic materials), Liszt produced about 400 pieces of music. In addition to something like 200 works for solo piano, he completed a substantial number of sacred choral works (including several masses and two oratorios), more than 70 songs and "melodramas" for voice and piano, a smaller number of secular choral pieces, a good-sized body of orchestral works (including the *Faust* and *Dante* symphonies and thirteen symphonic poems), dozens of pieces for organ, and a half-dozen large-scale works for piano and orchestra. Liszt wrote almost no chamber music, however; he completed no concertos for instruments other than the piano, and his considerable output for two pianos, four hands was restricted almost entirely to transcriptions. As an arranger, paraphraser, and transcriber of pre-existing works (many of them his own), Liszt produced hundreds of piano and orchestral scores. Most of his arrangements and transcriptions are of the highest quality, while many of his operatic paraphrases rank among the finest works of their kind. Nor should his musical legacy be conceived of exclusively in terms of his own compositions and transcriptions. Liszt took much from the musical world around him, and he gave much back. His "original" works (as well as his paraphrases and arrangements) were influenced by the works of Beethoven, Schubert, Rossini, and other figures, and he in turn influenced the likes of Grieg, Tchaikovsky, Wagner, Debussy, Bartók, and even Schoenberg.

Liszt's piano works may be divided into several categories: 1) "abstract" works like the Sonata in b minor; 2) etudes and "technical exercises"; 3) poetic works like the pieces that make up all three volumes of the *Années de pèlerinage*;

---

3   The number of Liszt's compositions depends on whether one counts as separate works the pieces that appear in collections and revisions as separate works. Even conservative estimates run to over 750 finished, unfinished, and lost works; see item 47, which lists 769 compositions, arrangements, and transcriptions.

4) works written in familiar forms: waltzes, marches, and so on; 4) works of markedly national or regional character; and 5) the disturbing works of his last years. His first completed compositions for piano were sets of variations, some of them based on tunes by other composers. Liszt matured quickly as a composer; by 1826 he had published the first version of what eventually became the *Etudes d'exécution transcendante* (or "Transcendental Etudes"), and during the 1830s he wrote pieces like *Lyon* (inspired by a rebellion of garment works in that city) and drafted his E-flat Major Concerto. Only after the 1840s, however, did he compose or publish most of the keyboard works familiar to audiences today: the Sonata in b minor, the final version of the "Transcendental Etudes," the two "St. Francis Legends," and an assortment of waltzes, ballades, marches, and "national" works—including the famous "Hungarian Rhapsodies." Finally, during the late 1870s and 1880s he experimented with unusual harmonies and textures in works like *Am Grabe Richard Wagners* and the *Bagatelle sans tonalité*. In addition to piano pieces, Liszt also finished several major organ works. Among his masterpieces for that instrument are the *Praeludium und Fuge über BACH* (also known as the "BACH" Prelude and Fugue), the Fantasy and Fugue on "Ad nos, ad salutarem undam," a tune used by Meyerbeer in his opera *Le prophète*, and two masses arranged for organ from his own vocal works.

Liszt's orchestral compositions are not numerous, but most of them are quite substantial. In addition to the symphonies and symphonic poems mentioned above, he completed two "scenes" from Lenau's *Faust*, the *Trois odes funèbres*, and several orchestral marches. Works scored by Liszt for piano and orchestra include two concertos, the *Totentanz*, a fantasy on themes from Beethoven's *Ruin of Athens*, and several other large-scale works. Liszt also prepared orchestral transcriptions of many of his own compositions, as well as of pieces by Cornelius, Schubert, and Weber (some with solo voice or piano). Except for a "Duo" sonata for violin and piano, however, virtually all of his chamber works are arrangements for string instruments or strings and piano of his own music.

Between the late 1830s and the early 1880s Liszt composed a substantial number of solo vocal works. This body of music includes two, three, and even four versions of songs like *Die Lorelei, Du bist wie eine Blume, Der König in Thule, Es muß ein Wunderbares sein*, and so on. He also set a number of French poems to music, including Victor Hugo's *Enfant, si j'étais roi*. Among his Italian songs are settings of three sonnets by Petrarch (also arranged for solo piano), and he set a few Hungarian, Russian, and English verses to music. Many of Liszt's songs are short, but a few are almost operatic in length and scope; *Jeanne d'arc au bucher*, for example, was arranged by the composer for soprano and large orchestra. *Der traurige Mönch*, one of his finest "melodramas," calls for a highly skilled narrator and lasts almost a quarter of an hour.

Liszt is often thought of principally as a keyboard and orchestral composer, but he wrote more choral than orchestral music. In addition to the oratorios mentioned above, he completed a festival mass in honor of the coronation of Franz Joseph I as King of Hungary. Works like the *Missa choralis* were subdued; others—like the published portions of his unfinished oratorio *St. Stanislaus*—were grandiose. His smaller choral pieces include several settings of such traditional texts as the *Te Deum, Ave Maria*, and *Ave maris stellae*. Most of these shorter works are musically conservative, but a few pieces—especially the *Via crucis* ("Stations of the Cross")—are filled with dissonant harmonies and quotations from a variety of sources, including Protestant hymn tunes.

Liszt's transcriptions—together with an enormous body of paraphrases, "reminiscences," and "partitions de piano" (or "piano scores"), all of them adapted more or less directly from the operatic and symphonic literature of his day—comprise hundreds of titles, about half his total output. A large number of these pieces are straightforward arrangements of his own and other composer's works; among the most successful of these are keyboard versions of all nine Beethoven symphonies, large portions of Wagner's operas and music-dramas, fifty of Schubert's finest songs, and so on. Especially faithful to their source are piano adaptations of organ preludes and fugues by J. S. Bach. Other pieces are fantasies rather than copies. Among these works are paraphrases of classical masterpieces like Mozart's *Don Giovanni* as well as Romantic operas by Verdi, Bellini, and Donizetti. Liszt arranged many of his fantasies and transcriptions for two piano, four hands, and he also arranged for solo piano ensemble pieces like the *Totentanz*.

Liszt was an author as well as a composer. Unfortunately, it is difficult to determine with precision what he himself wrote and what was written in whole or part by his associates, among them the Comtesse d'Agoult and the Princess Sayn-Wittgenstein. Evidence shows that Liszt's book-length testimonial to Chopin and his study of Hungarian Gypsy music were tampered with (or, perhaps, improved by) the Princess. Other works may be more his own; among these, the series of articles entitled *De la situation des artistes* and some of the concert reviews and "dramatic essays" published under his name deserve to be consulted more often. Nor should his voluminous correspondence be forgotten. Many of his 6,000-odd published letters make fascinating reading. They contribute substantially to our understanding of nineteenth-century musical life as well as to our knowledge of their author's activities and attitudes.

II: LISZT STUDIES PAST AND PRESENT

Two decades ago Alan Walker stated that, "Of all the great nineteenth-century composers, Liszt alone still remains to be fully explored" (item 31; p. xiii). A flood of books and articles has appeared since Walker wrote those words, but his statement still rings true. Liszt remains an enigmatic figure, more written about (and against) than understood. Today, of course, we understand him better than we once did. But much remains to be learned. The following survey of published Liszt literature describes some of the research already in print and points out directions researchers may wish to explore in the future.

§

The evolution of Liszt studies since the middle of the nineteenth century resembles the evolution of many other humanistic specialties during the same period. Like them, Liszt studies has gradually become both more comprehensive and more detailed. But Liszt studies has also evolved in its own way. A plethora of nineteenth-century publications had the effect of bringing research almost to a halt during the fifty years separating 1886 (the year of Liszt's death) and the 1930s. The so-called "Liszt legend"—the assumption that Liszt was a kind of musical saint—also stayed the hands of debunking biographers during those years, then drove some of them to attack their subject with more enthusiasm than common sense. Only since 1961 (the 150th anniversary of Liszt's birth), and especially since the mid-1970s, has Liszt studies won recognition throughout Europe and the United States as a field for reputable musicological investigation.

Documents associated with Liszt's family and childhood have been traced as far back as the seventeenth century (see items 385-386), and during the 1820s journalists occasionally reviewed Liszt's early public performances in Vienna and Paris (see items 1a, 199, 228, 271, 281, etc.). In 1829 the first true Liszt "study" appeared: an entry about Liszt in an encyclopedia devoted to famous Hungarians.[1] By the mid-1830s the European press reported the activities of Liszt the virtuoso and man-about-Europe with some regularity. The *Revue et gazette musicale de Paris*, for example, ran notices of Liszt's travels and activities, invited him to join its editorial board, and published his first forays into musical journalism (items 165b, 169-170, and 172-173). In the 1840s Liszt was the subject

---

[1] *Gemälde von Ungern* [sic], ed. Johann v. Csaplovics ("Erster Theil"; Pesth: Hartleben, 1829, pp. 264-265). Like other early Liszt studies—but by no means all of them—this one is identified in item 39.

of three full-fledged monographs: Christern's biography (item 365), Rellstab's account of Liszt's career and Berlin concerts of 1842 (item 366), and Schilling's biographical and musical essay (item 367). By 1847, when he left the concert stage, Liszt had already become a legend. Of course, a few of the stories even then in circulation about him were not entirely true. Consider the "Weihekuss" (or "kiss of consecration") Beethoven was supposed to have given the young prodigy at the conclusion of his 13 April 1823 concert in Vienna (and discussed at some length below). Joseph d'Ortigue told this tale in 1835 (in item 369), and it spread quickly across France and Germany (in item 396). Accounts of Liszt's largess also became legendary; these, however, were based more firmly on fact. Some of these accounts were reported in biographies and critical studies of the period; others, however, remained obscure until quite recently, when "Zeitungsforschung" (or "newspaper research") began to bring to light thousands of Liszt documents printed during the 1830s, 1840s, and 1850s. (See items 269-274, where some of these documents are reprinted and described.)

It was only during the last of these decades—the so-called "Weimar years"—that Liszt's compositions began to attract the attention of Europe's most influential critics. Richard Wanger, for example, took up his pen to praise his friend's first half-dozen symphonic poems (item 889), and Richard Pohl published a series of articles about the *Faust* and *Dante* symphonies, the symphonic poems, and some of the choral works (reprinted in item 227). Other journalists attacked the "New German School" (closely closely associated with Liszt and his Weimar circle) and ridiculed the so-called "Music of the Future." Eduard Hanslick, whose denunciations of musical programmism were disseminated in newspaper notices and reviews as well as *Vom musikalisch-Schönen*,[2] did much to transform Vienna into a bastion of anti-Liszt sentiment. Yet even in Vienna a few critics rushed to Liszt's defense; Leopold Zellner, for instance, published the first extended study of the "Gran" Mass, one of Liszt's most important sacred works (item 974).[3] We know almost nothing about how Liszt responded to criticism during the 1830s and 1840s, decades when virtually everything published about him was either complimentary or inconsequential. But he confessed on several occasions that encouragement from the likes of Wagner, Pohl, and Zellner did not fend off the attacks launched against him throughout Central Europe.[4] Meanwhile Liszt's reputation

---

[2] Recently republished into English as: Eduard Hanslick, *On the Musically Beautiful*, trans. Geoffrey Payzant (Indianapolis, Indiana: Hackett, 1986). It should be pointed out that Hanslick disliked Liszt's music but not Liszt himself, and he praised Liszt's keyboard performances.

[3] Like so much nineteenth-century periodical material, Zellner's publications have virtually disappeared from view. Yet they are important and extensive. Consider *Zellner's Blätter für Musik, Theater und Kunst* which, between 1855 and 1859, printed accounts of Liszt matinées at the Weimar Altenburg, articles about Liszt in Hungary and Czechoslovakia (some of them reprinted from *Pester Lloyd*, a German-language "Hungarian" newspaper), an article about Liszt's vocal music as a whole, and so on. The *Blätter* also ran the whole of Zellner's "Gran" Mass book.

[4] See Keith Johns, "Liszt at the Gewandhaus: A Study of Documents for the 26 February

as a pianist continued to grow, influencing virtually everything written about him during his lifetime (a phenomenon also discussed below).

After he "retired" from Weimar in 1858, Liszt for a time led a more secluded life. As a consequence, comparatively few important or influential accounts of him and his works appeared in print during those years—even during the mid-1870s, when he did so much for public musical life in Hungary (see items 479-480). Then Liszt was approached by Lina Ramann, a young author who offered to write a "definitive" account of his life and labors. The first volume of Ramann's *Franz Liszt als Künstler und Mensch* (item 3a) was published in 1880, six years before Liszt's death; corrections for some of its contents were supplied by Liszt himself (see item 226; pp. 385ff.). Shortly thereafter Marie Lipsius, who wrote under the pen name "La Mara," began preparing for press the first volumes of Liszt's collected correspondence (item 186) and literary works (item 165), albeit with the help of the Princess Sayn-Wittgenstein. La Mara and the Princess did their best in these publications to present flattering documentary portraits of their subject; it was their collaborations (and Ramann's biography) that finally consolidated the "Liszt legend."[5] Venerated until the day of his death as a "Grand Old Man" of music (if not of musical creativity), Liszt also received posthumous praise for his keyboard virtuosity as well as his support of artists everywhere. Several decades passed, however, before biographers like Julius Kapp (item 352) began to do more than rephrase Ramann's and La Mara's assessments of their hero's activities and artistic accomplishments.

During the fifty years that separated Liszt's demise from the early 1930s, little research about him appeared in print. Jean Chantavoine, one of the first important Liszt scholars, rediscovered the score of Liszt's opera *Don Sanche* (item 943), lost for decades in the archives of the Paris Opéra. August Stradal published articles about individual keyboard and orchestral compositions (items 768, 906, and so on), and Alfred Heuß did the same thing for some of the same pieces (e.g., item 897). In 1916 Peter Raabe, then a doctoral candidate at the University of Jena, completed the first serious study of Liszt's stylistic development (item 295); his researches led to his appointment as curator of the so-called "Liszt Museum" in Weimar (taken over after World War II by the Nationale Forschungs- und Gedenkstätten der Klassischen Deutschen Literatur). The 1920s also witnessed the publication of a few valuable monographs, among them Andor Sommsich's Hungarian-language biography (item 363).

Then, in the early 1930s, two bombshells burst over the heads of Liszt researchers. One of the explosions was set off by expatriate musicologist Emile Haraszti, who undertook systematic examination of documents associated with Liszt's early life in Paris. Haraszti's work laid the foundations for more reliable accounts of Liszt's youthful activities and attitudes (see item 254), but it also pro-

---

1857 Concert," *Journal of the American Liszt Society* 27 (1990), pp. 38-47. The second part of this article will appear in Volume 29 of the same periodical. (With regard to Liszt's feelings about his critics, see his letter to Ödön Mihalovich quoted on p. 9 of the present guide.)

5 Ramann has often been blamed for disseminating the "legend," but scholars have begun to exonerate her. See item 1a; p. 7, and item 277.

vided evidence upon which he erected a scaffolding of oversimplifications concerning Liszt's character and literary activities. Because Haraszti learned, for example, that Liszt had been assisted by the Comtesse d'Agoult in writing portions of the *Lettres d'un bachelier ès musique*, he concluded that none of Liszt's literary efforts could be genuine (see items 177-178). (Haraszti's statement that no holographs survive of Liszt's books and articles has been overturned by other researchers, among them Charles Suttoni and Mária Eckhardt. See item 170; pp. 238-245, and item 180.)

The other explosion was ignited by Wagner expert Ernest Newman, who announced—based on documentary research as well as exaggeration and distortion—that "the Master" was anything but saintly. Instead, Newman argued that Liszt had been "divided against himself," a disturbed personality whose pretentions to artistic greatness stopped just short of fraud (item 376). Newman's claims have been attacked time and again, but they continue to surface in popular biographies as well as scholarly debates. More damaging to Liszt studies as a discipline, though, was Newman's reliance on carefully selected, occasionally bowdlerized letters, reminiscences, and "eyewitness" accounts of his subject's activities and character. By implication, Newman (and many of his followers) repudiated an enormous body of more objective documentation: contemporary press clippings, for instance, or mss. of musical and literary materials. The appearance in 1931 of Raabe's much more accurate (if somewhat dry) two-volume survey of Liszt's life and music (item 2) did little to offset Haraszti's and Newman's more radical conclusions. The rise of Fascism in Europe during the later 1930s and the subsequent devastation caused by World War II also prevented for more than a decade any additional extensive Liszt researches.

After 1945 Liszt studies slowly began to recover strength. Hungarian scholars, for example, unearthed and published during the 1950s a number of Liszt's late piano pieces (see items 831, 837, and 841-842). Several of these works, reprinted in England by the British Liszt Society (in items 145a-b), inspired a view of Liszt as a precursor of musical modernism, especially of harmonic innovations and even atonality. Humphrey Searle popularized this view in several articles (items 748-749) as well as *The Music of Liszt* (item 602), the first full-length assessment of his subject's musical output and significance. Carl Dahlhaus also contributed to this theory in several influential publications (e.g., items 751, 867, 896, etc.). Of course, not every Liszt study written during these decades was equally important: more than a few books and articles by Eastern European specialists—among them Bence Szabolcsi's *Twilight of Franz Liszt* (item 17)—were tinged with Marxist-Leninist dogma. Despite censorship, however, Hungarian scholars continued to break ground. By 1960 plans had been formulated for a new complete edition of Liszt's music (item 137), and *Studia musicologica* devoted half of its 1963 issue to studies presented two years before in Budapest at a joint Liszt-Bartók conference (see items 64, 299, 336, and so on).

By the mid-1960s what German musicologist Andreas Holzschneider has called the "Liszt renaissance" of the post-war years was well underway (see item 122). Suddenly Liszt began to interest a generation of performers and scholars also involved with Mahler, Bruckner, and "authentic" Baroque music. Dozens of Liszt articles appeared in European magazines, and doctoral candidates in musicology—first in the United States, then in France, Germany, and Great Britain—began to choose Liszt dissertation topics with increasing frequency. The finest studies to appear during these years, especially since the mid-1970s, include Sharon Winklhofer's reevaluations of the B-minor Sonata (items 293-294). The 1970s also witnessed the birth of three Liszt periodicals: *Liszt saeculum* (which grew in the early 1970s out of the International Liszt Center newsletter edited by Lennart Rabes), the *Liszt Society Journal* (founded in London in 1975 and edited by Adrian Williams and Derek Watson), and the *Journal of the American Liszt Society* (established by Maurice Hinson in 1977 and edited since 1987 by Michael Saffle). Finally, three volumes of *Liszt-Studien* appeared in Austria and Germany during the 1970s and 1980s, edited (respectively) by Wolfgang Suppan and Serge Gut.

Liszt enthusiasm culminated in 1986, the centenary of Liszt's death, in a host of publications and presentations. Entire conferences were devoted to Liszt's life and output (see item 108), museums held Liszt exhibitions and printed catalogs of Lisztiana (items 83, 88-89, 91, etc.), and the groundwork was laid for the publication of a new and definitive catalog of his compositions,[6] a new edition of his literary works (item 166), and a new edition of his letters (announced in item 218). The last of these projects has already been abandoned, but the rest—when finished—will help researchers of the future find and interpret materials still unavailable to much of the Western musical community. Issues associated with musical form and expression have also begun to fascinate Liszt specialists. Richard Kaplan, for example, has pointed out characteristic aspects of sonata form in Liszt works once considered "formless" musical tales (see item 643), and Allan Forte has identified harmonic patterns of considerable experimental ingenuity (see item 747). Programmism itself has also begun to receive attention: Keith Johns, for instance, has suggested that Liszt's symphonic poems can be understood semiotically (see item 885), while Márta Grabócz has written related things about a number of the Master's mature piano pieces (see items 664-666).

§

Researchers continue to grapple with new Liszt discoveries. But these are not the only challenges they face. Old ideas die hard: the legends fostered by late nineteenth-century biographers and scholars were followed by the debunking exaggerations and distortions of Haraszti, Newman, and their ilk. Nationalism too—be it French, German, or Hungarian—has often infiltrated assessments of Liszt and his art. With notable exceptions, Liszt scholarship (at least until recently) has been more prolific than productive of lasting insights and discoveries. If it is to continue to build upon its successes, Liszt studies must also discredit the myths it once helped establish.

The first obstacle Liszt researchers face has already been mentioned: the sheer quantity and complexity of the surviving documentary legacy. Well-known documents require reinterpretation; new artifacts continue to come to light. The

---

[6] See the report by Mária Eckhardt mentioned in the "Preface" to this research guide.

"Weihekuss" story is a case in point. Scholars have been aware for decades that Beethoven knew something of the boy Liszt and the concert he presented on 13 April 1823 in Vienna; they have also been aware that early accounts of Liszt's career claim the young prodigy received the "kiss of consecration" at the conclusion of that concert—indeed, that Liszt himself mentioned a kiss in a letter he addressed in 1875 to Ilka Horowitz-Barnay.[7] Alan Walker tackled the "Weihekuss" legend scientifically (in item 1a; pp. 80-85), pointing out that Liszt may well have received a kiss from Beethoven in private, but that the older musician did not even attend the younger's performance. In an unfortunate review of Walker's work (item 130), Allan Keiler challenged the accuracy of some of Walker's statements without, however, contributing any new evidence of his own (see item 131).

Walker consulted many sources before arriving at his conclusions, but he overlooked important contemporary newspaper evidence that verified his conclusions: a review of the 13 April 1823 concert published originally in *Der Sammler* (and reprinted in item 40 [1986]; p. 279). Keiler made considerable noise about Walker's "failures," but he too overlooked the *Sammler* article. These authors turned primarily and as a matter of course to Liszt's letters to verify at least some of their statements. Letters, of course, contain valuable information about Liszt's activities and attitudes. Like other autobiographical documents, however, letters cannot always be trusted, even when their texts have been established (as far too many Liszt-letter texts have not!). Newspaper and magazine stories also suffer from limitations: perfunctoriness, bias, and (sometimes) outright dishonesty. Nevertheless, newspapers and magazines sometimes contain information unavailable in other primary sources. Written soon after the events they describe and by (presumably) impartial observers, periodical publications are frequently more accurate than reminiscences, more detailed than diary entries, more objective than much correspondence. As Alan Lee has observed, "The press in the nineteenth century was the most important single medium of the communication of ideas."[8]

Incidents like the "Weihekuss" story can be understood more fully only when new evidence (including newspaper evidence) is brought to light. The distortions of the "Liszt legend," on the other hand, requires that familiar but mutilated documents be restored to their original condition. La Mara and Ramann may have been well-intentioned, but their versions of Liszt's affairs required suppression, rearrangement, and even falsification of the facts in hand. The failings of La Mara's letters editions (items 186, 191, 197, etc.), for example, have never been fully rectified (see item 220); nor have those of other Liszt-letters editors (e.g., items 202-203). Plans for a new collected edition of Liszt's correspondence (see item 218) have been rejected by many of the foremost scholars in the field; in any event, such plans—calling for the publication of *every* surviving letter in strict chronological order, together with *every* textual variant and imaginable annotation—would have been virtually impossible to carry out. The "New Liszt Edition" of musical works (item 137), on the other hand, is well underway. Yet here too problems exist. None

---

[7] Reprinted in Theodor von Frimmel, *Beethoven Studien II: Bausteine zu einer Lebensgeschichte des Meisters* (Munich and Leipzig 1906), pp. 103-104.

[8] Alan Lee, *The Origins of the Popular Press, 1855-1914* (London 1976), p. 18.

of the "NLE" volumes issued to date exhibits the textual accuracy of other "Gesamtausgaben"; there are no "Forschungsberichte" (or "research reports") dealing with variant passages and editions, problems of interpretation, and the like; and early or "alternate" versions of important works have been deliberately excluded in favor of "definitive" versions (decisions argued over hotly in items 155-161). Only the new collected edition of Liszt's literary endeavors (item 166) promises scrupulous textual accuracy and suitable scholarly apparatus. Isolated but equally admirable studies—Ernst Burger's handsome iconography (item 281), for instance, or a number of dissertations devoted to individual musical documents and stylistic issues (items 315, 603, 607, and so on)—have also taught us a great deal about Liszt and his artistic legacy.

Haraszti, Newman, and other "debunkers" were successful in promulgating bizarre notions of Liszt's shortcomings because so much conflicting evidence had not yet been unearthed or was available only in mutilated editions. Advocates of musical nationalism have also failed for the most part to take into account the evidence at hand. Liszt's "world" encompassed rural Austro-Hungary in the years before the Congress of Vienna, the Paris of Victor Hugo, the London of Bernard Shaw, and the Budapest of October 1849 (engaged in a revolution which Liszt witnessed only from a distance) *and* of June 1867 (when Franz Joseph I was crowned king, an event for which Liszt provided the music). Some experts have rejected much of this "world." Thus Liszt's relationship with Hungary, which he himself repeatedly avowed and to which country he devoted so much service for so little recognition, has been played down even by Serge Gut (in item 18). Others have concerned themselves with certain national issues, setting others aside: consider Eleanor Perényi's marvellous account of the young Liszt as French Romantic hero (item 350), or Dezső Legány's two-volume chronicle of Liszt's Hungarian sojourns. (It could be argued that these authors' special concerns prevented them from exploring a broader range of events and evidence. But specialized studies are often more useful and reliable than general ones; compare Legány's painstaking researches, for instance, with Derek Watson's admirable but necessarily abbreviated summary of Liszt's entire life and output [item 21].) Finally, at the fringes of nationalist scholarship are those "research works" colored by invidious political and social doctrines: Nazi-inspired descriptions of a "German" Liszt (items 476-477), or Marxist-Leninist hymns of praise for a Liszt who anticipated so many aspects of the post-1845 "friendship" between Warsaw Pact countries and the Soviet Union. Yet Liszt *was* influenced by Germany and Russia; these cultures are responsible for his settings of Goethe's "Flohlied" and his transcriptions of Glinka and Cui. Who else could have confused Gypsy tunes with authentic folksongs, then arranged those tunes so magnificently, outfitting them with chord progressions that recall Berlioz and piano passagework similar to—if not necessarily derived from—Thalberg and Chopin? Alfred Brendel put it well: "Instead of 'specializing in himself,' Liszt presents [in his music] a panorama of style" (item 281; p. 8).

Finally, Liszt's contribution to the Western musical tradition continues to be debated by various factions. The day is almost past when his works can be dismissed out of hand as vulgar or worthless, yet issues of value remain to be resolved. Charles Rosen has written that "Good taste is a barrier to an understanding and appreciation of the nineteenth century," and that "only a view of Liszt that places the Second Hungarian Rhapsody in the center of his work will do him justice" (item 29). Here Rosen, who is right about so many things, begs the question by suggesting (rather than demonstrating) that the "Hungarian Rhapsodies" are negligible. A similar position has also been adopted by far less imaginative critics. As a pianist, these individuals maintain, Liszt was unsurpassed; as a composer, he never (or rarely) got his musical balloons off the ground. The notion here is that no one can be a great performer *and* a great composer (although Bach, Mozart, Beethoven, Brahms, Mahler, Rachmaninoff, Bartók, and a host of other musicians were precisely that). This assumption may have arisen because Liszt's works were judged originally in terms of Classical works rather than on their own terms; the compositions of Mozart and Beethoven are, after all, quite different in intention from Liszt's and written for a different kind of audience. As a performer, on the other hand, Liszt was evaluated at once in terms of his own accomplishments; indeed, he set standards that persist to the present day.[9]

Envy also enters into many observations about Liszt—just as, to quote Alfred Brendel at some length (item 281; pp. 7-8), it has entered into observations about Haydn:

> Liszt's early European success as virtuoso and improviser equalled that of Mozart; a few years later, his "genius of expression" (Schumann) and boundless pianistic skill made him, as a player, superior even to Chopin, Mendelssohn, or Clara Schumann. The combination of a lively mind, personal magnetism, masculine beauty, the social triumphs enjoyed by a privileged parvenu, and a love life bordering on scandal turned out to be, within one human being, barely forgivable. There was a conspicuous absence of mitigating circumstances such as Mozart's or Schubert's early death, Mozart's alleged impoverishment and unmarked "pauper's grave," Schubert's syphilis, Beethoven's deafness, Chopin's consumption, or Schumann's mental disorder—features that make the fame of a genius a great deal more gratifying, and guarantee its solidity. . . .
>
> Arguably, Liszt and Haydn are the most frequently misunderstood among major composers; their biographers afford little food for pity. . . . In old age, Haydn reigned over the musical world as its undisputed leading light. For this, the nineteenth century punished him—as it punished Liszt for his undisputed supremacy as a performer. . . . Not until our century did a greater number of composers—from Richard Strauss, Ravel, and Busoni to Schoenberg, Bartók, and Boulez—appreciate Liszt by taking him seriously.[10]

---

9   See Michael Saffle, "Liszt's Reputation: The Role of 'Rezeptionsästhetik'," *Atti del XIV congresso della Società Internationale de Musicologica,* ed. Lorenzo Bianconi et al. (Bologna 1990), Volume 3 ["Free Papers"], pp. 805-810.

10   Similar remarks about Liszt and the influence of his fame as a performer on his reputation as a composer appear in items 113-114. See also item 115, where ·Brendel's remarks—quoted in this chapter and Chapter I—appeared in print for the first time.

Idolized during his lifetime as a pianist even as he was damned as a composer (or at least damned with faint praise), then ignored by scholars for decades after his death, Liszt is at long last coming into his own. The considered judgment of the late twentieth-century musical establishment is that Liszt was not the least important of the great Romantic composers; that his works built upon the accomplishments of earlier masters and inspired those of masters to come; and that his long, uneven, and multifaceted life deserves reexamination if only for the conflicting attitudes and accomplishments it represents. As Aaron Copland has remarked, we are overdue in showing generosity to Liszt and his legacy:

> The world has had greater composers than this man, but the fact remains that we do him and ourselves a grave injustice in ignoring the scope of his work and the profound influence it has exerted on the contemporary musical scene.[11]

---

[11] Aaron Copland, "Liszt as Pioneer," *Copland on Music* (New York: W. W. Norton, 1963), pp. 124-125.

An Annotated Bibliography
of Liszt Studies

III: COMPREHENSIVE SURVEY STUDIES

Only a handful of scholars have attempted to evaluate all—or even a significant part—of the colossal phenomenon that was Liszt. Throughout this volume the term "survey studies" is used to refer to studies of Liszt's life and of his music-making. Most of the surveys discussed in this chapter are "comprehensive," devoted to all Liszt's activities and works. A few articles and anthologies dealing with both biographical and musical topics are also discussed below.

A small number of "borderline" studies devoted primarily (but not entirely) to Liszt's compositions are discussed in Chapter IX. Survey studies of Liszt's private and professional activities within one geographical area (e.g., Hungary) or related to one central organization or theme (e.g., Roman Catholicism) are discussed in relevant sections of Chapter X and cross-referenced below.

BOOKS AND MONOGRAPHS

Although incomplete, the finest survey of Liszt's life and works undertaken to date is:

1. Walker, Alan. *Franz Liszt*. 2 volumes. New York and London: Macmillan, 1983-1989. (Volume 3 in preparation.)
    ML410.L7W27
    1a. Volume 1: *The Virtuoso Years, 1811-1847.*
    1b. Volume 2: *The Weimar Years, 1848-1861.*
    Engagingly written and unusually detailed. Volume 1 (item 1a) deals with Liszt's family, childhood, youth, and "years of transcendental execution" (i.e., 1838-1847) as well as with the artist's earliest compositions. Illustrated with portraits, facsimile reproductions of documents, several maps, chronological tables, and scattered musical examples. Concludes with a valuable although eccentrically organized "bibliography" (actually a list of source materials) and an appendix devoted to Liszt's own summary of his concert repertory and preserved in D-WRgs Liszt ms. Z15. Volume 2 discusses in detail Liszt's life and compositions of the 1850s as well as new documentary evidence concerning his projected marriage with the Princess Carolyne zu Sayn-Wittgenstein (see item 547). Throughout these volumes Walker purports to take "nothing on trust as far as Liszt is concerned."

Widely praised, the original edition of item 1a won two international prizes for biography as well as criticism concerning errors of fact, narrative tone, and lack of musical analysis (see items 29 and 130-133). A worthwhile review by Rey M. Longyear of item 1b appeared in the *Journal of the American Liszt Society* 26 (1989), pp. 67-72.

A revised edition of item 1a was issued in 1987 in paperback by Cornell University Press. NB: Most published reviews of Walker's work, even those which appeared as late as 1988 (e.g., item 132), refer only to the original edition. Editions in Hungarian and other languages of both the 1983 and 1987 editions of item 1a have already been published or will appear in print in the near future. Part of item 1a dealing with Liszt's family appears in German translation as item 588. Also discussed in Chapter II (above).

NB: Whenever practical, Walker's volumes are cross-referenced throughout the present research guide.

The two finest completed *Liszt survey studies remain:*

2.   Raabe, Peter. *Franz Liszt*, rev. Felix Raabe; 2 volumes. Tutzing: Hans Schneider, 1968.
        ML410.L7R34 1968
            2a. Volume 1: *Liszts Leben.*
            2b. Volume 2: *Liszts Schaffen.*
Originally published in 1931 as a summary of its author's researches as curator of the so-called "Liszt-Museum" in Weimar. Careful and generally accurate in his correction of mistakes found in Ramann (item 3 below), Raabe is nevertheless somewhat cursory and occasionally dry. *Liszts Leben* (item 2a) concludes with a detailed chronological table of Liszt's personal life and professional career (discussed separately as item 373). *Liszts Schaffen* (item 2b) contains one of the finest catalogs of Liszt's compositions in print (discussed separately as item 48). Both volumes contain facsimile reproductions of holograph scores (e.g., the famous "Revolutionary Symphony" sketch), but few other musical examples. Volume 2 concludes with indexes and a bibliography heavily weighted in favor of German-language source materials. Raabe's *Wege zu Liszt*, an abridged version of this study, is described below as item 357.

NB: The 1968 edition of Raabe's unabridged two-volume study contains emendations prepared by the author's son Felix Raabe and printed as "supplements" to each volume. Although useful, the younger Raabe's statements are not always reliable.

3.   Ramann, Lina. *Franz Liszt als Künstler und Mensch.* 3 volumes. Leipzig:
        Breitkopf & Härtel, 1880-1894.
            ML410.L7R2
            3a. Volume 1: *Die Jahre 1811-1840.*
            3b. Volume 2: *Virtuosenperiode. Die Jahre 1839/40-1847.*
            3c. Volume 3: *Sammlung und Arbeit. Weimar und Rom. Die
                Jahre 1848-1886.*
        The "authorized" Liszt biography-*cum*-musical study, begun under
Liszt's supervision but completed after his death. An uneven work, full of
exaggerations and distortions probably introduced both by Ramann herself
and by the Princess Sayn-Wittgenstein. Despite its flaws, however,
Ramann's work contains information unavailable in other studies and reflects strongly the adoration accorded Liszt by his admirers during and after his lifetime. Ramann has recently been defended for her real virtues (see
items 41 and 277). Copiously illustrated with musical examples and quotations from sources of various kinds, including press notices of selected
Liszt concerts and the texts of Liszt letters. See also item 4 (below) and
Chapter II.

An English-language translation of part of this last work appeared as:

4.   Ramann, Lina. *Franz Liszt, Artist and Man: 1811-1840,* trans. E.
        Cowdery. 2 volumes. London: W. H. Allen, 1882. xxvi, 413pp.; and
        400pp. (often bound together).
            ML410.L7R22
        An uneven translation of item 3a (above). A catalog of Liszt's com-
positions to 1840 appears at the beginning of the first volume. Although
advertised, translations by Cowdery of Ramann's other volumes never
appeared in print.

The most important Russian-language summary of Liszt's life and works is:

5.   Mil'shtein, Yakov I[saakovich]. *F. List,* rev. ed.; 2 volumes. Moscow:
        "Muzyka," 1971.
            ML410.L7M5 1971   USSR 71-VKP
        A generally conservative survey study, copiously illustrated with musi-
cal examples. As one might expect, Mil'shtein provides a great deal of information about Liszt's Russian travels and his influence on Russian
composers. Volume 2 contains a detailed catalog of Liszt's compositions
(pp. 327-438), drawn almost entirely from Raabe's "Werkverzeichnis"
(item 48) and from Searle's 1954 *Grove* catalog (see item 54). Mil'shtein's
volumes also contain an index of persons, a chronological table of Liszt's
activities, and an extensive bibliography of secondary sources.
        In Russian. The original 1957 edition was also published in Hungarian
in 1964. A "review article" about this latter edition, written by Zoltán

Gárdonyi, appeared under the title "Egy jelentös Liszt-monográfiáról" in *Magyar zene* 6 (1965), pp. 258-265. In Hungarian.

Fourteen other book-length survey studies are listed below in alphabetical order (by author). Additional studies are cross-listed here and described in greater detail only in Chapters X-XI:

6.   Bălan, Theodor. *Franz Liszt*. Bucharest: Editura Muzicală, 1963. 404pp.
        ML410.L7B24 1963
        Discusses Liszt's life, character, piano performances, and contributions to keyboard technique in some detail. Bălan also provides a useful description of Liszt's 1846-1847 Balkan tours, complete with quotations from newspapers like *Albina Romînească* (pp. 349-366). Also contains photographic illustrations, numerous musical examples, and facsimile reproductions of several documents—among them, an album inscription in Liszt's hand dating from 1823. In Rumanian.
        NB: This volume should not be confused with a much less useful book having the same title and published by the same author, c. 1957 (157pp.).

7.   Chantavoine, Jean. *Liszt*. Paris: F. Alcan, 1920. 247pp.
        ML410.L7C4 1920
        An intelligent, now rather old-fashioned study of Liszt's life and works, written by the scholar who rediscovered the score of *Don Sanche* at the turn of this century (item 943) and who published several articles about Liszt's private affairs and musical style (items 566 and 674). Concludes with a compact catalog of Liszt's compositions (pp. 240-245) and a brief bibliography. In French.
        Earlier editions of Chantavoine's book also exist, and an edition apparently identical to the one published in 1920 appeared in 1950.

8.   Dalmonte, Rossana. *Franz Liszt: La vita, l'opera, i testi musicali*. Milan: Giangiacomo Feltrinelli, 1983. 389pp.
        ML410.L7D3 1983   ISBN 8-8071-80030
        An insightful study, illustrated with carefully chosen musical examples. One of Dalmonte's principal interests is the relationship between music and literature; the third part of her book contains the texts of virtually all Liszt's songs and choral works and the libretto of *Don Sanche* in the original French (pp. 199-370). Carefully indexed. Principal text in Italian.

*   Dömling, Wolfgang. *Franz Liszt und seine Zeit*.
        A musical study that also explores important aspects of Liszt's character and interpersonal relationships. Discussed below as item 606.

9.   Engel, Hans. *Franz Liszt*. Potsdam: Akademische Verlagsgesellschaft
     Athenaion, 1936. 132pp.
       ML410.L7E5
       An uneven, highly opinionated monograph by the scholar who sup-
     plied the Liszt *MGG* article (item 58). Illustrated with portraits and fac-
     similes of several mss. as well as with musical examples, the majority of
     them taken from keyboard and symphonic compositions. No bibliography
     or other scholarly apparatus, but several previously unpublished compos-
     itions appear as "appendices." Concludes with a comparatively extensive
     but outdated catalog of works (pp. 275-331).

10. Gavoty, Bernard. *Liszt: le virtuose, 1811-1848*. Paris: Julliard, 1980. 356pp.
       ML410.L7G35   ISBN 2-260-002225-0
       A readable account of Liszt's childhood, youth, and young manhood
     in Austro-Hungary and France. Gavoty draws extensively on French-
     language documentary sources; his evaluations of his subject's Paris per-
     formances are worthwhile, but his documentation is uneven. Concludes
     with a chronological table summarizing Liszt's early life (pp. 329-340), a
     brief catalog of compositions (pp. 341-348), a number of plates—most of
     which reproduce well-known pictures of Liszt and some of his
     contemporaries—and a bibliography. Portions of Gavoty's work are drawn
     from an unpublished "autobiographical" Liszt letter mentioned in item 41.
       NB: Gavoty died before he could write a second (and final) volume
     dealing with Liszt's later life and compositions. See item 131.

11. Göllerich, August. *Franz Liszt*. Berlin: Marquardt, 1908. xi, 331pp.
       ML410.L7G65
       An erratic testimonial to (and eyewitness account of) Liszt's genius and
     character, composed of biographical fragments, "character studies," and
     brief discussions of individual compositions. Much of this book is out-
     dated, but its facsimile reproductions of letters and certain illustrations are
     still useful. Contains musical examples and a catalog of Liszt's compos-
     itions (pp. 271-331).

12. Hamburger, Klára. *Liszt*. Translated by Gyula Gulyás; translation revised
     by Paul Merrick. Budapest: Corvina Kiadó, 1987. 243pp.
       ML410.L7H255 1987   ISBN 963-13-23056
       An admirable account of Liszt's life and compositions, revised from a
     volume of the same name published in 1980 in Hungarian (ISBN
     963-2-80774-X). Hamburger's scholarship is sound and her writing vigor-
     ous; her text abounds with excerpts from Liszt's correspondence and with
     references to important secondary studies by other scholars. Unfortunately,
     the quality of the English-language text is uneven. Contains musical ex-
     amples as well as a chronology of Liszt's life (pp. 201-207), a catalog of

works (pp. 208-227) borrowed from item 54, a bibliography of "important Liszt literature," and two indexes. Reviewed by Alan Walker in the *Times Literary Supplement* for 10 July 1987; also reviewed in item 132.

Not to be confused either with *Liszt Ferenc* (Budapest: Corvina, 1973), a Hungarian-language "preliminary" version of this work, nor with the author's earlier Liszt study (item 354).

13.   Horvath, Emmerich Karl. *Franz Liszt: Eine Studie auf der Grundlage der bekannten Quellen, Biographien und zeitgenössischen Darstellungen.* Eisenstadt: Nentwich, 1978-1986.

    ML410.L7H68

      13a. Volume 1: *Kindheit (1811-1827)*.
      13b. Volume 2: *Jugend.*
      13c. Volume 3: *Franz Liszt in Italien: Aufenthalt mit*
        Marie Gräfin d'Agoult von 1837 bis 1839.

A study of Liszt as man and artist based for the most part on primary sources, especially German-language materials. Horvath does not discuss Liszt's compositions in a systematic manner, but he does treat several musical topics in detail (e.g., Liszt's early performances and concert tours). Although somewhat cursory, Horvath's work is generally reliable and his third volume (item 13c) is especially fine. Illustrations and lists of sources but no musical examples. Item 13c is reviewed in item 132.

14.   Kraft, Günther. *Franz Liszt — Leben, Werk und Vermächtnis.* Weimar: Nationale Forschungs und Gedenkstätten der klassischen deutschen Literatur, 1961. 48pp.

    ML410.L7K82

A brief summary of Liszt's career and creative output, published as a "supplement" to item 32. Contains illustrations and a few musical examples.

*   Legány, Desző. *Ferenc Liszt and His Country, 1869-1873.*

The first volume of an outstanding two-volume series devoted to Liszt's activities in Hungary during the latter part of his life. Described in greater detail as item 479.

*   Legány, Desző. *Liszt Ferenc magyarországon, 1874-1886.*

The second volume of the series identified immediately above. Described in greater detail as item 480.

* Merrick, Paul. *Revolution and Religion in the Music of Liszt.*
A study of Liszt's character and output based on his involvement with extra-musical ideas. Described in greater detail as item 608.

* Prahács, Margit. "Franz Liszt und die Budapester Musikakademie."
An important study of Liszt's life and activities on behalf of the Academy of Music he helped establish in Budapest during the 1870s. Reprinted in German in item 30; described in greater detail as item 481.

15.   Rehberg, Paula, and Gerhard Nestler. *Franz Liszt: Die Geschichte seines Lebens, Schaffens und Wirkens.* Zurich: Artemis, 1961. 729pp.
      ML410.L7R345
A fulsome popular biography, supplemented with an appendix (pp. 514-599) devoted to well-known aspects of Liszt's compositional style and development. Illustrated with several portraits and photographs as well as a few musical examples. Includes an extended, albeit incomplete catalog of Liszt's musical and literary works (pp. 629-679).

16.   Stockhammer, Robert. *Franz Liszt im Triumphzug durch Europa.* Vienna: Österreichischer Bundesverlag, 1986. 187pp.
      ML410.L7S83 1986   ISBN 3-215-05649-6
A survey study that concentrates on Liszt's 1840s virtuoso tours, keyboard repertory, and transcriptions (pp. 19-148). Supplementary chapters deal with such topics as Liszt's childhood and youth, keyboard technique, etc. Opinions differ about the worth of this book: Lennart Rabes, in *Liszt saeculum* 38 (1986), pp. 116-117, questions its reliability and points out its lack of scholarly apparatus. Charles Suttoni (item 46), on the other hand, praises Stockhammer for his "well presented" account of Liszt's concert tours and for a "lean, concise prose style." Scattered musical examples as well as portraits and a brief bibliography.

17.   Szabolczi, Bence. *The Twilight of Ferenc Liszt*, trans. András Deák. Budapest: Akadémiai Kiadó, 1959. 134pp.
      ML410.L7S983
A heartfelt account of Liszt's last years, especially the time he spent in Hungary. Szabolczi supplements his observations with the complete texts of some of Liszt's late pieces (pp. 81-134), among them the *Csárdás obstiné* and *Ossa arida*. Also supplemented with observations of a Marxist-Leninist flavor.
Published in Hungarian under the title *Liszt Ferenc estéje* (Budapest 1956). Originally published under the same title in *Zenetudományi tanulmányok* 3 (1955), pp. 211-265; summaries in German and English, pp. 553-554. Also published in German- and Russian-language editions.

Also by Szabolczi, a short article that presents some item 17 material appeared under the title "Franz Liszts Lebensabend" in *Musik und Gesellschaft* (1956), pp. 16-17.

*   Westerby, Herbert. *Liszt, Composer, and His Piano Works.*
       A "borderline" study, generally classified as a monograph on Liszt's piano works but fitted out with biographical and general musical information. Described in greater detail as item 761.

Not all book-length Liszt survey studies are innovative or especially well-written. Many brief, less useful, or less reliable monographs also exist; the four volumes described below must stand for dozens of others:

18.   Gut, Serge. *Franz Liszt.* Artigues-prè-Bordeaux: Delmas, 1989. 432pp.
       ISBN 2-87706-042-X   [No LC number available]
       An ambitious survey study by the author of items 421, 569, 603, 700-701, 710, and other publications. Contains chapters about portions of Liszt's life and various kinds of compositions as well as chapters devoted to specialized topics (e.g., literary works, correspondence, relationship with Hungary, friendships with Berlioz, Chopin, Wagner, etc.). Gut's observations are supplemented with several portraits and numerous musical examples as well as appendices containing poems associated with some of Liszt's programmatic compositions, the text of his will (also reprinted in items 222-223), a detailed chronology of his life (pp. 476-539), and so on. Concludes with indexes and an extensive bibliography.
       Despite its merits, Gut's book is full of proofreading errors, outdated information, and—worst of all—material apparently borrowed without acknowledgement from a variety of secondary sources, among them item 31. A review by Alan Walker of Gut's work which discusses some of these failings appeared in the *Journal of the American Liszt Society* 26 (1989), pp. 37-51. NB: Gut cites a number of unfamiliar or unpublished secondary sources in his bibliography; a few of them are mentioned as or under items 165-166 and so on.

19.   Leroy, Alfred. *Franz Liszt: L'homme et son ouevre.* Musiciens de ous les temps, 5. Paris: Seghers, 1964. 191pp.
       ML410.L7L38
       An inferior Liszt survey study, characterized by reliance on previous publications rather than original research. Contains sections devoted to Liszt's life (pp. 11-86), works (pp. 89-175), and discographical information (pp. 183-187). Illustrated with a few portraits and other pictures but no musical examples. Concludes with a short bibliography.

20.   Taylor, Ronald. *Franz Liszt: The Man and the Musician*. New York: Universe Books, 1986. xv, 285pp.
        ML410.L7T35 1986   ISBN 0-87663-490-0
        A disappointing popular biography masquerading as a serious study of Liszt's life, character, and art. Taylor claims to discuss Liszt's compositions "primarily as creative expressions of his intellectual and spiritual energy, not as a body of music for analysis in its own technical terms." Unfortunately, his research is as superficial as his musical chitchat. Eight pages of illustrations and one or two musical examples.

21.   Watson, Derek. *Liszt*. New York: Schirmer Books, 1989. xii, 404pp.
        ML410.L7W35 1989   ISBN 0-02-872705-3
        A worthwhile, well-written, but extremely brief introduction to Liszt's career, character, and compositions. Watson reprints item 47 (the Searle/Winklhofer catalog of Liszt's works) almost without change (pp. 333-379); he also provides a calendar of Liszt's activities (pp. 312-332), a dictionary of individuals Liszt knew (pp. 380-384), and a selected bibliography. Illustrated with black-and-white plates as well as a large number of musical examples.

A number of less useful Liszt survey studies also appeared in print before World War I. Two examples of such studies are:

22.   Lüning, Otto. *Franz Liszt. Ein Apostel des Idealen*. Entire issue of *Neujahrsblatt der Allgemeinen Musik-Gesellschaft in Zürich* 84 (1896).
        ML5.N48
        A hymn of praise to Liszt's character and artistic accomplishments. Lüning deals with his subject's compositions almost entirely in terms of their "idealism" and their relationship to Liszt's life. No musical examples.

23.   Vogel, Bernard. *Franz Liszt: Abriss seines Lebens und Würdigung seiner Werke*. Musikheroen der Neuzeit, 6. Leipzig: Max Hesse, 1888. vi, 131pp.
        ML410.L7V7
        A musical monograph supplemented with a biographical sketch and chapters about Liszt's activities as author, conductor, pedagogue, and keyboard technician. Illustrated with musical examples and a portrait. Like others of its kind, Vogel's work is primarily interesting today for the light it casts on outmoded views of Liszt's life and compositions.

ARTICLES

Most articles about Liszt deal with specialized biographical or musical topics and are described below in Chapters IX-X. Articles of a general nature published in leading music encyclopedias are discussed in Chapter IV. Two "survey-study" articles, however, deserve special attention. Although published decades ago, they remain important because they present intriguing interpretations of Liszt's personality and artistic accomplishments:

24.   Schering, Arnold. "Über Liszts Persönlichkeit und Kunst." *Jahrbuch der Musikbibliothek Peters* 33 (1927), pp. 31-44.

An unusually intelligent introduction of Liszt's complex personality and contributions to nineteenth-century music. Includes references to Wagner's "triumph" over his sometime friend and father-in-law, Impressionistic elements in late piano pieces like the *Jeux d'eaux à la villa d'Este* from the third book of the *Années de pèlerinage*, and so on. According to Schering, Liszt will someday be considered "one of the most important bearers of nineteenth-century European musical culture."

25.   Schönberg, Arnold. "Franz Liszts Werk und Wesen." *Allgemeine Musik-Zeitung* [Berlin], 20 October 1911.

A loosely organized collection of musings on Liszt's "fanatical faith," "instinctive life," contributions to musical form, etc. Schoenberg's central argument seems to be that Liszt's "craftsmanly deftness, technique and play with materials [were] less remarkable . . . than the things behind them—the personality, the true artist-being, that draws from direct vision."

Reprinted in English in *Style and Idea: Selected Writings of Arnold Schoenberg*, ed. Leonard Stein (London: Faber & Faber, 1975), pp. 442-447.

Other important survey articles about Liszt include:

26.   Antcliffe, Herbert. "Liszt." *Art, Religion and Clothes*. The Hague: Hagel, 1927; pp. 81-92.

ML60.A57A67

An early, carefully considered challenge to the "Liszt legend" by a musical amateur who revered Liszt as "essentially a religious man," a great teacher, and a source of inspiration to figures like Hans von Bülow, Karl Klindworth, and Alexander Mackenzie. Often overlooked by researchers.

27.   Bergfeld, Joachim. "Franz Liszts Persönlichkeit und Kunst." In item 32;
        pp. 21-42.
            Describes important features of Liszt's life and artistic activities, in-
        cluding the uneven quality of his compositional output. Bergfeld refers in
        passing to much of the Liszt literature published before 1961 as well as to
        studies of such "related" composers as Richard Strauss and Hans Pfitzner.
        No musical examples.

*Many worthwhile Liszt articles about Liszt's life and music have appeared in news-
papers, concert programs, private publications, etc. One example is described below:*

28.   Schumann, Karl. "Virtuose—Visionär — Europäer. Franz Liszts Leben: ein
        Gang von der Wiener Klassik zur Moderne." *Süddeutsche Zeitung* (2-3
        August 1986), "Feuilleton."
            Introduces general readers to Liszt's activities as composer, performer,
        and pedagogue. Schumann's observations pertain especially to 1986
        'Liszt-year' celebrations in Europe. Illustrations.

*Finally, an unusually provocative sketch of Liszt's character and musical accom-
plishments deserves more attention than it has often received:*

29.   Rosen, Charles. "The New Sound of Liszt." *New York Review of Books*
        31/6 (12 April 1984), pp. 17-20.
            Ostensibly a review of Walker's *Franz Liszt: The Virtuoso Years* (item
        1a, 1983 edition). Actually a survey of Liszt's contributions to musical lit-
        erature and style, punctuated with observations about the artist's character.
        Although an admirer of some of Liszt's music, Rosen maintains that much
        of it is banal. Several illustrations. Discussed in Chapter II.

ANTHOLOGIES AND "READERS"

*Although not always "comprehensive" in character, book-length anthologies and
"readers" devoted to Liszt's accomplishments must be considered survey studies of
a kind.*
    Among Liszt "readers" are two of outstanding importance:

30.   *Franz Liszt: Beiträge von ungarischen Authoren,* ed. Klára Hamburger.
        Budapest: Corvina, 1978. 336pp.
            ML410.L7F735   ISBN 963-13-0088-9
            A valuable collection of studies published originally in Hungarian, or
        published here for the first time and in German. Contains German-
        language texts of items 111-112, 337, 385, 481, 630, 633-634, 746, and 812
        (dealing with Liszt's family, the *Faust* symphony, harmony, etc.) as well

as an article by Bálint Sárosi about Hungarian Gypsy music *not* discussed below. Illustrated with 24 black-and-white plates and numerous musical examples. Concludes with bibliographic information about the studies themselves and with an index of names. Reviewed as an anthology in item 110.

31.   *Franz Liszt: The Man and His Music*, ed. Alan Walker. New York: Taplinger, 1970. xiv, 471pp.
    ML410.L7W28   ISBN 0-80082-990-5
    A "Liszt reader," consisting of contributions solicited from prominent British performers and scholars. Contains items 381, 673, 750, 772, 824, 864, 914, 931, 946, 987, 1041, and 1066 (dealing with Liszt's personality, compositional style, relationship with twentieth-century music, etc.). Illustrated throughout with musical examples and a few black-and-white portraits and facsimile reproductions. Concludes with an index and a "complete" catalog of Liszt's works—actually, a rearranged and somewhat improved version of Searle's 1954 *Grove* catalog (see item 54).

A number of museum catalogs and memorial publications also contain articles about Liszt; these publications are described for the most part in Chapter IV. Five somewhat more important anthologies devoted exclusively to such articles are described below in alphabetical order (by title):

32.   *Franz Liszt* [pamphlet]. Weimar: Nationale Forschungs und Gedenkstätten der klassischen deutschen Literatur, 1961. 32pp.
    ML410.L7D48
    An anniversary publication dealing primarily—and briefly—with Liszt's life and musical activities in and around Weimar, although attention is also paid to Liszt's relationships with other artists. Contains items 574, 692, and 1044 as well as an article closely related to item 464. Item 14 was issued as a "supplement" to this volume. Several illustrations.

33.   *Franz Liszt*, ed. Heinz-Klaus Metzger and Reiner Riehn. Musik-Konzepte, 12 (1980). 127pp.
    ML410.L7F73x   ISBN 3-883-77047-7
    A short collection of articles devoted to Liszt's personality, literary works, and compositional style. Contains items 125, 598, 861, and 870 as well as musical examples and additional illustrations.

34.   *Franz Liszt a jeho Bratislavskí priatelia: Práce z konferencie konanej 5. októbra 1973 v Bratislave.* Hudobné tradície Bratislavy a ich tvorcovia, 2. Bratislava: Vydavateľstvo Obzor, 1975. 232pp.
        ML410.L7F7
        A series of short papers, most of them about Liszt's relationship with Bohemia and Bohemian music and composers, presented in October 1975 at a conference in Bratislava. Contains items 217, 25,8, 275 437, and 675 as well as articles on topics peripheral to Liszt studies. Concludes with an appendix containing 73 illustrations, among them portraits of Liszt and other musicians, facsimiles of press clippings and other documents, etc. In Czech and German throughout, with interleaved Russian-language abstracts.

35.   *Franz Liszt zum 150. Geburtstag. Festschrift zu den Bayreuther Lisztfeiern 1961.* Bayreuth: Emil Mühl, 1961. 62pp.
        No LC number available. OCLC files provide holdings information. See also Library of Congress card 85-853994.
        An anniversary pamphlet consisting of addresses by public officials from Austria and Germany as well as items 27, 474, and 697. Except for Bergfeld's survey and Liszt-Wagner studies (items 27 and 697), however, this pamphlet is not very useful. Illustrated with several plates. See also item 71.

36.   *Liszt.* Entire issue of *Silences* [Paris] 3 (July 1986).
        ISBN 2-7291-0222-1   [No LC number available]
        A collection of essays—some outstanding, some of indifferent quality—dealing with many aspects of Liszt's life, activities, and creative accomplishments. Contains item 383 as well as articles closely related to items 190, 311, 521, 598, 701, 1000, and 1014. Also contains articles too superficial to be discussed below. Of special interest to Liszt "hobbyists" is a true/false quiz (Philippe A. Autexier, "Vrai ou faux? Questionnaire-jeu sur Liszt," pp. 264-266) devoted to exploding many of the misunderstandings surrounding Liszt and his contemporaries. Attractively, if somewhat eccentricially illustrated. Numerous musical examples.

Among other, less useful Liszt anthologies is the following volume:

37.   *Weimarer Liszt-Studien. Bericht über die wissenschaftliche Konferenz "Das Weimarer Schaffen Franz Liszts und seine Ausstrahlung auf die Weltmusikkultur,"* ed. Uta Eckhardt et al. Weimar: Arbeitskreis "Franz Liszt," 1987. 171pp.
        [No LC or ISBN numbers available]
        A comparatively unimportant collection. Contains 17 short conference papers, only five of which (items 668, 895, 901, 904, and 950) are described

below. References to other papers in this volume appear under items 181, 240, 452, 675, and so on. No illustrations and virtually no musical examples. Published too late to be included in item 40.

Several Liszt anthologies have been published only in Hungarian. Among these is the *Liszt kiskönyvtár* ["Little Liszt Library"], issued in two volumes (1982 and 1984) by the Liszt Ferenc Társaság of Budapest. This irregular periodical contains item 694 as well as studies mentioned under items 440 and 456. No illustrations.

Finally, one uneven "Liszt reader" also deserves to be mentioned here, if only for part of its contents:

38.   *Liszt.* Collection génies et réalités [no number]. Paris: Hachette, 1967. 287pp.
        ML410.L7L56
        A popular work, handsomely bound but virtually worthless for research purposes. Only Bernard Rajben's Liszt discography is discussed separately below (item 104). Another article contains musical examples. Illustrated with portraits, sheet-music covers, etc.; some illustrations in color.

IV: REFERENCE WORKS

Reference works include bibliographies, indexes of musical works (sometimes called "thematic indexes," especially when outfitted with musical incipits), encyclopedia articles (which sometimes contain indexes and bibliographic information), collection and exhibition catalogs, discographies, and research reports of various kinds. Some of these works are "comprehensive" (i.e., they contain information about all or at least most aspects of Liszt's life and musical activities). Others are highly specialized.

Because of their value to researchers, virtually every important *Liszt bibliography, index, and catalog is described below. Less valuable bibliographies and discographies, many of them appended to other works, are omitted. Some of these latter items are mentioned in passing in Chapters III and XI. The only published Liszt iconographical index is also described below; iconographies proper are described in Chapter VIII.*

BIBLIOGRAPHIES

The only reasonably complete guide to literature about Liszt published before and during 1936 is:

39. Koch, Lajos. *Liszt Ferenc bibliográfiai kisérlet/Franz Liszt: Ein bibliographischer Versuch.* Budapest: Székesfőváros Házinyomdája, 1936. 108pp.
     ML410.L7K56
     The most extensive bibliography of secondary Liszt studies in print. Contains about 5,000 entries, many of them referring to otherwise obscure German- and Hungarian-language newspaper and magazine articles. Despite its size, however, this "bibliographic essay" omits many pre-1936 studies, especially concert reviews and letters by Liszt published in periodicals. Introduction in German and Hungarian; includes German-language summaries of many Hungarian publications.
     Reprinted (as a separate volume) from the *Jahrbuch der Stadtbibliothek Budapest* for 1935.

With the exception of the present volume, the most complete guide to post-1936 Liszt studies is:

40.   Saffle, Michael. "Liszt Research since 1936: A Bibliographic Survey." *Acta musicologica* 58 (1986), pp. 231-281.

A supplementary article appeared as: "The 'Liszt-Year' 1986 and Recent Liszt Research." *Acta musicologica* 59/3 (September-December 1987), pp. 271-299.

Identifies and briefly discusses most of the books, monographs, articles, and dissertations about Liszt that have appeared in print since the publication of item 39 (above). Much of the present volume is based on this article and its 'Liszt-Year' supplement. The second section of "Liszt Research" also reprints and discusses a little-known review, originally published in *Der Sammler*, of Liszt's 13 April 1823 "Weihekuss" concert in Vienna. The second section of "The 'Liszt-Year' 1986" contains corrections to the original article.

NB: Almost without exception, the contents of both articles have been incorporated into the present volume.

An exceptionally valuable bibliographic guide to Liszt's published correspondence deserves the closest attention:

41.   Suttoni, Charles. *Liszt Correspondence in Print: An Expanded, Annotated Bibliography.* Entire issue of the *Journal of the American Liszt Society* 25 (1989).

Identifies thousands of Liszt letters published since the mid-nineteenth century. An introductory essay summarizes important problems facing students of Liszt's correspondence. Concludes with valuable indexes of Liszt's correspondents and of publishers and/or editors of individual collections.

A completely revised version of the original bibliography, which appeared under the title "Franz Liszt's Published Correspondence: An Annotated Bibliography" in *Fontis artes musicae* 26 (1979), pp. 191-234. This article is occasionally bound and cataloged as an independent publication [ML134.L774S9].

NB: *Suttoni's bibliography is cited here and elsewhere in the present volume in lieu of virtually all of its contents.*

The only published index to pictures of and about Liszt remains:

42.   Csatkai, André. "Versuch einer Franz Liszt-Ikonographie." *Burgenländische Heimatblätter* 5/2 (May 1936), pp. 34-67.

Identifies 351 paintings, etchings, lithographs, figurines, etc., portraying Liszt throughout his life. Includes limited information about the provenance of some Liszt illustrations. Valuable but somewhat difficult to obtain: the *Heimatblätter* is a rare publication in the United States.

For several years a series of iconographical articles appeared in *Franz Liszt Kring*, a comparatively little-known Netherlands periodical. See Door Ad de Ray, "Listz-Iconographie" [sic]; 2 (1980), pp. 11-13; 4 (1982), pp. 10-12; and so on. Commentary in Dutch.

Four specialized Liszt research tools are described below in alphabetical order (by author):

43. Arnold, Ben, and Allan Ho. "Liszt Research and Recordings, 1982-1984." *Journal of the American Liszt Society* 15 (1984), pp. 105-138.

Supplements in the *Journal of the American Liszt Society* 16 (1984), pp. 35-52; 17 (1985), pp. 24-38; 18 (1985), pp. 36-46; 19 (1986), pp. 23-42; and 20 (1986), pp. 4-29.

Identifies secondary sources according to categories (i.e., "Books," "Articles," "Scores," etc.). More recent materials, as well as updated and corrected entries, appear in the "Supplements." Studies, scores, and recordings issued before 1982 are mentioned only if revised and reissued after that date. Especially useful for discographers.

44. Eckhardt, Mária [P.]. "Studies and Articles on F. Liszt in 'Studia musicologica: [Academiae] Scientiarum Hungaricae', 1961-1980." *Journal of the American Liszt Society* 10 (1981), pp. 9-14.

A catalog of *Studia musicologica* articles, studies, and reviews published about Liszt during the 1960s and 1970s. Draws in part on the register of that magazine prepared by Zsuzsanna Szepesi and András Wilheim for *Studia musicologica* 21 (1979), pp. 1-77.

NB: Certain studies mentioned in Eckhardt's catalog, notably reviews, are *not* included in the present study.

45. [Rabes, Lennart.] "Index of Letters Published for the First Time in the 'ILC-Quarterly' and 'Liszt saeculum'." *Liszt saeculum* 32/2 (1983), pp. 81-86.

Identifies fifty-odd letters—among them twelve by Liszt—according to recipient, date, incipit, publication information, and provenance (collection). Illustrated with facsimiles of some original holographs. NB: Other letters have appeared in *Liszt saeculum* since this index appeared in print. See item 41 for more detailed information about *Liszt saeculum* letter publications.

46.   Suttoni, Charles. "Liszt: A Centenary Miscellany of Books and Catalogs." *Journal of the American Liszt Society* 21 (1987), pp. 62-66.
       Names and describes important 1986 "Liszt-Year" monographs issued by publishers in France, Germany, Belgium, and Hungary.

INDEXES OF MUSICAL WORKS

Almost all of the Liszt indexes published to date are devoted to his own versions of his compositions, paraphrases, and transcriptions. Although imperfect, the most complete and generally reliable of these indexes is:

47.   Searle, Humphrey, and Sharon Winklhofer. [Catalog of Liszt's Compositions]. In: *Chopin, Schumann, Liszt.* The New Grove Early Romantic Masters, 1 (New York and London: W. W. Norton, 1985), pp. 322-368.
       ML390.T28 1985   ISBN 0-393-01691-9
       The most accurate and complete version of Humphrey Searle's *New Grove* catalog (item 54), revised by Sharon Winklhofer immediately after Searle's death. Unfortunately, Winklhofer's revisions are limited in scope and not always correct. More reliable information about certain mss. and collections appears in item 48 (below). Illustrated with a few musical examples. NB: Winklhofer also revised Searle's *New Grove* Liszt article; see item 57.
       Like other published guides to Liszt's music, the Searle/Winklhofer catalog is based in part on archival catalogs like those prepared by Raabe for what today is D-WRgs. Other ms. catalogs of Liszt pieces have recently been discovered, among them a catalog of piano pieces in the hand of the Princess Carolyne Sayn-Wittgenstein [F-Pn Doc. R 607]. Mentioned in item 1b; p. 370n. Described in detail by Mária Eckhardt in "Párizsi Liszt-dokumentum 1849-ből," *Zenetudományi dolgozatok* (1978), pp. 79-93.

An older, somewhat less complete, but invaluable index also deserves careful attention:

48.   Raabe, Peter. "Verzeichnis aller Werke Liszts nach Gruppen geordnet." In item 2b; pp. 241-364.
       The best "thematic catalog" of Liszt's compositions ever published. Although partially out of date, Raabe's index contains more information about many mss. and sheet-music publications than the Searle/Winklhofer index discussed above (item 47). Illustrated with a few musical examples.

Liszt himself was involved in the preparation of two catalogs of his published compositions:

49.   *Thematisches Verzeichnis der Werke von F. Liszt. Von dem Autor verfasst.* Leipzig: Breitkopf & Härtel, 1855. 97pp.
        ML134.L77
        An advertising prospectus prepared by Breitkopf & Härtel with Liszt's assistance. Provides incipits for important compositions published before 1855 as well as information about literary works and "Liszt portraits." (Facts about the preparation of this catalog may be found in item 1b; pp. 365 and 365n.)

50.   *Thematisches Verzeichnis der Werke, Bearbeitungen und Transkriptionen von F. Liszt.* "Neue vervollständigte Ausgabe." Leipzig: Breitkopf & Härtel, 1877. 162pp.
        ML134.L7A3
        A revised version of item 49 (above), containing additional entries and musical incipits. Neither edition contains information about unpublished Liszt works. Furthermore, neither edition addresses systematically the issue of which editions of his works Liszt preferred.
        A reprint of the revised catalog was issued in 1965 by H. Baron of London.

Four other important indexes are described below in alphabetical order (by author):

51.   Friwitzer, Ludwig. "Chronologisch-systematisches Verzeichnis sämtlicher Tonwerke Franz Liszts," *Musikalische Chronik* [Vienna] 5/3-8 (5 November 1887 — 31 January 1888), pp. 33ff.
        A fulsome catalog of compositions published before the composer's death in 1886. Contains useful information about early editions and publishers, most of which also appears in items 47-48. No incipits or musical examples.

52.   Ho, Allan. "Tentative Revisions to Searle's *New Grove* Catalog of Liszt's Works for Two Pianos and Piano Four-Hands." *Journal of the American Liszt Society* 14 (1983), pp. 24-29.
        Corrects and supplements relevant entries for item 57. Contains otherwise little-known information about Liszt's arrangements of his own *Festpolonaise*, the *Concerto pathétique* (based on the *Grosses Konzertsolo* of the late 1840s), *Héroïde funèbre*, and so on. Concludes with a bibliography of relevant secondary sources.

53.   Schnapp, Friedrich. "Verschollene Kompositionen Franz Liszts." *Von deutscher Tonkunst: Festschrift zu Peter Raabes 70. Geburtstag*, ed. Alfred Morgenroth. Leipzig: C. F. Peters, 1942; pp. 119-152.
        ML55.M55
        Identifies 95 works Liszt purportedly began or completed which were subsequently lost. In recent years some of the works Schnapp mentions have been rediscovered and even published—e.g., the fourth *Valse oubliée*; a fantasy on themes from Rossini's *Siège de Corinthe* (see item 309). Includes a facsimile reproduction of an otherwise lost work: Liszt's youthful Sonata in f minor.

54.   Searle, Humphrey. [Catalog of Liszt's Compositions.] In item 57; pp. 51-72.
        A revised version of the catalog originally published in Volume 5 of the fifth edition of *Grove's Dictionary of Music and Musicians* (1954), pp. 263-314. Supplemented by Winklhofer's revisions for item 47, this catalog remains the finest guide to Liszt's works published since item 48. Illustrated with a few musical examples.

Two less important indexes to Liszt's works also deserve to be mentioned here:

55.   Morhange-Morchane, Marthe. *Liszt*. Text by Joseph Bloch. Thematic Guide to Piano Literature, 5. New York: G. Schirmer, 1988. 126pp.
        [No LC or ISBN numbers available]
        A catalog of published Liszt piano pieces, with worthwhile comments about many of them by Joseph Bloch. Includes tables, most of them devoted to ranking kinds of compositions (etudes, character pieces, dance pieces, etc.) according to technical difficulty. Also includes 270 single or multiple melodic incipits as well as information about individual works. No bibliography or index.

56.   Suppan, Wolfgang. "Blasorchesterbearbeitungen Liszt'scher Werke." *Liszt-Studien* 1 (1977), pp. 179-202.
        Identifies some of the best-known arrangements of Liszt works for wind instruments by other composers, among them transcriptions of the "Hungarian Rhapsodies," *Tasso*, the piano concertos, and so on. Includes several musical examples as well as a measure-by-measure comparison of arrangements of *Les préludes* by German wind specialists Grossmann, Müller, Kotter, and Villinger. Suppan's notes contain valuable bibliographic citations, almost all of them from German-language sources.

ENCYCLOPEDIA ARTICLES

Articles about Liszt in so-called "popular" encyclopedias are virtually worthless for serious researchers, but a few music encyclopedias and dictionaries contain articles of value. Among the best of these are:

57.   Searle, Humphrey. "Franz Liszt." *The New Grove Dictionary of Music and Musicians*, ed. Stanley Sadie. London: Macmillan, 1980; Volume 11, pp. 28-74.

   ML100.N48   ISBN 0-333-23111-2

   Drawn to a considerable extent from Searle's earlier *Grove* article (identified under item 54), now out of date. Contains item 54 as well as material revised and republished as item 47. Despite his pioneering efforts on Liszt's behalf, including his book-length study of Liszt's music (item 602), Searle was no musicologist; in item 134, Winklhofer observed that even this revised version of his work is filled with factual errors and "suspect opinions." Supplemented by a few musical examples. (With regard to a French-language edition of Searle's article, see item 132.)

58.   Engel, Hans. "Franz Liszt." *Die Musik in Geschichte und Gegenwart*, ed. Friedrich Blume. Kassel: Bärenreiter, 1949-1986; Volume 8 [1960], cols. 964-988.

   ML100.M92

   A somewhat old-fashioned survey of Liszt's life and professional activities as composer, pianist, pedagogue, and musical man-of-affairs. Illustrated with facsimile reproductions of mss. and documents and with several portraits of the composer. Engel takes sides on many controversial issues in Liszt studies, among them the role of traditional sonata-allegro structural principles in compositions like the B-minor Sonata and *Les préludes* (see also item 9). Concludes with a brief catalog of Liszt's works and a bibliography heavily biased in favor of German-language secondary-source materials.

   Numerous corrections and some additional information appear in *MGG* supplement "E-Z," cols. 1142-1144.

Among briefer Liszt articles, these are especially useful:

59.   "Franz (Ferencz) Liszt." *Baker's Biographical Dictionary of Musicians*, 7th edition; rev. Nicholas Slonimsky. New York: G. Schirmer, 1984; pp. 1368-1372.

   ML105.B16 1984   ISBN 0-02-870270-0

   Summarizes important events in Liszt's life and basic facts about his musical works and compositional style. Slonimsky's vigorous editorial style makes this article good reading. Concludes with a catalog of compositions.

60.   "Franz Liszt." *Riemann Musik-Lexikon*, 12th rev. edition; ed. Wilibald
        Gurlitt. Mainz and New York: B. Schotts Sons, 1961; Volume 2
        ["Personenteil L-Z"], pp. 80-84.
            ML100.R52 1959
        A short account of Liszt's career and compositions, published in the
        most recent edition of the foremost German-language music reference
        works. Concludes with a short catalog of works and a bibliography.
            Updated information and bibliographic citations appear in the supple-
        mentary 1975 *Ergänzungsband* [L-Z], pp. 67-70.
            Older encyclopedia articles about Liszt may also be useful to special-
        ists. See, for example, the lengthy description of Liszt's life and musical
        activities in Volume 5 of Fétis's *Biographie universelle des musiciens*, 2nd
        ed. (Paris: Didot, 1870), pp. 318-324.

COLLECTION AND EXHIBITION CATALOGS

*Catalogs of Lisztiana in public and private collections, as well as catalogs published
in conjunction with special Liszt exhibitions, often contain valuable information about
artifacts of all kinds: letters, musical mss., sheet-music, portraits, periodical literature, musical instruments, and so on. Descriptions of musical editions, individual
letters, and mss. are described (respectively) in Chapters V and VII-VIII. Discussions of individual Liszt instruments are described in Chapter XX.*

Catalogs of Permanent Collections

*A few important permanent Liszt collections (e.g., those of the Bibliothèque
Nationale, Paris) have never been described in print. Other collections, however, have
been described many times—including collections that have ceased to exist, at least
in their original form.*

*Among catalogs of existing collections, those described below are unusually de-
tailed and useful:*

61.   Eckhardt, Mária [P.]. *Franz Liszt's Music Manuscripts in the National
        Széchényi Library, Budapest*, ed. Zoltán Falvy. Budapest: Akadémiai
        Kiadó, 1986. 252pp.
            ML134.L7E313 1986   ISBN 963-05-4177-7
        A superbly detailed catalog of 78 Liszt mss. and scores, illustrated with
        facsimile reproductions of documentary materials and with musical exam-
        ples. Based to a certain extent on her other studies (e.g., items 297-298),
        Eckhardt's book also incorporates information published in *Studia
        musicologica* and other periodicals. This catalog thus constitutes an intro-
        duction to Liszt's art and Liszt mss., not merely to certain documents.
        Outfitted with tables, transcriptions of musical passages, and a valuable
        bibliography.

Distributed in the United States by Pendragon Press as Studies in Central and Eastern European Music, 2.

Not to be confused with Eckhardt's "Liszt Ferenc és magyar kortársai az Országos Széchényi Könyvtár dedikált Liszt-zeneműveinek tükrében," published in *Orságos Széchényi Könyvtár Evkölnyve* (1973), pp. 87-130. This article identifies and describes handwritten dedications in H-Bn editions. In Hungarian, with German-language summary (pp. 128-130).

62.   Eckhardt, Mária [P.]. *Liszt Ferenc hagyatéka/Franz Liszt's Estate*. Volume 1: *Könyvek/Books*. Budapest: Liszt Ferenc Zeneművészeti Főiskola, 1986. 213pp.

ISBN 963-0-17309-3 (I)   [No LC number available]

A volume-by-volume description of 273 publications from Liszt's personal library, preserved today in the collections of the Budapest Academy of Music. This splendid detailed study also contains an introductory essay by Margit Prahács as well as 24 plates reproducing book pages, some of which include marginal comments in the composer's hand. Contains several appendices as well as indexes of names and titles. In Hungarian and English. Reviewed in item 132.

Other valuable catalogs of permanent Liszt collections, including others of Hungarian holdings, are described or cross-listed below—first by city or region, then alphabetically (by author or title):

<u>A. Basel</u>

63.   Schanzlin, Hans Peter. "Liszt in Basel und die Liszt-Dokumente in der Universitätsbibliothek Basel." *Liszt-Studien* 2 (1981), pp. 163-171.

Provides information about Liszt's visits to Switzerland as well as informal descriptions of a few musical mss., autograph letters, and pieces of memorabilia (among them a signed copy of the *Faust* symphony) owned by the Basel University Library. Illustrated with a facsimile of an "Albumblatt" and a caricature-sketch of Liszt playing whist, one of his favorite amusements.

<u>B. Bratislava</u>

64.   Hrabussay, Zoltán. "Neznáme rukopisy Franza Liszta na Slovensku." *Hudobnovedné studie* 4 (1960), pp. 177-196.

Discusses Liszt's involvement with the Zamoyski family and describes a series of letters Liszt addressed to Ludmilla Gizycka-Zamoyska between 1871-1880. Hrabussy also includes information about mss. of several short Liszt pieces, including a "Ländler" and the *Air cosaque*. Facsimiles, some accompanied by Czech translations. In Czech; summaries in Russian and German.

Another discussion of these documents by Hrabussay appeared in *Studia musicologica* 5 (1963), pp. 125-129. NB: As of 1960 the documents in question were owned by the Slovakian Central Archive, Bratislava, and the Zamoyska-Wielopolska family of Bratislava-Petrzalka (formerly Preßburg-Engerau).

C. Brussels

*   *Lettres autographes conservées à la Bibliothèque Royale Albert Ier. — Ferenc Liszt.*

A collection of letters rather than a catalog per se. Described in greater detail as item 200.

D. Budapest

*   Eckhardt, Mária [P.]. *Franz Liszt's Music Manuscripts in the National Széchényi Library, Budapest.*

Described as item 61.

*   Eckhardt, Mária [P.]. *Liszt Ferenc hagyatéka/Franz Liszt's Estate.*

Described as item 62.

65.   Eckhardt, Mária [P.]. *Liszt Ferenc Memorial Museum. Liszt Ferenc Academy of Music, Budapest. Catalogue.* Budapest: Liszt Ferenc Memorial Museum and Research Center, 1986. 84pp.

ISBN 963-01-7469-3   [No LC number available]

Describes 175 pieces of Lisztiana, including important holograph mss., concert programs, portraits, and pieces of furniture owned by Liszt during several periods of his life. Eckhardt's introductory material includes English-language texts of Legány's 1984 article "Liszt's Homes in Budapest" (item 484), János Kárpáti's article on Liszt pianos (item 1080), and pamphlets by Kálmán d'Isoz (item 68) and Margit Prahács (see item 69). Illustrated with color and black-and-white photographs as well as with facsimile reproductions of a few letters and musical holographs. Concludes with a useful bibliography.

66. Eckhardt, Mária [P.]. "Liszt Ferenc Zeneműkéziratai Főiskola Liszt Ferenc emlékmúzeumában." *Zenetudományi dolgozatok* (1986), pp. 235-260.

Identifies some 60 Liszt holographs owned by the Ferenc Liszt Memorial Museum of the Academy of Music, Budapest. Concludes with 18 facsimile reproductions of ms. pages, including leaves from the *Via crucis* and several Liszt transcriptions of Schubert songs. In Hungarian.

NB: Eckhardt has recently published other Hungarian-language catalogs and bibliographies dealing with Liszt's letters. Among these bibliographies is "Liszt Ferenc levelei az MTA Zenetudományi Intézetének Major-gyűjteményében," which appeared in *Zenetudományi dolgozatok* (1987), pp. 281-302.

67. Gábry, György. "Franz Liszt-Reliquien im Nationalmuseum Budapest." *Studia musicologica* 17 (1975), pp. 407-423.

Describes several Liszt relics, including two wreaths overlaid with gold or silver, a medal minted at Pest in 1873, the famous "Ehrensäbel" presented to Liszt in Pest early in 1840, and the Broadwood piano once owned by Beethoven. Illustrated with eight pages of photographs.

A Hungarian-language version of this article appeared as "Liszt Ferenc emléktárgyai a Magyar Nemzeti Múzeumban," *Folia historica* [Budapest] 5 (1977), pp. 121-137. Includes a German-language summary (p. 131).

68. d'Isoz, Kálmán. *Liszt szobájának kalauza.* Budapest: Liszt Ferencz Zene-művészeti Főiskola, 1925. 16pp.

ML410.L7Z4664m   [Sometimes cataloged as ML141.B9 L5]

Describes the contents of the Liszt room at the Academy of Music, Budapest. In Hungarian.

Out of date but reprinted in English in item 65.

69. Prahács, Margit. *Chambre commémorative de François Liszt* [Catalog]. Budapest: "Ecole Supérieure de Musique François Liszt," 1956. 15pp.

ML410.L7B87

Identifies 271 artifacts owned by the Franz Liszt Academy of Music in Budapest. Illustrated with portrait photographs, facsimiles of diplomas, musical examples, and so on.

NB: This pamphlet should not be confused with Prahács's "Introduction to the Catalog of the Liszt Memorial Rooms of the Academy of Music" (1968), reprinted in English in item 65.

E. The Burgenland (Austria)

70.   Eckhardt, Mária [P.], and Cornelia Knotik. *Franz Liszt und sein Kreis in Briefen und Dokumenten aus den Beständen des Burgenländischen Landesmuseums.* Wissenschaftliche Arbeiten aus dem Burgenland, 66. Eisenstadt: Burgenländisches Landesmuseum, 1983. 160pp.
         ML410.L7F75 1983   ISBN 3-85405-084-4
         A catalog of 121 documents (principally letters) owned by the Burgenland District Museum of Eisenstadt. Reproduces the complete texts of these documents as well as German-language translations of "foreign" source materials. Supplemented with several photographs and facsimile reproductions as well as indexes of correspondents and names mentioned in the work itself. Reviewed in item 132.
         NB: Many of the documents described by Eckhardt and Knotik were written by figures other than Liszt (e.g., the Princess Sayn-Wittgenstein, Richard Wagner, Liszt's nephew Eduard von Liszt, and so on).

71.   Klampfer, Josef. *Liszt-Gedenkstätten im Burgenland.* Burgenländische Forschungen, 43. Eisenstadt: Michael Rötzer, 1961. 129pp.
         ML410.L77K63
         A description of Liszt momuments in Eisenstadt and Raiding, among them 669 artifacts owned by the Haydn-Museum. Published in conjunction with the 150th anniversary of Liszt's birth at the latter town. Also contains an outline of Liszt's life (pp. 77-95), a list of compositions (pp. 96-120), and photographs of Austrian Liszt "memorials."
         Additional information about these "memorials" is available in items 86-89 as well as in Hans Wastl, "Die Franz Liszt-Gedächtnisstätte in Raiding," printed in item 35; pp. 11-12.

72.   Krajasich, Peter, and Johann Steuer. *Liszt-Museum Raiding.* Eisenstadt: E. & G. Horvath, 1981. 68pp.
         ISBN 3-85405-069-0   [No LC number available]
         Identifies 272 ms. facsimiles, sheet-music covers, and other artifacts on permanent exhibition in the house where Liszt was born. Illustrated with black-and-white plates, including photographs of the museum itself. Prefaced by a short essay entitled "Liszts Aufenthalte in Raiding," pp. 9-15.

73.   Schenk, Erich. "Das Geburtshaus Franz Liszts zu Raiding im Burgenland." *Österreichische Musikzeitschrift* 25 (1970), pp. 229-232.
         An informal "catalog," presented as a biographical sketch with interpolated italicized references to artifacts in Raiding collections.

74.   Schenk, Erich. "Die Franz Liszt-Gedächtnissstätte zu Raiding." *Burgen-ländische Heimatblätter* 23 (1961), pp. 91-95.
        A short account of Liszt's childhood in and visits to Raiding. Less interesting than item 73 (above).

F. Nürnberg

75.   Gottwald, Clytus. "Die Liszt-Autographe des Germanischen Nationalmuseums in Nürnberg." *Musikforschung* 35 (1982), pp. 166-172.
        Describes musical mss. owned by the German National Museum, Nuremberg, including Hs. 107016 (an orchestral draft of *Tasso* in August Conradi's hand), holographs of *Die Ideale*, and several sketches. No illustrations or musical examples.

G. Rome

76.   Eősze, László. *119 római Liszt dokumentumok*. Budapest: Zeneműkiadó, 1980. 184pp.
        ML410.L7E58
        Identifies and reproduces 119 letters, musical mss., and other documents currently owned by eight libraries and archives in Rome. Eősze's volume draws heavily on studies by Hamburger (item 211) as well as on items 77-78 (below). Illustrated with facsimile reproductions and a few musical examples; concludes with a short bibliography. In Hungarian; original documents in French, German, Italian, and Latin; summary in English.
        NB: Eősze overlooked or ignored more than 100 documents owned by Vatican archives and concerned with Liszt's plans to marry the Princess Sayn-(Wittgenstein. With regard to these documents, see item 1b; especially pp. 566-582, and item 255.)

77.   Eősze, László. "Római Liszt-kéziratok és dokumentumok." *Magyar zene* 20 (1979), pp. 165-172.
        A preliminary and extremely abbreviated version of item 76 (above). In Hungarian.

78.   Eősze, László. "Unbekannte Liszt-Handschriften und Dokumente aus Rom." *Liszt-Studien* 2 (1981), pp. 55-62.
        An abbreviated version of item 76, concentrating on musical mss. and avoiding all but the briefest references to and quotations from letters and other biographical sources.

H. Szekszárd (Hungary)

79.   Vendel-Mohay, Lajosné. *Liszt-emlékek Szekszárdon.* Szekszárd: Múzeumi
         Füzetek, 1986. 152pp.
              ISBN 963-01-7227-5   [No LC number available]
         Describes and reprints (in their original languages and in Hungarian)
         the texts of 43 Liszt letters owned by the Szekszárd Museum, most of them
         addressed to Baron Anton Augusz. Illustrated with facsimile reproductions
         of almost all the letters as well as portraits of Augusz, Ede Reményi, Pál
         Rosty, and other contemporary Hungarian figures. Concludes with a brief
         bibliography and index. Commentary in Hungarian. NB: Item 184 con-
         tains the bulk of the Liszt-Augusz correspondence.

I. Vienna

*   Legány, Deszö. *Franz Liszt: Unbekannte Presse und Briefe aus Wien,
         1822-1886.*
         A useful collection of letters and press-clippings preserved today in
         Viennese archives and newspapers. Described below as item 199.

J. Washington, D.C.

80.   Waters, Edward N. *Liszt Holographs in the Library of Congress.*
         Washington, D.C.: Library of Congress, 1979. 12pp.
              ML410.L7L5
         Identifies 89 mss., printer's proofs, and inscribed editions belonging to
         America's largest collection of Lisztiana. Unfortunately, Waters's work is
         fragmentary; even some of the mss. mentioned in items 47 and 54 are
         missing from this pamphlet. No illustrations or musical examples.
         A much more complete catalog of Liszt scores and letters owned by the
         Library of Congress will be published in the near future.

*   *The Letters of Franz Liszt to Olga von Meyendorff.*
         A collection of letters rather than a catalog. Described in greater detail
         as item 203.

K. Weimar

81.   Saffle, Michael. "Unpublished Liszt Works at Weimar." *Journal of the
         American Liszt Society* 13 (1982), pp. 3-24.
         Provides information about 87 Liszt compositions preserved in one or
         more holograph copies in the collections of the Goethe- und Schiller-
         Archiv, East Germany. Illustrated with a facsimile reproduction of

D-WRgs Liszt ms. I78b, an orchestral transcription by the composer of his youthful *Allegro di bravura*.

NB: Since the early 1980s a number of the pieces mentioned in this article have been published, most of them in the so-called "New Liszt Edition" (item 137). A revised version of this catalog will appear in a future issue of the *Journal of the American Liszt Society*.

No "official" catalog of D-WRgs holdings has ever been published, but an introduction of sorts to some D-WRgs Liszt materials appeared as "Franz Liszt's handschriftlicher Nachlaß im Goethe- und Schiller-Archiv" in *Informationen* [Nationale Forschungs- und Gedenkstätten der Klassischen Deutschen Literatur] 2 (1986). Not seen but cited in item 41.

82.   Weilguny, Hedwig. *Das Liszthaus in Weimar*. Weimar: Nationale Forschungs- und Gedenkstätten der klassischen deutschen Literatur, 1970. 64pp.
        ML410.L7W44
One of several short books by Weilguny with the same title, all of which contain histories of the Hofgärtnerei, Liszt's home in Weimar from 1869-1886, and introductions to its post-World War II contents. Printed as a tourist souvenir rather than a work of scholarship. Illustrated with several photographs.

Weilguny also published "Liszt-Stätten in Weimar" in *Musik und Gesellschaft* (1961), pp. 596-598. Illustrated with photographs of the Hofgärtnerei facade and parlor. NB: A somewhat different book, bearing the same title but written by Willy Handrick, appeared as *Das Liszthaus in Weimar* (n.d.; 32pp.)

Catalogs of Temporary Exhibitions

Exhibition catalogs are especially valuable for information about artifacts generally unavailable to the public. The most widely available of these catalogs are described below first by city or region, then alphabetically (by author or title):

A. Brussels

83.   *Franz Liszt, 1811-1886*. Brussels: Bibliothèque Royale Albert Ier, 1986. 42pp.
        ISBN 2-87093-031-3   [No LC number available]
Briefly describes 211 artifacts displayed at the Royal Library from 17-29 November 1986. Often misleading—e.g., entry 111 (a quotation from Liszt's letter of 11 January 1842 to the Comtesse d'Agoult) is identified by the heading "Robert Schumann (1810-1856)"! Illustrated with 9 plates of portraits, sheet-music covers, buildings, etc.

B. Budapest

84.   Bártha, Denes. *Exposition Fr. Liszt dans la grande salle du Musée National Hongrois: Catalogue et introduction.* Budapest: Hungarian National Museum, 1936. 51pp.
>   British Library shelf number Ac. 7301/11 [No LC number available]
>   Describes artifacts displayed in the National Museum, Budapest, in celebration of the fiftieth anniversary of Liszt's death. Corrected and updated by Eckhardt in item 85 (below). No illustrations.

85.   Eckhardt, Mária [P.]. "Az 1936-os Liszt-kiállítás dokumentumainak nyomában." *Magyar zene* 25 (1984), pp. 141-153.
>   A "supplement" to and set of corrections for item 84 (above). In Hungarian.

C. The Burgenland (Austria)

86.   *Album d'un voyageur. F. Liszt Gedächtnisausstellung anlässlich der 170. Wiederkehr seines Geburtsjahres,* ed. János Kárpáti and Peter Krajasich. Eisenstadt: Amt der Burgenländischen Landesregierung, 1981. 87pp.
>   ISBN 3-85405-074-7   [No LC number available]
>   Identifies 249 artifacts exhibited in Eisenstadt in 1981 to mark the 170th anniversary of Liszt's birth in the Austrian Burgenland. Includes the texts of eight otherwise unpublished Liszt letters as well as eight colored plates, black-and-white illustrations of mss., sheet-music editions, and so on. Prefaced with a useful, although incomplete calendar of Liszt's travels. Introduction in German and Hungarian; the rest in German only.

87.   *Der Wunderknabe aus Raiding,* ed. Hans Rosnak. Eisenstadt: Belvedere, 1985. 88pp.
>   [No LC or ISBN numbers available]
>   A publication honoring the 100th anniversary of Liszt's death in 1886. Contains more than a dozen short articles about Liszt, the Burgenland, etc., as well as an illustrated catalog of Liszt's association with "the Burgenland" (including the nearby cities of Sopron, Hungary, and Bratislava, Czechoslovakia). Also contains portraits, facsimile reproductions of documents, photographs of monuments, and other relevant illustrations—some of high quality and in color.

88.   *Franz Liszt: Ein Genie aus dem pannonischen Raum. Kindheit und Jugend.*
        Eisenstadt: Burgenländisches Landesmuseum, 1986. 168pp.
            ISBN 3-85405-098-4   [No LC number available]
            A catalog of 184 artifacts exhibited during 1986 by the Burgenland
        Regional Museum. Contains items 391, 407-409, 412, 414, 588, and 735
        as well as an article about nineteenth-century Vienna by Thomas Leibnitz,
        and other short studies. Handsomely illustrated with numerous portraits
        and photographs, many in color. Reviewed in item 132.

89.   *Franz-Liszt-Gedenkjahr 1986.* Entire "1986" issue of the *Burgenland —
        Jahrbuch für ein Land und seine Freunde.* Eisenstadt: Belvedere, 1985 [sic].
        82pp.
            [No LC or ISBN numbers available]
            A memorial anthology, similar in format to item 88 (above). Contains
        anniversary essays, several short articles—most of them dealing with topics
        of only peripheral interest to Liszt researchers and *not* identified separately
        below—and a variety of color and black-and-white illustrations. An ap-
        pendix provides biographical sketches of Austrian citizens who took part
        in 1986 Liszt celebrations.

90.   *Katalog   der   Franz   Liszt-Ausstellung   im   Haydnmuseum   des
        Burgenländischen Heimat- und Naturschutzvereins in Eisenstadt, 1936.*
        Eisenstadt, 1936. [19pp.]
            Typescript copy in US-Wc: ML141.E36L5
            Describes 148 pieces of Lisztiana (mss., portraits, pieces of sheet-music,
        and so on) exhibited at Eisenstadt during the fiftieth anniversary of
        Liszt's death. Of limited interest; most of the artifacts identified were bor-
        rowed for the exhibition from other collections. NB: Today this museum
        is known as the Burgenländisches Landesmuseum; see items 86 and 88.

D. Krems (Austria)

91.   *Anna Maria Liszt. Die Mutter des Musikers — ein Leben in Briefen.* Vienna:
        L. Wetzl, 1986. 41pp.
            [No ISBN or LC numbers available]
            Identifies 68 artifacts (letters, mss., pieces of sheet-music, photographs,
        etc.) displayed at the Historisches Museum, Krems, from 24 April — 30
        September 1986 as part of the regional Franz Liszt Festival. Also contains
        items 398 and 400 as well as an article closely related to item 268, portraits,
        boxed quotations, documentary facsimiles, and additional quotations from
        Liszt family correspondence.

E. Stockholm

92.   Kazemi, Changiz. "The Liszt Exhibition in Stockholn, 1986." *Liszt
        saeculum* 38 (1986), pp. 41-62.
        Describes about 100 Liszt portraits, letters, musical mss., and other
        pieces of memorabilia exhibited at the Stockholm Music Museum,
        Sweden, from 8 June — 30 September 1986. Includes reproductions of the
        exhibition brochure cover and of facsimiles of several letters, mss., sheet-
        music pages, and concert advertisements, including a poster for Liszt's 30
        March 1840 concert at the Gewandhaus, Leipzig.

Catalogs of Defunct Collections

*Like exhibition catalogs, catalogs of now-defunct collections may contain informa-
tion unavailable in other publications. Among such catalogs are two devoted to some
of the Liszt documents belonging since World War II to the Nationale Forschungs-
und Gedenkstätten der Klassischen Deutschen Literatur in Weimar:*

93.   Bachmann, "Professor" [?Franz]. "Das Liszt-Museum in Weimar." *Neue
        Musik-Zeitung* 21 (1900), pp. 269-270 and 280.
        Discusses Liszt's associations with the Hofgärtnerei in Weimar and the
        transformation of that building into the so-called "Liszt Museum," today
        known officially as the "Liszthaus" (see item 82). Illustrated with the
        well-known Louis Held photograph of Liszt in the Hofgärtnerei. Although
        the Liszthaus still stands, its collections were partially transferred to the
        Goethe- und Schiller-Archiv and the Weimarer Stadtbibliothek following
        World War II.
        NB: The precise authorship of this article is uncertain. Franz
        Bachmann was a prominent contributor to German-language music peri-
        odicals around the turn of the century.

94.   Mirus, Adolf. *Das Liszt-Museum zu Weimar und seine Erinnerungen*, 3rd
        edition. Leipzig: Breitkopf & Härtel, 1892. 64pp.
        ML410.L7M53
        Traces the history and describes the contents of the so-called
        "Liszt-Museum," now part of the Nationale Forschungs- und
        Gedenkstätten der Klassischen Deutschen Literatur in Weimar. Also pro-
        vides information and anecdotes about aspects of Liszt's career, quotations
        from letters, diplomas, poems, etc. Illustrated with four pictures of Liszt
        and his Weimar homes.

Two published descriptions of other defunct Liszt collections also deserve attention:

95. Jerger, Wilhelm. "Die Handschriften Franz Liszts aus dem Nachlaß von August Göllerich in Linz." *Musikforschung* 29 (1976), pp. 288-294.

 Describes Göllerich's collection of Lisztiana, which included a number of letters and telegrams, some photographs, and mss. of *Die Vätergruft* and *Der 129. Psalm* (among other compositions). No illustrations or examples, but some letters are reprinted in full. NB: Since this article appeared the Göllerich collection has been auctioned off, much of it by Stargardt's firm in Marburg. The present whereabouts of some items is unknown.

96. Wolf, Sándor. *Franz Liszt. Katalog des Franz Liszt-Gedächtnisszimmers der Sammlung Wolf in Eisenstadt 1936.* Vienna: Sándor Wolf, 1936. 9pp.
 ML141.E36W6

 A privately-printed prospectus, illustrated with several Liszt portraits. Also includes three Liszt letters (Nos. 51-53). Outdated, Wolf's collection having been dismantled long ago. Illustrated with three portraits.

Lisztiana in Other Collection Catalogs

Dozens of museum and auction catalogs mention letters, musical mss., and other Liszt documents. Among such catalogs readily available to researchers, the following items are especially interesting:

97. Albrecht, Otto E. *A Census of Autograph Music Manuscripts of European Composers in American Libraries.* Philadelphia: University of Pennsylvania Press, 1953. xvii, 331pp.
 ML135.A2A4

 Contains brief descriptions (pp. 164-172) of 48 Liszt mss. owned by or on permanent loan to the Pierpont Morgan Library, the Curtis Institute of Music, Stanford University, etc. (With regard to the Morgan Library, see item 100.) No illustrations or musical examples. Some of Albrecht's entries are out of date.

98. Deaville, James [A.]. "The C. F. Kahnt Archive in Leipzig: A Preliminary Report." *Notes* 42 (1985-1986), pp. 502-517.

 Evaluates the present state of the Kahnt archives in Leipzig. Deaville also describes an engraver's copy of *Die Legende von der heiligen Elisabeth* (with holograph corrections by Liszt) as well as engraver's scores corrected by Mahler. Illustrated with several facsimiles; concludes with a short catalog of other documents by Liszt, Mahler, Raff, etc., owned today by the Leipzig Staatsarchiv.

99.   *Manuskripte — Briefe — Dokumente von Scarlatti bis Stravinsky. Katalog der Musikautographen-Sammlung Louis Koch*, ed. by Georg Kinsky. Stuttgart: Felix Krais, 1953. xxii, 360pp.
        ML138.K63
        Contains brief descriptions (pp. 239-242) of 10 documents, including a holograph draft of Liszt's *Requiem für die Orgel* and several letters. Also contains descriptions of Liszt holographs preserved in two autograph albums (pp. 322 and 340-341), including an album formerly owned by Carolyne zu Sayn-Wittgenstein. No facsimiles or musical examples.

100.   Turner, J. Rigbie. "Nineteenth-Century Autograph Music Manuscripts in The Pierpont Morgan Library: A Check List." *19th Century Music* 4 (1981), pp. 49-69 and 157-183.
        Identifies mss. of about 20 Liszt works (pp. 160-162) owned by or on loan to the Pierpont Morgan Library, including a holograph of the Sonata in b minor: the so-called "Lehman ms." No musical examples. (With regard to the Lehman ms., see also items 147, 162, and 293-294.)
        Turner's catalog has also been published as a book (New York: Pierpont Morgan Library, 1982; ISBN 0-87598-077-5), with a preface by Charles Ryskamp and a facsimile of a page from a ms. of the *Totentanz*.

Finally, an abbreviated catalog published by the Liszt Museum of Sopron, Hungary, provides a little information for biographers and scholars:

101.   *A Soproni Liszt Ferenc Múzeum és kiállításai*. Győr, 1966. 48pp.
        [No LC number available]
        Identifies a bust of Liszt (reproduced on p. 16) and mentions a handful of Liszt mss. and programs of Sopron Liszt concerts (p. 41).
        Published descriptions of Sopron exhibits contain surprisingly little information about Liszt artifacts. Attila Környei's "Internacionalisták visszaemlékezései a Soproni Liszt Ferenc Múzeum gyűjteményéből," published in *Arrabona* 13 (1971), pp. 417-504, for example, praises ten natives of Sopron honored for activities on behalf of the Soviet Union but says nothing about Liszt.

DISCOGRAPHIES

Very few attempts have been made to date to identify and discuss recordings of Liszt's music. Brief lists of phonorecords appear in a few survey studies and biographies; the finest of these lists are identified in Chapter III. Other short Liszt discographies are identified in reference works like the International Bibliography of Discographies, *ed. David Edwin Cooper (Littleton, Colorado: Libraries Unlim-*

*ited, 1975), p. 101. Additional discographical information, together with descriptions
of 100 selected Liszt recordings, may be found in the appendix.*
  The three studies described below are comparatively detailed and complete:

102.   Fagan, Keith. "Liszt on Compact Disks: A Survey." *Journal of the Amer-
       ican Liszt Society* 22 (1987), pp. 68-71; 23 (1987), pp. 106-109; and 26
       (1989), pp. 56-61.
          Identifies and evaluates most important CDs devoted to Liszt's key-
       board music, choral compositions, songs, etc. Among Fagan's choices are
       CD transfers of recordings that appeared originally on phonorecords and
       cassette tapes. NB: The installment that appears in Volume 24 of the
       journal in question does *not* deal with recordings of Liszt works.
          Readers interested in reviews of Liszt recordings should consult
       Fagan's numerous contributions to the *Liszt Society Journal.* See also item
       135 and the appendix.

103.   Holcman, Jan. "Liszt in the Records of His Pupils." *Saturday Review of
       Literature* 44 (23 December 1961), pp. 45-47 and 57.
          A surprisingly useful article of Liszt recordings on LPs, published as
       part of a tribute to the composer shortly after the 150th anniversary of his
       birth. Contains a catalog (p. 46) identifying dozens of recordings made by
       Liszt pupils. NB: By 1961 some of the performances identified in this cat-
       alog had been distributed in as many as 24 different versions, but only one
       version of each performance is identified by label and catalog number.
       (With regard to other recordings by Liszt pupils, see the appendix.)

104.   Rajben, Bernard. "Catalogue commenté et discographie critique." In item
       38; pp. 271-287.
          An annotated survey of selected Liszt recordings made before the
       1970s. Useful primarily because so little other information is available
       about this topic.

RESEARCH REPORTS AND RELATED STUDIES

*Research reports vary widely in length, contents, and attitude. Some are short, an-
ecdotal accounts of "what's happening" in Liszt studies; others are serious discussions of complex issues involving archival materials or interpretive dilemmas.
Reports dealing exclusively with musical editions or with editing Liszt's works for
publication are described in Chapter V. A few articles pertaining to biographical research are described in Chapter IX. Related studies (including reviews and reports)
are described at the end of this chapter.*

Research Reports

Three of the most detailed and influential Liszt research reports published to date are:

105.   Haraszti, Emile. "Le problème Liszt." *Acta musicologica* 9 (1937), pp. 123-136; and 10 (1938), pp. 32-46.

An evaluation of pre-1936 Liszt research based on the assumption that Liszt's life and music constitute "the most complex problem in the history of modern music." Haraszti supports that hypothesis with discussions of: early Liszt biographies, including Ramann's (item 3); the reliability of the published Liszt correspondence (e.g., item 186); Raabe's failure (in item 2) to consult French-language sources; the importance of Liszt's contributions to nineteenth-century piano technique, and so on. Throughout this and other of his studies Haraszti maintains that France, especially Paris, and French Romanticism "determined the development of Liszt's uniqueness," a claim that has been questioned by many scholars. Other claims by Haraszti about Liszt scholarship are summarized in item 119.

106.   Legány, Dezső. "New Directions in Liszt Research." *Journal of the American Liszt Society* 20 (1986), pp. 125-136.

Suggests that future Liszt researchers will have to address such topics as: the character of Liszt's biographers, not just Liszt himself; the dates of Liszt's letters, published as well as unpublished; slanders aimed at Liszt's memory by Ernest Newman (especially in item 376); and so on. Legány praises a number of studies, including Suttoni's 1979 bibliography of Liszt's published correspondence (see item 41) and describes attempts to establish a Liszt Research Center in Budapest—now a reality. See also item 107 (below).

107.   Legány, Dezső. "Some Problems in Liszt Research." *Journal of the American Liszt Society* 7 (1980), pp. 17-26.

Evaluates Raabe's *Franz Liszt* (item 2) and its limitations; problems with Liszt's published correspondence; press materials and Liszt scholarship; the provenance and authenticity of Liszt's literary works; catalogs of Liszt's compositions; and Liszt's concerts in Pozsony during 1874.

The only book-length "research report" on Liszt studies appeared recently under the title:

108.   *Liszt heute. Bericht über das internationale Symposion in Eisenstadt, 8.-11. Mai 1986*, ed. Gerhard J. Winkler and Johannes-Leopold Mayer. Wissenschaftliche Arbeiten aus dem Burgenland, 78. Eisenstadt: Rötzer, 1987. 167pp.

ISBN 3-85405-104-2   [No LC number available]
Consists of 14 papers presented at the "Liszt heute" symposium held at Eisenstadt in May 1986. With two or three exceptions, these papers deal with Liszt research and its effects on Liszt's reputation throughout the Western world: Austria, England and the United States, France, Germany, Hungary, etc. Contains scattered musical examples and bibliographic citations in the form of endnotes.

NB: Because this collection was designed as a research report of a special kind, its contents are *not* discussed individually below.

Twenty-one more limited research reports and related studies are described below in alphabetical order (by author and/or title). Three other articles, cross-referenced below, are described in greater detail in Chapter IX or at near the end of the present chapter:

109.   Altenburg, Detlef. "Franz Liszt (1811-1886). Bilanz eines Gedenkjahres." *Musica* 41 (1986), pp. 508-513.

A survey of Liszt studies published shortly before and during the centenary celebration of the composer's death. Limited almost entirely to German-language publications.

110.   Autexier, Phillippe A. "Actualité de la recherche Lisztienne en Hongrie." *Revue de musicologie* 67 (1981), pp. 80-89.

A study-by-study review of Hamburger's *Franz Liszt: Beiträge aus ungarischen Authoren* (item 30). Hamburger's anthology and Autexier's summary call to mind what Gerald Abraham once called "Musicology's language curtain" (i.e., the barrier of understanding that prevented, at least until recently, the dissemination in Western Europe and the United States of research originally published in Eastern European languages).

111.   Bartók, Béla. "Liszt problémák." *Nyugat* 29 (1936), pp. 171-179.

An influential essay by twentieth-century Hungary's foremost composer. Bartók deals with the popularity of Liszt's music, its influence on musical history, and Liszt's relationship with Hungary and Hungarian music. In Hungarian.

Published in English under the title "Liszt Problems [1936]" in *Béla Bartók Essays*, ed. Benjamin Suchoff (New York: St. Martin's Press, 1976), pp. 501-510. Reprinted in Hungarian in *Zenetudományi tanulmányok* 3 (1955), pp. 17-26 (with summaries in English, German, and French: pp. 548-549); and in German in item 30; pp. 122-132. See also item 112 (below).

NB: Bartók's essay appeared originally in a censored version. Discussions of the censored passages appear in *Journal of the American Liszt Society* 21 (1987), pp. 26-30; and 22 (1987), p. 88.

112.   Bartók, Béla. "Liszt zenéje és a mai közönség." *Népművelés* 6/17-18 (October 1911), pp. 359-362.

A much shorter essay than "Liszt Problems." Deals primarily the Master's compositions and turn-of-the-century taste and contends that "the public today has not yet got used to" Liszt's music. In Hungarian.

Published in English under the title "Liszt's Music and the Public of Today" in *Béla Bartók Essays* (described in item 111 above), pp. 451-454. Reprinted in Hungarian in *Zenetudományi tanulmányok* 3 (1955), pp. 13-16 (with summaries in English, German, and French: p. 547). Also published in English in the *New Hungarian Quarterly* 2/1 (January 1961), pp. 5-8; in Italian in *Nuova rivista musicale italiana* 4 (1970), pp. 913-916; and in German in item 30; pp. 118-121.

113.   Bekker, Paul. "Franz Liszt Reconsidered," trans. Arthur Mendel. *Musical Quarterly* 28 (1942), pp. 186-189.

An attempt at counteracting the abrasive Liszt studies of Newman (item 376) and others devoted to destroying the so-called "Liszt legend" and a review of the research that went into those studies. Bekker contends that many people find Liszt's music uncongenial because they cannot acknowledge his genius and noble character. Published posthumously. See also item 114 (below).

114.   Bekker, Paul. "Liszt and His Critics." *Musical Quarterly* 22 (1936), pp. 277-283.

A defense of Liszt as a composer, based on Bekker's contention that widespread failure in recognizing "all-inclusive cultural element[s]" in his creative work resulted in much of the antagonism that work has faced during the nineteenth and early twentieth centuries. Bekker also argues that Liszt's ability as a performer actually interfered with his reputation as a composer, an argument easily substantiated by anyone familiar with criticism of Liszt's music published during his lifetime.

115.   Brendel, Alfred. "The Noble Liszt." *New York Review of Books* 33/18 (20 November 1986), pp. 3, 6, 8.

A short, well-written defense of Liszt's reputation by one of the finest pianists of the century. Maintains that nineteenth-century critics punished Liszt "for his undisputed supremacy as a performer." Many of Brendel's observations reappear in item 271; pp. 7-8 as well as articles like "The Penalties of Being a True Celebrity," the *Times* [London] (3 November 1986), pp. 16b-g. Excerpts from item 281 are quoted in Chapter II.

116.   Cook, Nicholas. "Liszt — 100 Years On." *Musical Times* 127 (1986), pp. 372-375.

Primarily a discussion of Liszt's influence on twentieth-century music. Cook maintains that "the heart of Liszt's modernity lies in his conception of music being essentially psychological." Illustrated with several musical examples, including a passage from the *Carrousel de Madame Pelet-Narbonne*, and with references to well-known Liszt studies.

117.   Dömling, Wolfgang. "'Kein Klavierspieler für ruhige Staatsbürger.' Zum 100. Todestag von Franz Liszt." *Österreichische Musikzeitschrift* 41 (1986), pp. 65-71.
    Evaluates the reputation Liszt established as a virtuoso performer and composer of virtuoso piano music, especially during the the late 1830s and 1840s. Illustrated with Charles Renouard's 1886 drawing of Liszt at the keyboard.

*   Gut, Serge. "La recherche Lisztienne depuis 1982."
    A review of the original edition of item 1a and of other individual studies rather than a research survey per se. Described in greater detail as item 132.

118.   Gray, Cecil. "Franz Liszt." *Contingencies and Other Essays*. New York and London: Oxford University Press, 1947; pp. 77-92.
    ML60.G795
    An intelligent review of problems created by early Liszt researchers and scholars. Gray attacks what he considers anti-Liszt sentiment in England; among other points, he maintains that charges of "lack of formal cohesion" and "reliance on programmatic ideas alien to music" in Liszt's music are unjustified. Avoiding the "Liszt legend," however, Gray also admits that at least some Liszt pieces "[merit] the denigratory epithets" of the harshest critics.

*   Hamburger, Klára. "'Musicien humanitaire'."
    More an apostrophe to Liszt's personality and artistic contributions to nineteenth-century cultural life than a review of research. Described in greater detail as item 377.

119.   Haraszti, Emile. "Liszt Literature Fifty Years after His Death." *Hungarian Quarterly* 1 (1936), pp. 312-321.
    Unlike many other research reports, a study-by-study evaluation of important Liszt publications before 1936, including monographs by Zoltán Gárdonyi (items 727-728) and Andor Sommsich (item 363). Rather surprisingly, Haraszti fails to mention the distortions and outright errors in

Newman's and Sitwell's studies (respectively, items 376 and 361). See also item 105.

120.   Helm, Everett. "Franz Liszt, das ewige Enigma — Warum?" *Liszt-Studien* 2 (1981), pp. 13-22.
         Reviews the "enigma" of Liszt's personality and discusses as part of that process a number of important documents and studies, including Marie d'Agoult's novel *Nélida*, Chantavoine's Liszt survey study (item 8), Haraszti's biography (item 351), Walker's *Franz Liszt: The Man and His Music* (item 31), and so on.

*   Helm, Everett. "Franz Liszt — ein Opfer seiner Biographen?"
         Deals with Liszt's complex personality as well as with a number of important publications. Described in greater detail as item 384.

121.   Hinson, Maurice. "The Present State of Liszt Studies Related to his Piano Works." *Piano Quarterly* 23 (1975), pp. 50-56.
         A bibliographic survey of keyboard studies prefaced by an introduction. Somewhat cursory but useful for specialists interested in this enormous topic.
         Reprinted in the *Liszt Society Journal* 2 (1977), pp. 27-28.

122.   Holschneider, Andreas. *Was bedeutet uns Franz Liszt?* Veröffentlichungen der Joachim Jungius-Gesellschaft der Wissenschaften, 31. Göttingen: Vanderhoeck & Ruprecht, 1977. 18pp.
         ML410.L7H66   ISBN 3-525-8557-5
         Grapples with the so-called "Liszt renaissance" of the 1950s and 1960s. Holschneider claims that only today can we view such figures as Liszt and Mahler with relative objectivity. Although he acknowledges the appearance of a post-World War II "flood" of Liszt publications in England and Hungary, Holschneider ignores other studies—including American doctoral dissertations dealing with Liszt's music.

123.   Kárpáti, János. "Das Erbe Franz Liszts und die ungarische Musikwissenschaft." *Musik und Gesellschaft* 6 (1956), pp. 453-456.
         Evaluates a few of the numerous contributions Hungarian scholars have made to Liszt studies and to music in general, and singles out studies by Aladór Tóth (see item 128) and Bence Szabolczi (item 17) for special praise.

124. Kolleritsch, Otto. "Bemerkungen zur neuen Liszt-Rezeption." *Studia musicologica* 25 (1983), pp. 135-143.

    Traces the growth of interest in Liszt and his music from the nineteenth century to the 1980s. Kolleritsch discusses briefly Raabe's survey study (item 2) as well as specialized musical studies by Heinemann (item 655), Schwarz (item 846), and Torkewitz (item 613). Like Holschneider (in item 122), Kolleritsch compares recent interest in Liszt's music to the "Mahler revival" of the 1960s. Limited to German-language publications.

125. Nagler, Norbert. "Das Liszt-Bild — ein wirkungsgeschichtliches Missverständnis?" In item 33; pp. 115-127.

    Challenges researchers to abandon preconceived views of Liszt by "reading across the grain" in the search for the real pianist and composer. Nagler includes as evidence for his arguments quotations from well-known books and articles. Bibliographic citations in more than fifty footnotes.

126. Orga, Ates. "Franz Liszt: Time for Reassessment." *Musical Opinion* 96 (1973), pp. 511-515 and 621-622.

    Identifies lacunae in Liszt research before the 1970s. Among other topics, Orga discusses the unusual character of some late Liszt piano pieces and praises Walker's "Liszt reader" (item 31).

127. Roberts, Wesley. "Has it Been Ten Years Already? Surveying the First Decennium of the 'Journal of the American Liszt Society'." *Journal of the American Liszt Society* 21 (1987), pp. 59-61.

    Describes the origins of this important publication and evaluates some of the articles that appeared in its first 20 volumes.

128. Tóth, Aladór. "Liszt Ferenc a magzar zene útján." *Zenetudományi tanulmányok* 3 (1955), pp. 27-54.

    A review of Hungarian contributions to Liszt scholarship that draws heavily on the author's volume *Liszt Ferenc a magyar zene útján* (Budapest 1939). Tóth maintains that "flourish and chauvinistic self-deception" blinded Hungarians during the 1930s to the "profound musical traditions" revealed in Liszt's own work as well as the music of Bartók and Kodály. In Hungarian; abstracts in German and English (pp. 549-550).

129. Waters, Edward N. "Sur la piste de Liszt." *Notes* 27 (1970-1971), pp. 665-670.

    A chatty account of European excursions undertaken to track down little-known Liszt artifacts. Among other discoveries, Waters located in the British Library, London, a holograph draft of the last "De la situation des artistes" essay published by Liszt in 1835 in the *Revue et gazette musicale* (reprinted in items 165 and 169). Also discusses Liszt studies prior to 1970, individual Liszt studies, and how the Library of Congress acquired the Rosenthal-Liszt collection.

Related Studies (especially reviews)

Studies other than research reports per se *also evaluate portions of the Liszt literature. Most book reviews deal in detail only with a single publication, but a few extraordinary reviews attempt much more. One review of this kind, which deals especially with Walker's* Franz Liszt: The Virtuoso Years, 1811-1847 *(item 1a), is discussed in Chapter III (item 29). Another review of Walker's work—and Walker's reply—deserve special attention:*

130.   Keiler, Allan. "Liszt Research and Walker's 'Liszt'." *Musical Quarterly* 70 (1984), pp. 374-403.

A commentary on recent directions in Liszt research as well as a review of the 1983 edition of item 1a. Keiler criticizes Walker for his "anecdotal" approach to biography as well as isolated errors of fact. Walker's spirited rebuttal, which demolishes many of Keiler's criticisms, is described below (item 131) as well as in Chapter II.

Keiler apparently presented the portions of this review dealing with Liszt's 13 April 1824 "Weihekuss" concert at the 1986 Cleveland meeting of the American musicological Society. See also item 575.

131.   Walker, Alan. [Reply to Allan Keiler's] "Liszt Research and Walker's 'Liszt'." *Musical Quarterly* 71 (1985), pp. 211-219.

A delightfully written counterthrust aimed at item 130 (above) as well as certain tendencies in writing about music. Includes a little information about the unpublished third volume of Walker's biography.

Two other reviews of Walker's book also contain important information about mss., source materials, and the evolution of Liszt studies as a musicological specialty:

132.   Gut, Serge. "La recherche Lisztienne depuis 1982." *Revue de musicologie* 74 (1988), pp. 81-96; and 75 (1989), pp. 76-100.

At once a critique of item 1a (1983 edition) and other studies published prior to 1982 and a collection of comments about items 12, 13c, 62, 70, 88, 224, 226, 253, 281 (original German edition), 461, 521, 606, 608, and 995. Also reviews a French-language edition of item 57.

133.	Mueller, Rena [Charnin]. [Review.] *Journal of the American Musicological Society* 37 (1984), pp. 185-196.

A cautious evaluation of Walker's work: occasionally complementary, more often contradictory. Mueller discusses in some detail Walker's use of documentary materials, especially those pertaining to the Liszt-d'Agoult liaison and, even more especially, D-WRgs ms. Z15. NB: Some of Mueller's corrections were *not* dealt with in the 1987 revised edition of item 1a.

A review of special interest to students of Liszt thematic catalogs as:

134.	Winklhofer, Sharon. "The Grove of Academe." [Review.] *19th Century Music* 5 (1982), pp. 257-262.

Criticizes Searle's *New Grove* Liszt article (item 57), claiming that its pages "are littered with subjective assumptions and misrepresentations which modern scholarship cannot substantiate." Concludes with corrections for many of the first 351 entries in Searle's revised catalog of Liszt's works (item 54). (With regard to these corrections, see also item 47.)

Finally, one of the only reports dealing with recordings of Liszt's music:

135.	Fagan, Keith. "Liszt and One Hundred Years of Recording." *Journal of the American Liszt Society* 20 (1986), pp. 33-37.

A synopsis of issues involving Liszt's compositions and various kinds of sound recordings. Interesting primarily because so little has been published on this topic. No detailed discographical information.

V: MUSICAL EDITIONS AND RELATED STUDIES

Most of the enormous number of compositions, paraphrases, and transcriptions Liszt worked on during his lifetime have been published, some in dozens—even hundreds—of editions. A complete catalog of these editions would thus run to thousands of entries. The publications discussed below constitute either the most complete collected editions of Liszt's works currently available, or editions noteworthy either for their format (e.g., facsimile editions) or their contents (e.g., works published recently for the first time). Research studies devoted exclusively to individual editions or to problems associated with preparing Liszt's compositions for press are described at the end of this chapter.

COLLECTED EDITIONS

No "complete" edition of Liszt's music has yet appeared in print. The most complete edition published to date remains:

136.   *Grossherzog Carl Alexander Ausgabe der musikalischen Werke Franz Liszts,* issued by the "Franz Liszt-Stiftung." Five published series of volumes; incomplete. Leipzig: Breitkopf & Härtel, 1907-1936.
   M3.L48
   136a. Series I, volumes 1-13: Orchestral works (including three works for piano and orchestra).
   136b. Series II, volumes 1-10, 12: Works for piano solo.
   136c. Series V, volumes 3, 5-7: Sacred vocal works.
   136d. Series VII, volumes 1-3: Works for solo voice.
   136e. Transcriptions, volumes 1-3.
   Widely known among Lisztians as the "Collected Edition," "Old Liszt Edition," or simply "GA" (for "Gesamtausgabe," or "collected edition"), this handsome series reprints all Liszt's symphonic poems, most of his original piano works, most of his songs, and many sacred works. Omitted were his organ works, several of his works for piano and orchestra, and virtually all his paraphrases and arrangements other than his Beethoven symphony transcriptions and his transcriptions from Wagner's operas. Each volume is accompanied by scanty editorial notes; some volumes contain "alternate versions" of individual passages or even entire pieces, but other versions are ignored. Illustrated with a few facsimile reprod-

uctions of ms. pages but no detailed descriptions of source materials. Gradually being replaced by the "New Liszt Edition" or "NGA" (item 137 below).

Reprinted by Gregg International in 1966 and by Belwin-Mills during the 1970s. (With regard to the first of these reprint editions, see item 163. With regard to editorial practices in the piano-music volumes, see Ferruccio Busoni, "Die Ausgaben der Liszt'chen Klavierwerke," reprinted in *Von der Einheit der Musik* [Berlin 1922], pp. 45-67.)

Well underway, but by no means finished, is what promises to be a much more complete edition of Liszt's musical works:

137.   *Franz Liszt. Neue Ausgabe sämtlicher Werke/Ferenc Liszt: New Edition of the Complete Works*, ed. Imre Sulyok et al. Budapest: Editio Musica, 1970-.
        M3.L722
        Widely known as the "New Liszt Edition" or "NGA" (for *Neue Gesamtausgabe*, or "new collected edition"). In progress. The volumes published to date contain virtually all Liszt's original works for solo piano, including many pieces also available in item 136 (above).
        Despite many fine qualities, "NLE" volumes are often outfitted with imperfect critical notes. Many volumes also omit early versions of important works (e.g., the 1839 edition of the "Transcendentals"). Reviewers have drawn attention time and time again to some of these problems (e.g., in items 159-161). (With regard to these problems, especially the decision by "NLE" editors to exclude early versions of certain works from their series, see items 154ff. and Chapter II.)
        Distributed in Western Europe by Bärenreiter and in the United States by Theodore Presser. NB: *Scholars should check "NLE" volumes to see whether they contain critical notes.* Many of the volumes on sale in Western Europe and America omit them.

Several incomplete editions of Liszt's music have appeared in the Soviet Union since World War II. Perhaps the most important of these editions is:

138.   *F. List. Opernye transkriptsii dlia fortep'iano*, ed. V. S. Belov and K. S. Sorokin. 7 volumes, bound as 6. Moscow: "Gos. Muz. Izd.," 1958-1968.
        M22.L77B4
        A valuable edition of Liszt's operatic transcriptions and paraphrases. Difficult to obtain; fortunately, some of its contents have been reprinted in items 139-140 (below). Not to be confused with other Soviet Liszt editions, including *Vengerskie rapsodii* (an edition of the "Hungarian Rhapsodies" published in 1965), *Sochineniia dlia fortep'iano* (collected piano works published in five volumes from 1960-1975), and so on.

Russian-language title and contents pages but little or no commentary in any language.

NB: The *New Grove* catalog of Liszt's compositions (item 54) gives "Gosudarstvennoe Muzykal'noe Izdatel'stvo" (or "Gos. Muz. Izd.") as the title for the opera-transcription series. This is the name of the Soviet State Music Publishing House, not of a printed edition of music.

Other editions of collected Liszt works include:

139.   Liszt, Franz. *Complete Piano Transcriptions from Wagner's Operas*, ed. Charles Suttoni. New York: Dover, 1981. 160pp.

   M34.L774W13   ISBN 0-486-24126-2

Adapted from item 138 (above). Contains transcriptions from such works as *Rienzi, Tannhäuser, Lohengrin, Tristan und Isolde*, and *Parsifal* as well as an informative introduction. See also items 140 (below) and 1018.

140.   Liszt, Franz. *Piano Transcriptions from French and Italian Operas*, ed. Charles Suttoni. New York: Dover, 1982. 247pp.

   M22.L77P4   ISBN 0-486-24273-0

Also adapted from item 138. Contains paraphrases from operas by Handel, Mozart, Meyerbeer, Rossini, Donizetti, Bellini, Verdi, Gounod, and Tchaikovsky. See also item 1018.

141.   Liszt, Franz. *Werke für Klavier zu 2 Händen*, ed. Emil von Sauer. 12 volumes. Leipzig: C. F. Peters, 1917.

   M22.L77

A widely-used performance edition of Liszt's most familiar works for solo piano. Includes the "Hungarian Rhapsodies" and "Transcendental Etudes" (1852 version). Excludes the B-minor Sonata, the Beethoven symphony transcriptions, many operatic paraphrases, and so on. A Liszt pupil himself, von Sauer added to his teacher's musical texts performing directions considered necessary today by many performers.

Reprinted after 1945 by the London and New York City branches of the C. F. Peters Co.

142.   Liszt, Franz. *Sämtliche Orgelwerke/The Complete Works for Organ*, ed. Martin Haselböck. 10 volumes. Vienna: Universal-Edition, 1985-.

   M3.1.L57H3

An important collection of music, much of it the finest of its kind composed during the nineteenth century. In addition to presenting material not yet published in "NLE" volumes (item 137), Haselböck's edition supplants those of Straube and Margittay.

NB: When the present research guide went to press Haselböck's edition remained incomplete, the "Forschungsbericht" (Volume 10) not having appeared in print.

Three collected editions of Liszt contributions to keyboard technique also deserve attention:

143. Liszt, Franz. *Technische Studien für das Pianoforte*, ed. Alexander Winterberger. 12 volumes. Leipzig: G. Schuberth, 1887.
M3.3L77T4
Presents keyboard exercises written by Liszt during the last decades of his life and published for the first time a year after his death. Not to be confused either with item 144 (below), which contains some of the same material, or with the *Liszt-Pedägogium* (item 1037) edited by Lina Ramann and originally published in 1901.

144. *The Liszt Studies*, ed. Elyse Mach. New York and London: Associated Music Publishers, 1973. xxvi, 85pp.
MT225.L777
Includes materials borrowed from item 143 (above) as well as translations from Boissier's account of Liszt's pedagogical practices (item 232). Also includes reminiscences by Liszt's great-granddaughter, Mme. Blandine Ollivier de Prévaux. An eccentric study aimed at a popular market. No index or bibliography.

* *Liszt-Pädagogium.*
An anthology prepared for advanced students of Liszt's piano music by several famous performing artists. Described in greater detail as item 1037.

SPECIAL EDITIONS

First Editions

Since 1945, several Liszt works have appeared in print for the first time, or have been reprinted for the first time since their original publication. Among the most important of these publications are:

145.   *Liszt Society Publications*. London: Schott, 1950-; and Aylesbury, England: Bardic 1987-.
        M3.L77L5
          145a. Volume 1:   *Late Piano Works.*
          145b. Volume 2:   *Early and Late Piano Works.*
          145c. Volume 3:   *Hungarian and Late Piano Works.*
          145d. Volume 4:   *Dances for Piano.*
          145e. Volume 5:   *Various Piano Pieces.*
          145f. Volume 6:   *Selected Songs.*
          145g. Volume 7:   *Unfamiliar Piano Works.*
          145h. Volume 8:   Overture to *King Lear* by Berlioz; trans. Liszt.
          145i. [Volume 9]:   Piano Piece No. 1 in A-flat Major.

Miscellaneous collections, mostly of piano pieces not available elsewhere during the 1950s, 1960s, and early 1970s. Important primarily for bringing Liszt's later works to the attention of performers in Europe and America. Unevenly edited and generally void of information about sources, editing techniques, etc. The Berlioz/Liszt transcription (item 145h), for example, contains no specific reference to the D-WRgs Liszt ms. from which it was taken.

Another recent "premiere" publication of an otherwise obscure Liszt composition is:

146.   Liszt, Franz. *Grande fantaisie symphonique* ["Lélio" fantasy] for piano and orchestra. Arranged for two pianos by Manfred Thiele; edited textually by Reiner Zimmermann. Leipzig: Breitkopf & Härtel, 1981. 85pp. [score].
        M1011.L77G77 1981

A stopgap edition of an important work. Like the *Liszt Society Publications* discussed above (item 145), this volume is valuable primarily for making little-known music more widely available. Orchestral parts are available for rental from the Breitkopf offices in Leipzig.

A commendable review of the "Grande fantasie" edition, written by Ralph P. Locke, appeared in *Notes* 41 (1984-1985), pp. 383-385.

Facsimile Editions

A few Liszt works have been published in facsimile editions. The most important and best-known of these editions is undoubtedly:

147.   Liszt, Franz. *Klaviersonate h-Moll. Faksimile nach dem im Eigentum von Robert Owen Lehman befindlichen Autograph*, with "Final Thoughts" by Claudio Arrau. Munich: G. Henle, 1973. 38pp.
        M23.L774

A full-color facsimile edition of the so-called "Lehman ms." deposited in the Pierpont Morgan Library, New York City. A handsome publication marred, according to some experts, by inadequate color definition and other technical problems. Detailed discussions of the "Lehman ms." itself may be found in items 293-294. A discussion of the facsimile edition itself is described as item 162.

Six other Liszt facsimile editions are described below in alphabetical order (by title):

148.   Liszt, Franz. *Cinque melodie ungheresi per pianoforte*, ed. Pietro Scarpini. Torino: Fratelli Pozzo-Salvati-Gros, 1963. 17pp.
          ML96.5L77
          Two colored, foldout facsimiles of the complete musical text for Liszt's *Ungarische Volkslieder*. NB: No references to Scarpini's edition appear either in item 47 or item 134.

149.   *Es war einmal ein König . . . Goethes Flohlied in der Vertonung von Franz Liszt. Faksimile-Ausgabe mit Anmerkungen zum Goethe-Verständnis und zu einigen Goethe-Kompositionen Liszts*, ed. Hans Rudolf Jung. Weimar: Nationale Forschungs- und Gedenkstätten der Klassischen Deutschen Literatur, 1961. 14pp., facsimile.
          ISBN 3-7443-0033-1   [No LC number available]
          A facsimile reproduction of D-WRgs Liszt ms. E7, somewhat reduced in size. Accompanied by an essay explaining the provenance of the ms. itself, Liszt's interest in Goethe's life and poetry, his settings of other Goethe texts, and so on. Illustrated with about a half-dozen printed musical examples.

150.   *Faksimile der Notenhandschrift "Es muß ein Wunderbares sein . . ." von Franz Liszt*, ed. Hans Rudolf Jung. Weimar: Nationale Forschungs- und Gedenkstätten der Klassischen Deutschen Literatur, 1986. 8pp, facsimile.
          ISBN 3-7443-0008-0   [No LC number available]
          A reproduction in a single leaf of D-WRgs Liszt ms. D86, inserted into an essay about the ms. itself, Liszt's relationship to the solo-song traditions of the nineteenth century, and so on. The cover reproduces a Liszt medallion cast during the 1850s.

151.   Liszt, Franz. *Nonnenwerth. Lied für eine Singstimme und Klavier. 2. bisher unveröffentliche Fassung*, ed. Otto Goldhammer. Weimar: Nationale Forschungs- und Gedenkstätten der Klassischen Deutschen Literatur, 1961.
          Rare: US-Wc shelf number M1621.L [case]
          A facsimile edition of D-WRgs Liszt ms. D94, supplemented with a complete transcription of the music and an essay by Otto Goldhammer. Additional musical examples.

152.   Liszt, Franz. *XIX. Magyar rapszóda zongorára.*/*XIX. Ungarische Rhapsodie für Klavier.*/*XIX. Hungarian Rhapsody for piano solo (1885)*, ed. Mária [P.] Eckhardt. Budapest: Editio Musica, 1985. 39pp.
    Folio ML96.5.L77   [No ISBN number available]
    A handsome, full-color reproduction of H-Bn Mus. ms. 353. Concludes with a postscript by Eckhardt. The entire edition is large enough, if not always clear enough, to be read from at the keyboard.

153.   Liszt, Franz. *Revive Szégedin!*, ed. Klára Hamburger. Szeged 1986. No numbered pp.
    ISBN 963-7581-60-X   [No LC number available]
    Consists of a brief introductory essay (in Hungarian), followed by two facsimiles of this march (one bound, the other merely inserted). The bound facsimile reproduces a ms. written entirely by Liszt; the inserted facsimile a ms. in another hand, with Liszt's corrections. See also item 1007.

RELATED STUDIES (INCLUDING REVIEWS)

Preparing Liszt's musical works for publication is a task discussed in a number of articles and editorial introductions. Four of these studies involve editorial decisions for "NLE" volumes. These studies are listed below in chronological order:

154.   Goldhammer, Otto. "Die neue Liszt-Ausgabe. Der kulturelle Beitrag der Deutschen Demokratischen Republik zum Liszt-Jahr 1961." *Beiträge zur Musikwissenschaft* 2/3-4 (1960), pp. 69-85.
    A summary of proposed German contributions, especially by the Goethe- und Schiller-Archiv, to Series I "NLE" volumes (item 137). Includes information about "NLE" editorial policies. Since the 1960s, however, "NLE" editors have reformulated several of their most fundamental policies.
    Additional information about "NLE" editorial policies appeared in a pamphlet by Zoltán Gárdonyi and Otto Goldhammer entitled *Franz Liszts musikalische Werke. Richtlinien für die Edition* (Budapest and Weimar 1961).

155.   Gárdonyi, Zoltán. "Hauptprobleme der neuen Liszt-Ausgabe." *Liszt-Studien* 1 (1977), pp. 73-79.
    A summary of "NLE" editorial policies of the 1960s and early 1970s, including the decision to publish only final versions of compositions known to exist in earlier versions. Many of Gárdonyi's statements reappear, albeit in different wording, in the introductory words found at the beginning of each "NLE" Series I volume.

156.   Boronkay, Antal. "Frühe und endgültige Fassungen von Liszt-Werken in der neuen Liszt-Ausgabe." *Liszt-Studien* 1 (1977), pp. 47-51.
         Describes Boronkay's "NLE" editorial work, problems associated with individual Liszt mss., and aspects of such compositions as the *Großes Konzertsolo*, the *Praeludium und Fuge über BACH* (the so-called "BACH" prelude and fugue) for solo piano, and the B-minor Sonata. Illustrated with the opening measures of the last work.

157.   Sulyok, Imre. "The New Liszt Edition." *New Hungarian Quarterly* 26/99 (Autumn 1985), pp. 188-194.
         A restatement of "NLE" editorial policies, including the decision to publish at least a few preliminary versions of works later revised and republished by Liszt. Illustrated with a facsimile reproduction of H-Bn Mus. ms. 274, containing additions to "Hungarian Rhapsody" No. 2.
         A very slightly different version of this article appeared under the same title but without facsimile illustration in the *Journal of the American Liszt Society* 19 (1986), pp. 5-9.

Among reviews of "NLE" volumes is the following brief survey:

158.   Howard, Leslie. "The New Liszt Edition." *Music and Musicians* (October 1986), pp. 14-15.
         A review of "NLE" Series I publications and the music contained in those volumes. Howard mentions musicological weaknesses in the volumes he discusses, but he also praises the "NLE" as a whole for legibility, format, and—of course—some of the pieces themselves. Illustrated with a drawing of Liszt done by George T. Tobin, and with a photograph of Liszt in his seventies.

Reviews of Liszt editions sometimes comment on editorial procedures, or correct misprintings, or identify and discuss source materials overlooked by the editors of the editions themselves. Three such reviews of "NLE" Series I and II volumes are described below in alphabetical order (by author):

159.   Ho, Allan. [Review.] *Notes* 40 (1983-1984), pp. 886-888.
         Evaluates "NLE" Series I/15-16, Liszt's transcriptions for piano of his own compositions. Ho praises aspects of these volumes; he also points out compositions overlooked or omitted by NLE editors (among them, works described in item 81).

160. Rucker, Patrick. [Review.] *Journal of the American Liszt Society* 24 (1988), pp. 113-116.

Examines and describes differences between "NLE" Series II texts of Liszt-Schubert transcriptions and the texts of the original editions. Illustrated with musical examples from Diabelli's edition of *Das Wandern* (c. 1847) and portions of the same transcription in "NLE" format.

161. Saffle, Michael. [Review.] *Notes* 44 (1987-1988), pp. 815-817.

Deals with "NLE" Series I/13 and 18, especially with questionable editing practices and the contents of one US-Wc Liszt ms.

Two studies of other important Liszt editions also deserve attention:

162. Longyear, Rey M. "The Text of Liszt's B Minor Sonata." *Musical Quarterly* 60 (1974), pp. 435-450.

A description of the "Lehman ms.," reproduced in facsimile in item 147. Sharon Winklhofer (in items 293-294) has objected to some of Longyear's conclusions on the grounds that the facsimile edition is inadequate for scholarly purposes.

163. Searle, Humphrey. "The Breitkopf Collected Edition of Liszt's Works." Published at the end of the Gregg reprint of item 136 (Series VII, Volume 3). 38pp.

A comparatively detailed survey of the "Old Liszt Edition" (item 136), evidently intended as an introduction to Liszt's music as a whole. Concludes with a catalog (pp. 6-38) of the composer's works, adapted from Searle's 1954 *Grove Dictionary* catalog (see item 54). A little-known publication, ignored by most reference works on Liszt and inadvertantly omitted from item 40. The Music Division of the Library of Congress keeps a copy on the Reading Room reference shelves.

Finally, a very few studies of editions prepared by Liszt of other composers' works have also appeared in print. Among them is:

164. Veszprémi, Lili. "Liszt — Bartók — Weiner a Mondschein-szonátáról." *Parlando* 21/5 (May 1979), pp. 8-12.

Compares three editions of Beethoven's Sonata, Op. 27, No. 2. In Hungarian.

Similar studies by Veszprémi have appeared in *Parlando*, Hungary's best-known music-education journal. See, for example, her article "Liszt — Bartók — Weiner Beethoven két legkönnyebb szonátájától," *Parlando* 21/9 (September 1979), pp. 1-7. Also in Hungarian.

VI: LITERARY WORKS AND RELATED STUDIES

Liszt's literary works include several books, a number of lengthy articles, and a variety of concert reports, reviews, and miscellaneous publications. The precise authorship of some of these works remains in doubt, since the Comtesse d'Agoult and the Princess Sayn-Wittgenstein (respectively) almost certainly drafted portions of the "Bachelor" letters and the monograph on Hungarian music (actually Gypsy music). Today, however, it is generally accepted that Liszt himself wrote at least some of the books and articles published under his name. Studies dealing with this and related issues are described below and in Chapter X.

COLLECTED EDITIONS

Although incomplete, two collected editions of Liszt's literary works have been or are being published:

165.   *Franz Liszt. Gesammelte Schriften*, ed. Lina Ramann. 6 volumes. Leipzig: Breitkopf & Härtel, 1881-1899.
       ML410.L7A7
       165a. Volume 1: *Friedrich Chopin.*
       165b. Volume 2: *Essays und Reisebriefe . . .*
       165c. Volume 3: *Dramaturgische Blätter.*
       165d. Volume 4: *Aus der Annalen des Fortschritts.*
       165e. Volume 5: *Streifzüge: kritische, polemische und zeithistorische Essays.*
       165f. Volume 6: *Die Zigeuner und ihre Musik in Ungarn.*

An unfortunately bowdlerized collection of Liszt's principal literary works, translated into German and published without scholarly apparatus of any kind. Items 165b-e contain most of Liszt's shorter essays but not all of them; Ramann either made no attempt to track down all of her subject's literary efforts or deliberately excluded some of them from her edition. In German throughout, despite the fact that most of Liszt's published literary efforts appeared originally in French.

    Other editions of the *Gesammelte Schriften* also exist (e.g., a "Volksausgabe" in 4 volumes issued by Breitkopf & Härtel in 1910). A collection of articles taken from item 165 appeared under the editorship of Wolfgang Marggraf as *Schriften zur Tonkunst* (Leipzig: Reclam, 1981).

Not seen; cited in item 18. La Mara's edition is also mentioned in Chapter II.

166.   *Franz Liszt: Sämtliche Schriften*, ed. Detlef Altenburg et al. Wiesbaden: Breitkopf & Härtel. In press.
     166a. Volume 5: "Dramaturgische Blätter."
     ISBN 3-7651-0236-9   [No LC number available]
     A new, comprehensive, and highly scholarly edition of Liszt's literary works. NB: Additional volumes of this series should be available by the time the present guide appears in print. All volumes in French and German (if appropriate).
     Much of Altenburg's work with Liszt's literary works was anticipated in his unpublished doctoral dissertation, *Studien zum Musikdenken und zu den Reformplänen von Franz Liszt* (University of Cologne 1980). Cited in item 18 and a few other, recent Liszt studies.

SPECIAL EDITIONS

Several of Liszt's books and essays have appeared in editions of their own. Among these are facsimiles of mss. and early editions, collections of essays and reviews, and translations of individual literary works.

Facsimile Editions

167.   Liszt, Franz. *De la Fondation-Goethe à Weimar/Zur Goethe-Stiftung in Weimar*, ed. Otto Goldhammer and Heinz Holtzhauer. Weimar: Nationale Forschungs- und Gedenkstätten der Klassischen Deutschen Literatur, 1961. 61 + 7pp.
     PT2145.G6L5 1961
     A facsimile of Liszt's original proposal for an arts foundation honoring the memory of Johann Wolfgang Goethe. Includes lengthy essays about Liszt's life and works, the original French-language text of the essay, and a German-language translation. (With regard to Liszt's plans for the Foundation, see item 596.)

168.   Liszt, Franz. *Lohengrin et Tannhäuser de Richard Wagner*, with a preface by Jacques Bourgeois. Paris: Adef-Albatros [1980].
     [No LC or ISBN numbers available]
     A fascimile of a volume originally published in French in 1851. Bourgeois's preface includes information about Liszt's essays, their publication history, and their considerable influence on Wagner's reputation. In French throughout.

Anthologies

169.   Liszt, Franz. *Pages romantiques*, ed. Jean Chantavoine. Paris: F. Alcan, 1912. xii, 290pp.

ML410.L7A14

Contains most of the articles published under Liszt's name between 1835-1840 in the *Revue et gazette musicale* [Paris]. Especially valuable because Ramann's edition of Liszt's "complete" literary works (item 165) consists entirely of German translations. NB: Some of Liszt's "Bachelor" essays were omitted from Chantavoine's volume; see item 170 (below). In French throughout.

Reprinted in 1985 by Éditions d'aujourd'hui of Plan de la Tour [Var], with a preface by Serge Gut.

When the present research guide went to press, no other anthologies of Liszt's literary works had appeared in print. Individual Liszt essays or portions of them, however, have been reprinted several times; portions of "Berlioz and his 'Harold' Symphony," for example, were included in *Source Readings in Music History From Classical Antiquity through the Romantic Era*, ed. Oliver Strunk (New York: W. W. Norton, 1950), pp. 846-873. An English-language translation of Liszt's tribute to Paganini appeared in the *Liszt Society Journal* 7 (1982), pp. 41-42. See also *Divagazioni di un musicista romantico*, a collection of Liszt's writings edited by Raoul Meloncelli (ISBN 8-885026-25-7) and printed in Italian. Like item 169, this anthology includes only some of the "Bachelor" letters.

Editions of Individual Literary Works

170.   Liszt, Franz. *An Artist's Journey: Lettres d'un bachelier ès musique, 1835-1841*. Translated and annotated by Charles Suttoni. Chicago and London: University of Chicago Press, 1989. xxvii, 260pp.

ML410.L7A3 1989   ISBN 0-2264-8510-2

A painstakingly annotated, lively translation of Liszt's "Bachelor" essays originally published in the *Revue et gazette musicale* [Paris] and elsewhere. Contains several essays missing from items 165b and 169 (above). Illustrated with 22 portraits, photographs, maps, and other visual aids; outfitted with copious notes, index, and bibliography. NB: This volume also contains translations of George Sand's "Letter of a Voyager to Liszt," essays by other nineteenth-century literary figures, and Liszt's essay on church music. (With regard to English-language translations of this last essay, see items 536 and 973.)

171.   Liszt, Franz. *Frederic Chopin*, trans. Edward N. Waters. New York: The
        Free Press, 1963. vii, 184pp.
            ML410.C54L738
        A readable English-language version of Liszt's *F. Chopin*, originally
        published in the 1850s in part as a memorial to the Polish composer's life
        and work. Includes an essay about the monograph's history and some of
        its textual problems. Some of the ideas presented in this essay also appear
        in item 184.

172.   Liszt, Franz. "De la situation des artistes." *Liszt Society Journal* 9 (1984),
        pp. 29-30.
        Introductory comments in English by Eunice Mistarz, followed by the
        French-language text of Liszt's essay, reproduced from British Library
        Add. ms. 33965, fols. 237-242. Unfortunately incomplete, the editor having
        omitted Liszt's marginal notes to the typesetter for the edition published
        in the *Revue et gazette musicale* and reprinted in item 169.

173.   "Liszt the Writer: Impressions of Genoa and Florence," trans. Adrian
        Williams. *Liszt Society Journal* 11 (1986), pp. 39-43.
        An English-language version of two "Bachelor" articles published in
        1839 under Liszt's name in *L'Artiste* and omitted from Ramann's and
        Chantavoine's anthologies (items 165b and 169) but included in item 170.
        Illustrated with a view of Genoa, a portrait of sculptor Lorenzo Bartolini,
        a picture of Bartolini's studio in Florence, and the Bartolini bust of Liszt.

STUDIES OF LITERARY WORKS

Only one extended evaluation of Liszt's literary endeavors has ever appeared in print:

174.   Schemann, Ludwig. "Liszt als Schriftsteller." *Bayreuther Blätter* 10 (1887),
        pp. 285-330.
        A wordy summary of Liszt's literary efforts, written in 1885-1886 but
        published as a tribute to him shortly after his death in the latter year. In-
        teresting primarily for students of nineteenth-century music criticism and
        "Rezeptionsgeschichte." (With regard to these topics, see also items 175
        [below], 177-178, 180, and relevant portions of items 166-167 and 170.)

*Among shorter surveys of Liszt's literary works, the following articles are especially
interesting:*

175.   Altenburg, Detlef. "Die Schriften von Franz Liszt: Bemerkungen zu einem
        zentralen Problem der Liszt-Forschung." *Festschrift Arno Forchert zum*

60. Geburtstag am 29. Dezember 1985, ed. Gerhard Allroggen and Detlef Altenburg. Kassel: Bärenreiter, 1986; pp. 242-251.

    ISBN 3-761-80776-7   [No LC number available]

Discusses problems associated with Liszt's literary efforts, including their authenticity, the limitations of Ramann's "complete" edition (item 165), philological characteristics of individual publications, the reception of individual works by the musical world, etc. Includes numerous references to primary and secondary sources in the form of footnotes. NB: Altenburg's observations anticipate the publication in the immediate future of item 166a and additional volumes in that series.

176.   Hübsch-Pfleger, Lini. "Franz Liszt als Schriftsteller." *Musica* 15 (1961), pp. 534-537.

A brief introduction to Liszt's literary interests and output as well as to his possible collaboration with d'Agoult and Sayn-Wittgenstein. (With regard to this last issue, see item 1b; pp. 368-396, as well as items 177-178 [below], 180, etc.)

*   Bauer, Marion. "The Literary Liszt."

As much a study of Liszt's literary interests as of the books and articles published under his name. Described in greater detail as item 526.

The authenticity of Liszt's literary works was debated with special fervor in several essays written during the 1930s and 1940s. Among these are:

177.   Haraszti, Emile. "Franz Liszt: Author Despite Himself." *Musical Quarterly* 33 (1947), pp. 490-516.

Argues that the Comtesse d'Agoult and the Princess Sayn-Wittgenstein served as the "ghost writers" who produced the books and articles published under Liszt's name. Haraszti made skillful use of source materials available during the 1940s, but his contention that none of Liszt's essays survives in his own handwriting was disproved almost two decades ago by Waters (in item 129) and, more recently, by Eckhardt (in item 180). Includes quotations from Liszt's correspondence as well as from selected literary works. Discussed in Chapter II.

Not to be confused with item 178 (below), or with other publications by Haraszti, including "Die Authorschaft der literarischen Werke Franz Liszts," *Ungarische Jahrbücher* 21 (1941), pp. 173-236.

178.   Haraszti, Emile. "Franz Liszt, écrivain et penseur." *Revue de musicologie* "Série speciale" No. 2 (July 1943), pp. 19-28; and No. 3 (1944), pp. 12-24.

Another discussion of Liszt's literary works as well as his literary interests.

Two other articles deal with published and unpublished documents relating to Liszt's literary output:

179.   Deaville, James [A.]. "A Checklist of Publications of Liszt's Writings, 1849-1879." *Journal of the American Liszt Society* 24 (1988), pp. 86-90.
        Identifies dozens of Liszt literary works—among them his books about Chopin (see item 165a) and Gypsy music (see item 165f) and his most important Wagner essays—by their places of first publication.

180.   Eckhardt, Mária [P.]. "New Documents on Liszt as Author." *New Hungarian Quarterly* 25/93 (Autumn 1984), pp. 1-14.
        Demonstrates conclusively that Liszt played a role in writing at least some of the books and articles published under his name. Eckhardt illustrates her discussion with facsimiles of six documents belonging to the Goethe- und Schiller-Archiv, Weimar; the Bibliothèque Nationale, Paris; the Liszt Ferenc Museum of Sopron, Hungary; and an unnamed private collection. Each document includes at least Liszt's signature; three of them represent holograph fragments from *F. Chopin* (see items 165a and 171), and from a draft of Liszt's obituary of Paganini (see item 169).
        Reprinted under the same title but without facsimile illustrations, in the *Journal of the American Liszt Society* 18 (1985), pp. 52-66.

Five studies of Liszt's literary works, most of them dealing with concert reviews or reviews of published music, are described or cross-referenced below in alphabetical order (by author):

*   Bangert, Mark. "Franz Liszt's Essay on Church Music . . ."
        Contains a complete English-language translation of Liszt's essay as well as observations on its gestation and significance. Described in greater detail as item 536.

181.   Berg, Michael. "Der Künstler als Kritiker: Anmerkungen zu Liszts Schumann-Essay." *Musik und Gesellschaft* 36 (1986), pp. 347-349.
        Discusses Liszt's 1855 article about Robert Schumann and his music in light of Liszt's other literary works, especially the 1835 "De la situation des artistes" essays. Among other topics, Berg mentions the possibility that Liszt's essay was intended as a reply to issues raised by Eduard Hanslick in his famous book about the "musically-beautiful." Illustrated with several photographs.
        A second, less significant article by Berg appeared under the title "Zu Franz Liszts kritikkritischen Ideen" in item 37; pp. 153-158.

182.   Lowens, Irwing. "Liszt as Music Critic." *Journal of the American Liszt Society* 6 (1979), pp. 4-9.

Describes Liszt's work as a critic between 1834-1840 and 1849-1859 in light of the collaboration he received at least occasionally from d'Agoult and Sayn-Wittgenstein. Includes quotations from items 171 and 177.

183.   Reuss, Eduard. "Liszt als Kritiker." *Neue Zeitschrift für Musik* 78 (1911), pp. 173-175, 192-194, 208-210, and 230-232.

Deals with Liszt's Schumann and Wagner essays as well as his 1837 article about Thalberg for the *Revue et gazette musicale*. Reuss wanders from topic to topic, considering many issues of peripheral interest to Lisztians (e.g., Schopenhauer's impact on nineteenth-century culture). No illustrations, extended quotations, or specific citations of secondary sources.

184.   Waters, Edward N. "'Chopin' by Liszt." *Musical Quarterly* 47 (1961), pp. 170-194.

Describes the origins and character of Liszt's book-length tribute to his Polish colleague (item 165a). Reproduces a letter addressed to Liszt by Sainte-Beuve on 31 March 1850 (reprinted from item 191). Also includes lengthy quotations from item 171.

Finally, several nineteenth-century discussions of individual Liszt literary works continue to interest specialists. Among such discussions is:

185.   Adelburg, August von. *Entgegnung auf die von Dr. Franz Liszt in seinem Werke "Des Bohemiens et de leur musique en Hongrie" aufgestellte Behauptung, dass es keine ungarische Nationalmusik gibt.* With a foreword by Alexander von Czeke. Pest: Lampel, 1859. 30pp.

British Museum shelf number 7896.b.6 [No LC number available]

Attacks Liszt's book about "Gypsy music" (reprinted as item 165f) for implying that nineteenth-century Hungary possessed no other traditional music. Discussed at greater length in item 1a; p. 341n.

Another monograph about Liszt's "Gypsy Music" book, written by one Sámuel Brassai, was published at Kolozsvár in 1860 and in Hungarian under the title *Magyar-vagy Czingány-Zene? Elmefuttatás Liszt Ferencz "Czigányokról irt Könyve felett.* Not seen; cited in item 1b; p. 584.

VII: LETTERS AND RELATED STUDIES

Although an enormous amount of Liszt's correspondence remains unpublished, thousands of letters have already appeared in print. It is impossible to identify this literature in the present volume, much less evaluate it in detail. Instead, almost all of Liszt's published correspondence is reviewed in item 41. The books and articles described below have been selected because of their importance, or because they exemplify various kinds of Liszt-letters studies. Collected editions are described first, followed by other Liszt letters publications and by studies relating to Liszt's correspondence. Letters written by Liszt have appeared in many kinds of studies, including some of the publications described in Chapter VIII. Other letters appear in survey studies (Chapter III), biographies (Chapter IX), and specialized biographical studies (Chapter X).

COLLECTED EDITIONS

No comprehensive collected edition of Liszt's correspondence has appeared in print, although a plan has been proposed to publish such an edition (see item 218). The closest approach to a complete edition of Liszt letters remains:

186.   *Franz Liszt's Briefe*, ed. "La Mara" [pseud. Marie Lipsius]. 8 volumes. Leipzig: Breitkopf & Härtel, 1893-1905.
ML410.L7A3
        186a.   Volume 1: *Von Paris bis Rom.*
        186b.   Volume 2: *Von Rom bis an's Ende.*
        186c.   Volume 3: *An eine Freundin* [Agnès Street-Klindworth].
        186d-g.   Volumes 4-7: *An Fürstin Carolyne Sayn-Wittgenstein.*
        186h.   Volume 8: *1823-1886. Neue Folge zu Bde. I und II.*
The largest single published collection of Liszt correspondence. Includes 2492 letters, among them letters dating from every period of Liszt's life and addressed to virtually all his correspondents. Unfortunately unreliable; full of editorial suppressions (indicated, however, in almost every instance) and occasional errors. Published in French- and German-language editions, even though Liszt wrote most of his letters in French. No critical apparatus or bibliographic citations, although indexes of names appear in items 186b-e and 186g-h. Item 186e also contains Liszt's will (reprinted in item 1b; pp. 557-563, as well as in items 222-223). An heroic

effort, only now being replaced by a new Liszt-letters edition (see item 218). (With regard to La Mara's editorial work, see the introduction to item 41. With regard to the textual integrity of item 186c, see item 220 as well as comments in Chapter II.)

An abridged edition of this collection also appeared as:

187.   *Letters of Franz Liszt,* trans. Constance Bache. 2 volumes. London: H. Grevel, 1894.
  ML410.L7A31, vols. 1-2.
  An English-language translation of items 186a-b (above). Although no more reliable than its model, Bache's translation does contain four letters missing from La Mara's volumes. Available in several reprint editions.

At least three other, extensive collections of Liszt letters addressed to a variety of correspondents deserve to be consulted regularly by Liszt researchers:

188.   *Franz Liszt: Briefe aus ungarischen Sammlungen, 1835-1886,* ed. Margit Prahács. Kassel: Bärenreiter, 1966 [Also published in Budapest]. 484pp.
  ML410.L7A314
  After item 186 the largest collection of Liszt's correspondence, and certainly the best. Contains 605 fully annotated and indexed letters printed in Prahács's text. Supplemented with 160 pages of commentary containing an 14 additional letters (pp. 312, 336, 338, 342, 353, 355, 375, 380, 385, 404, 426, 434, 440, and 447). Concludes with indexes of names and topics.
  Fine anthologies of Liszt letters have also appeared in Hungarian. The best of these is: *Liszt Ferenc válogatott levelei (1824-1861),* ed. Mária Eckhardt (Budapest: Zeneműkiadó, 1989; ISBN 963-330-677-9). This volume includes indexes of pieces by Liszt as well as of persons and places referred to in the 160 letters it reprints. Illustrated with several facsimiles, including one of a note dated 10 June 1826 and reproduced from a ms. owned by the Bibliothèque Nationale, Lyon.

189.   *Franz Liszt in seinen Briefen. Eine Auswahl,* ed. Hans Rudolf Jung. Frankfurt: Athenäum, 1988. 523pp.
  ISBN 3-610-08470-7   [No LC number available]
  Contains 170 letters, some of them never previously published, including four letters by Liszt's father Adam. Illustrated with 16 black-and-white plates of portraits, facsimile ms. pages, sheet-music covers, and so on. Concludes with more than 150 pages of detailed commentary, information about the source of each letter, and a useful index.
  Originally published in 1987 by Henschel of East Berlin. For additional information about some of the source materials used by Jung in both the Frankfurt and East Berlin texts of this anthology, see Gerhard J.

Winkler's review in the *Journal of the American Liszt Society* 23 (1988), pp. 113-115.

A curiosity today, Eduard Reuß's [or Reuss's] anthology *Franz Liszt in seinen Briefen* (Stuttgart: Greiner & Pfeiffer, n.d.; ML410.L7R58) appeared around the turn of the century and presented excerpts from item 186 grouped according to recipients. In German throughout.

190.   *Franz Liszt. Correspondance: Lettres choisis*, ed. Pierre-Antoine Huré and Claude Knepper. Paris: Jean-Claude Lattès, 1987. 596pp.

     ML410.L7A4 1987   [No ISBN number available]

     Not seen. According to items 41 and 46, it contains more than 400 letters and constitutes a "notable contribution to the literature, not only for itself, but [because] it corrects omissions and errors found in earlier editions of Liszt letters to his mother Anna Liszt [item 197], to Marie d'Agoult [item 194], and [to] Agnès Street-Klindworth [item 186c]." In French throughout.

     A much shorter Huré-Knepper collection of Liszt correspondence, based on D-WRgs holographs, appeared under the title "Huit lettres inédites" in item 36; pp. 16-35.

Another extremely important collection of correspondence consists of letters addressed to Liszt by family members, friends, and colleagues:

191.   *Briefe hervorragender Zeitgenossen an Franz Liszt*, ed. La Mara. 3 volumes. Leipzig: Breitkopf & Härtel, 1895-1904.

     ML410.L7L52

       191a. Volume 1: *1824-1854.*

       191b. Volume 2: *1855-1881.*

       191c. Volume 3: *1836-1881. Neue Folge.*

     Next to *Franz Liszt's Briefe* (item 186), the largest published collection of Liszt letters. Includes 798 missives addressed to the composer between 1824-1886, although comparatively few items date from his last years. The letters themselves are printed in French or German, according to the language they were written in. No bibliography or critical apparatus, aside from brief biographies of correspondents.

Editions of Liszt's correspondence with Richard Wagner and with the Comtesse d'Agoult also deserve special attention:

192.   *Briefwechsel zwischen Wagner und Liszt*, ed. Erich Kloss. 3rd enlarged edition. 2 volumes. Leipzig; Breitkopf & Härtel, 1910.

     ML410.W1A362 1912

     Contains 351 letters exchanged by the two composers between 1841-1882. The second volume concludes with an index of names. Letters

in French and German, with German-language translations of French letters printed in appendices.

   NB: Earlier editions of the Liszt-Wagner correspondence, also published by Breitkopf & Härtel, are far less reliable; they were prepared
(anonymously) by Cosima, Liszt's daughter, very shortly after her father's
death in 1886. Translations made during the 1890s by Francis Hueffner
(into English) and L. Schmidt-Lacant (into French) were based on the
pre-Kloss texts. The Kloss edition is also available in a 1943 French-
language version edited by G. Samazeuilh. See also item 193 (below).

193.   *Franz Liszt — Richard Wagner Briefwechsel*, ed. Hanjo Kesting. Frankfurt
       a.M.: Insel, 1988. 757pp.
          ML410.L7A4 1988   ISBN 3-458-14369-6
       A new, somewhat sparsely annotated edition of the Liszt-Wagner let-
       ters published in several editions (see item 192 above). Includes 20 letters
       omitted from other editions. Concludes with German-language trans-
       lations of French texts and with an index of names.

194.   *Correspondance de Liszt et de la Comtesse d'Agoult*, ed. Daniel Ollivier. 2
       volumes. Paris: Bernard Grasset, 1933-1934.
          ML410.L7A32 1933-1934
       Contains 566 letters exchanged by Liszt and Marie (Comtesse)
       d'Agoult, his lover and the mother of his three children. Important in part
       because Liszt-d'Agoult letters could not be included in items 186a and
       186h. The Liszt-d'Agoult *Correspondance* includes Liszt's copies of letters
       to several miscellaneous correspondents and to the committee charged
       with erecting a memorial to Beethoven in Bonn. Another unreliable edi-
       tion, soon to be replaced by item 195 (below). No apparatus, except for
       an index of names, and no detailed bibliographic information.

       A German-language edition of the first volume, edited by Käthe Illich,
       was published in Berlin in 1933 under the title *Briefe an Marie Gräfin
       d'Agoult*.

195.   *Correspondance de Liszt et de Marie d'Agoult*, ed. Jacqueline Bellas. Paris:
       In press.
          [No ISBN number available]
       A revision of item 194 (above), consisting of 562 letters (including
       about a dozen previously unknown documents), extensive annotations,
       chronological information, and a biographical index.

Eight other valuable collections of Liszt letters are described or cross-referenced below in alphabetical order (by title or author):

196.   *Correspondance de Liszt et de sa fille Madame Emile Ollivier, 1842-1862*, ed. Daniel Ollivier. Paris: Bernard Grasset, 1936. 341pp.
        ML410.L7A28
        Contains 179 letters addressed by Liszt not only to his daughter Blandine (later Mme Olliver), but to his other children Cosima and Daniel as well as the children as a group. Concludes with an index of names.
        Much of this volume's contents appeared originally in the *Revue de musicologie* 105 (1935), pp. 836-868; and 106 (1936), pp. 111-144.

*   Eckhardt, Mária [P.], and Cornelia Knotik. *Franz Liszt und sein Kreis in Briefen und Dokumenten aus den Beständen des Burgenländischen Landesmuseums.*
        A museum catalog as well as a collection of letters written by Sayn-Wittgenstein, Liszt's nephew Eduard von Liszt, Richard Wagner, etc. Described in greater detail as item 70.

197.   *Franz Liszt: Briefe an seine Mutter*, ed. La Mara. Leipzig: Breitkopf & Härtel, 1918. 156pp.
        ML410.L7A39
        A German-language edition of 102 letters addressed by Liszt to his mother between 1827-1866. Unfortunately, French-language texts of most of these letters remain unpublished. NB: New letters addressed by Anna Liszt to her son and other relatives, and by Liszt to his mother, have recently appeared in print; see item 268.

198.   *Franz Liszts Briefe an Baron Anton Augusz, 1846-1878*, ed. Wilhelm von Csápo. Budapest: Franklin, 1911. 233pp.
        ML410.L7A37
        Contains 117 letters preceded by the editor's reminiscences of Liszt ("Aus meinen Erinnerungen"; pp. 1-38). Illustrated with facsimile reproductions of several mss., including an "Albumblatt" dating from 1839 and a Liszt portrait (as frontispiece). Most of the letters are printed in French, although some were written in and appear in German. (With regard to other Liszt-Augusz letters, see item 79.)
        An Hungarian-language edition of this volume was also published in 1911 under the title *Liszt Ferencz levelei báró Augusz Antalhoz*.

199.   *Franz Liszt: Unbekannte Presse und Briefe aus Wien, 1822 — 1886*, ed.
        Dezső Legány. Wiener musikwissenschaftliche Beiträge, 13. Vienna and
        Graz: Hermann Böhlaus, 1984. 265pp.
           ML410.L7F72 1984   ISBN 3-205-00543-0
           A valuable collection of letters (and press clippings) preserved in eight
        Viennese libraries and archives. Among 210-odd items of correspondence
        are some seventy letters addressed to Bösendorfer between 1870-1886.
        Legány provides valuable comments about each document as well as
        bibliographic citations and an index.
           Reviewed in detail in item 429.

200.   *Lettres autographes conservées à la Bibliothèque Royale Albert Ier. —
        Ferenc Liszt*, ed. Yves Lenoir. Fontes musicae Bibliothecae Regiae
        Belgicae, 1. Brussels: Royal Belgian Library, 1986. 32pp.
           ISBN 2-87093-033-X   [No LC number available]
           A collection of seven letters published in facsimile, in their original
        French texts, and in Flemish translations. Includes a previously unpub-
        lished note addressed on 16 September 1826 to one Paultre de Lamothe.

201.   *Lettres de Liszt à Agnès Street-Klindworth*, ed. Pauline Pocknell. Ottawa:
        University of Ottawa Press. In press.
           [No ISBN number available]
           Announced as a complete, uncensored edition of Liszt's letters to
        Klindworth, originally published in deliberately falsified versions as item
        186c (see item 1b; pp. 209ff, as well as items 41, 220, etc.). In English and
        French.

*   Vendel-Mohay, Lajosné. *Liszt-emlekék Szekszárdon.*
           A catalog of Liszt-Augusz letters in the Szekszárd Museum, Hungary.
        Includes facsimile reproductions of the letters themselves as well as their
        French- or German-language texts, translations into Hungarian, and
        Hungarian-language commentary. Described in greater detail as item 79.
        See also item 198.

Two recent but disappointing collections of letters should be used with care:

202.   *The Letters of Franz Liszt to Marie zu Sayn-Wittgenstein*, ed. Howard E.
        Hugo. Cambridge, Massachusetts: Harvard University Press, 1953. x,
        376pp.
           ML410.L7A365
           A surprisingly poor collection, full of errors and rash editorial opinions.
        Contains a number of letters originally printed in items 186d-g as well as

in several periodical publications. Concludes with critical notes and an index.

Reviewed at some length by Jacques Barzun in the *Musical Quarterly* 40 (1954), pp. 110-115.

203. *The Letters of Franz Liszt to Olga von Meyendorff, 1871-1886, in the Mildred Bliss Collection at Dumbarton Oaks*, ed. William Tyler and Edward N. Waters. Washington, D.C.: Dunbarton Oaks, 1979.

ML410.L7A363   ISBN 0-88402-078-9

Another lacklustre publication. Tyler and Waters provide comparatively little information about the provenance and contents of these letters, their index is disappointing, and no French-language texts accompany their translations.

A much more detailed discussion of this collection, written by Mária Eckhardt, appeared in *Studia musicologica* 22 (1980), pp. 468-474. See also item 41.

Finally, one important collection of Liszt correspondence has a rather misleading title:

204. *Franz Liszt — L'artiste, le clerc. Documents inédits*, ed. Jacques Vier. Paris: Éditions du Cèdre, 1950. 158pp.

ML410.L7A18

A miscellaneous collection of Liszt letters, including more than two dozen addressed to his mother Anna before her death in 1866. Also includes the texts of letters to Marie d'Agoult, Jules Janin, Maurice Schlesinger, and other important figures in Liszt's life. (With regard to articles about many of these figures, see Chapter X.)

EDITIONS OF INDIVIDUAL LETTERS

Individual Liszt letters have been published in a variety of formats (e.g., as magazine articles, in newspapers, in museum catalogs, and so on). Virtually all periodical Liszt-letter publications are identified by Charles Suttoni (item 41). Ironically, the most interesting series of such publications is Suttoni's own:

205.   Suttoni, Charles. "Liszt's Letters." *Journal of the American Liszt Society* 2-20 (1977-1986).

> 205a. "Liszt to Alfred Jaëll and the E-flat Concerto"; 2 (1977), pp. 32-34.
>
> 205b. "Liszt's Letters (2): The 'Hungarian Rhapsodies'"; 3 (1978), pp. 27-29.
>
> 205c. "Liszt's Letters (3): The Goethe Centenary"; 4 (1978), pp. 57-59.
>
> 205d. "Liszt's Letters (4): Isolation in Geneva"; 5 (1979), pp. 75-78.
>
> 205e. "Liszt's Letters (5)"; 6 (1979), pp. 34-36.
>
> 205f. "Liszt's Letters (6): 'Reminiscences of Norma'"; 7 (1980), pp. 77-79.
>
> 205g. "Liszt's Letters: Anton Rubinstein at Weimar"; 8 (1980), pp. 75-76.
>
> 205h. "Liszt Letters: The Tonsure and Minor Orders"; 9 (1981), pp. 95-98.
>
> 205i. "Liszt's Letters: Carl Gille"; 10 (1981), pp. 71-76.
>
> 205j. "Liszt's Letters: An Alpine Interlude"; 11 (1982), pp. 42-46.
>
> 205k. "Liszt Letters: Emile Deschamps"; 12 (1982), pp. 63-65.
>
> 205m. "Liszt Letters: Carolyne Wittgenstein on Their Publication"; 13 (1983), pp. 116-119.
>
> 205n. "Liszt's Letters: Lamennais' Paroles d'un croyant"; 14 (1983), pp. 71-73.
>
> 205p. "Liszt's Letters: A Little-known Letter to Schumann"; 15 (1984), pp. 174-177.
>
> 205q. "Liszt's Letters: A Traveling Gypsy Troupe"; 16 (1984), pp. 112-114.
>
> 205r. "Liszt's Letters: Perseus, Cellini and Berlioz"; 17 (1985), pp. 97-106.
>
> 205s. "Liszt's Letters: A List for Herbeck (hereto unpublished)": 18 (1985), pp. 137-138; and 19 (1986), p. 149.
>
> 205t. "Liszt's Letters: Valérie Boissier"; 19 (1986), pp. 146-149.
>
> 205u. "Liszt's Letters: A Last Note to Nourrit"; 20 (1986), pp. 136-139.

Each article in this worthwhile series includes a Liszt letter in both its original language and English, together with introductory observations and annotations. Most of Suttoni's articles are illustrated with facsimile reproductions from letters mss. or early editions. Item 205s reproduces a page entitled "Liste der verlangten Musikalien" missing from the Liszt-

Herbeck letter of 11 October 1859, at least insofar as it appeared originally in item 186.

Post-1975 publications of Liszt letters were omitted from the original 1979 version of item 41. Among such omissions was the following citation, included in the present chapter not only because it was overlooked in item 40 in its English-language version, but because it exemplifies the kind of "unpublished" Liszt-letters items that have plagued specialists for decades:

206.   Bodo, Árpád [sic]. "Discovery of Letter by Liszt." *Liszt Society Journal* 4 (1979), p. 30.

Introduces, then reprints in English the text of a note Liszt addressed to Amalie von Fabry on 21 November 1879. Also published [?in Hungarian] in an unidentified issue of *Dunántuli Napló*. Like other "unpublished" Liszt letters, however, this one had already appeared in print; see Imre Achátz, "Ein unveröffentlicher Liszt-Brief im Archiv des Komitats Baranya," *Studia musicologica* 20 (1978), pp. 405-412. Letter in German. See also item 41; entry 800.

In addition to several cross-referenced studies, four other recent periodical Liszt-letters publications are described below in alphabetical order (by author or editor):

207.   Eckhardt, Mária [P.]. "Liszt in his Formative Years — Unpublished Letters, 1824-1827." *New Hungarian Quarterly* 27/103 (Autumn 1986), pp. 93-107.

Describes and reprints in their original French texts eight early Liszt letters preserved in the collections of the Richard Wagner Archives, Bayreuth. Illustrated with a facsimile of a letter addressed by Liszt on 3 April 1824 to Comtesse Eugénie de Noirberne. Also includes two letters by Adam Liszt. Numerous and detailed endnotes.

208.   Eckhardt, Mária [P.]. "Une femme simple, mère d'un génie européen: 'Anna Liszt / Quelques aspects d'une correspondance'." *Revue musicale* 405-406-407 (1987), pp. 199-214.

A bibliographic survey of the Liszt/Anna Liszt correspondence. Includes a table of all known letters addressed by these individuals to each other (pp. 206-214) as well as the text of a letter Anna Liszt wrote her son on 13 February 1849. No illustrations or facsimile reproductions. Quotations in French and German; the bulk of the article in French.

209.   Jung, Hans Rudolf. "Einige Lebens- und Schaffensprobleme Franz Liszts in den Jahren 1859 bis 1861 — Dargestellt unter Verwendung

unveröffentlichter Briefe des Komponisten." *Liszt-Studien* 3 (1986), pp. 56-69.

Deals with Liszt's difficulties in Weimar during the late 1850s, his compositional activities during those years, and his resignation as director of the Hoftheater. Jung quotes from previously unpublished letters written by Liszt during 1859-1860 and owned by the Goethe- und Schiller-Archiv, Weimar, and the Deutsche Staatsbibliothek, East Berlin. Some of the documents quoted in this article also appear in items 189 and 199. Useful bibliographic citations in the form of endnotes.

*   Kürthy, András. "L'histoire du rapport de Liszt et de la Casa Ricordi refletée par leur correspondance."

Reprints 11 Liszt letters in their original French- and Italian-language texts. Described *under* (not as) item 582. Published too late to be described independently in the present research guide.

Other studies, like the one below, describe letters previously published only in fragmentary form:

210.   Saffle, Michael. "An 'Unpublished' Liszt Letter to Franz Xaver Witt." *Journal of the American Liszt Society* 24 (1988), pp. 91-95.

Identifies and discusses a letter addressed by Liszt to the founder of the German Cecilianist movement on 15 July 1874 and omitted from "Vierzehn Original-Briefe Liszts an Witt," ed. Karl Weinmann, in *Musica sacra* 46 (1913), pp. 289-295. Contains the letter's original German-language text and an English-language translation as well as a partial facsimile of the letter itself. NB: Portions of this letter—including a fragmentary facsimile—appeared without commentary in item 584.

Many studies devoted to Liszt "documents" are actually letters studies. Most works of this kind treated in the present volume are described in Chapter VIII, but one is identified and discussed below:

211.   Hamburger, Klára. "Documents — Liszt à Rome." *Studia musicologica* 21 (1979), pp. 319-344.

Summarizes the provenance and reproduces the contents of several Liszt letters, including one addressed to Wilhelm Speyer of Frankfurt a.M. in March 1843 (Rome: Biblioteca Nazionale ms. 158-41). Illustrated with facsimiles of this letter and several others pertaining to Liszt's life during the 1860s.

An Hungarian-language version of Hamburger's article appeared under the title "Római Liszt-dokumentumok" in *Magyar zene* 19 (1978), pp. 55-75.

In addition to recent publications, older articles like the example described below also contain valuable information about and examples of Liszt's correspondence:

212.   Raff, Helene. "Franz Liszt und Joachim Raff im Spiegel ihrer Briefe." *Musik* 1 (1901-1902), pp. 36ff.

Discusses the relationship Liszt and Raff enjoyed during most of their lives. Helene Raff illustrates her reminiscences with the complete texts of more than 50 letters, most of them Liszt's and only two of them published in item 186. Important not only for the letters themselves but for Helene Raff's reinteration of her husband's belief that he "taught" Liszt how to write for the orchestra. (With regard to this last topic, see items 295-296.)

Finally, individual Liszt letters have appeared in obscure publications, or in publications devoted primarily to other topics and composers. Studies of these kinds are described in Chapter X, and almost all of them containing complete Liszt letters are identified in item 41. Two studies inadvertently omitted from that item are described below:

213.   Biba, Otto. "Franz Liszt und Anton Bruckners 3. Symphonie." *Bulletin [of the] International Bruckner-Gesellschaft* 15 (1979), pp. 30-31.

Not seen. According to RILM 13 (1979), entry 2731, this article discusses a previously unpublished Liszt letter to Bösendorfer recommending Bruckner's piece for performance. The letter is undated but reached Vienna on 20 August 1880.

214.   Scholcz, Peter. "Een onbekende Liszt-brief." *Franz Liszt Kring* 9 (November 1988), pp. 3-4.

Discusses, reprints in its original French and in Dutch translation, and reproduces in facsimile (p. 4) a letter Liszt addressed to Elisabeth Reekers-Borge on 18 April 1875. Commentary in Dutch.

NB: *Franz Liszt Kring* is one of several specialized Liszt periodicals omitted from many standard reference works.

RELATED STUDIES

In addition to letters themselves, scholars have also published studies of Liszt's epistolary habits, attitudes, and output. Among these studies is a pamphlet-length survey of Liszt as letter-writer:

215.   Bondeville, M. Emmanuel. *Un grand epistolier Franz Liszt.* Paris: Dirmin-Didat, 1978. 13pp.
         ML410.L7B63
         The text of a lecture delivered on 15 November 1978 before the Académie des Beaux-Arts. Bondeville deals rather superficially with Liszt's letters, literary studies, and contacts with certain literary figures. Illustrated with a lithograph of Liszt dating from 1832.

Two worthwhile studies of the letter-sketchbooks Liszt used during much of his life deserve close attention:

216.   Eckhardt, Mária [P.]. "Zur Frage der Liszt'chen Briefkonzeptbücher." *Liszt-Studien* 2 (1981), pp. 43-54.
         Describes Liszt's "letter-sketchbooks," based on an examination of H-Bn ms. Mus. 376 (which contains drafts of more than 300 letters Liszt wrote between January 1877 and May 1878) as well as other documents preserved in the Library of Congress and Weimar archives. Illustrated with six facsimile reproductions, five taken from the "Budapest Sketchbook" (identified above) and one taken from a letter Liszt addressed to Baron Augusz on 8 June 1877.

217.   Kraft, Günther. "Franz Liszt v zrkadle svojich skicárov/Franz Liszt im Spiegel seiner Konzeptbücher." In item 34; pp. 109-122.
         An introduction to Liszt's letter-sketchbooks based on discussion of Weimar Staatsarchiv document "Hausarchiv Carl Alexander Nr. 1622," identified by Eckhardt in item 216 (above). Kraft intended to publish a longer article about Weimar Liszt letter-sketchbooks in *Beiträge zur Musikwissenschaft*, but his death several years ago put an end to this plan.

Finally, three important studies of—or proposals for—editions of Liszt's letters have recently appeared in print:

218.   Knepper, Claude. "Le project d'édition intégrale de la correspondance de Franz Liszt." *Revue musicale* 405-406-407 (1987), pp. 347-364.
         Announces the publication of a new complete edition of Liszt's correspondence, a Herculean undertaking. Presented at the 1986 Paris Liszt conference, Knepper's plans have not materialized. The difficulties associ-

ated with such an undertaking are discussed in the introduction to item 41 as well as Chapter II.

219.   Bónis, Ferenc. "Liszt und Wagner-Briefe an Mosonyi in Kodálys wissenschaftlicher Bearbeitung." *Musikforschung* 39 (1986), pp. 317-334.

Traces the history and describes the significance of several letters edited by Zoltán Kodály for publication during the 1920s. Includes the complete texts of two letters Liszt addressed to Mosonyi during 1857 and 1862 as well as two Wagner letters addressed to Mosonyi in 1863 and 1865. Illustrated with a complete facsimile reproduction of Liszt's 29 April 1857 letter as well as facsimiles of Kodály's hand- and typewritten transcripts and with a table of corrections for several pages of item 188. Both Liszt letters contain musical examples, reproduced in handwritten copies apparently prepared by the author.

220.   Winklhofer, Sharon. "Editorial Censorship in Liszt's Letters to Agnès Street-Klindworth." *Journal of the American Liszt Society* 9 (1981), pp. 42-49.

Discusses editorial suppression in the published text of item 186c, based on a study of copies of Liszt letters presented in D-WRgs. The "Freundin" in the title of this latter publication was Agnès Street-Klindworth, a confidante of Liszt's later years and his lover. (With regard to the Liszt-Agnès affair, see also item 552.) Winklhofer describes how and why La Mara and the Princess Sayn-Wittgenstein conspired to falsify materials soon to be made available in their original form (as item 201).

VIII: DOCUMENT AND SOURCE STUDIES

Even excluding his letters, Liszt's documentary legacy is staggeringly large. Much of this legacy is biographical; Liszt wrote little about himself, but others made up for this "deficiency" with thousands of newspaper articles, reports, concert reviews, diary entries, reminiscences, poems, and so on. Liszt also left us hundreds of musical documents, including mss., corrected proof copies, printed music, autographed sheet-music copies, and fragmentary compositions.

The most important Liszt source and document studies are reviewed below. Studies of Liszt's literary works and letters are evaluated separately in Chapters VI-VII. A small number of facsimile editions of musical mss. are discussed in Chapter V; others are evaluated below.

AUTOBIOGRAPHICAL DOCUMENTS

Liszt's only "autobiography" is reprinted in:

221. Kapp, Julius. "Autobiographisches von Franz Liszt." *Musik* 11 (1911-1912), pp. 10-21.

    Contains the original French text of an encyclopedia article Liszt re-wrote on galleys supplied by the editor of the *Biographie des contemporains* (Paris: Giaeser & Co.) in 1881. Kapp also reproduces the texts of four Liszt letters as well as a letter addressed to Liszt by the Viennese critic Eduard Hanslick on 8 October 1854.

Other non-epistolary, autobiographical documentary publications include:

222. *Liszts Testament*, ed. Friedrich Schnapp. Weimar: Hermann Böhlaus, 1931. 31pp.
    ML410.L7A112

    Reproduces the complete text of the testament Liszt completed on 14 September 1866. Includes information about what happened to some of the objects Liszt left various individuals. Also includes several letters and a facsimile reproduction of the cover of a holograph copy of the *Trois odes funèbres* as a frontispiece. See also item 1b; pp. 557-563, and item 223 (below).

223.   Liszt, Franz. *Mein letzter Wille*, ed. Emmerich Karl Horvath. Eisenstadt: Horvath, 1970. 31pp.
        [No LC number available]
        Another transcription of the testament also reproduced in item 222 (above). Like Schnapp, Horvath provides information about the present whereabouts of objects Liszt mentioned in his will but more up to date. Illustrated with a number of portraits, including pictures of Liszt being buried at Bayreuth and of the Liszt memorial at Raiding, Austria.

224.   Liszt, Franz. *Tagebuch 1827. Im Auftrag der Stadt Bayreuth*, ed. Detlef Altenburg and Rainer Kleinertz. 2 volumes. Bayreuth: Neff, 1986.
        ISBN 3-7014-0229-9   [No LC number available]
        A facsimile reproduction of a document owned by the Richard Wagner-Archiv, Bayreuth (Volume 1) and an annotated transcription (Volume 2). Liszt's "diary" is actually a day-book, full of seemingly random but nevertheless interesting jottings on various topics. Both volumes are handsomely boxed and represent Bayreuth's nod in Liszt's direction during the 1986 centennial celebrations. Reviewed in item 132.

Documentary anthologies of several kinds are described later in the present chapter. One collection of autobiographical Liszt documents, however, must be mentioned here:

225.   *Liszt: A Self-portrait in His Own Words*, ed. David Whitwell. Northridge, California: Winds, 1986. vii, 242pp.
        ML410.L7A163 1986   [No ISBN number available]
        A summary of Liszt's life, character, and activities drawn from the composer's letters, essays, and other documents. Includes observations made by Liszt on the Jews, the peoples of various nations, and a variety of individuals—among them, Bach, Ludwig II of Bavaria, Tolstoy, and Wagner. No scholarly apparatus, bibliography, or index.

REMINISCENCES

Much of what we know about Liszt comes from reminiscences and other eyewitness acounts of his life and musical activities. Sources like these continue to be discovered on a regular basis. Among such discoveries, for example, are passages from Theresa Brunswick's diary dealing with Liszt's tour of Hungary and the Balkans; these have been reproduced in facsimile and evaluated by Mária Hornyák in "Liszt in Martonvásár (11 Mai 1846)," published in Studia musicologica *30 (1988), pp. 333-341. NB: Like several other recent Liszt studies mentioned below, this one appeared too late to be described independently.*

Perhaps the finest collection of Liszt reminiscences to appear during the last decade is:

226.   Ramann,   Lina.   *Lisztiana: Erinnerungen   an   Franz   Liszt   in Tagebuchblättern, Briefen und Dokumenten aus den Jahren 1873-1886/87,* ed. Arthur Seidl and Friedrich Schnapp. Mainz and New York: B. Schott's Sons, 1983. 475pp.
         ML410.L7R315   ISBN 3-79571-782-5
         A fascinating volume of reminiscences and documents of various kinds, complete by 1895 but left unpublished at Ramann's death. Among other things, *Lisztiana* contains a number of Liszt letters, an index of selected items of Liszt correspondence (pp. 455-458), the questionnaires (pp. 385-408) Liszt completed for Ramann's three-volume study of his life and music (item 3), and a catalog of Liszt's works mentioned in Ramann's text. Illustrated with photographs, musical examples, and facsimile reproductions of several documents. Reviewed in item 132.

An equally important volume of reminiscences and reports also deserves careful attention:

227.   Pohl, Richard. *Franz Liszt. Studien und Erinnerungen.* Gesammelte Schriften über Musik und Musiker, 2. Leipzig: Bernhard Schlicke, 1883. xv, 402pp.
         ML410.L7P7
         An anthology of articles about Liszt, many of them reminiscences of personal encounters. Also contains Pohl's lengthy accounts of Liszt and the 1853 Karlsruhe and 1857 Aachen music festivals (see item 599) as well as articles about the symphonies, symphonic poems, and choral works (items 876, 882, 888, 965, and 971), a description of his resignation in 1859 from the directorship of the Weimar Hoftheater, and a letter addressed to Pohl on 5 November 1853. (With regard to other portions of this volume, see items 1081 and 1083.)
         Reprinted in facsimile in 1973 by Dr. Martin Sändig of Wiesbaden [ISBN 3-500-28270-9].

228.   *Portrait of Liszt By Himself and His Contemporaries,* ed. Adrian Williams. Oxford, England: The Clarendon Press, 1990. xiii, 746pp.
         ML410.L7W55 1989 [sic]   ISBN 1-19-816150-6
         A massive collection of press clippings, reminiscences, reports of individual performances, and other biographical documents. Williams has divided his material among chapters devoted to individual years or groups of years in Liszt's life; he also provides a running commentary and copious bibliographic citations. Illustrated with more than two dozen mostly familiar black-and-white portraits, facsimile reproductions of manuscript pages, and other pictures. A valuable reference work that can also be read

as a biography, Williams's book suffers only from its reliance on French and English sources. Concludes with an index of names and composition titles.

Twenty-five other Liszt "reminiscences" are described or cross-referenced below in alphabetical order (by author and/or title):

229.   Barnett, Elise Braun. "An Annotated Translation of Moriz Rosenthal's 'Franz Liszt, Memories and Reflections'." *Current Musicology* 13 (1972), pp. 29-37.

Reprints in English Rosenthal's article "Franz Liszt: Erinnerungen und Betrachtungen," which appeared originally in *Musik* 11 (1911-1912), pp. 46-51.

230.   Beale, Willert. "Memories of John Orlando Parry." *Liszt Society Journal* 9 (1984), pp. 16-18.

An eyewitness account of Liszt's British tours of 1840-1841. Parry, who accompanied Liszt on these tours, also left a diary described as item 440. Walker (item 1a; pp. 361) reproduces the 23 November 1840 entry from that diary. Illustrated with a portrait of Parry completed c. 1845.

231.   Boise, Otis B. "An American Composer Visits Liszt." *Musical Quarterly* 43 (1957), pp. 316-325.

An autobiographical account of Boise's visits with Liszt during 1876-1877, the advice about composition he received, and his recollections of Raff and some of Liszt's piano pupils. Illustrated with a photograph of Boise, and with a facsimile of a Liszt letter addressed to Boise and dated 20 July 1876.

232.   Boissier, Valérie. *Liszt pédagogue. Leçons de piano données par Liszt à Mlle. Valérie Boissier à Paris en 1832*, ed. "Caroline Butini" [also known as Mme Auguste Boissier]. Paris: H. Champion, 1927. 96pp.
ML410.L7B62

A handsomely printed transcription of Mlle Boissier's 1832 diary, one of the most valuable eye-witness accounts of Liszt's pedagogical practices ever published. Illustrated in this edition with a portrait of Mme Auguste Boissier, and with several famous diagrams Liszt drew for his pupil to illustrate ways of playing the piano. NB: Mlle Boissier is better-known to students of nineteenth-century *belles lettres* as Catherine Valérie, Comtesse de Gasparin.

Translations of the diary have appeared in several languages, including German and Spanish. Excerpts from them also appear in Elyse Mach's "Recollections of the Young Liszt as Teacher," *Piano Quarterly* 23/89

(Spring 1975), pp. 12-16; and in other publications. The 1930 German-language edition of *Liszt pédagogue* includes the text of a letter written by Liszt in 1855 missing in the original volume. Otherwise unpublished portions of Mlle Boissier's diary may be found in the first volume of *La comtesse Agénor de Gasparin et sa famille*, ed. Caroline Barbey-Boissier (Paris 1902). This last volume not seen; cited in item 41.

233.   Borodin, Alexander P. *Vospominaniia o F. Liste*. Moscow: "Gos. Muz. Izd.," 1953. 56pp.
          ML410.L7B642
       Reminiscences derived from letters Borodin sent his wife in 1877 that describe, among other things, his visits with Liszt in Weimar. In Russian.
       Portions of Borodin's reminiscences, also adapted from his correspondence, have also appeared in English; see item 240.

234.   Czerny, Carl. *Erinnerungen aus meinem Leben*, ed. Walter Kolneder. Collections d'études musicologiques, 46. Strassbourg: P. H. Hertz, 1968. 78pp.
          ML410.C99A3
       Contains a fascinating account of Liszt's youthful musical talent and training (pp. 27-29), recorded by one of nineteenth-century Europe's most important piano pedagogues. Also includes the text of a letter Liszt wrote Czerny during September 1852. Despite the place of publication, in German throughout.
       An English-language translation of the Liszt portions of this document appeared under the title "Recollections from My Life" in the *Musical Quarterly* 42 (1956), pp. 314-316.

235.   d'Agoult, Marie. *Meine Freundschaft mit Franz Liszt: Ein Roman der Liebe aus dem Memoiren einer berühmten Frau*. Translated by Egas von Wenden; introduction by Siegfried Wagner. Dresden: Reissner, 1930. 256pp.
          [No LC number available]
       A posthumous d'Agoult "reader," consisting of excerpts from her written remarks about Liszt. Illustrated with several plates, most of them portraits of d'Agoult at various ages as well as with a facsimile of her handwriting.
       Rare, at least in the United States. The *National Union Catalog*, pre-1956 imprints series, Vol. 5, p. 233, gives only a Dewey shelf-number [780.9 L774ya] for this volume. See also item 248.

236.   "1886: Liszt's Last Months and Death. A Selection of Contemporary
        Impressions." *Liszt Society Journal* 11 (1986), pp. 102-110.
            An anthology of excerpts from well-known reminiscences of Liszt's last
        months (January-July 1886), taken from recollections by August Stradal
        (item 250) as well as from the London *Times*, the Budapest "Musical
        Journal" *Zenelap*, etc. Illustrated with photographs of Liszt taken in
        London in April 1886, in Luxembourg in July 1886, and on his deathbed
        in Bayreuth, as well as a contemporary sketch of Liszt's Bayreuth funeral,
        3 August 1886.

237.   Fay, Amy. *Music-Study in Germany*, ed. Fay Peirce. New York:
        Macmillan, 1913. 352pp.
            ML417.F284
            Contains delightful, often-quoted remarks about Liszt, many of his
        more important pupils, and 1870s Weimar.
            Fay returned to the United States after completing her "German
        studies," then vanished into comparative obscurity. A volume of her cor-
        respondence appeared recently under the title *More Letters of Amy Fay:
        The American Years, 1879-1916*, ed. Margaret W[illiam] McCarthy
        (Detroit: Information Coordinators, 1986).
            Among other Fay reminiscences is "Musical Hours in Weimar with the
        Pianists of the Future," reprinted in the *Inter-American Music Review* 7/2
        (Spring-Summer 1986), pp. 79-83. NB: This article was originally pub-
        lished on 20 July 1876 in the Boston *Daily Advertiser* under the pen-name
        "Zero."

238.   Friedheim, Arthur. *Life and Liszt: The Recollections of a Concert Pianist*,
        ed. Theodore L. Bullock. New York: Taplinger, 1961. viii, 335pp.
            ML417.F89A3
            Contains valuable information about Liszt and his pedagogical activ-
        ities. Also contains chapters entitled "Liszt the Conductor," "Liszt the
        Pianist," and "Liszt the Composer." Illustrated with photographs of Liszt,
        the Hofgärtnerei in Weimar, and Friedheim himself. Reprinted in item 246.
            NB: Only the first sixteen of Friedheim's chapters deal exclusively or
        substantially with Liszt. The rest of this book is an account of
        Friedheim's subsequent concert career, compiled from previously unpub-
        lished mss. by Bullock.

*   Göllerich, August. *Franz Liszts Klavierunterricht von 1884-1886.*
            An extremely detailed account of Liszt's Weimar piano classes and
        musical opinions. Discussed in greater detail as item 1047.

239. Gottschalg, Alexander Wilhelm. *Franz Liszt in Weimar und seine letzten Lebensjahre. Erinnerungen und Tagebuchnotizen nebst Briefen des Meisters*, ed. Carl Alfred René. Berlin: Glaue, 1910. viii, 158pp.
ML410.L7G68
Personal observations by one of Liszt's closest friends and sometime musical collaborator. Contains discussions about Liszt's relationships with Hoffmann von Fallersleben, the Princess Sayn-Wittgenstein, and Wagner. Gottschalg also reprints 48 letters Liszt addressed to him between 1862-1883 (pp. 57-127). Illustrated with portraits of Liszt and Gottschalg.

240. Habets, Alfred. *Borodin and Liszt*, trans. Rosa Newmarch. London: Digby, Long & Co., 1895. 192pp.
ML410.B73H13
Contains "Liszt, as Sketched in the Letters of Borodin" (pp. 107-192), a collection of some or all of Borodin's letters to his wife, as well as part of a letter Borodin addressed to César Cui on 12 June 1881. Illustrated with several portraits.
Often confused with item 233 and related collections of letters (see item 41; entry 510). Passages from Borodin's letters also appear in David Lloyd-Jones's "Borodin on Liszt," *Music & Letters* 42 (1961), pp. 217-226. A brief review by Tamara Burde of Borodin's Liszt reminiscences also exists: see "Liszt in Erinnerungen von Alexander Borodin" in item 37; pp. 159-166.
The 1890s edition of Habets's book was reprinted in 1977 in facsimile by AMS Press of New York City (ISBN 0-404-12938-2).

241. Lachmund, Carl von. *Mein Leben mit Franz Liszt: Aus dem Tagebuch eines Liszt-Schülers*, ed. Mabel Wagnalls. Eschwege: Schroeder, 1970. 316pp.
ML417.L15A3
Lachmund's recollections of Liszt and his circle in the form of diary entries from 1882-1884. An appendix identifies Liszt's pupils by name (pp. 297-308). Illustrated with a number of portraits, reproductions of photographs, three facsimiles of Liszt letters, facsimiles of Lachmund diary pages, etc.

242. Lenz, Wilhelm von. *The The Great Piano Virtuosos of Our Time*, ed. Philip Reder. London and New York: Regency Press, 1971. 169pp.
ML397.L57 1971
Presents von Lenz's fascinating first-hand account of Liszt in Paris during the late 1820s. Portions of von Lenz's testimony have been challenged by Walker (in item 1a; pp. 135-136), but Walker also repeats many of the Russian's intriguing observations.

Translated from *Die grossen Pianovirtuosen unserer Zeit aus persönlicher Bekanntschaft: Liszt — Chopin — Tausig* (Berlin: B. Behr, 1872). The original edition of the English-language translation identified above, now rather scarce, appeared in 1899.

243.   "Liszt Through the Decades of His Life: A Selection of Contemporary Impressions." *Liszt Society Journal* 11 (1986), pp. 2-21.

A biographical sketch in the form of quotations from such figures as Liszt's father Adam Liszt, Valérie Boissier (item 232), Jules Janin, Otto Roquette, and others. Illustrated with several well-known portraits of Liszt and his contemporaries.

Since 1975 the *Liszt Society Journal* has published similar collections of vignettes, most of them available from other published sources—e.g., "Sketches of the Master," selected and translated by Adrian Williams in the *Liszt Society Journal* 1 (1975), pp. 17-18. See also item 228.

244.   Liszt, Eduard von. "Skizzenartige Darstellung des Lebenslaufs Abbé Franz Liszt's, 1811-1886, von seinem Cousin." *Liszt saeculum* 36-37 (1985-1986), pp. 16-30.

A deceptive title: this is neither a biographical sketch nor a set of reminiscences; it is a chronological table similar to those described in Chapter IX. NB: Eduard von Liszt's work is quite similar to item 373. Did Raabe base his "Zeittafel" on this chronological outline?

245.   Pictet, Adolphe. *Une course à Chamounix. Conte fantastique.* Paris: Benjamin Duprat, 1838. 195pp.

PQ 2382 + P138.C6

Describes Liszt's 1835 visit to Switzerland with the Comtesse d'Agoult and retinue. Quoted at some length by several biographers and scholars, including Walker (item 1a; esp. pp. 220ff.) and Perényi (item 350). One of Pictet's most famous passages, a description of Liszt improvising on an organ at Freibourg (pp. 186ff.) should be read in light of similar reminiscences. See, for example, B. de Miramonde Fitz-James, "Une improvisation de Liszt," *Les amis de l'orgue* "Numéro spécial" 30-31 (June-September 1937), pp. 66-70, which describes how Liszt played the organ for Autran in a deserted church at midnight.

The original edition of Pictet's book is rare in America; copies exist in several European libraries, including F-Pn and D-F. Reprinted in Geneva by the "Journal de Genève" press (1930).

*   Rellstab, Ludwig. *Franz Liszt: Beurteilungen — Berichte — Lebensskizze.*
         Berlin: Trautwein, 1842.
             Includes Rellstab's impressions of Liszt's 1841-1842 Berlin concerts.
         Described in greater detail as item 366.

246.   *Remembering Franz Liszt*, ed. Michael Grant. New York: Limelight Edi-
         tions, 1986. xxiv, 375pp.
             ML410.L7R37 1986   ISBN 0-87910-113-X
             Contains English-language texts of *Life and Liszt* by Arthur Friedheim
         (item 238) and *My Memories of Liszt* by Arthur Siloti (item 249) as well
         as an introductory essay by the editor.

247.   Robert, Walter. "Two Chapters from Waldemar Meyer's 'Aus einem
         Künstlerleben." *Journal of the American Liszt Society* 20 (1986), pp. 50-55.
             Discusses Meyer's visits with Liszt and reproduces his accounts of
         those visits, including remarks about rehearsals for and performances of
         Wagner's *Ring des Nibelungen* in Bayreuth, 1875-1876.

248.   "Stern, Daniel" [pseud. Marie d'Agoult]. *Mémoires (1833-1854)*, with an
         introduction by Daniel Ollivier; 5th ed. Paris: Calman Lévy, 1927. xii,
         246pp.
             PQ2152.A38Z32 1927
             D'Agoult's published reminiscences of her years with Liszt—among
         them, the well-known "Journal des Zyi" (pp. 173-180) as well as many
         other passages pertinent to Liszt scholarship. Walker (item 1a; pp. 259ff.)
         has questioned the veracity of these *Mémoires.*
             Not to be confused with d'Agoult's *Souvenirs*, which describe her ex-
         periences of 1806-1833. See item 235.

249.   Siloti, Alexander. *My Memories of Liszt.* Edinburgh: Methuen Simpson,
         n.d. 76pp.
             ML410.L7S51
             An eyewitness account of Liszt's last years, written by one of his most
         celebrated pupils. Illustrated with a couple of portraits and facsimile re-
         productions of several musical mss. Reprinted complete in item 246.
             Siloti's book is virtually identical with his article "Meine Erinnerungen
         an Franz Liszt" (trans. Sophie Korsunska), published in the *Zeitschrift des
         Internationalen Musikgesellschaft* 14 (1913), pp. 294-318.

250.   Stradal, August. *Erinnerungen an Franz Liszt*. Bern: P. Haupt, 1929.
         173pp.
         ML410.L7S85
         Another eyewitness account of Liszt in old age, recording events dating
         for the most part from 1885-1886. Stradal, one of Liszt's numerous piano
         pupils, includes sketches of Liszt as man (pp. 167-173) and teacher (pp.
         157-166). Illustrated with several well-known portraits of Liszt and two
         musical examples.

251.   Wagner, Richard. *My Life*. Edited by Mary Whittal; translated by Andrew
         Gray. Cambridge and New York: Cambridge University Press, 1983. ix,
         786pp.
         ML410.W1W146 1983   ISBN 0-521-22929-4
         A famous—some might say infamous—autobiographical statement ad-
         dressed to the "friends" of the man who was, by turns, Liszt's friend,
         musical mentor-disciple, enemy, and son-in-law. Contains dozens of im-
         portant passages dealing with the earliest Liszt-Wagner encounters, Liszt's
         productions of *Tannhäuser* and *Lohengrin* in Weimar, Liszt's and
         Wagner's attitudes toward each other, etc. Cited here in lieu of numerous
         German-language editions.

One misleading title also deserves to be mentioned here:

252.   Wagner, Cosima. *Franz Liszt. Ein Gedenkblatt von seiner Tochter*, 2nd
         edition. Munich: F. Bruckmann, 1911. 126pp.
         ML410.L7W14
         A "souvenir" commemorating the centenary of Liszt's birth as well as
         an account of Cosima's relationships with both her father (Liszt), her
         husband (Richard Wagner), and the Princess Sayn-Wittgenstein. Supple-
         mented by excerpts from a variety of letters. NB: Despite Cosima's pur-
         ported authorship, this publication was actually prepared by Hans von
         Wolzogen and published originally as "Zu Liszts Briefen an die Fürstin
         Carolyne Sayn-Wittgenstein" in the *Bayreuther Blätter* 23 (1900), pp.
         622ff.

STUDIES AND COLLECTIONS OF BIOGRAPHICAL DOCUMENTS

*Working with these "reminiscences," as well as with other contemporary accounts
of Liszt's activities, scholars have produced a variety of documentary biographical
studies. Among these are the studies of Liszt letters described in Chapter VII. Other
studies dealing with documentary materials are described throughout Chapter X.*

Documentary Anthologies

*Few Liszt documentary anthologies have appeared in print. (One collection of
autobiographical documents is described above as item 225.) The largest anthology
of prose documents appeared recently under the title:*

253.   *Liszt et son temps. Documents choisis, présentés et annotés*, ed. Paul-
         Antoine Huré and Claude Knepper. Paris: Hachette, 1987. 699pp.
         ISBN 2-0-011770-0   [No LC number available]
         A kind of "documentary biography" consisting of running commentary
         interspersed with quoted materials pertaining to Liszt's personal and pro-
         fessional activities. Occasionally useful but generally disappointing; most
         of the documents Huré and Knepper quote from are either already familiar
         to Lisztians, or inadequately annotated, or both. On pp. 142-143, for ex-
         ample, Huré and Knepper reproduce only part of Liszt's October 1841
         letter to the Princess Belgiojoso; the complete letter was published in
         Autour de Mme d'Agoult et de Liszt, pp. 180-183 (one of many letters
         omitted from the present volume but described in item 41). In French
         throughout. Reviewed in item 132.

Other outstanding documentary studies also deserve to be mentioned here:

*   Burger, Ernst. *Franz Liszt: A Chronicle of His Life in Pictures and Docu-
         ments.*
         The finest Liszt iconography in print, Burger's book also contains a
         great deal of purely documentary material. Described in greater detail as
         item 281.

*   *Portrait of Liszt*, ed. Adrian Williams.
         Described as item 228.

Studies of Previously Unpublished Documents

*Publications dealing with previously unpublished Liszt letters are described in
Chapter VII (although some of the studies described immediately below and
throughout Chapter X also contain previously unpublished letters). Among studies
of other unpublished or otherwise little-known Liszt documents (e.g., mss., press
clippings, certificates, trinkets, etc.) is the following exceptionally important
monograph:*

254.   Haraszti, Emile. "Liszt à Paris: Quelques documents inédits." *Revue
         musicale* 165 (April 1936), pp. 241-258; and 167 (July-August 1936), pp.
         5-16.

A ground-breaking study of miscellaneous documents pertaining primarily to Liszt's early Paris years. Reproduces and comments on letters of introduction Liszt received from Bretfeld and de la Ferté; letters and notices published during the 1820s in *La pandore*, the *Journal des débats*, and other newspapers; other letters by Liszt's father Adam Liszt; and so on. Includes photographs of the tomb of Liszt's mother Anna Liszt as well as of a number of posters, portraits, and concert programs. In French throughout.

Another important monograph is due to be published in the immediate future:

255.   Walker, Alan. *Liszt Documents in Vatican Archives* [working title]. American Liszt Society Studies Series, 1. Stuyvesant, New York: Pendragon. In press.
         [No LC or ISBN numbers available]
         Identifies, reprints, and discusses dozens of documents associated with Liszt/Sayn-Wittgenstein marriage plans of the 1850s and early 1860s. Walker's discoveries have proved conclusively that the Princess could have married Liszt, and that the Hohenlohe family probably convinced Liszt to reject her. Documents in Latin and other languages, with English-language translations.
         One of the documents scheduled to appear in this study may be found (in both Latin and English) in item 547. (With regard to other Vatican Liszt documents, see also item 548.)

Fifteen other studies of previously unpublished Liszt biographical documents are described or cross-referenced below in alphabetical order (by author or title):

*   Calza, Edvige. *Interpretazione letteraria dei Preludi di Chopin attribuita a Liszt.*
         Reproduces in facsimile a letter purportedly written by Liszt about how to perform Chopin's piano preludes. Described in greater detail as item 1072. Commentary in Italian.

256.   Chailley, Jacques. "Documents relatifs aux 'Préludes' de Liszt." *Revue musicale* 405-406-407 (1987), pp. 307-335.
         A miscellany of source materials bearing on item 345 and the genesis of *Les préludes*. Includes letters addressed by Liszt to several individuals (including Autran, author of the poems for *Les quatre élémens*, on which Liszt's unfinished "first draft" of *Les préludes* was based). Also contains press clippings associated with Liszt's concert tours of 1844-1845 and three letters addressed by the Princess Sayn-Wittgenstein to Autran during 1856-1857.

* Eckhardt, Mária [P.]. "Diary of a Wayfarer."
Among other documents, Eckhardt reproduces passages from a pocket diary Liszt kept during 1835. Described in greater detail as item 516.

257. "Ein Liszt-Dokument aus der 1840er Jahren." *Studia musicologica* 4 (1963), pp. 191-193.
Traces the provenance and summarizes the contents of a certificate purportedly written by Liszt in praise of Carl Jean's pianos and dated 22 August 1847. A facsimile reproduction of this "testimonial" appears as an illustration.

258. Gábry, György. "Lisztove vzt'ahy k Bratislave v zrkadle mad'arských pamiatok/Liszts Beziehungen zu Bratislava im Spiegel ungarischer Dokumente." In item 34; pp. 133-144.
Devoted to Hungarian documents associated with Liszt's visits to nineteenth-century Preßburg (today, Bratislava, Czechoslovakia). Not to be confused with item 259 (below). No illustrations.

259. Gábry, György. "Neuere Liszt-Dokumente." *Studia musicologica* 10 (1968), pp. 339-352.
Describes memorabilia exhibited at the National Museum, Budapest, in 1956—among them, a letter by Friedrich Weitzmann describing how he acquired a lock of Liszt's hair. Illustrated with two facsimile reproductions of letters and with several photographs, including one of the hair.
Observations by Gábry about these materials also appeared in Hungarian as "Liszt Ferenc és C. F. Weitzmann" in *Magyar zene* 24 (1983), pp. 305-311. NB: This latter article is illustrated with facsimile reproductions of harmonic progressions written in Weitzmann's hand and discovered among releted Liszt documents. See also Dennis Hennig, "Musical Puzzles, Photographic Canons, and Enharmonic Caterpillars: Liszt's Visiting Cards," *Journal of the American Liszt Society* 27 (1990), pp. 32-37.

* Hamburger, Klára. "Documents — Liszt à Rome."
Described in greater detail as item 211.

260. Haraszti, Emile. "Trois faux documents sur Fr. Liszt." *Revue de musicologie* 42 (1958), pp. 193-216.
Identifies and discusses misleading references to Liszt's relationships with Franck, Musorgsky, and Schumann. In French throughout.
Márta Papp's article "Liszt and Musorgsky: The Genuine and False Documents of the Relationship Between the Two Composers," published

in *Studia musicologica* 29 (1987), pp. 267-284, reviews some of the same material. Papp also reproduces a facsimile of a letter Liszt addressed to Vasili Bessel on 25 May 1873. Published too late to be included in item 40 and described independently in the present research guide.

261.   Kovács, Mária. "Documents sur Liszt en Belgique." *Studia musicologica* 23 (1982), pp. 157-162.

Deals with Liszt's several visits to Belgium. Kovács reprints two Liszt letters written in the 1880s. Illustrated with two facsimile reproductions. Originally published in Hungarian under the title "Ismeretlen Liszt-levelek" in *Magyar zene* 21 (1980), pp. 182-189.

A recent supplementary study by Kovács, received too late to be described independently in the present chapter, appeared as: "Des manuscripts de Liszt à Morlanwelz [also known as Mariemont]" in *Studia musicologica* 30 (1988), pp. 321-332. Among other documents, this article describes a previously unknown Belgian ms. of *Aux cyprès de la Villa d'Este*. Illustrated with facsimiles of this ms. as well as with three additional musical examples.

262.   *Liszt tanulmányok*, ed. Zsuzsa Dömötör, Mária Kovács, and Ilona Mona. Budapest: Zeneműkiadó, 1980. 153pp.

ML410.L7L63   [No ISBN number available]

Reviews documents pertaining to Liszt's first Hungarian tour and discusses such related topics as "Franz Liszt and the Age of Hungarian Reform, 1839-1840." Concludes with a chronological table of Liszt's early Hungarian activities. In Hungarian.

263.   Murányi, Robert [Árpád]. "Unknown Liszt Relics." *Studia musicologica* 4 (1962), pp. 201-209.

A study of miscellaneous documents, including a letter written by Liszt on 29 September 1881, a rosary, a portrait of the composer, and so on. Illustrated with six pages of photographs and documentary facsimiles.

A second article by Murányi, devoted to other artifacts, appeared in Hungarian under the title "Ismeretlen Liszt emlékek" in *Magyar zene* 5 (1964), pp. 528-532. In Hungarian.

264.   Papp, Márta. "Moszkvai archivumok Liszt-dokumentumai." *Magyar zene* 27 (1986), pp. 29-38.

Describes Liszt letters written in 1841 and 1879-1880 as well as a short composition entitled *Ne brani menia, moi drug* on a poem by Alexander Tolstoy. In Hungarian.

265.   Tauberová, A. "Franz Liszt in der zeitgenössischen Dokumentation und Ikonographie aus der Slowakei." *Studia musicologica* 28 (1986), pp. 225-236.

Deals with documents associated with Liszt's visits to present-day Czechoslovakia in 1839, the 1870s, and the 1880s: concert posters, press clippings, signed pieces of sheet-music, etc. Illustrated with six facsimiles, including a photograph of Liszt taken by Kozmata of Prague.

266.   Walker, Alan. "Daniel Liszt: Two Unpublished Documents." *Liszt saeculum* 36-37 (1985-1986), pp. 51-56.

An abbreviated version of item 404, Includes a facsimile reproduction of the first page of a Latin essay for which Daniel won an important prize in 1856 (p. 55).

267.   Zientarski, Władysław. "Gnieźnienskie autografy Franciszka Liszta." *Muzyka* [Warsaw] 18/4 (1973), pp. 53-57.

Refers exclusively to two notes, addressed by Liszt to Cardinal Czacki in 1882, owned today by an archive in Gniezno. Two facsimiles but no references to musical mss. or other kinds of documentary materials. In Polish.

A few publications about other individuals reprint documents relevant to Liszt's life and activities. Among such publications is a collection of letters written by Liszt's mother:

268.   Hamburger, Klára. "Madame Liszt (Versuch eines Bildnisentwurfs auf Grund von unbekannten Dokumenten." *Studia musicologica* 27 (1985), pp. 325-378.

Describes and evaluates 21 letters written by Anna Liszt to Liszt's daughter Blandine and to Emile and Démosthène Ollivier between 1859-1865. Illustrated with 17 pages of facsimiles.

Related studies by Hamburger have appeared in Hungarian as "Liszt Anna. Arcképvázlat Liszt Ferenc édesanyjáról, ismeretlen dokumentumok fényében," *Magyar zene* 27 (1986), pp. 126-166; and "A Liszt-család levelestárából," *Magyar zene* 28 (1987), pp. 141-172. Hamburger's researches into these letters have also been published in German under the title "Madame Liszt. Versuch eines Portraits von bisher unveröffentlichten Dokumenten" in item 91; pp. 20-26.

Newspaper Articles and Press Clippings

News articles and announcements, feature articles, and concert reviews scattered throughout nineteenth-century European and American newspapers and magazines tell us a great deal about Liszt's life, creative endeavors, and reputation. Among the most important studies of these materials are two monographs by one of Hungary's finest Liszt scholars:

269.   Legány, Dezső. "Liszt in Rom — nach der Presse (Erster Teil)." *Studia musicologica* 19 (1977), pp. 85-107.

A study of newspaper reports describing Liszt's Roman activities during the latter part of his life, especially 1861-1865. Legány provides quotations from several newspapers, including *L'osservatore Romano, Pesti napló,* and *Eptacordo* as well as a valuable review of secondary sources touching on Liszt's years in Rome, and on Roman life during the 1860s (pp. 85n-86n).

NB: Despite its subtitle, no further installments of this study have appeared in print.

*   Legány, Desző. *Franz Liszt: Unbekannte Presse und Briefe aus Wien, 1822-1886.*

Includes dozens of newspaper clippings, most of them associated with Liszt's concerts in Vienna. Described in greater detail as item 199.

Ten other studies of Liszt documents originally published in newspapers are described or cross-referenced below in alphabetical order (by author):

*   Arnold, Ben, and Michael Saffle. "Liszt in Ireland (and Belgium): Reports from a Concert Tour."

Described as item 499.

270.   Bellas, Jacqueline. "Du fantastique au merveilleux: Liszt, fils d'Hoffmann, chez M. de Pontmartin." *Missions et démarches de la critique. Mélanges offerts au professeur J. A. Vier.* Paris: Klincksieck, 1973; pp. 157-170.

Not seen. According to RILM 10 (1976); entry 5675, this article deals in part with a story published in *Le ménestrel* in June 1845 based on a description of concerts Liszt gave at Avignon the previous month and apparently written by Count Armand de Pontmartin, Liszt's host in that city.

NB: RILM gives the language of this article as German; it *must* be French.

*   Florán, Juan. "Liszt the Player of Chamber Music."

Includes press reports of Liszt's 1830s performances in Paris with Urhan and Batta. Described in greater detail as item 1067.

271. *Franz Liszt in Paris. Eine Rezension aus dem Jahre 1824*, ed. Friedrich
Schnapp. Weimar: Hermann Böhlaus, 1930. 14pp. + supplement.
ML410.L7S34
A handsome edition of A. Martainville's well-known review, originally
published in *Le Drapeau blanc* on 9 March 1824. Illustrated with a ms.
facsimile "supplement" and accompanied by an afterword written by Peter
Raabe. Commentary in German.
Martainville's review appears substantially complete and in English in
item 1a; pp. 99-101. It also appears in German in item 281; p. 34.

*   "From 'The Musical World'," ed. Dudley Newton.
Clippings from one of England's most important nineteenth-century
music magazines, published more as souvenirs of Liszt's British visits than
as "source materials." Described in greater detail as item 441. See also
items 442-443, which are similar in format.

*   Khvostenko. V. "List v Russii."
A collection of newspaper articles dealing with Liszt's Russian concerts
of 1842-1843. Described in greater detail as item 511.

272. Pándi, Marianne. "Liszt Ferenc az egykorú magyar sajtó tükrében: hírek
és recenziók a Honművészben." *Magyar zene* 9 (1968), pp. 75-80.
Deals with reports about Liszt's activities in Paris during the 1830s, as
reported in *A Hon*, the *Pester Zeitung*, etc. Reproduces about a dozen recital programs in French. The bulk of the article, however, in Hungarian.

273. Saffle, Michael. "Lisztiana in Early American Music Magazines." *Journal
of the American Liszt Society* 22 (1987), pp. 62-67.
Describes references to Liszt printed in American periodicals like the
Musical World and New York Musical Times before 1861. Includes a facsimile page from that publication illustrating what may have been the first
"original" Liszt study, written by an American in 1853.

274. Szerző, Katalin. "Contemporary Reports on Liszt in the Gazetta Musicale
di Milano (1870-86)." *Studia musicologica* 29 (1987), pp. 245-257.
Evaluates articles about Liszt in one of Europe's most important music
periodicals. Includes quotations from a number of articles in the original
Italian. Concludes with a short bibliography.
Other versions of this article appeared as: "'Il celebre maestro . . . '
Reports on Liszt in the 'Gazetta musicale di Milano' in the Years
1870-1886," *Periodica musica* 5 (1987), pp. 24-31; and "'Il celebre maestro
. . . ' Egykorú tudósítások Lisztről a Gazzetta musicale di Milano

hasábjain (1870-1886)," *Magyar zene* 27 (1986), pp. 39-48. The last in Hungarian.

*   Wright, William. "Press Reviews of Liszt's Concerts in Scotland."
       Described in greater detail as item 514.

Miscellaneous Biographical Document Studies

Only a few studies of Liszt's handwriting have appeared in print. Among these is an article by the author of the best Russian-language Liszt survey study:

275.   Mil'shtein, Yakov [Isaakovich]. "O niektorých zvláštnostiach hudobných rukopisov Franza Liszta/Über einige Besonderheiten der Handschriften Liszts." In item 34; pp. 47-66.
        A brief, somewhat superficial survey of Liszt's handwriting. NB: A more detailed discussion of this topic was presented by Sharon Winklhofer some years ago at a meeting of the New York State chapter of the American musicological Society.

Many scholars consider handwriting "analysis" intellectually suspect. The following monograph lends credibility to that opinion:

276.   Gille-Maisani, J.-Ch. *Écritures de compositieurs, de Beethoven à Debussy. Musique et graphologie.* Paris: Dervy-Livres, 1978. xi, 215pp.
        ML93.G54   ISBN 2-850-76068-4
        Describes famous Romantic and post-Romantic composers, including Liszt (pp. 79-92), by analyzing their handwriting. Includes seven facsimile pages of letters Liszt wrote on 13 March 1825, 22 May 1855, 15 May 1882, 16 February 1885, etc. An eccentric, carefully documented study; useful for its facsimiles (if for nothing else), but full of references to astrology and arcane source materials.

Four other studies devoted to Liszt biographers and biographical documents are described below in alphabetical order (by author and/or title):

277.   Rieger, Eva. "So schlecht wie ihr Ruf? Die Liszt-Biographin Lina Ramann." *Neue Zeitschrift für Musik* 147/7-8 (July-August 1986), pp. 16-20.
        Reevaluates Ramann and her Liszt publications, based on the hypothesis that Ramann was "a well-integrated personality, able to fight when challenged on important issues." Rieger also discusses briefly the character and extent of Ramann's two most important Liszt studies: *Franz Liszt als Künstler und Mensch* (item 3) and *Lisztiana* (item 226). Illustrated

with facsimiles of two Ramann questionnaires and with a portrait of Ramann herself. (With regard to Ramann's reputation, see also Chapter II.)

278.   Vörösmarty, Mihály. "To Ferencz Liszt," trans. Alan Dixon. *New Hungarian Quarterly*. 27/103 (Autumn 1986), pp. 139-141.

A verse translation of Mihály Vörösmarty's tribute to Liszt, originally published in 1841.

Several other translations into English of Vörösmarty's ode also exist. See, for example, Patrick Rucker, "Vörösmarty's Ode to Liszt" in the *Journal of the American Liszt Society* 20 (1986), pp. 42-48. (This article includes a brief introductory essay about the poet and his contributions to Hungarian literature.) Yet another translation appeared in the 1937 Universal-Edition publication of Zoltán Kodály's *Ode to Franz Liszt*, with English-language text by Elisabeth M. Lockwood [plate No. 10862]. The original poem has been published several times, among them in *Zenetudományi tanulmányok* 3 (1955), p. 11.

279.   "Views and Reviews." *Musical Quarterly* 22 (1936), pp. 354-361.

A description of Christern's pioneering Liszt biography (item 365), together with a biographical sketch of Christern, a facsimile reproduction of a page from his book containing holograph corrections in Liszt's hand, and an explanation of how Liszt's copy of Christern was purchased by the Library of Congress. Concludes with an incomplete catalog of Liszt's emendations in the DCl copy (pp. 358-360).

280.   Winklhofer, Sharon. "Lisztiana in Cosima Wagner's Diaries, 1869-1877." *Journal of the American Liszt Society* 7 (1980), pp. 27-34.

Summarizes Cosima's attitudes toward her father, as revealed in the diaries published for the first time about a decade ago. Winklhofer pays special attention to Cosima's divorce from Hans von Bülow and her newfound liaison with Wagner, as well as to Cosima's personality and her faithful record of life's "ironies."

ICONOGRAPHICAL STUDIES

Iconographical materials associated with Liszt include hundreds—if not thousands—of portraits, medallions, statues, figurines, stamps, coins, cartoons, etc., etc. A number of books and articles devoted to these materials have appeared in print since 1936. Without doubt the most complete, handsome, and reliable of these studies is:

281.   Burger, Ernst. *Franz Liszt: A Chronicle of His Life in Pictures and Documents*. Translated by Stewart Spencer; foreword by Alfred Brendel. Princeton, New Jersey: Princeton University Press, 1989. 358pp.
ML410.L7B913 1989   ISBN 0-691-09133-3
An outstanding collection of 650 Liszt documents, portraits, and related materials—photographs, facsimiles of musical mss., letters, and press clippings, cartoons, caricatures, and so on—beautifully printed in both black-and-white and color. Supplemented by extensive commentary and a table of activities for each year of Liszt's life. Burger's volume thus could be considered both an iconographical study and a documentary biography. Concludes with notes, bibliographical citations, an appendix containing English-language translations of document texts reproduced in illustrations (pp. 335-344), and information about the provenance of the illustrations—many of which, it turns out, belong to the author's own collection.
Originally published as *Franz Liszt. Eine Lebenschronik in Bildern und Dokumenten* (Munich: Paul List, 1986). Reviewed in this form by Alan Walker in the *Times Literary Supplement* for 10 July 1987; also reviewed in item 132. NB: The original edition contained errors corrected in the English-language edition.
Other essays about Liszt by Brendel appear in that author's *Nachdenken über Musik* (Munich: Piper, n.d.). See also references to newspaper articles by Brendel in item 40.

The only catalog of iconographical Lisztiana remains:

*   Csatkai, Andre. "Versuch einer Franz Liszt-Ikonographie."
Identifies pictures and statues of Liszt completed before 1936. Described in greater detail as item 42.

Nine other Liszt iconographies are described below in alphabetical order (by author, authors, and/or title):

282.   Bártha, Dénes von. *Franz Liszt, 1811-1886: Sein Leben in Bildern*. Leipzig: Bibliographisches Institut, 1936. 46pp.
ML410.L7B28
A small book consisting of an introductory essay and 46 black-and-white reproductions of Liszt portraits, pictures of places where he lived, mss. of compositions he wrote, and so on. Bártha's book has been superceded by more recent publications, including studies by Burger (item 281) and by László and Mátéka (item 286).

283. Bory, Robert. *La vie de Franz Liszt par l'image précedée d'une introduction biographique par A. Cortot.* Paris: Horizons de France, 1936. 249pp.
ML410.L7B662
A somewhat drab survey of Liszt's life in the form of numerous black-and-white illustrations. Also includes facsimiles of four Liszt letters as well as other documents. Students of twentieth-century pianism in general and of Alfred Cortot in particular may wish to consult that artist's introductory essay. Also printed in 1936 at Geneva.

284. Fodor, András. *Liszt Ferenc arcai. Fotóportrék.* Budapest: Múzsák Közm űvelődési Kiadó, ?1986. 53pp.
ISBN 963-564-276-8   [No LC number available]
Consists of 56 photographs of Liszt taken between 1854-1886, introduced by a brief essay and followed by a bibliography of sources and an index of names. Text in Hungarian.

285. Füssmann, Werner, and Béla Mátéka. *Franz Liszt: Ein Künstlerleben in Wort und Bild.* Langensalza: J. Beltz, 1936. xv, 301pp.
ML410.L7F9
A handsome Liszt picture-book, containing 315 carefully identified black-and-white illustrations. Supplemented by a bibliography. Mátéka also collaborated on item 286 (below), which should not be confused with his 1936 collaboration with Füssmann.

286. László, Zsigmond, and Béla Mátéka. *Liszt Ferenc élete képekben és dokumentumokban.* Budapest: Zeneműkiadó, 1978. viii, 195pp.
ML88.L48L45   ISBN 963-330-249-8
An important study, containing 378 numbered illustrations (portraits, mss. facsimiles, sheet-music covers, etc.). Different from other László-Mátéka publications—for example, *Franz Liszt. A Biography in Pictures* (London: Barrie & Rockliff, 1968)—and not to be confused with them. Text in Hungarian.

287. Raabe, Peter. *Weimarer Lisztstätten.* Weimar: Hermann Böhlaus, 1932. 8pp.
ML410.L7R136
A visual survey of "Liszt places" in Weimar, including the Altenburg, Hofgärtnerei, etc. Illustrated with 12 rather poor black-and-white photographs. Issued by the "Franz Liszt Bund."

288.   Szelényi, István. *Liszt Ferenc élete képekben*, 3rd. ed. Budapest:
        Zeneműkiadó, 1961. 70pp.
            ML410.L7S988
            Consists of an introductory biographical essay and 88 illustrations,
        many of them portraits. In Hungarian.

289.   Weilguny, Hedwig, and Willy Handrick. *Franz Liszt*, 6th ed. Leipzig:
        Volksverlag Weimar, 1980. 176pp.
            ML88.L48W4   [No ISBN number available]
            A handsome volume of pictures, most of them familiar to students of
        Liszt's life and work. Similar to item 290 (below) but more complete and
        more handsomely printed. Includes facsimiles of Liszt letters and other
        documents as well as a bibliography.

290.   Weilguny, Hedwig, and Willy Handrick. *Franz Liszt: Biographie in
        Bildern.* Leipzig: Deutscher Verlag für Musik, 1961. 168pp.
            ML88.L48W4 1961
            Contains 164 illustrations of Liszt, his loved ones, some of his ac-
        quaintances, places where he lived, etc., supplemented with an introduc-
        tory essay by Weilguny (pp. 7-40).

*Several dozen Liszt postal stamps have been issued by more than a dozen nations
since the 1930s. The finest study of these stamps and their illustrations is:*

291.   Danek, Victor B. "Liszt (and his Contemporaries) on Stamps." *Journal
        of the American Liszt Society* 23 (1988), pp. 3-18.
            Identifies and discusses 30 Liszt stamps issued during the past fifty
        years or so by Albania, Austria, Hungary, Luxembourg, and so on. Also
        identifies stamps featuring portraits of Berlioz, Chopin, Mendelssohn,
        Wagner, and other Liszt contemporaries. Illustrated with eight black-and-
        white plates reproducing virtually every Liszt stamp ever issued as well as
        details of several portraits possibly used as models by German stamp
        engravers.

Another brief study is also worth consulting:

292.   Moore, Herbert. "Paraphrase on Franz Liszt." *Scott Stamp Monthly*
        (September 1986), pp. 12-13.
            A philatelist's tribute to Liszt, illustrated with enlarged reproductions
        of five Liszt stamps and a well-known lithograph of Liszt conducting the
        premiere performance of *Die Legende der heiligen Elisabeth* in Hungary.

Liszt stamps have been reproduced in iconographies and music magazines. See, for example, "Some Further Philatelistic [sic] Items in Connection with the Liszt Centenary," *Liszt saeculum* 40 (1987), pp. 3-4.

STUDIES OF MUSICAL DOCUMENTS

No part of Liszt's musical documentary legacy is more valuable or revealing than scores, sketchbooks, and certain copies of sheet-music relating to his compositional endeavors. Studies of these and other documents are described below; these studies, however, should not be confused with musical catalogs, which are discussed in Chapter IV. Modern and facsimile Liszt editions, as well as studies related to them, are described in Chapter V. Studies of Liszt's compositions, rather than of editions of them, are described (according to genre) in Chapters XIII-XIX.

Manuscript Studies
(excluding sketchbook and revisions studies per se)

Liszt's surviving musical holographs include sketchbooks, drafts of various kinds, "Albumblätter," annotated scores and pieces of sheet-music, corrected engraver's copies, and so on. The studies described immediately below deal with complete or near-complete ms. drafts of published compositions. Studies devoted to Liszt's sketchbooks and to revisions for published compositions are described in separate sections later in this chapter.

Among the finest Liszt music manuscript studies is:

293.   Winklhofer, Sharon. *Liszt's Sonata in B Minor: A Study of Autograph Sources and Documents*. Ann Arbor Studies in Musicology, 29. Ann Arbor, Michigan: UMI Research Press, 1980. 298pp.
         ML410.L7W56   ISBN 0-8357-1119-6
         A painstaking discussion of the history of Liszt's B-minor Sonata, based to a considerable extent on an examination of the so-called "Lehman ms." owned by the Pierpont Morgan Library, New York (reproduced in facsimile as item 147). Winklhofer considers this document "a revealing source of information about the composer's creative process"; she incorrectly asserts that "such an approach is new in Liszt studies," overlooking Mária Eckhardt's *Studia musicologica* and *Magyar zene* articles (items 297-298) and Saffle's Stanford University dissertation (item 609). Winklhofer's generalizations from evolutionary tendencies in the "Lehman ms." to others of Liszt's are often unjustified; in other respects, hers is a splendid documentary study, examining—among other things—Liszt's use of "collettes" (or "pasteovers") and their contents. Illustrated with rejected, previously unpublished passages from the ms. Outfitted with an excellent bibliography and index. See also item 294 (below).

294.   Winklhofer, Sharon. *The Genesis and Evolution of Liszt's "Sonata in B Minor": Studies in Autograph Sources and Documents*. Dissertation: University of California at Los Angeles, 1978. 522pp.

A longer, more diffuse study than item 293 (above), and not to be confused with it.

Summarized in DAI 39/5 (November 1978), p. 2613A; reprinted in the *Journal of the American Liszt Society* 5 (1979), p. 90.

Two other very important, comparatively lengthy Liszt music manuscript studies are:

295.   Raabe, Peter. *Die Entstehungsgeschichte der Orchesterwerke Franz Liszts*. Dissertation: University of Jena, 1916. 54pp.
ML410.L7R13

One of the first detailed studies of Liszt manuscript materials. Among other topics, Raabe examines and refutes Helene Raff's claims (in item 212) that her husband actually orchestrated Liszt's early symphonic poems. Raabe's monograph is illustrated with an unfortunately small number of passages transcribed from what today are D-WRgs Liszt mss. of *Tasso* and several other symphonic poems. See also item 296 (below).

296.   Haraszti, Emile. "Les origines de l'orchestration de Franz Liszt." *Revue de musicologie* 34 (1952), pp. 81-100.

A valuable survey of Liszt's early orchestral works, especially the influence of Conradi and Raff on compositions like *Tasso* and *Ce qu'on entend sur la montagne*. Illustrated with examples taken from D-WRgs Liszt mss. B22 and A2b. Unfortunately, much of Haraszti's argument and virtually all his examples appear to have been borrowed from Raabe, especially from item 295 (above).

Nineteen studies of individual Liszt mss. or groups of related mss. are described or cross-referenced below in alphabetical order (by title and/or author):

*   Chantavoine, Jean. "Die Operette 'Don Sanche.' Ein verloren geglaubtes Werk Franz Liszts."

Describes the rediscovery and discusses Liszt's music for *Don Sanche*, his only opera. Described in greater detail as item 943.

297.   Eckhardt, Mária [P.] "Die Handschriften des Rákóczi-Marsches von Franz Liszt in der Széchényi Nationalbibliothek, Budapest." *Studia musicologica* 17 (1975), pp. 347-405.

Describes H-Bn Mus. mss. 16, 22, 23, and 5.829 and discusses the complicated history of these documents, all of them arrangements of the famous "Rákóczi" tune. Lavishly illustrated with musical examples and facsimile reproductions, including a complete transcription of H-Bn Mus. ms. 22, dating from 1840. An outstanding study, not entirely superceded by Eckhardt's catalog of Széchényi Liszt holographs (item 61).

A similar article by Eckhardt appeared under the title "Liszt Rákóczi indulójának kéziratai az Országos Széchényi Könyvtárban" in *Magyar zene* 17 (1976), pp. 161-189. In Hungarian.

298.   Eckhardt, Mária [P.]. "Ein Spätwerk von Liszt: der 129. Psalm." *Studia musicologica* 18 (1976), pp. 293-333.

An important study of H-Bn Mus. mss. 4.809 and 5.632, holograph drafts of settings by Liszt of Psalm CXXIX. Eckhardt also discusses the history of Liszt's unfinished setting of the *De profundis*, as well as mss. owned by the Goethe- und Schiller-Archiv, Weimar, and the Library of Congress. Illustrated with facsimiles and musical examples, among them the complete solo version of Liszt's "Psalm" preserved in H-Bn Mus. ms. 4.809. and a complete facsimile reproduction of ms. 5.632.

299.   Helm, Everett. "A Newly Discovered Liszt Manuscript." *Studia musicologica* 5 (1963), pp. 101-106.

Explains how Helm acquired the ms. of "Madrigal," an early version of the fifth *Consolation* for solo piano evidently completed in 1844. Helm also compares melodic, rhythmic, harmonic, and other details in both versions of this work. No musical examples.

300.   Hilmar, Ernst. "Kritische Betrachtungen zu Liszts Transkriptionen von Liedern von Franz Schubert: Allgemeines und Spezielles zur Niederschrift des 'Schwanengesangs'." *Liszt-Studien* 1 (1977), pp. 115-123.

Discusses differences between the published text of Liszt's *Schwanengesang* transcriptions and mss. MH 10087/c and 10088/c owned by the Vienna National Library. Hilmar also refers to other A-Wn mss.; unfortunately, he illustrates his arguments only with a single unidentified facsimile (p. 122).

301.   Johns, Keith [T.]. "More on 'Tasso,' with some Notes on a Little-known Manuscript of Liszt's 'Lamento e Trionfo' for Piano Duet preserved in the Deutsche Staatsbibliothek, East Berlin." *Journal of the American Liszt Society* 17 (1985), pp. 20-23.

Discusses portions of D-WRgs Liszt mss. A2a-c, 22c, and N5 as well as holographs owned by the Germanisches Nationalmuseum, Nürnberg, and the old German National Library. Includes short musical examples taken from several of these documents.

302.   Jung, Hans Rudolf. "Zum Autograph des 'Arbeiterchors' von Franz Liszt. Anmerkungen zur Bedeutung dieses Werkes im Schaffen des Komponisten." *Burgenländische Heimatblätter* 50 (1988), pp. 111-117.

Discusses the genesis and character of Liszt's musical tribute to the revolution of 1848-1849, scored for male chorus with piano accompaniment and written to words by Johann Philipp Kaufmann. Includes the text of a brief letter Liszt addressed to Karl Haslinger in Vienna. Illustrated with a facsimile of the first page from Liszt's ms. of the work (M. H. 6779/c) owned by the Stadt- und Landesbibliothek, Vienna, and with a reproduction of the first page from the 1954 Hungarian "first edition" of the work.

303.   Kecskeméti, István. "Die Eigenschrift der italienischen Fassung der 'Hymne de l'enfant' von Franz Liszt." *Studia musicologica* 13 (1971), pp. 333-345.

Describes the provenance and contents of H-Bn Mus. ms. 4.050, a version with Italian-language text of Liszt's *Hymne de l'enfant* completed in 1865. Illustrated with three facsimiles of the ms. as well as with other musical examples and a Liszt portrait dating from 1866.

304.   Kecskeméti, István. "Two Liszt Discoveries." *Musical Times* 115 (1974).
         304a. "An Unknown Piano Piece"; pp. 646-648.
         304b. "An Unknown Song"; pp. 743-744.

Describes two discoveries: holographs of a *Siegesmarsch* composed by Liszt c. 1870, and of *Quand du chants*, a song composed in 1852 (respectively, H-Bn Mus. mss. 5.589 and 5.108). Both articles include fragmentary facsimile reproductions from the documents they describe.

Hungarian-language articles virtually identical with items 304a-b appeared (respectively) as "Egy ismeretlen Liszt-dal" in *Magyar zene* 15 (1974), pp. 17-25; and "Liszt Ferenc ismeretlen zongoradarabja" in *Magyar zene* 14 (1973), pp. 347-372. These articles are illustrated (respectively) with complete facsimiles of H-Bn Mus. mss. 5.108 and 5.598.

305.   Kecskeméti, István. "Unbekannte Eigenschrift der XVIII. Rhapsodie von Franz Liszt." *Studia musicologica* 3 (1962), pp. 173-179.

Describes H-Bn Mus. ms. 3.276, a previously unknown draft of "Hungarian Rhapsody" No. 18. Includes a "critical report" describing differences between the ms. and published versions of the work. Illustrated with facsimile reproductions from the ms. in question, and with musical examples.

A Hungarian-language version of this article appeared under the title "Liszt XVIII. rapszódiájának ismeretlen kézirata" in *Magyar zene* 5 (1964), pp. 191-194.

*   Longyear, Rey M. "The Text of Liszt's B Minor Sonata."
     Devoted as much, if not more, to the Henle facsimile edition of the so-called "Lehmann ms." of the Sonata than to the ms. itself. Described in greater detail as item 162.

306.   Mueller, Rena [Charnin]. "Reevaluating the Liszt Chronology: The Case of 'Anfangs wollt ich fast verzagen'." *19th Century Music* 12/2 (Fall 1988), pp. 132-147.
     Reviews and evaluates kinds of Liszt ms. materials before undertaking a careful look at a recently discovered autograph source for *Anfangs* in Bayreuth's Haus Wahnfried. Among other topics tackled by Mueller is the role played by Conradi, Raff, and other copyists of Liszt mss. in preparing definitive musical texts of *Anfangs* and other songs. Illustrated with seven multipartite musical examples and two facsimile reproductions of Bayreuth and D-WRgs documents.

307.   Murányi, Robert [Árpád]. "Neue Liszt-Handschriften in der Széchényi Nationalbibliothek." *Studia musicologica* 27 (1985), pp. 305-324.
     Describes two holograph documents: a ms. of *Ungarns Gott* and a printed copy of the *Rheinweinlied* with comments in Liszt's hand. Illustrated with two facsimile reproductions and the complete musical text of the *Ungarn's Gott* arrangement for baritone, clarinets, trumpets, trombones, tuba, and timpani (pp. 309-322).

308.   Nugent, George. "'Die Glocken von Marling': A Source Recovered." *Journal of the American Liszt Society* 20 (1986), pp. 81.
     Identifies a holograph draft of *Die Glocken von Marling* owned by the George Arents Research Library at the University of Syracuse. The ms. itself is reproduced in facsimile in "A Liszt Manuscript at Syracuse," *Syracuse University Library Associates Courier* 21/2 (Fall 1986), pp. 90-92.

309.   Reich, Nancy B. "Liszt's Variations on the March from Rossini's 'Siège de Corinthe'." *Fontis artes musicae* 23 (1976), pp. 102-106; and 26 (1979), pp. 235-236.
     Traces the provenance and examines the contents of a ms. completed by Liszt in 1830 and currently owned by the Manhattanville College Library in Purchase, New York. Illustrated in the first installment (1976) with a complete facsimile reproduction of the ms. itself.
     Reprinted—unfortunately, without the facsimile reproductions that accompany the original—in the *Journal of the American Liszt Society* 7 (1980), pp. 35-41.

310.   Schnapp, Friedrich. "Liszt: A Forgotten Romance," trans. Humphrey
        Searle. *Music & Letters* 34 (1953), pp. 232-235.
           Describes *Romance*, a previously unknown early version of the *Ro-
        mance oubliée* "discovered" by Schnapp among Busoni's papers in Berlin
        (but identified previously by Raabe in item 48; entry 66a). Supplemented
        with observations about Liszt's penchant for revisions and harmonic sense
        but no musical examples. Concerning the musical quality of *Romance*,
        Schnapp observes merely that "it seems impossible to give an objective
        judgment on music so highly 'subjective'."

311.   Szitha, Tünde. "Liszt's 'Unknown' French Songs." *Studia musicologica*
        29 (1987), pp. 259-265.
           Discusses several works, among them a previously little-known version
        of *Le juif errant* and a French-language version of *Nonnenwerth*.
           Other versions of this article appeared as "Liszt Ferenc 'ismeretlen'
        francia dalai" in *Magyar zene* 27 (1986), pp. 49-82 [in Hungarian]; and as
        "Mélodies françaises inconnues" in item 36; pp. 36-43. The Hungarian
        version reprints the complete *Juif errant* score (pp. 55-82).

312.   Waters, Edward N. "Liszt's 'Soirées de Vienna'." *Quarterly Journal of the
        Library of Congress* 6/2 (February 1949), pp. 10-19.
           Explains how the Library of Congress acquired a holograph draft of the
        Liszt/Schubert *Soirées musicales*. Illustrated with a ms. facsimile.
           Subsequent issues of the Library of Congress *Quarterly Journal of
        Current Acquisitions* contain briefer accounts of the provenance and con-
        tents of other US-Wc Liszt mss.

313.   Winkler, Gerhard J. "Noch einmal: Franz Liszts 'XX. Ungarische
        Rhapsodie'. Rekonstruktion einer Unterstellung." *Burgenländische
        Heimatblätter* 48 (1986), pp. 176-184.
           Describes a holograph ms. of the so-called "Hungarian Rhapsody No.
        20" deposited in the Burgenland Regional Museum by the Rudolf Otte
        Foundation. Winkler demonstrates that this piece is virtually identical with
        No. 9 from Liszt's *Magyar dallok*. (On this topic see also item 328.) Il-
        lustrated with a facsimile page from the "Otte" ms. and with the opening
        pages of two published versions of this work.

Finally, one recent Liszt manuscript study replaces an older, much poorer one:

314.   Papp, Géza. "Unbekannte Verbunkos-Transkriptionen von Franz Liszt."
        Studia musicologica 29 (1987), pp. 183-218.
           Identifies and describes a notebook Liszt used to jot down Gypsy
        tunes. (The ms. is owned today by the Wagner Archives, Bayreuth: Shelf-

number "Ch 1 Mappa Originalmanuskripte von Franz Liszt Nr. 1.") Illustrated with 12 pages of facsimiles, 18 musical examples, and an appendix reproducing a handwritten transcription of the notebook's "Verbunkos" contents (pp. 206-218).

An extraordinarily vague discussion of this ms. appeared decades ago; see Otto Goldhammer, "Liszt, Brahms und Reményi" (*Studia musicologica* 5 [1963], pp. 89-100). Goldhammer failed even to identify the ms. in question or reproduce passages from it!

Sketch Studies
(excluding revisions studies per se)

Only a few Liszt sketchbooks survive, all of them owned by the Goethe- und Schiller-Archiv, Weimar. Liszt also left unbound sketches for some of his compositions, but only studies of sketches associated with his operatic plans—as well as sketchbook studies—are described below. Studies of pieces drafted in whole or part in the sketchbooks are described in Chapters XIII-XIX.

Recent studies of these sketchbooks include:

315.   Mueller, Rena [Charnin] *Liszt's "Tasso" Sketchbook: Studies in Sources and Revisions*. Dissertation: New York University, 1986. xiii, 418pp.
        [No LC number available]
        A detailed discussion of "how Liszt composed, exploring diverse works presented in a Weimar sketchbook (ms. N5), and placing them in the context of Liszt's life and of the other primary sources for his music" (DAI 47/8 [February 1987], p. 2792A). Mueller's primary object of investigation is D-WRgs Liszt ms. N5 (the "Tasso" sketchbook), but she also discusses *Tasso* itself, portions of the *Harmonies poétiques et religieuses*, the *Ernani* transcriptions, and Liszt's "reminiscences" of *La favorite* and *Robert le diable*. Illustrated with musical examples. Concludes with a useful bibliography and four appendices, two of which identify 34 Liszt copyists and 104 kind of Liszt music papers. Also contains facsimile reproductions of several manuscript pages.
        Summarized in DAI, as cited above. Material derived from this dissertation reappears in items 334 and 316 (below).

316.   Mueller, Rena [Charnin]. "Liszt's Tasso Sketchbook: Studies in Sources and Chronology." *Studia musicologica* 28 (1986), pp. 273-293.
        Derived from item 315 (above). In addition to tabulating the contents of D-WRgs Liszt ms. N5 (pp. 280-283), Mueller provides cursory descriptions of the other eight D-WRgs Liszt sketchbooks. No facsimiles or musical examples, but p. 276 contains a diagram of the sketchbook's physical structure.

A short survey article dealing with all nine D-WRgs Liszt sketchbooks also deserves attention, if only for its musical examples:

317.   Kókai, Rezső. "Liszt Ferenc vázlatkőnyveiröl." *Magyar muzsika* (1935), pp. 12-21.
        A pioneering description of the "N" series D-WRgs Liszt sketchbooks, illustrated with a few musical examples. In Hungarian.

Three other Liszt sketchbook studies are identified below:

318.   Johns, Keith [T.]. "Franz Liszt's N6 Sketchbook held at the Goethe-Schiller Archive in Weimar." *Journal of the American Liszt Society* 20 (1986), pp. 30-33.
        A brief but intelligent survey of D-WRgs Liszt ms. N6, which contains musical notations made by Liszt during the early 1830s. Concludes with a catalog of sketches for "major" Liszt works contained in this document. See also item 319 by the same author.

*   Johns, Keith [T.]. "More on 'Tasso' . . ."
        Deals with several documents, including D-WRgs Liszt ms. N5, the so-called "Tasso sketchbook" (see also items 315-316). Described in greater detail as item 301.

319.   Johns, Keith [T.]. "The 'N' Series of Liszt's Sketchbooks." *Journal of the American Liszt Society* 19 (1986), pp. 20-22.
        Outlines the contents of D-WRgs Liszt mss. N1-2, a pair of sketchbooks dating from several periods of Liszt's life and containing themes which later appeared in *Tasso*, volumes of the *Années de pèlerinage, Via crucis*, and the Sonata in b minor. No musical examples.

Liszt completed only one youthful opera, but he planned to compose several mature dramatic works. Among studies of the sketches and drafts associated with these un-finished operas are:

320.   Szelényi, László. "Liszts Opernpläne: Ein wenig bekanntes Kapitel aus dem Schaffen des Komponisten." *Liszt-Studien* 1 (1977), pp. 215-224.
        A brief account of Liszt's plans for *Le corsaire, Sardanapal*, and *Jankó*. Illustrated with several short musical examples from surviving sketches as well as excerpts from the Overture to Liszt's only completed opera *Don Sanche*.
        Translated into English as "Liszt's Opera Projects" in the *Liszt Society Journal* 3 (1978), pp. 27-30, and illustrated with three musical examples. Another article, written by "I. Szelényi," appeared in Hungarian under the

title "Liszt operatervei" in *Új zenei szemle* 6/7-8 (July-August 1955), pp. 10-18. Illustrated with three examples, including a fragment of Liszt's unfinished opera *Saranapole*.

321. Szelényi-Farago, László. "Liszts Opernpläne." *Neue Zeitschrift für Musik* 125 (1964), pp. 518-521.

Similar to item 320 (above). NB: The author's names differ in these studies, but the presence of almost identical musical examples suggests that the same person may have drafted both works.

Studies of Drafts and Revisions

Liszt revised hundreds of his compositions, some of them as many as half a dozen times. He also prepared two or more draft mss. for many of his works. Studies of Liszt drafts and revisions per se are described below. (Studies devoted to individual mss. and to sketchbooks and individual sketches are described above.) Studies of individual works revised by Liszt, not the revisions themselves, are described in Chapters XIII-XIX.

No book-length survey of all Liszt's revisions and drafts has appeared in print, but at least one article attempts to grapple with these materials:

322. Souter, Kenneth. "Liszt's Revisions." *Liszt Society Journal* 8 (1983), pp. 9-11.

An extremely cursory introduction to what, in effect, are hundreds of published and unpublished sketches, drafts, revisions, and "alternate" versions. Souter mentions several versions of *Nonnenwerth*—a piece Liszt arranged both for solo piano and for voice and piano. No musical examples.

Two dissertations also grapple with larger numbers of individual revisions and drafts:

*   Hansen, Bernard. *Variationen und Varianten in den musikalischen Werken Franz Liszts.*

A study of source materials that, in effect, covers almost the whole of Liszt's enormous compositional output. Described in greater detail as item 607.

*   Saffle, Michael [B]. *Franz Liszt's Compositional Development . . .*

Examines revisions for some of Liszt's piano and organ pieces, symphonic works, concerti, and chamber compositions. Described in greater detail as item 609.

Twenty-eight other studies of individual Liszt revisions and drafts are described or cross-referenced below in alphabetical order (by author):

323.   Bonner, Andrew. "Liszt's 'Les préludes' and 'Les quatre élémens': A Reinvestigation." *19th Century Music* 10 (1986), pp. 95-107.

    Contradicts Raabe (item 295), Haraszti (items 296 and 329), and others concerning the transformation of Liszt's unfinished choral pieces *Les quatre élémens* into the symphonic poem *Les préludes*. Bonner draws supporting evidence from several unpublished Liszt letters as well as from D-WRgs Liszt mss. A 3a-c and N6 (the latter one of Liszt's few surviving sketchbooks). Supplemented by a diagrammatic outline of Liszt holographs dating from 1844-1856. Illustrated with facsimile reproductions of several ms. pages and two musical examples. See also item 345.

324.   Claus, Linda. "An Aspect of Liszt's Late Style: The Composer's Revisions for 'Historische, Ungarische Portraits'." *Journal of the American Liszt Society* 3 (1978), pp. 3-18.

    Describes four movements of the "Hungarian Portraits" preserved in mss. acquired in 1966 by the Library of Congress. Claus observes that "all . . . Liszt's additions of one measure or more [of music] occur at major points of articulation—beginning, end, or interior sectional devisions." She also notes, however, that it is impossible today to determine how many of these additions merely correct mistakes made by copyists in lost ms. sources. Copiously illustrated with musical examples and documentary facsimiles—unfortunately, many of them almost illegible.

*   Conway, James Bryant. *Musical Sources for the "Etudes d'exécution transcendante"*.

    Deals to a considerable extent with Liszt's revisions for the second and third versions of these elegant works. Described in greater detail as item 789.

325.   Dart, William J. "Revisions and Reworkings in the Lieder of Franz Liszt." *Studies in Music* [Australia] 9 (1975), pp. 41-53.

    A disappointing survey of one of the most complex problems in Liszt studies: the evolution and character of dozens of individual songs. Dart claims correctly, however, that Liszt generally revised his songs "for the purpose of musical economy and subtlety." Illustrated with 32 musical examples and an incomplete table of Lieder revisions.

326.   Eger, Patricia. "Another Liszt Revision." *Journal of the American Liszt Society* 18 (1985), pp. 107-121.
         Examines differences between a handwritten copy made by Liszt of Chopin's Sonata in b minor (held in the Rocheblave Collection, Paris) and Chopin's published work. Eger concludes that "Liszt's revision neither adds nor subtracts measures," but "enriches the right hand and reduces the left hand to eighth notes" in measures 207ff. Illustrated with several comparatively lengthy musical examples as well as a facsimile page of Liszt's "revision."

*   Fowler, Andrew. "Franz Liszt's 'Petrarch Sonnets' . . ."
         Deals with motivic materials shared by piano and piano-vocal settings of several Liszt works. Described in greater detail as item 638.

327.   Friedheim, Philip. "First Version, Second Version, Alternative Version: Some Remarks on the Music of Liszt." *Music Review* 44 (1983), pp. 194-202.
         An intriguing discussion of selected Liszt song revisions, including those made for the final version of *Im Rhein, im schönen Strome*. Also includes brief references to several keyboard works. Friedheim contents that the "philosophical point" of Liszt's revisions is "that there is no such thing as an ultimate interpretation, or a final version, of any composition [by Liszt or by other composers]." Five musical examples.

328.   Gárdonyi, Zoltán. "Eine unbekannte Liszt-Rhapsodie? Zum Druck einer frühen Werkfassung." *Musica* 25 (1971), pp. 153-154.
         Concludes that the composition published by Rudolf Otte as Liszt's "Hungarian Rhapsody No. 20" is actually a draft for *Magyar dallok* No. 9. See also item 313.

*   Hansen, Bernard. "'Nonnenwerth': Ein Beitrag zu Franz Liszts Liedkomposition."
         As much a survey of the original song's origins and character as a study in revisions and alternate versions. Described in greater detail as item 939.

329.   Haraszti, Emile. "Genèse des préludes de Liszt qui n'ont aucun rapport avec Lamartine." *Revue de musicologie* 5 (1953), pp. 111-140.
         Traces the origins of the symphonic poem *Les préludes* to choruses Liszt wrote on texts from Autran's *Quatre éléments* in the 1840s. Among other documents, Haraszti discusses in some detail D-WRgs Liszt mss. S9, S10, S11, and S11a. Illustrated with several facsimile reproductions and with a number of musical examples.

330.   Haselböck, Martin. "Von der Erst- zur Urfassung — Neue Erkenntnisse
        zu Liszts Präludium und Fuge über B-A-C-H." *Musik und Kirche* 56
        (1986), pp. 219-224.
            Primarily an examination of D-WRgs mss. of the first version the
        "BACH" prelude and fugue in light of registration indications and possi-
        bilities. Illustrated with several musical examples taken from the published
        score and with photographs of two organs known to Alexander
        Winterberger, for whom "BACH" was written.

331.   Heinemann, Ernst Günther. "Liszts 'Angelus' — Beobachtungen zum
        kompositorischen Entstehungsprozess." *Musik. Edition. Interpretation.
        Gedenkschrift Gunther Henle*, ed. Martin Bente. Munich: G. Henle, 1980;
        pp. 213-217.
            ML55.H44 1980   ISBN 3-8732-8032-9
            Describes compositional changes in surviving mss. of *Angelus*, taken
        from the third volume of the *Années de pèlerinage*. Heinemann maintains
        that, despite these changes, there was no smoothing out of the musical
        material; consequently, Liszt's piece still seems uneven. No musical ex-
        amples.

332.   Hughes, William H., Jr. *Liszt's "Première Année de pèlerinage: Suisse." A
        Comparative Study of Early and Revised Versions*. Dissertation: University
        of Rochester, 1985. xii, 311pp.
            ML95.3H894
            Deals with Liszt's alterations and improvements for seven pieces found
        in the first volume of the "Years of Pilgrimage" collection: *Chapelle de
        Guillaume Tell, Au lac de Wallenstadt, Pastorale,* and so on. Among other
        topics, Hughes also discusses the circumstances of Liszt's life during the
        1830s and 1840s, nineteenth-century pianos, and interpretive indications
        in the mss. and scores he examined. Numerous musical examples.
            Summarized in DAI 46/4 (October 1985), p. 832A; reprinted in the
        Journal of the American Liszt Society 18 (1985), p. 181.

*   Jiránek, J[aroslav]. "Liszts Beitrag zur Musiksprache der Romantiker."
            In part a study of the evolution of two numbers from Liszt's Etudes,
        Op. 1, into *Vision* and *Wilde Jagd* from the "Transcendental Etudes" of
        the 1850s. Described in greater detail as item 612.

333.   Lozza, Giuseppe. "La doppia versione del Lied di Liszt 'Der
        Fichtenbaum'." *Nuova rivista musicale italiana* 20 (1986), pp. 387-399.
            Deals with two versions of a song Liszt revised during the middle years
        of his career. Illustrated with 11 musical examples. In Italian.

*   Main, Alexander. "Liszt after Lamartine: 'Les préludes'."
Primarily a discussion of the program of *Les préludes* and its relationship to Lamartine's ode, but Main also refers to D-WRgs mss. of *Les quatre élémens* and their relationship to Liszt's symphonic poem. Described in greater detail as item 909.

334.   Mueller, Rena [Charnin]. "Le cahier d'esquisses du 'Tasso' et la composition des 'Harmonies poétiques et religieuses'." *Revue musicale* 405-406-407 (1987), pp. 11-28.
Part discussion of the evolution of the revised *Harmonies*, part documentary study devoted to uncovering source materials dealing with that evolutionary process. No facsimiles or musical examples but numerous references to D-WRgs and other archival Liszt mss., especially the "N" series of D-WRgs sketchbooks.

335.   Schenkman, Walter. "The 'Venezia e Napoli' Tarantella: Genesis and Metamorphosis." *Journal of the American Liszt Society* 6-8 (1979-1980).
> 335a. "The Liszt-Cottrau Connection"; 6 (1979), pp. 10-24.
> 335b. "The Transition from 'Tarantelles' to 'Tarantella'"; 7
> (1980), pp.42-58.
> 335c. "The Specifics of the Changes between 'Tarantelles'
> and 'Tarantella'"; 8 (1980), pp. 44-59.

Describes in detail the genesis of and revisions for the work best-known today as the *Tarantella* from Liszt's *Venezia e Napoli* (revised version). Item 335a deals with Guillaume Cottrau, from four of whose canzonas ("Fenesta ca lucive," "Lo Guarracino," "Fenesta vascia," and "Michelemmà") Liszt drew thematic materials for the original *Tarantelles*. According to Schenkman, Liszt makes at least one "incongruous" alteration in material borrowed from his Italian predecessor. Item 335b deals with revisions for the *Tarantelles*; Schenkman explains that Liszt outgrew the disparity between "pianist" and "composer" pointed out to him by Ernest Legouve in 1840, and that changes in the original *Tarantelles* involved virtually every aspect of their musical character. Item 335c consists of a detailed comparison of the two versions of this composition. Schenkman pays special attention to the musical content of Liszt's revisions—to Liszt's "new and better ways of musical expression" which he believes demonstrate Liszt's willingness to undertake a fundamentally "un-Romantic" Illustrated throughout with musical examples.

*   Schütz, Georg. "Form, Satz- und Klaviertechnik in den drei 'Grossen Etüden' von Franz Liszt."

More a study of the "Transcendentals" and of their compositional characteristics than of their various versions. Described in greater detail as item 790.

336.   Somfai, László. "Die Metamorphose der 'Faust-Symphonie' von Liszt." *Studia musicologica* 5 (1963), pp. 283-293.

Not to be confused with items 337-338 (below). A shorter, less "scientific" study, containing different musical examples.

337.   Somfai, László. "Die musikalischen Gestaltwandlungen der Faust-Symphonie von Liszt." *Studia musicologica* 2 (1962), pp. 87-137.

A much more detailed study than item 336 (above). Traces the evolution of the *Faust* symphony from surviving drafts to completed orchestral score, especially in D-WRgs Liszt mss. N4, W12 a-b, and A14 a-b, and especially in the holograph draft preserved in H-Bn Mus. ms. 260. Somfai also discusses the psychological character of Liszt's musical portraits and problems associated with the choral ending appended only at a comparatively late date to the last movement of this work. Illustrated with a single facsimile reproduction and 41 musical examples.

Translated from Somfai's Hungarian-language article "Liszt Faust-szimfóniájának alakváltásai," published in *Magyar zene* 1/6 (June 1961), pp. 559-573; and 1/7-8 (August-October 1961), pp. 78-102. Reprinted in English in *Nineteenth-century Music*, ed. Ellen Rosand (New York: Garland, 1985); pp. 176-208. Also reprinted in German in item 30; pp. 292-324.

338.   Somfai, László. "Metamorphoses of Liszt's Faust Symphony." *New Hungarian Quarterly* 2/3 (July-September 1961), pp. 75-83.

Not to be confused with items 336-337 (above). A much shorter study of compositional genesis and written for the layman. No musical examples.

339.   Stradal, August. "Das 'Album d'un voyageur' und 'La première année de pèlerinage' ('La Suisse') von Franz Liszt." *Neue Musik-Zeitung* 33 (1912), pp. 41-43, 153-154, 195-196, 214-215, 255-257, 296-298, 355-356, 394-395, 436-437, and 476-478.

A piece-by-piece, measure-by-measure comparison of Liszt's earlier *Album d'un voyageur* pieces with the later versions that became Book I of the "Years of Pilgrimage" collection. Although published before World War I, Stradal's study has never been superceded. Illustrated with dozens of musical examples.

340.   Tagliavini, Luigi Ferdinando. "La prima versione d'un lied di Liszt in una fonte sinora sconosciuta. L'album musicale della poetessa russa Evdokija Rostopčina." *Rivista musicale italiana* 19 (1984), pp. 277-297.

Describes an early version of *Dichter, was Liebe sei* preserved in an album once owned by the Russian poet Evdokija Rostopčina. Illustrated with facsimile reproductions of the album (pp. 40-41) and three musical examples. An appendix describes the contents of the album itself, which also contains pieces ascribed to Donizetti and Beethoven. In Italian.

341.   Torkewitz, Dieter. "Die Erstfassung der 'Harmonies poétiques et religieuses' von Liszt." *Liszt-Studien* 2 (1981), pp. 220-236.

Compares the two published versions of Liszt's *Harmonies* and discusses the evolution of his musical style. Torkewitz also refers to D-WRgs Liszt ms. N6, as well as to studies by Kókai (item 317) and other scholars. Illustrated with 21 musical examples in the form of an appendix.

342.   Turner, Ronald. "A Comparison of two Sets of Liszt-Hugo Songs." *Journal of the American Liszt Society* 5 (1979), pp. 16-31.

Identifies revisions for four songs Liszt wrote on texts by Victor Hugo and discusses those revisions in terms of compositional development. Musical examples.

343.   Williamson, John. "The Revision of Liszt's 'Prometheus'." *Music & Letters* 67 (1986), pp. 381-390.

Discusses the history of Liszt's choruses on texts from Herder's *Entfesselten Prometheus* and the *Prometheus* symphonic poem. Williamson describes motivic and programmatic links between these compositions; he mentions the "iron control that Liszt kept over the copying, revision and orchestration of his work" but gives Joachim Raff credit for orchestrating much of the 1850 version of the "Prometheus Overture." Illustrated with eight multipartite musical examples, a table of D-WRgs Liszt mss. associated with the works in question, and facsimiles of 2 consecutive leaves from D-WRgs Liszt ms. A5a.

344.   Wuellner, Guy. "Franz Liszt's 'Liebestraum' No. 3: A Study of 'O lieb' and its Piano Transcription." *Journal of the American Liszt Society* 24 (1988), pp. 45-73.

Examines virtually every change Liszt made in transforming—not merely "transcribing"—a song into a piano solo. Wuellner also speculates about the well-known *Liebestraum* No. 3 as a characteristically Romantic work. More than two dozen musical examples.

Finally, a study devoted to studies *of some of Liszt's drafts and revisions:*

345.   Chailley, Jacques. "Quel fut l'inspirateur des 'Préludes' de Liszt?" *Revue musicale* 405-406-407 (1987), pp. 37-55.

    Evaluates positions taken by scholars over several decades, especially Bonner (item 323), Haraszti (items 296 and 329), and Main (in item 905) concerning the inspiration for the program of Liszt's symphonic poem *Les préludes*. Chailley finally decides against Main and in favor of the notion that at least parts of *Les préludes* were based on Liszt's unfinished Autran choruses. Illustrated with several tables and three musical examples. (With regard to documents concerning Liszt, Autran, and the genesis of *Les préludes*, see item 256.)

Studies of Printed Music

Most of the articles published about Liszt's printed music deal either with editions or with the compositions contained in that music. These studies are described (respectively) in Chapters V and XIII-XIX.

    Two articles about printed Liszt musical materials deal with a lost concerto that may recently have been rediscovered:

346.   Hinson, Maurice. "Long Lost Liszt Concerto?" *Journal of the American Liszt Society* 13 (1983), pp. 53-58.

    Suggests that the "Concerto in Hungarian Style" purportedly written by Liszt during the latter years of his life is actually Tchaikovsky's *Hungarian Melodies* for piano and orchestra. Illustrated with four examples from Tchaikovsky's score. NB: Hinson's theory was first proposed in 1962 by Margit Prahács in item 347 (below).

347.   Prahács, Margit. "Liszts letztes Klavierkonzert." *Studia musicologica* 4 (1962), pp. 195-200.

    Suggests that Liszt's reference to a "lost" concerto in an 1885 letter to Sophie Mentor actually refers to the composition published under Tchaikovsky's name as *Hungarian Melodies*. Prahács reproduces a facsimile of the letter in question (pp. 196-197).

Two other studies of printed Liszt musical materials also deserve attention:

348.   Röckl, Sebastian. "Ein unbekanntes Männerquartett Franz Liszts (mit Musikbeilage)." *Zeitschrift für Musik* 96 (1929), pp. 332-333.

    Describes the origins of *Trinkspruch*, a short work for male chorus composed between 18 October 1843 and 19 January 1844 and published as a supplement to Röckl's article. Also reproduces the text of a letter addressed by Liszt to Count Franz Pocci from Weimar on 19 January 1844.

349.   Sonneck, O. G. "Liszt's Huldigungs Marsch and Weimar's Volkslied."
        Musical Quarterly 22 (1936), pp. 326-338.

   Describes problems associated with a little-known score by Raff for
military band of Liszt's *Huldigungs-Marsch*. Raff's arrangement also in-
corporates the so-called "Weimars Volkslied" tune in its trio section.
Sonneck uses extensive quotations from Liszt's correspondence and a
number of musical examples to demonstrate that Raff's arrangement of the
march precedes Liszt's published orchestral score by some six or seven
years (1853 vs. 1858-1859). Includes among other musical examples the
complete "Volkslied," scored by Liszt for unaccompanied male chorus.

IX: BIOGRAPHIES AND CHARACTER STUDIES

Hundreds of Liszt biographies have appeared in print. Some are mere sketches of the artist's life; others are lengthy, complex studies. Among the most reliable "lives" of Liszt are portions of several multi-volume survey studies described in Chapter III. Valuable biographical information also can be found in items described in Chapters VII-VIII. Other, more specialized biographical studies are described below in Chapter X.

BIOGRAPHIES

Modern Biographical Studies

Reliable, readable accounts of Liszt's life can be found today in virtually every book store and library. Unfortunately, however, most of the Liszt biographies published during the past fifty or sixty years are unreliable popularizations of their subject's accomplishments. Two outstanding exceptions to this situation are:

350.   Perényi, Eleanor. *Liszt: The Artist as Romantic Hero.* Boston: Little, Brown, 1974. x, 466pp.
ML410.L7P3   ISBN 0-3166-9910-1
A brilliant interpretive work, based almost exclusively on letters Liszt exchanged with colleagues and with d'Agoult and Wittgenstein. Although issued as a popular publication, this book deserves the most serious attention; Rena Mueller called it "extraordinarily worthwhile" in a review published in *Current Musicology* 20 (1975), pp. 96-104. Perényi promulgates the thesis that "Liszt was the first musician to benefit from the Romantic cult of genius," and that it was this cult—French Romanticism at its most extravagant—which "even now . . . obscures his stature as one of the innovators of nineteenth-century music." Unfortunately, Perényi has little to say about her subject after 1861; instead, she leaves Liszt at the threshold of old age. Illustrated with several portraits; concludes with a short bibliography. Mentioned in Chapter II.

351.   Haraszti, Emile. *Franz Liszt*. Paris: A. & J. Picard, 1967. 306pp.
        ML410.L7H29
        A book-length miscellany, compiled from Haraszti's papers after his
        death in 1958. Describes much of Liszt's life but ignores his childhood and
        other important topics. Although uneven, this volume reflects its author's
        extensive knowledge of primary sources, especially French-language mate-
        rials. Some chapters are especially valuable—among them, those dealing
        with Liszt and Balzac, and with the representation of Liszt in Balzac's
        Béatrix and d'Agoult's *Nélida*. Contains an introduction by André
        Schaeffner and several illustrations.

Liszt biographies often overlooked by specialists include:

352.   Kapp, Julius. *Liszt, eine Biographie*. Berlin: Schuster & Loeffler, 1909.
        607pp.
        ML410.L7K33
        A valuable volume, first published before World War I and reprinted
        many times; unfortunately, post-1911 editions do not contain the docu-
        mentary material found in the original publication. Full of valuable anec-
        dotes about Liszt and his associates as well as an extensive bibliography
        (pp. 547-600), a catalog of Liszt's compositions, occasional illustrations
        and documentary facsimiles, and more than two dozen otherwise unpub-
        lished Liszt letters.

353.   Walker, Alan. *Liszt*. London: Faber & Faber, 1971. 108pp.
        ML410.L7W29   ISBN 0-571-09120-2
        A short biography published as a book for young people. Not to be
        confused with the Walker's splendid study of Liszt's early and middle years
        (items 1a-b). Illustrated with portraits and photographs of Liszt and his
        surroundings, facsimiles of various documents, and so on.

*Ten additional Liszt biographies are described below in alphabetical order (by au-
thor). Three even more important studies, described in Chapter III, are cross-
referenced among them:*

354.   Hamburger, Klára. *Liszt Ferenc*. Budapest: Gondolat, Kiadó, 1966. 483pp.
        ML410.L7H255 1980   ISBN 963-2-80774-X
        More or less "straight" biography; not to be confused with broader,
        even more reliable studies by the same author (see item 12). Concludes
        with a bibliography and catalog of Liszt's works (pp. 413-456). In
        Hungarian.

355.   Helm, Everett. *Franz Liszt in Selbstzeugnissen und Bilddokumenten.*
        Hamburg: Rowohlt, 1972. 160pp.
            ML410.L7H37
        A compact account of Liszt's life and activities, supplemented by ex-
        cerpts from a variety of sources. Illustrated with small, black-and-white
        reproductions of portraits, facsimiles of several mss., etc. Concludes with
        an abbreviated catalog of Liszt's works and a short bibliography.

*   Horvath, Emmerich Karl. *Liszt.*
        A series of three volumes covering Liszt's life and musical activities
        from birth through the late 1830s. Described in greater detail as item 13.

356.   Koronghy, Clara von. *Die Musik war sein Leben: Gedenkbuch für Franz
        Liszt.* Eisenstadt: Horvath, 1984. 168pp.
            ML410.L7K75 1984   [No ISBN number available]
        A biographical study-*cum*-reminiscence, describing Liszt's relationships
        with several Austrian families, including the Hennigs and Vetzkos.
        Koronghy also deals with Liszt's family (pp. 15-21) and travels (especially
        within Austro-Hungary, pp. 43-66) as well as iconographical issues (pp.
        155ff.). Amply illustrated with black-and-white photographs.

*   Raabe, Peter. *Franz Liszt.*
        The volume of this set remains one of the most objective accounts of
        Liszt's life ever published. Described in greater detail as item 2a. See also
        items 357 (below) and 373.

357.   Raabe, Peter. *Wege zu Liszt.* Deutsche Musikbücherei, 13. Regensburg:
        Gustav Bosse, 1943. 167pp.
            ML410.L7R13
        Much shorter than item 2a and almost entirely biographical. Includes
        some references to individual compositions and musical style but no
        musical examples.

358.   Rostand, Claude. *Liszt,* trans. John Victor. London: Calder & Boyars,
        1972. 192pp.
            ML410.L7R7213
        Essentially a biography in the form of a year-by-year chronicle of
        Liszt's life, although four of its eight chapters present a superficial sum-
        mary of Liszt's reputation as a pianist and his compositional output. Il-
        lustrated with portraits and a few melodic musical examples as well as a
        facsimile example of F-Pn ms. 175, a table of key signatures Liszt prepared

near the end of his life for some unknown reason. Includes a short catalog of works and a bibliography.

Originally published in French in 1960 by Editions du Seuil of Paris.

359.   Rueger, Charles. *Magie in Schwarz und Weiß: Franz Liszt*. Berlin: Erica Klopp, 1986. 277pp.

ML410.L7R77 1986   ISBN 3-7817-1827-1

Suttoni (in item 46) correctly considers this study a "popularly oriented and generously illustrated biography" that presents Liszt as a "'European,' viewed against the supra-national cultural currents" of his time.

360.   Schibli, Sigfried. *Franz Liszt: Rollen, Kostüme, Verwandlungen*. Munich: Piper, 1986. 170pp.

ML410.L7S35 1986   ISBN 2-492-15238-4

Explores the hypothesis that Liszt adopted a number of disguises, self-consciously playing the successive parts of virtuoso, Kapellmeister, and cleric. Schibli also deals cursorily with Liszt's correspondence and with several compositions, including the B-minor Sonata. Illustrations include reproductions of portraits, paintings, caricatures, and a handful of short musical examples.

361.   Sitwell, Sacheverall. *Liszt*, rev. ed. New York: Dover Books, 1967. 400pp.

ML410.L7S62 1967

Elegantly written but unfortunately ill-documented and inaccurate. Sitwell considers Liszt interesting above all as a performer (p. xxi) and only incidentally influential as a creative force in nineteenth-century music. The original 1934 edition concludes with an abbreviated catalog of Liszt's works (pp. 338-357), a chronological outline of his life, an outdated bibliography, and four appendices devoted to the lives of Alkan, Sivori, John Field, and Walter Bache. A fifth appendix quotes the same part of Haweis's *Musical Life* also quoted at length at the end of item 350. Revisions made by Sitwell in old age were confined to a seven-page postscript dated "1955." See also item 381.

362.   Sogny, Michel. *L'admiration créatrice chez Liszt*. Paris: Buchet-Chastel, 1975. 186pp.

ML410.L7S653

A biography fleshed out with psychoanalytic speculation (pp. 99-105) as well as with the texts of several "unpublished" letters (pp. 149-175). NB: Most of these letters appeared in print long ago, some in such obvious places as *Franz Liszt's Briefe* (item 186). Supplemented by a chronological outline of Liszt's activities and a bibliography.

Derived from Sogny's dissertation *Le processus de l'esprit créateur chez Liszt* (Paris 1974). See *French Language Dissertations in Music: An Annotated Bibliography*, ed. Jean Gribensk (Stuyvesant, New York: Pendragon Press, 1979), pp. 191-192.

363.   Sommsich, Andor. *Liszt Ferenc élete*. Budapest: Magyar Irodalmi Társaság, 1925. 480pp.

Rare. The Boston Public Library is said to own a copy of this volume.

A commendable work, now out of date. Haraszti praised Sommsich in his 1936 evaluation of published Liszt literature (item 119), and Hungarian scholars still cite him from time to time. His book contains a list of compositions and a bibliography especially useful for pre-1918 Hungarian-language publications (pp. 475-478). Illustrated with a frontispiece Liszt portrait. In Hungarian.

*   Walker, Alan. *Franz Liszt*.

The best English-language biography-*cum*-musical study in print. Two volumes have appeared to date; these are described in greater detail as items la-b.

A few lengthy biographical articles have also appeared in print. Among these is:

364.   Rehberg, Paula. "Franz Liszt — Ein Künstlerleben." *Österreichische Musikzeitschrift* 16 (1961), pp. 416-428.

A rather fulsome sketch of the artist's life drawn from the book-length study published by Rehberg and Gerhard Nestler (item 15). Illustrated with a lithographic portrait of Liszt finished in 1824.

Early Biographical Studies

In general, recent Liszt biographies are more reliable than earlier studies. A few nineteenth-century biographies, however, contain valuable information about Liszt's character and activities. These studies include:

365.   Christern, J. W. *Franz Liszt. Nach seinem Leben und Werke aus authentischen Berichten dargestellt*. Leipzig: Schuberth, 1842. 43pp.
       ML410.L7Z2846M

The first important book-length biography of Liszt, containing valuable information about the artist's early concert tours. Concludes with a one-page catalog of pieces Liszt completed before c. 1841.

The Library of Congress owns a copy containing emendations and corrections in Liszt's hand (described in item 279). Additional information about this copy [US-Wc shelf number ML95.L68 case] and facsimile reproductions of some of its pages are scattered throughout item 1a. Mentioned in Chapter II, as are items 366-367 (below).

366.   Rellstab, Ludwig. *Franz Liszt. Beurteilungen — Berichte — Lebensskizze.*
        Berlin: Trautwein, 1842. iv, 76pp.
           ML410.L7R35
        A valuable source of information about Liszt's concert career, especially his Berlin performances of the early 1840s. The bulk of this book, in fact, consists of a report about Liszt's 1842 Berlin visit (pp. 29-56) and of reviews—occasionally revised and edited—which originally published in the *Vossische Zeitung* (pp. 1-28). No illustrations or musical examples.

367.   Schilling, Gustav. *Franz Liszt: Sein Leben und Wirken aus nächster Beschauung.* Stuttgart: Stoppani, 1844. xvi, 267pp.
           ML410.L7Z833M
        Another early biography of interest. Schilling provides a great deal of information about Liszt's early virtuoso concert tours. Illustrations of several kinds but no systematic discussion of musical issues.

One of the most interesting older Liszt biographies remains:

368.   La Mara. *Franz Liszt*, 13th ed. Leipzig: Breitkopf & Härtel, 1920. 77pp.
           ML410.L7L774
        A popular work by the author of the "authorized" Liszt biography (item 3). Illustrated with a portrait of Liszt as a frontispiece; supplemented with a catalog of works (pp. 57-78), including some bibliographic entries. No musical examples or discussion.

Among early Liszt biographies are several works cited primarily because they provided information adopted wholesale by the authors of subsequent studies. Perhaps the most famous of these publications is:

369.   d'Ortigue, Joseph. "Franz Liszt." *Revue et gazette musical de Paris* 2/24 (14 June 1835), pp. 197-204.
        An "legendary" account of Liszt's early life, complete with the famous "Weihekuss" tale discussed in Chapter II and argued over in items 1a, 130-131, 576, etc.
        Transformed into German by one Herr Flechsig (who is also sometimes credited with writing it) and published in the *Neue Zeitschrift für Musik* 4 (1836). This translation is discussed separately as item 396. Also discussed in Chapter II.

Not all early Liszt biographies are reliable; some can only be considered curiosities today. Three examples are described below in alphabetical order (by author):

370.   Duverger, J. *Notice biographique sur Franz Liszt*, ed. M. E. Pascallet; 2nd ed. Paris: Amyot, May 1843. 66pp.
          Rare: US-Wc shelf number ML410.L7D9
          A poor work, full of small errors—e.g., the date of Liszt's honorary doctorate from the University of Königsberg is given as 1841, instead of 1842. Like other biographical "notices," this pamphlet testifies to the hunger of nineteenth-century music lovers for information about Liszt—reliable or otherwise. Includes the texts of letters Liszt wrote in 1838-1839. Apparently published previously in the *Revue générale.*
          NB: "Duverger" may have been a pen name for the Comtesse d'Agoult. See item 41; entry 434.

371.   Ledos de Beaufort, Raphael. *Franz Liszt. The Story of His Life, to Which Are* [sic] *Added Liszt as a Littérateur by T. Carlaw Martin.* London: Oliver Ditson, 1887. 233pp.
          ML410.L7L3 1887
          A cheap popular biography, issued in several editions and under several titles, at least one of which (London 1886) contains Nadine Helbig's essay "Liszt in Rome" (see item 504). Another edition appeared under the title *The Abbé Liszt: The Story of his Life* (London ?1866). The 1887 London edition concludes with a list of compositions (pp. 228-231) and a roll-call of "principal pupils" (pp. 232-233).

372.   Nohl, Louis. *Life of Liszt*, trans. George P. Upton. Chicago: A. C. McClurg, 1889. 198pp.
          ML410.L7N85
          A lacklustre biography outfitted with an appendix containing some intriguing source materials: a letter written by Adam Liszt in 1824, a review of "Don Sancho" [sic] published in the *Harmonicon* in 1825, and so on.
          A 1970 reprint of this volume (Detroit: Gale Research Co.) includes a Liszt portrait; the original edition lacks illustrations as well as musical examples.

Biographical Tables and Outlines

Several valuable diagrammatic outlines of Liszt's life have appeared in print since the 1930s. Perhaps the best of these publications is:

373.   Raabe, Peter. "Zeittafel." In item 2a; pp. 274-318.
          Summarizes Liszt's life and times in three columns—the first devoted to compositions, the second to activities and relationships, and the third

to contemporary events. Generally accurate and unusually detailed, this table provided much of the information for a similar table in item 18; pp. 476-539. See also item 244.

Other biographical outlines and tables include:

374.   Nádor, T. *Liszt Ferenc életének krónikája.* Nagy muzsikusok életének krónikája, 12. Budapest: Zeneműkiadó, 1975. 344pp.
        ML410.L7N2   ISBN 963-3-30084-3
        A year-by-year, often day-by-day "chronicle" of Liszt's life and activities, supplemented by a few musical examples. Often sketchy and less reliable than Raabe's table (item 373 above).

*   Burger, Ernst. *Franz Liszt: Eine Lebenschronik in Bildern und Dokumenten.*
        Contains tables identifying important events in virtually every year of Liszt's life. Described in greater detail as item 281.

*   Gut, Serge. *Franz Liszt.*
        Includes a chronological outline of Liszt's life (pp. 476-539). Described in greater detail as item 18.

*   Liszt, Eduard von. "Skizzenartige Darstellung . . ."
        Described in greater detail as item 244.

375.   Cooper, Frank. "Franz Liszt: A Life in Outline." *American Organist* 20/7 (July 1986), pp. 52-55.
        A short year-by-year survey of Liszt's life, written for non-specialists and of little value.

CHARACTER STUDIES

Liszt has been served better by biographers than by students of human nature. Few studies of his character exist, and none of them tackles all the problems associated with its complex subject. The most famous of these studies—and, almost every Lisztian would agree, the most disreputable—is:

376.   Newman, Ernest. *The Man Liszt: A Study of the Tragi-comedy of a Soul Divided Against Itself.* London: Cassell, 1934; and New York: Charles Scribner, 1935. Both xxii, 313pp.
         ML410.L7N4
         A dishonest, poorly argued, yet extremely influential attack on the so-called "Liszt legend" (discussed at some length in Chapter II). Although Newman considered his subject an "extraordinary man . . . perhaps the most elusive psychological problem in all music," he discussed him with a remarkable lack of sympathy. Illustrated with a few portrait photographs. Prefaced with a list of sources (pp. xviii-xxii).
         Reprinted in 1970 in a facsimile edition issued by Victor Gollancz of London. Carl Engel's biting attack on Newman's work appeared under "Views and Reviews" in the *Musical Quarterly* 21 (1935), pp. 230-240. See also Chapter II.
         NB: Newman's opinions about Liszt were not always negative. See the "Study of Liszt," reprinted in the *Liszt Society Journal* 8 (1983), pp. 32-33.

Seven other character studies are described below in alphabetical order (by author):

377.   Hamburger, Klára. "'Musicien humanitaire'." *New Hungarian Quarterly* 27/103 (Autumn 1986), pp. 85-92.
         An apostrophe to Liszt's character as well as his artistic contributions to nineteenth-century cultural life. Asserts that nineteenth-century Europe could not tolerate "such a radiant spirit" as Liszt and thus defaced his memory. Also reviews the contents and implications of some published Liszt letters as well as biographies by Raabe (item 2a) and Haraszti (item 351).

378.   Knotik, Cornelia. "'Génie oblige'. Selbstdarstellung und Stilisierung der Person Franz Liszts." *Österreichische Musikzeitschrift* 41 (1986), pp. 77-82.
         Describes Liszt's artistic, nationalistic, and clerical "posturing" apart from his accomplishments as composer, performer, and pedagogue. Illustrated with two portraits of the artist—one as "Abbé," the other in Hungarian costume. An intriguing study, unfortunately on the short side.

379.   Quéro, Robert. *Franz Liszt (1811-1886). Étude psycho-pathologique.* Dissertation: University of Bordeaux, 1932. 147pp.
         [No LC number available]
         Not seen. References to this study are scattered through the Liszt literature and, according to the *National Union Catalog, Pre-1956 Imprints,* Vol. 477, p. 150, the Yale University library once owned a copy. The present author was unable to locate the copy purportedly owned by H-Bn.

380.   Schramek, Rudolf. "Franz Liszt: Eine psychologische Untersuchung über
         Leben und Werk." *Archiv für die gesamte Psychologie* 92 (1934), pp. 45-84.
              A psychological examination of Liszt's personality and fluctuations in
         his artistic output. Schramek believes the later 1850s (especially 1857) were
         Liszt's "peak" years as a composer because his life in Weimar with the
         Princess Sayn-Wittgenstein fed his creative energies. Illustrated with several
         intriguing graphs.

381.   Sitwell, Sacheverell. "Liszt: A Character Study." In item 31; pp. 1-21.
              Drawn for the most part from Sitwell's book-length study of Liszt's life
         and character (item 361).

382.   Suarès, André. "Liszt le magnanime." *Revue musicale* "Numéro special"
         (1 May 1928), pp. 5-17.
              A flattering sketch of Liszt's character, similar to a number of short
         articles omitted from the present study. Well-intended but cursory and
         possibly too "enthusiastic" in tone.

383.   Suarès, André "Liszt, le magnanime." In item 36; pp. 142-147.
              Not to be confused with item 382 (above). The publishers of *Silences*,
         in which the present article appeared, identify its source as a previously
         unedited F-Pn ms.

Finally, one research report devoted exclusively *to the published Liszt biographical
literature also deserves to be mentioned here:*

384.   Helm, Everett. "Franz Liszt: ein Opfer seiner Biographen?" *Festschrift für
         einen Verleger. Ludwig Strecker zum 90. Geburtstag*, ed. Carl Dahlhaus.
         (Mainz: B. Schott, 1973), pp. 167-177.
              ML55.S848F5 1973
              Reviews Liszt's life in order to assess evidence for and against the so-
         called "Liszt legend." Helm concludes that although the Comtesse
         d'Agoult and Princess Sayn-Wittgenstein must have helped Liszt with his
         literary works, the composer himself must bear some of the burden for the
         legend. Numerous source citations.

X: SPECIALIZED BIOGRAPHICAL STUDIES

Many of the book-length biographies of Liszt published to date have been disappointing, but specialized biographical studies of various kinds have filled many gaps in our knowledge of his character and affairs. The most important of these studies are described below. Biographies proper and character studies are described in Chapter IX.

ANCESTORS AND FAMILY

Genealogical Studies

Liszt's ancestry has been traced with care by several outstanding scholars. The best summaries of that ancestry include:

385.   Békefi, Ernő. "Franz Liszt. Seine Abstammung — seine Familie," trans. Klára Litkei. In item 30; pp. 7-48.
   ML410.L7B297
   A thorough study of Liszt's ancestors, tracing the family back through father Adam, grandfather Georg Adam [List], and great-grandfather Sebastian [Liszt], and through mother Maria Anna *neé* Lager, maternal grandfather Mathias Lager, Jr., and maternal great-grandfather Mathias Lager, Sr. Békefi also deals briefly with peripheral family members.
   Originally published in Hungarian as *Liszt Ferenc származása és családja* (Budapest: Zeneműkiadó, 1973). Illustrated in this version with facsimiles of genealogical documents missing from the more accessible German-language version. NB: This latter title should not be confused with item 386 (below).

386.   Csekey, István. *Liszt Ferenc származása és hazafisága.* Budapest: Franklin Nyomda, 1937. 36pp.
   Rare: the Austrian National Library owns a copy (shelf-number 147.091-B. 25, 9)
   The first "scientific" study of Liszt's family background and ties to Hungary. Among other topics, Csekey deals with the rumor proposed by nineteenth-century newspapers like *Buda-Pesti rajzolatok* and the *Pester Tageblatt* that Liszt was descended from nobility. (On this last topic, see

item 385 (above) as well as item 1a; pp. 30-31, and items 587-588. Includes two fold-out tables. In Hungarian.

*   Lindmann, Stig. "Anteckningar kring Liszt."
       Despite its title, a sketch of Liszt's childhood activities as well as of his closest relatives. Described in greater detail as item 418.

387.   Liszt, Eduard von. *Franz Liszt: Abstammung, Familie, Begebenheiten.* Vienna: W. Braumüller, 1937. xiv, 111pp.
       ML410.L7Z4957
       A valuable account of Liszt's immediate ancestors, complete with anecdotes about many of them. Eduard von Liszt, a distinguished lawyer and civil servant, was Franz Liszt's nephew and corresponded regularly with his uncle for several decades. Illustrated with 18 portraits of family members. Accompanied by an appendix containing two letters addressed by the young Liszt to his father.

388.   Liszt, Eduard von. "Stammtafel der Familie Liszt." *Österreichische Musikzeitschrift* 16 (1961), p. 429.
       A diagrammatic summary of information available in items 385-387 (above). NB: The "Stammtafel" also appeared as a pamphlet with four-page introduction (Vienna 1940).

389.   Wamser, Heinrich. "Abstammung und Familie Franz Liszts." *Burgenländische Heimatblätter* 5/2 (May 1936), pp. 24-34.
       A less detailed summary of Liszt's family. Useful primarily for several facsimile reproductions of genealogical documents (printed between pp. 52-53).

Family and Childhood

Studies of Liszt's relationship with family members cannot always be distinguished neatly from the genealogical studies described above. Those studies described below deal for the most part with events after 1811; many of them also deal with Liszt's children or other relations.

The only book-length study devoted exclusively to Liszt's family and to his early years is:

390.   László, Zoltán. *Az ifjú Liszt, 1811-1839*. Budapest: Zeneműkiadó, 1962.
         174pp.
              ML410.L7L37
         A detailed description of Liszt's family, childhood, experiences in Paris
         and Vienna, and first "transcendental" concert tours. Illustrated with a
         number of black-and-white photographs but no musical examples. In
         Hungarian.

Among other studies devoted in part to the same material are:

*   Walker, Alan. *Franz Liszt: The Virtuoso Years, 1811-1847*.
         Covers the same time-span as item 390 (above) as well as Liszt's tours
         after 1839 and much of his early musical development. Described in greater
         detail as item 1a.

*   Horvath, Emmerich Karl. *Franz Liszt*.
         Deals with Liszt's life from birth to c. 1839. Described in greater detail
         as items 13a-c.

*Studies dealing with Liszt's parents (especially their activities after 1811), children,
or other relatives are described below under individual sub-headings:*

A. Liszt's father Adam Liszt

Three recent studies of the life and character of Liszt's father deserve close attention:

391.   Winkler, Gerhard J. "Adam Liszt — Charakterstudie eines Vaters." In item
         88; pp. 60-75.
         A concise, intelligent account of Adam Liszt's personality and re-
         lationship with his son. Illustrated with a facsimile of H-Bn "Acta
         musicalia" ms. 170, fol. 530/31, a letter Adam Liszt addressed in July 1819
         to Esterházy Prince Nikolaus II, which is also quoted in other studies (e.g.,
         the *Haydn Yearbook* 13-16 [1982-1985], pp. 183ff.).
         Most discussions of Liszt's father include quotations from his corre-
         spondence, especially the letters he exchanged with Carl Czerny. Early
         "editions" of these letters include La Mara's "Aus Franz Liszts erster
         Jugend. Ein Schreiben seines Vaters mit Briefen, Czerneys an ihn," *Musik*
         5/3 (1905-1906), pp. 15-29; and *Classisches und Romantisches aus der
         Tonwelt* (Leipzig: Breitkopf & Härtel, 1892), pp. 233-262. See also C. F.
         Pohl, "Aus Franz Liszts Jugendleben," *Münchener Propylaen* 1 (1869), pp.
         145ff.; translated as "Incidents of Franz Liszt's Youth" in the *Monthly
         Musical Record* 1 and 2 (1871-1872). Like other publications containing
         Liszt letters, these are identified and described in item 41. See also János
         Hárich [also given as "Johann Harich"], *Liszt Ferenc családja és az*

Esterházy hercegek (Budapest 1934), a short pamphlet describing Adam Liszt's relationship with the Eszterházy family in terms of H-Bn "Acta musicalia" documents. In Hungarian.

392.   Winkler, Gerhard J. "Adam Liszt und Franz Liszt. Zur Anatomie einer folgenreichen Vater-Sohn Beziehung." *Studia musicologica* 28 (1986), pp. 11-19.

Deals with Adam Liszt's character as well as with his son's ancestry and youthful circumstances. Similar in several respects to item 392 (above). No lengthy documentary quotations or illustrations.

393.   Winkler, Gerhard J. "Franz Liszts Kindheit. Versuch eines biographischen Grundrisses." *Musikforschung* 39 (1986), pp. 335-340.

Similar in content to items 391-392 (above). Winkler challenges the opinions of other scholars, including Walker (in item 1a), concerning the probity and familial disinterestedness of a father who lived off his son's earnings for several years. Footnotes identify virtually everything published before 1986 about Liszt's ancestors and family.

Other studies of Adam Liszt's activities and character include:

394.   Csekey, István. "Franz Liszts Vater: Nach bisher unveröffentlichten Dokumenten dargestellt." *Musik* 29/9 (June 1937), pp. 631-635.

A pioneering discussion of three "Acta musicalia" documents (Nos. 3500, 3506, and 4216) also reprinted in whole or part in items 1a, 391, 410, and so on. No illustrations.

Since Csekey completed this study several documents associated with Liszt's father have come to light. Among them is a report of Adam Liszt's participation in an 1810 concert conducted in Eisenstadt by Beethoven. See Johann Harich [also given as "János Hárich"], "Beethoven in Eisenstadt," *Burgenländische Heimatblätter* 21 (1959), pp. 168-188, esp. pp. 183-185.

395.   Haraszti, Emile. "Deux franciscains: Adam et Franz Liszt." *Revue musicale* 174 (1937), pp. 269-271.

Discusses Liszt's lifelong interest in St. Francis of Assisi and the order he founded as well as Adam Liszt's unsuccessful Franciscan novitiate. (With regard to Adam and Franz Liszt's "Franciscan" interests, see item 537. See also László Bucsi, "Liszt és a magyar ferencesek" in *Magyar zene* 28 [1987], pp. 50-52.)

One misleading title occasionally encountered in the Liszt literature is correctly identified below:

396.   ["Adam Liszts Tagebuch."] See the *Neue Zeitschrift für Musik* 4 (1836), pp. 13-16, 19-21, 23-24, 27-30, 31-33, and 39-40.

A translation into German by E. Flechsig for the *Neue Zeitschrift* of d'Ortigue's 1835 biography (item 369), purportedly based in part on diaries kept by Adam Liszt; the diaries themselves were reported lost during Liszt's lifetime. Quotations from the diaries appear in a number of scholarly studies, including item 1a.

B. Liszt's mother Anna Maria Liszt

Four excellent articles about Liszt's mother are described below in alphabetical order (by author):

397.   Eckhardt, Mária [P.]. "Une femme simple, mère d'un génie européen: 'Anna Liszt / Quelques aspects d'une correspondance'." *Revue musicale* 405-406-407 (1987), pp. 199-214.

A sketch of the life and character of Anna Liszt, followed by an index to her surviving correspondence with her famous son (pp. 206-214). Eckhardt also reprints two complete texts of a letter addressed by Anna Liszt to Franz Liszt on 13 February 1849 (the first in German, the second in French). (With regard to Anna Liszt's correspondence, see items 197, 208, and so on.)

398.   Horvath, Emmerich Karl. "Hochzeit und Leben in Raiding." In item 91; pp. 17-19.

A brief but well-documented sketch of Anna Liszt's life, especially her years with husband Adam and son Franz in Raiding. Includes descriptions of Anna Liszt originally published by Eduard von Liszt, Lina Ramann, August Göllerich, etc.

Information about Anna Liszt's ancestors and life also appears in Walter Dobner's "Blau-gelbe Liszt-Spuren. Zur mütterlichen Herkunft von Franz Liszt" in item 91; pp. 7-8.

399.   Legány, Dezső. "Liszt's Inheritance." *Liszt Society Journal* 12 (1987), pp. 2-7.

Describes Anna Liszt's character and explains how she "inspired" her son during the early years of his musical career. Contains a good-quality, black-and-white reproduction of the only known photograph of Anna Liszt.

400.   Leibnitz, Thomas. "Franz Liszt und seine Mutter: Zur Geschichte einer Beziehung in Briefen." In item 91; pp. 9-16.
    Evaluates Liszt's relationship with his mother, based on published and unpublished correspondence.

C. Liszt's children Blandine, Cosima, and Daniel

Two full-length monographs about Liszt's children have appeared in print:

401.   Bory, Robert. *Liszt et ses enfants. Blandine, Cosima, Daniel d'après une correspondance inédite avec la Princesse Marie Sayn-Wittgenstein.* Paris: R. A. Correa, 1936. 227pp.
    ML410.L7B648
    Describes Liszt's uneasy relationship with his children, in part through some 60 letters written between 1853-1860. Bory also reprints the complete text of a letter Liszt addressed to his daughters on 14 September 1855—a document printed only in part in other sources. Profusely illustrated.

402.   Rain, Henriette. *Les enfants du génie: Blandine, Cosima et Daniel Liszt.* Paris: Presses de la Renaissance, 1986. 347pp.
    ML410.L7R17 1986   ISBN 2-85616-364-5
    A mass-market "biography" of the artist and his children, written up almost like a novel and supported with only a few bibliographic citations. No illustrations.
    A detailed review of this volume by Pauline Pocknell, published in the *Journal of the American Liszt Society* 20 (1986), pp. 152-161, corrects a number of errors and supplies English-language translations of two important letters. According to Pocknell, "The definitive biography of Blandine, Cosima and Daniel Liszt still awaits its writer."

At least two articles have been devoted solely to Daniel Liszt's life and activities:

403.   Bellas, Jacqueline. "Liszt . . . prénom Daniel." *Revue musicale* 405-406-407 (1987), pp. 215-234.
    A detailed biographical sketch of Daniel Liszt (1839-1859), illustrated with copious quotations from letters and other documents, many of them previously unpublished.

404.   Walker, Alan. "A Boy Named Daniel." *New Hungarian Quarterly* 27/101 (Spring 1986), pp. 204-220.
    A spirited description of the life and character of Liszt's only son. Walker illustrates his observations with facsimile reproductions of previously unpublished baptismal records, photographs of Daniel and his tomb,

a relief of Daniel (anon.; c. 1857), and three letters addressed by Daniel to his father between 1848-1857. Yet another Daniel document appears in facsimile reproduction in item 266.

Reprinted in the *Journal of the American Liszt Society* 20 (1986), pp. 56-80.

One other article deals with an incident from Daniel's life:

405.   Brody, Elaine. "All in the Family: Liszt, Daniel and Ary Scheffer." *Nineteenth-Century French Studies* 13 (1985), pp. 238-243.

A short account of Liszt's relationship with his son and his attempt to introduce Daniel to Ary Scheffer, a well-known Dutch painter responsible for an outstanding Liszt portrait. Includes the text of a letter Liszt sent Scheffer on 17 October 1855.

Rumors have credited Liszt with a number of illegitimate children, but only one of these spurious offspring has been described in a book of his own:

406.   Berthoud, Dorette. *Davila, fils de Liszt? Sa vie, son oeuvre, le secret de ses origines d'après ses lettres, les documents réunis par sa fille, la générale Perticari est quelques sources nouvelles.* Neuchâtel: La Baconnière, 1956. 291pp.

ML410.L7Z2583M

A curiosity, written to support claims that Dr. Carlos Davila was a child of Liszt's and the Comtesse d'Agoult. Not seen but mentioned in several Liszt bibliographies and in item 1a; pp. 24-25.

D. Liszt's grandfather Georg Adam Liszt

A single short article has been devoted to this Liszt progenitor:

407.   Tobler, Felix. "Georg Adam Liszt. Seine Tätigkeit als Schulmeister, Notär und Bediensteter der Esterházyschen Zentralverwaltung (1774-1811)." In item 88; pp. 15-23.

Describes the ancestors and affairs of Liszt's paternal grand-father, Georg Adam Liszt [or List]. Tobler refers to ecclesiastical histories of the Burgenland and to documents owned by archives housed in Eisenstadt and nearby towns. No illustrations.

E. Liszt's Childhood

A number of studies have dealt exclusively with Liszt's childhood, his early years in Raiding (now in Austria) and his experiences in Vienna—especially his encounters there with Czerny and Beethoven. Two studies, for example, have been devoted to the Meierhof, Liszt's boyhood home:

408.   Meyer, Wolfgang. "Der Meierhof in Raiding — der Schauplatz von Liszts Kindheit." In item 88; pp. 47-53.

    An architectural description of the house Liszt first lived in and its renovations following his death. Illustrated with a nineteenth-century sketch of the building made by one Grünes, and with several floorplans.

    NB: An excellent color photograph of the Meierhof as it appears today is printed at the end of item 88.

409.   Prickler, Harald. "Franz Liszts Geburtsort und Geburtshaus." In item 88; pp. 29-46.

    Traces the history of Raiding from the late sixteenth century to the present day and the origins and activities of Liszt's Burgenland ancestors. Illustrated with a useful "family tree" (pp. 30-31). Some of Prickler's endnotes correct minor errors in item 1a.

Other studies deal with Liszt's earliest experiences in Raiding and Vienna. The best of these include:

410.   Fábián, Imre, and Arisztid Valkó. "Aus Franz Liszts Jugend." *Österreichische Musikzeitschrift* 16 (1961), pp. 430-436.

    Discusses Liszt's earliest musical experiences. Valuable primarily because Fábian and Valkó reprint the entire texts of several H-Bn "Acta musicalia" documents—e.g., No. 170, a letter Adam Liszt sent Prince Esterházy on 4 August 1819 on behalf of his son. Illustrated with facsimiles of parts of "Acta musicalia" Nos. 3500 (a request addressed by Adam Liszt to Prince Esterházy on 13 April 1820) and 3325.

    Another study of "Acta musicalia" Liszt documents by Valkó appeared in Hungarian under the title "A Liszt család a levéltári iratok tükrében" in *Magyar zene* 1/4 (February 1961), pp. 388-399; and 1/5 (March 1961), pp. 498-507.

411.   Harich, Johann. "Franz Liszt — Vorfahren und Kinderjahre." *Österreichische Musikzeischrift* 26 (1971), pp. 503-514.

    Deals with Liszt's father and grandfather as well as important incidents from Liszt's own childhood. Drawing on "Acta musicalia" documents, Harich also traces Liszt's ancestry back to his great-grandfather, Sebastian List. Includes a facsimile reproduction of H-Bn "Acta musicalia" No. 3325, a letter addressed by Antonio Salieri to Prince Esterházy on behalf of the young Liszt, then his pupil. An English-language translation of this letter appears in item 1a; pp. 74-75.

Still other studies deal exclusively with Liszt's experiences in Vienna after 1819 and especially during 1822-1823:

412.   Leibnitz, Thomas. "Wien (1822/23)." In item 88; pp. 96-102.
        An account of Adam and Franz Liszt's sojourns in Vienna after 1819, Liszt's studies with Czerny, Liszt's first Viennese concerts, and so on. Illustrated with a facsimile reproduction Liszt's first published composition: a variation on Diabelli's famous Waltz tune.

413.   Deutsch-German, Alfred. *Franz Liszt und seine Familie in Wien.* Vienna: Josef Rosler, 1906. 3pp.
        Rare: the National Széchényi Library, Budapest, owns a copy of this pamphlet.
        Describes some of Liszt's adventures in Vienna, 1822-1824. Cited in item 1a, p. 452; a much longer version of this publication appeared in the *Neue Musik- und Literatur-Zeitung* [Vienna] 3/12 (15 September 1906). Not seen; cited on the cover page of the version described here, and in item 39; p. 17.

Liszt's encounters with Czerny and Beethoven have also been the subject of specialized studies:

414.   Wehmeyer, Grete. "Carl Czerny (1791-1857) — Der Klavierlehrer von Franz Liszt." In item 88; pp. 103-115.
        Examines Liszt's relationship with Czerny in Vienna and afterwards. Includes quotations from Czerny's autobiography (item 234) and from the published and unpublished Liszt-Czerny and Adam Liszt-Czerny correspondence. Illustrated with a lithograph of Czerny prepared by Joseph Kriehuber in 1828.

415.   Gardavský, Č. "Liszt und seine tschechischen Lehrer." *Studia musicologica* 5 (1963), pp. 69-76.
        A brief discussion of Liszt's musical relationship with his teacher and friend during the young musician's early years in Vienna.
        Several other studies of the Liszt-Czerny relationship have appeared in print, among them: H. Vilma Hoffmann, "Liszt és Czerny," *Új zenei szemle* 3/10 (October 1952), pp. 13-18. In Hungarian.

416.   Nohl, Walther. "Der elfjährige Liszt und Beethoven." *Neue Musikzeitung* [Stuttgart] 48 (1927), pp. 307-309.
        A pioneering attack on the "Weihekuss" legend discussed in Chapter II. Nohl quotes passages from Beethoven's conversation books for

March-April 1823. Cited in item 1a and other authorities, now out of date. (With regard to Liszt and Beethoven, see items 130-131, 417, and 596.)

417.   Suttoni, Charles. "Young Liszt, Beethoven and Madame Montgolfier." *Studia musicologica* 28 (1986), pp. 21-34.

   Describes little-known incidents in Liszt's early life, including his relationship with Jenny Montgolfier. Suttoni reproduces whole and in facsimile a letter Liszt wrote to Madame Montgolfier in 1826 which, in part, bears witness to the young artist's admiration for Beethoven.

Finally, among less valuable studies of these topics is the article described below:

418.   Lindman, Stig. "Anteckningar kring Liszt." *Musikrevy* [Helsingborg, Norway] 41 (1986), pp. 177-180.

   A synopsis of Liszt's childhood and "relations"—including d'Agoult, his children, and the Princess Sayn-Wittgenstein. Valuable exclusively for its facsimile reproductions of several important documents, including the program for Liszt's 13 April 1823 Vienna concert and several portraits.

TRAVELS AND INTERNATIONAL ACTIVITIES

General Studies

Liszt spent much of his life travelling; at one time or another he visited virtually every part of continental Europe and made occasional excursions into Great Britain, Ireland, Russia, and Turkey. No study devoted exclusively to these travels as a whole has ever been published, but a useful introduction to most of them may be found in:

419.   Kárpáti, János. "Liszt the Traveller." *New Hungarian Quarterly* 27/103 (1986), pp. 108-118.

   An outline of Liszt's numerous journeys, not merely his concert tours of the 1830s and 1840s. Kárpáti believes Liszt travelled so much "because [he was] driven by a kind of Faustian insatiability," wanting "to incorporate everything, to be left out of nothing." Illustrated with 10 plates (two in color) reproducing portraits of Liszt and some of his contemporaries, title pages from first editions of his published compositions, facsimile reproductions of certain documents, and so on—among them, a letter addressed by Berlioz to Liszt in 1836.

*   Stockhammer, Robert. *Franz Liszt im Triumphzug durch Europa.*
           Devoted in large part to Liszt's virtuoso tours of 1838-1847. Contains
a sketchy chronological table of 1840s concerts (pp. 171-175) and travel
information of various kinds. Described in greater detail as item 16.

*An exhibition of Liszt's travel memorabilia also contains a summary of his
excursions:*

*   *Album d'un voyageur . . .*
           Contains a preliminary "catalog" of Liszt's principal voyages through-
out his life. Described in greater detail as item 86.

*Three other studies devoted to "Liszt as traveller" are described below in alphabet-
ical order (by author):*

420.   Autexier, Philippe A. "Musique sans frontières? Les choix des programmes
           de Liszt pour ses concerts de la période virtuose." *Revue musicale*
           405-406-407 (1987), pp. 297-305.
           Compares hundreds of concert programs played by Liszt during the
1840s in France and Germany to demonstrate that national elements influenced choices of certain selections—e.g., Liszt's preference for playing
Schubert in Germany. Illustrated with several valuable tables identifying
several dozen selections most frequently performed by Liszt—among them,
the *Grand galop chromatique* (!). No musical examples.

421.   Gut, Serge. "Nationalisme et supranationalisme chez Franz Liszt." *Revue
           musicale* 405-406-407 (1987), pp. 277-286.
           Treats of Liszt's fondness for several countries—especially France,
where he grew up, and Hungary, his native land—as well as his lifelong
internationalism. In terms of these arguments, Gut's article is relevant to
any student of Liszt's travels and international activities, although it discusses none of Liszt's national involvements in any detail.

422.   Timbrell, Charles. "On the Trail of Liszt, Chopin and Sand: 1833-1847."
           Piano Quarterly 34/135 (Fall 1986), pp. 49-56.
           Describes Liszt's visits to Geneva, Chamonix, Nohant, and so on. Il-
lustrated with photographs of some of these places as they exist today.
Timbrell includes quotations from a variety of letters and documents, including Sand's *Lettres d'un voyager* (see item 170) and Pictet's *Une Course
à Chamounix* (item 245).

Specialized Studies: Liszt and Individual Countries

Virtually everything else published about Liszt's travels is limited in scope or chronology. The finest of these studies are described below according to the country *or geographic area Liszt visited or considered visiting. The countries and areas themselves are listed under sub-headings in alphabetical order:*

A. America

Although Liszt never visited the United States, he numbered many Americans among his acquaintances and pupils. The only study devoted to Liszt's decades-long relationship with America and Americans is:

423.   Lowens, Irving. "Liszt and America." *Journal of the American Liszt Society* 4 (1978), pp. 4-10.
         Documents early references to Liszt and performance of his works in the United States between 1840 and the 1890s. Among other sources, Lowens quotes from John W. Moore's *Complete Encyclopaedia of Music*, published in 1854, and from "reminiscences" published by several of Liszt's American pupils. Concludes with a brief description of two offers extended to Liszt to visit the New World—one in 1874 or 1875 to attend a performance of the so-called "Gran" Mass in Cincinnati, the other (by Steinway & Co.) to undertake a concert tour of Atlantic seaboard cities for $100,000.

*   Saffle, Michael. "Lisztiana in Early American Music Magazines."
         Described as item 273.

B. Austria

In Liszt's day "Austria" did not exist. Consequently, it is difficult today to separate "Austrian" Liszt studies from studies dealing with other areas of what once was the Austro-Hungarian empire. One study that considers both Austrian and Hungarian topics is:

424.   Legány, Dezső. "Österreichisch-ungarische Beziehungen im letzten Zeitabschnitt des Lebens von Liszt." *Kontakte österreichischer Musik nach Ost und Südost*, ed. Rudolf Flotzinger. Grazer musikwissenschaftliche Arbeiten, 3. Graz: Akademische Druck- und Verlagsanstalt, 1978; pp. 7-16.
         ML2461.K66   ISBN 3-2010-1043-X
         An introduction to Liszt's relationships with natives or residents of Austro-Hungary during the last years of his life.

Five other pamphlets and articles dealing with visits Liszt paid to cities and towns located in present-day Austria are described below in alphabetical order (by author):

425.   Bolte, Theodor. *Franz Liszts Aufenthalt in Wien.* Vienna: Wilhelm Fischer, 1912. 20pp.

      Rare: the Liszt Research Centre, Budapest, owns a copy of this pamphlet.

      Deals with Liszt's visits to Vienna from the 1820s to the 1880s (not, as its title might be taken to imply, with a single visit). Includes about a half-dozen black-and-white illustrations.

426.   Stockhammer, Robert. "Die Weiner Konzerte Franz Liszts." *Österreichische Musikzeitschrift* 16 (1961), pp. 437-442.

      An introduction to the numerous concerts Liszt presented in Vienna during almost sixty years of his life, especially those of the late 1830s and 1840s. Supplanted by Stockhammer"s own Liszt biography (item 16).

      Eyewitness descriptions of Liszt's 1830s Vienna concerts were published in 1941 in Hungarian under the title *Liszt Ferenc árvízi hangversenyei Bécsben 1838/9*, ed. Béla Csuka. The author of these accounts was Teréz Walker (Madame Ferenc Pulszky). Not seen; cited in item 41. Other brief accounts of individual performances—among them Norbert Tschulik's "Vor 100 Jahren: Franz Liszt spielte im Wiener Musikverein," *Österreichische Musikzeitschrift* 29 (1974), pp. 34-35, which deals with the 13 January 1874 concert—are scattered throughout the literature.

427.   Suppan, Wolfgang. "Franz Liszt und die Steiermark." *Studia musicologica* 5 (1963), pp. 301-310.

      Describes Liszt's trips to Graz, and to Marburg in Styria (today Maribor, Yugoslavia) during June 1846 and the performances he gave during those visits. Illustrated with reproductions of two programs from 1840s posters.

      Another article by Suppan with the same title appeared in the *Mitteilungen des Steirischen Tonkünstlerbundes* 53/54 (July-December 1972), pp. 1-8. Not seen but identified in RILM 7 (1973); entry 670.

428.   Sylvester, Hans. "Franz Liszt und das Burgenland." *Burgenländische Heimatblätter* 5/2 (May 1936), pp. 21-24.

      A brief account of Liszt and the area where he was born and grew up. Sylvester includes information about visits Liszt paid to the Burgenland after he and his father moved to Vienna in 1822.

      Several shorter articles on Liszt and Burgenland places also exist—among them, Viktor Jovanovic's "Liszt in Eisenstadt," *Burgenländische Heimatblätter* 3-4 (1934-1935), p. 82. NB: The term "Burgenland"

is a modern Austrian political designation; in Liszt's day the area around
Raiding and Eisenstadt was at least as much Hungarian as Austrian.

429.   Walker, Alan. "Liszt and Vienna." *New Hungarian Quarterly* 26/99
        (Autumn 1985), pp. 253-259.
            Primarily a review of Legány's anthology of Liszt letters and press
        clippings in Viennese collections (item 199) as well as a survey of Liszt's
        relationship with a city he both loved and hated.
            Reprinted in the *Journal of the American Liszt Society* 19 (1985), pp.
        10-20.

C. The Balkans (i.e., present-day Bulgaria, Rumania, and Yugoslavia)

*Liszt travelled through the Balkans when much of that region belonged to Austro-
Hungary. Subsequent political developments, including the Stalinization of much of
that region after 1945—made thàt area difficult for researchers to work in. Furthermore, many of the studies written by Marxist sympathizers about Liszt and Balkan
lands have little value (e.g., S. Petrov, "Proizvedeniia Ferentsa Lista v Bolgarii,"
Studia musicologica 5 [1963], pp. 249-253; in Russian). Three more reliable
studies, described or cross-referenced below in alphabetical order (by author), deal
with places located today in Bulgaria, Rumania, and Yugoslavia:*

430.   Beu, Octavian. *Franz Liszt în tara noastră* . Sibiu: Krafft & Drotleff, n. d.
        99pp.
            ML410.L7B45
            Summarizes Liszt's visits during the mid-1840s to portions of present-
        day Rumania. Beu reproduces facsimiles from newspaper pages, musical
        mss., Liszt's Rumanian passport, etc. Other illustrations include a color
        portrait of Liszt, entitled "Amica Liszt" and painted by one Carol Pop de
        Satmari, bound as a frontispiece. In Rumanian.
            Other studies of Liszt and the Balkans include: István Lakatos, *Liszt
        Ferenc Kolozsváron* (Kolozsvár 1944; in Hungarian).

431.   Hoffman, A., and N[icolae] Missir. "Sur la tournée de concerts de Ferenc
        Liszt en 1846-47 dans le Banat, la Transylvanie et les Pays Roumains."
        Studia musicologica 5 (1963), pp. 107-124.
            Describes Liszt's Balkans concert tour of November 1846—June 1847.
        Includes a table listing the dates, places, and programs for many individual
        concerts (pp. 121-124). Hoffman and Missir quote in translation from
        concert notices and reviews originally published in such newspapers as
        Romînească ; they also reprint information from item 430 (above). (With
        regard to press coverage of Liszt's Rumanian travels, see items 1a and 6.)
            A second article on the same topic, but written by Missir alone, ap-
        peared in Rumanian under the title "Turneul de concerte întreprins de

Franz Liszt în 1846-1847" in *Studii si Cercetări de istoria artei* 8/2 (1961), pp. 490-504. A third article, this one devoted exclusively to Liszt's November 1846 concerts in Arad, appeared in Hungarian as: Lajos Pintér, "Liszt Ferenc Áradi hangversenyei," *Magyar zene* 28 (1987), pp. 189-199. Neither of these articles was available when the two parts of item 40 went to press.

*   Suppan, Wolfgang. "Franz Liszt und die Steiermark."
       Mentions Liszt's visit to present-day Maribor, Yugoslavia, in June 1847. Described in greater detail as item 427.

D. Belgium

Liszt's visits to Belgium were comparatively infrequent and unimportant. Only one study devoted exclusively to them has appeared in print:

432.   Vander Linden, A. "Liszt et la Belgique." *Studia musicologica* 11 (1969), pp. 281-290.
       Deals with Liszt's Belgian sojourns of the 1840s and 1880s. Includes observations Fétis made about Liszt, quotations from Liszt's correspondence, and documentary evidence (e.g., the text of Liszt's diploma as honorary president of the Brussels Musical Society).
       An essay entitled "Liszt en Antwerpen" appeared Andre M. Pols, *Von de Altenburg naar de Hofgärtnerei (een loofdstuk uit het leven van Liszt)* (Antwerp: S. V. Lectura, 1932), pp. 89-104. This essay includes the text of a letter Liszt addressed to Otto Menzel on 29 May 1884 and mentions Liszt's visits to Belgium in 1854, 1864, and so on. Text in Flemish. Helene Bock related an interesting Liszt anecdote in "Liszts Aufenthalt in Dinant," *Neue Musik-Zeitung* [Stuttgart] 14 (1893), p. 130. (With regard to Liszt in Dinant, see also item 499.)

E. Czechoslovakia

The nation we know today as Czechoslovakia encompasses several areas and cultures, among them Bohemia and its capital city, Prague. The most complete introductions to Liszt's relationship with Bohemia and her capital are:

433.   Buchner, Alexander. *Franz Liszt in Bohemia*, trans. Roberta Samsour. London: Peter Nenill, 1962. 190pp.
       ML410.L7B85
       A valuable study of Liszt's involvement with Bohemia's musical and cultural life during much of the nineteenth century. Buchner describes his subject's Bohemian concerts in some detail; he also discusses the music of Smetana, Janáček, and other Czech composers. Illustrated handsomely

with 167 photographs, including facsimile reproductions of letters, musical mss., etc., as well as portraits of Liszt and his Czech contemporaries.

NB: The German-language edition of this book, published in Prague in 1962, includes a survey of Liszt's relationship with Bohemia based on almost 250 letters (pp. 187-206) missing from other editions. Buchner also published in German an article entitled "Liszt in Prag," *Studia musicologica* 5 (1963), pp. 27-36.

434.   Plevka, Bohumil. *Liszt a Praha.* Prague: Editio Supraphon, 1986. 137pp.
        ML410.L7P55   [No ISBN number available]
        Primarily a study of Liszt's 1840 and 1846 Prague concerts, although Plevka also includes information about his subject's correspondence with prominent Czech composers, including Smetana. Illustrated with facsimile reproductions of concert programs and musical mss. Concludes with an index. In Czech; summaries in German (pp. 130-131) and Hungarian (pp. 132-133).

Liszt made a number of visits to the city known today as Bratislava and known to nineteenth-century Austro-Hungary as Preßburg. Three studies devoted to Liszt's relationship with this city are described below in alphabetical order (by author):

435.   Orel, Dobroslav. *František Liszt a Bratislava; na základě nevydané korrespondence Fr. Liszta a kněžny C. Wittgensteinové.* Bratislava: Filosofická Fakulta University Komenského, 1925. iii, 72pp.
        B18.S6B73, roč. 3, Čis. 36
        An account of Liszt's relationship with the city of Bratislava as well as a collection of 40 letters written by Liszt between 1869-1886. Orel also reprints the texts of letters addressed by the Princess Sayn-Wittgenstein to Jan Batka. Concludes with eight illustrations, among them facsimiles of Liszt letters. Commentary in Czech; letters in their original languages.
        Published in the series "Bratislava. Univerzita. Filozofické faculta. Sborník, roč 3, Čislo 36 [10]." Hence the LC call number given above.

436.   Furch, František. "Liszt in Bratislava." *Musik und Gesellschaft* 11 (1961), pp. 603-606.
        Deals with visits Liszt made to the city he knew as "Preßburg" in 1820, 1858, and the 1880s. No illustrations.

437.   Nováček, Zdenko. "Franz Liszt a Bratislava/Franz Liszt und Bratislava." In item 34; pp. 7-20.
        Another account of Liszt's relationship with Preßburg. In Czech and German; summary in Russian. (A short article by Nováček dealing primarily with Czech musical figures is described as item 743.)

438.   Zagiba, Franz. "Franz Liszt und Preßburg." *Burgenländische Heimatblätter* 14 (1952), pp. 164-170.
        Somewhat more carefully researched than item 437 (above).

F. Denmark

Liszt had even less to do with Denmark than with Belgium. The only study devoted exclusively to Liszt's 1841 Danish concert tour is:

439.   Johnsson, Bengt. "Liszt og Danmark." *Dansk musiktidsskrift* 37 (1962), pp. 79-82; and 38 (1963), pp. 81-86.
        Describes Liszt's contact with Danes (especially Hans Christian Andersen) during his visit to Copenhagen in June-July 1841. Johnsson reprints portions of concert reviews and notices from several nineteenth-century Danish newspapers. In Danish.

G. England (see also "Great Britain," "Ireland," and "Scotland")

Liszt visited England several times during his childhood and virtuoso tours; he also made a "farewell" visit in March 1886, shortly before his death. Most studies of these visits deal with only one or two of them, although one elusive title may be more comprehensive.[1] The best of these studies are described below in alphabetical order (by title and/or author):

440.   "'Fantastic Cavalcade': Liszt's British Tours of 1840 & 1841 from the Diaries of John Orlando Parry." *Liszt Society Journal* 6 (1981), pp. 2-16; and 7 (1982), pp. 16-26.
        An extremely entertaining eyewitness account of Liszt's 1840-1841 British tours, written by the performer/composer who accompanied him on them. Transcribed from two handwritten volumes owned by the University Library of Wales in Aberystwyth (mss. 17717 and 17718). Quotations and a facsimile page from these volumes appear in item 1a, pp. 359-365.
        An Hungarian-language synopsis of Liszt's British tours (including Scotland and Ireland) appeared as: Dezső Legány, "Liszt Albionban," *Liszt kiskönyvtár* 2 (1984), pp. 19-35. (With regard to this last article, see item 37. See also items 499 and 514.)

---

[1] Gerald S. Bedbrook, *Liszt in London* (?New York: Dobson, 1981); ISBN 0-234-72105-7. Not seen and apparently never published. Cited in *Books in Print: 1985-1986*, Vol. 5 ("Titles," H-P), p. 2977. Orders sent to the publisher by the present author were neither filled nor acknowledged. Cited nevertheless in item 40. (Item 496 may somehow have been assigned the ISBN number quoted above, then mistitled in *Books in Print.*)

441.   "From 'The Musical World'," ed. Dudley Newton. *Liszt Society Journal* 9 (1984), pp. 31-33.

Supplements in the *Liszt Society Journal* 10 (1985), pp. 8-11; and 11 (1986), pp. 52-55.

Excerpts from the British music magazine *The Musical World* dealing with Liszt's visits to England, 1840-1841. Also contains a few miscellaneous clippings, including translated passages from a French periodical dealing with Liszt's 1842 Berlin concerts, clippings from *The Musical World* of 1838-1839 dealing with Liszt's literary works and Vienna concerts, and so on. No illustrations or musical examples.

442.   "Liszt's British Tours: Reviews and Letters." *Liszt Society Journal* 8 (1983), pp. 2-8.

Supplements in the *Liszt Society Journal* 9 (1984), pp. 2-15 ["Liszt's British Tours (ii): Reviews and Miscellanea"]; 10 (1985), pp. 6-7; 11 (1986), pp. 44-51; and 12 (1987), pp. 22-23.

A collection of press clippings and other documents associated with Liszt's tours of England, Scotland, and Ireland during 1840-1841. Includes reviews, notices, and poems from such papers as the *Hampshire Advertiser & Salisbury Guardian*, the *Somerset Country Gazette*, and so on, as well as from Liszt's published correspondence with the Comtesse d'Agoult (items 194-195). Illustrated in the first installment with a sketch of Liszt made by Nancy Mérienne (?late 1830s) and a photograph of a ballroom in Bath where Liszt played in 1840 as well as with a facsimile of an advertisement from the *Bath Herald* of 29 August 1840. Illustrated in the second installment with a view of the Montpellier Rotunda at Clifton, the Assembly Rooms in Cheltenham, etc.

443.   "Liszt's Playing in London in 1840 & 1841: Some Contemporary Opinions." *Liszt Society Journal* 6 (1981), pp. 16-18.

A brief, anonymous introduction, followed by clippings from *The Athenaeum*, a weekly London magazine of arts and sciences. The three clippings (16 May, 13 June, and 4 July 1840, and 19 June 1841) all deal with Liszt's British tours of those years.

444.   Newton, Dudley. "Liszt and his Glass: Some Pianistic Alterations." *Liszt Society Journal* 13 (1988), pp. 40-60.

Identifies and evaluates reviews of performances Liszt gave in London during 1840-1841, couched in the form of a reply to remarks about Liszt's pianism published by Adrian Williams in the *Liszt Society Journal* 12 (1987), pp. 60-61. Newton quotes from a variety of documents, including minutes of a meeting of the Directors of the Philharmonic Society, London, held on 6 June 1840. Concludes with eight musical examples.

Williams replied to Newton's observations on pp. 60-63 of the *Liszt Society Journal* 13 (1988).

445.   Williams, Adrian. "Liszt's Last Visit to England: A Miscellany of Eye-Witness Reports." *Liszt Society Journal* 5 (1980), pp. 15-26.

A collection of quotations from Sir George Grove, Constance Bach, Bram Stoker, etc., concerning Liszt's April 1886 London sojourn. Not to be confused with item 446 (below).

A number of *Monthly Musical Record* articles and notices pertaining to Liszt's last years (1885-1886) are reprinted in *Liszt saeculum* 36-37 (1985-1986), pp. 31-50.

446.   Williams, Adrian. "Liszt's Last Visit to London: April 1886." *New Hungarian Quarterly* 27/103 (Autumn 1986), pp. 131-138.

A blow-by-blow account of Liszt's 1886 visit to England, including numerous but incomplete quotations from a variety of newspapers and magazines (e.g., *Musical Times*, the *Times* of London, the *Daily Telegraph*, the *Pall Mall Gazette*, etc.). Anecdotes include accounts of Liszt's private performances for Queen Victoria and the Duchess of Cambridge.

H. France

Liszt made his home in France during much of his life, and he visited that country many times after leaving it in 1844. No single study deals comprehensively with Liszt and French topics, although several biographies (especially item 351) concern themselves with it. Perhaps the most readable introduction to Liszt's association with his adopted "native" land is:

447.   Tiersot, Julien. "Liszt in France." *Musical Quarterly* 22 (1936), pp. 284-294.

A somewhat superficial summary of Liszt's involvement with France and the French people. Among other topics Tiersot mentions the young Liszt's arrival in Paris, his liaison with Marie d'Agoult, his lifelong fondness for French ideas and people, and French premieres during Liszt's old age of such works as the "Gran" Mass and *Die Legende von der heiligen Elisabeth*. Illustrated with the 1824 Leprince engraving of Liszt at the keyboard, dated 13 March 1825 and signed by the composer.

Eleven additional studies of Liszt visits to France and relationships with French culture and individuals include are described below in alphabetical order (by author):

448.   Bellas, Jacqueline. "Un virtuose en tournée . . . (Franz Liszt dans le Sud-Ouest en 1844)." *Littératures VIII* [Annales de la Faculté de Lettres, Université de Toulouse] 9 (1960), pp. 5-50.
        PN 3.T64 No. 8
        A detailed account of Liszt's 1844 French concert tour, fleshed out with quotations from a wealth of source materials. Bellas provides day-by-day calendars for her subject's visits to Toulouse (25 August-5 September), Bordeaux (7 September-6 October), and Pau (7-21 October 1844). Certain details of her work are corrected—or at least supplemented—by other scholars, including Walker (item 1a) and Autexier (item 522). No illustrations or musical examples.

449.   Carrières, Marcel. *Franz Liszt en Provence et en Languedoc en 1844.* Beziers: Claude Borreda, 1981. 39pp.
        ML410.L77C316   [No ISBN number available]
        A well-researched account of Liszt's visits to and concert performances in Lyon, Avignon, Toulon, etc., between June-August 1844. Includes the text of a letter Liszt wrote to Lambert Massart on 26 August 1844. Carrières also provides a calendar of Liszt's 1844 concerts (pp. 33-34) as well as quotations from obscure press clippings and a bibliography.
        Other articles also review Liszt's several visits to Lyon, among them Antoine Sallès, "Liszt à Lyon, 1826, 1836, 1837, 1844, 1845," *Revue musicale de Lyon* 9 (1911-1912), pp. 18-27. The same study also appeared as a pamphlet (Paris: E. Fromont, 1911).

450.   Eckhardt, Mária [P.]. "Liszt à Marseille." *Studia musicologica* 24 (1982), pp. 163-197.
        Describes Liszt's relationship with Marseille and her citizens from 1825-1866. Includes quotations from Liszt's correspondence and other documents as well as lengthy concert reviews originally published during July-August 1844 in *Sud* and *Sémaphore*, both Marseille newspapers.
        An Hungarian-language version of this article appeared as "Liszt Marseille városában" in *Magyar zene* 22 (1981), pp. 259-284.

451.   Goubault, C. "Les trois concerts de Franz Liszt à Rouen (1825, 1832, 1841)." *Revue internationale de musique française* 13 (1984), pp. 90-94.
        A brief survey of three Liszt visits to Rouen.

452.   Hamburger, Klára. "Megnyílik-e számára a halhatatlanság kapuja? (A Párizsi szaksajtó az élő és halott Liszt Ferencről, 1886-ban)." *Magyar zene* 25 (1984), pp. 52-58.

Deals with Liszt's final visit to Paris in April 1886. A valuable study, written in Hungarian. A similar article, also written by Hamburger, appeared in German under the title "'Ob sich ihm wohl je die Pforte der Unsterblichkeit erschließt?'—Über die Pariser Presse während Liszts letzter Anwesenheit 1886"; see item 37, pp. 110-122.

453.   Keeling, Geraldine. "Liszt's Appearances in Parisian Concerts, 1824-1844." *Liszt Society Journal* 11 (1986), pp. 22-34; and 12 (1987), pp. 8-22.

Describes dozens of recitals Liszt played or participated in between 1824-1844. In addition to places, dates, and other historical information, Keeling provides bibliographic citations for reviews published in newspapers and music magazines of the time. Illustrated with poorly-reproduced portraits of Giuditta Pasta, Cinti-Damoreau, and Henri Herz—all of whom appeared with Liszt on one of more of the concerts in question. Also illustrated with facsimiles of the title page from *Le ménestrel* (29 January 1837) and the cover from *Esmeralda*, a piece of sheet-music by Mlle Louise Bertin for which Liszt supplied a piano accompaniment.

454.   Machard, Roberte. "Franz Liszt et Avignon." *Revue de musicologie* 62 (1976), pp. 132-138.

Summarizes Liszt's visits to Avignon during 1845 and reprints articles about Liszt originally published in *Le mémorial de Vaucluse* (11 May 1845) and other local papers. Mauchart's observations are supplemented by facsimile reproductions of a letter Liszt wrote to Marmand de Pontmartin on 9 May 1845, and of a playbill for Liszt's 8 May 1845 recital. (With regard to the Liszt-Pontmartin letter, see item 270.)

455.   Photiadès, Constantin. "En Avignon, avec Liszt et Berlioz." *Revue musicale* "Numéro special" (1 May 1928), pp. 18-32.

Describes some of Liszt's activities in France during the late 1830s and early 1840s. Includes seven Liszt letters owned (at least at one time) by the Musée Calvet, Avignon, as well as a letter by Berlioz. Illustrated with two portraits.

456.   Prod'homme, J. G. "Liszt et Paris." *Revue musicale* "Numéro special" (1 May 1928), pp. 105-123.

A sketch of Liszt's almost life-long association with the French capital. Prod'homme quotes from several published Liszt letters as well as from press clippings and other documents.

Two Prod'homme articles with similar titles appeared as "Liszt en France" in the *Nouvelle revue de Hongrie* (1936), pp. 322-332; and as "Liszt à Paris" in the *Revue musicale* 11 (1911), pp. 479-483. A somewhat more fulsome account of Liszt's relationship with the French capitol, written by Mária Eckhardt, was published as: "Liszt és Parizs," *Liszt kiskönyvtár* 1 (1982), pp. 15-36. In Hungarian.

457.   Serra, Roch. "Liszt en Alsace." *Liszt saeculum* 41/42 (1988), pp. 5-10.
       Consists entirely of press clippings from *Currier du Haut-Rhin* and other papers as well as diary entries and poems associated with Liszt's 1845 tour of Strasbourg, Colmar, Mulhouse, and other Rhenish cities. Illustrated with a facsimile program for Liszt's Thann concert of 6 July 1845.

458.   Wangermée, Robert. "Conscience et inconscience du virtuose romantique: à propos des années Parisiennes de Franz Liszt." *Music in Paris in the Eighteen-Thirties/La musique à Paris dans les années mil huit cent trente*, ed. Peter Bloom. Musical Life in 19th-Century France, 4. Stuyvesant, New York: Pendragon, 1987; pp. 553-573.
       ML270.8P2M76 1987   ISBN 0-918-72871-1
       Discusses Liszt's life and activities in 1830s Paris as well as the history and purpose of his literary works. Wangermée quotes extensively from the "Bachelor" and "De la situation" essays (often as reprinted in item 169) as well as from periodicals like the *Revue musicale* and *Revue des deux mondes*. In French, with an English-language abstract (pp. 571-573).

One study of Liszt's French tours is quite difficult to locate:

459.   Blanc, C. "Le centenaire des concerts donnés par Franz Liszt à Pau, 1844-1944." *Bulletin de la Société des Sciences, Lettres et Arts de Pau* (1945).
       Not seen. Cited in item 1a, p. 408n; apparently unavailable in the United States. Not even the Liszt Ferenc Research Centre in Budapest has a copy.

I. Germany

Liszt spent as much—perhaps more—time in Germany than in any other part of Europe. No monograph deals with all of Liszt's German experiences, but two volumes have been devoted to his activities in and around Weimar during the late 1840s, 1850s, and early 1860s:

*   Walker, Alan. *Franz Liszt: The Weimar Years, 1848-1861.*
Covers virtually every aspect of Liszt's longest and best-known
German sojourn. Described in greater detail as item 1b.

460.   Marggraf, Wolfgang. *Franz Liszt in Weimar.* Weimar: Tradition und
Gegenwart, 23. Weimar: Buchdruckerei Weimar, 1972. 48pp.
ML410.L7M37
A readable account of Liszt's tenure as Kapellmeister to the Court at
Weimar as well as his other visits to Goethe's city. Like item 462, this
study is shot through with Marxist "interpretation." Illustrated with
black-and-white photographic reproductions of portraits, landscapes,
medallions, and so on. Concludes with information about these illus-
trations and a very brief bibliography.
A shorter survey of Liszt's Weimar activities appeared as: Karl-Heinz
Köhler, "Skizzen zum Werken Franz Liszts in Weimar," *Bulletin:
Musikrat der DDR* (?1986), pp. 14-22.

*Two other studies deal with Liszt's professional activities in Weimar between
1848-1861:*

461.   Huschke, Wolfram. *Musik im klassischen und nachklassischen Weimar.*
Weimar: Hermann Böhlaus, 1982. 240pp.
ML284.8.W4H9 1982   [No ISBN number available]
Contains an unusually reliable and well-written account of Liszt's ac-
tivities as composer, conductor, and general musical factotum to the
Weimar court (pp. 116-185). Thoroughly documented, Huschke presents
a great deal of information not available elsewhere. NB: The greater part
of Huschke's work deals with other figures—among them Johann
Nepomuk Hummel, Liszt's predecessor and acquaintance. Reviewed in
item 132.

462.   Kraft, Günther. "Das Schaffen von Franz Liszt in Weimar." *Studia
musicologica* 5 (1963), pp. 193-210.
A survey of influences on Liszt's compositions of the 1850s—among
them, his plans for a Goethe Foundation, his enthusiasm for the
Hungarian uprisings of the late 1840s, his sympathy with "workers" (exemplified in the *Arbeiterchor* for male chorus and keyboard
accompaniment), and so on. Quotations from a number of Liszt letters
but no musical examples. (With regard to the Goethe Foundation project,
see item 1b; pp. 126-129ff., and item 596. (With regard to the
Arbeiterchor, see item 302.)

Other studies have dealt with Liszt in and around Weimar from more specialized points of view. Five of these studies are described below in alphabetical order (by author):

463.   Bamberg, Edward von. "Liszts Rucktritt von der Weimarischen Opernleitung." *Deutsche Rundschau* 190 (1922), pp. 66-78 and 190-199.

An account of the administrative and artistic circumstances behind Liszt's resignation from the directorship of Weimar's Stadttheater in December 1858. No extended quotations from eyewitnesses or contemporary newspapers or magazines.

464.   Eberhardt, Hans. "Franz Liszt und Sondershausen." *Archiv für Musikwissenschaft* 43 (1986), pp. 201-217.

Describes Liszt's visits to Sondershausen from the mid-1850s to 1886. A much less detailed article by Eberhardt on the same topic and with the same title appeared im item 32; pp. 29-32.

465.   Johns, Keith T. "A Concert in Jena." *Liszt Society Journal* 13 (1988), pp. 29-30.

Describes the first major concert outside (but close to) Weimar of Liszt's symphonic poems. Includes quotations from advertisements and reviews published in the *Neue Zeitschrift für Musik* and the Jena *Wochenblätter*.

466.   Jung, Hans Rudolf. "Das Wirken Johann Nepomuk Hummels und Franz Liszts in Weimar." *Liszt-Studien* 2 (1981), pp. 78-89.

Discusses some of the material covered in item 1b; pp. 84-88, as well as musical life in Weimar during the mid-nineteenth century. Draws extensively on the published Liszt correspondence. No musical examples.

467.   Keiler, Allan. "Liszt and the Weimar Hoftheater." *Studia musicologica* 28 (1986), pp. 431-450.

A short survey of Liszt's involvement with Weimar and its musical establishment until the beginning of the 1860s, followed by discussions of Liszt's activities at the Hoftheater as operatic producer and conductor. Among related topics, Keiler also refers to little-known documents preserved today in the Weimar Staatsarchiv (not to be confused with the Goethe- und Schiller-Archiv, which owns hundreds of original Liszt mss.). Finally, Keiler evaluates Liszt's abilities as an orchestral conductor. No musical examples.

Liszt gave more than 250 concerts in Germany during the early and mid-1840s. The present author is currently completing a book about them, and preliminary findings have been reported in:

468.   Saffle, Michael. "Liszt in Germany: Problems and Discoveries." *Mitteilungen der Alexander von Humboldt-Stiftung* 48 (December 1986), pp. 15-23.

      Describes Liszt's German tours of 1840-1845, their importance to musical history, and their influence on the growth of Liszt's reputation. Illustrated with two portraits of Liszt, a map of Germany dating from the early nineteenth-century, facsimile reproductions of several documents, and pictures of towns visited by Liszt during his travels.

      NB: Researches described in this article will appear in *Liszt in Germany: 1840-1845* in the near future.

Three other studies of Liszt's 1840s German visits are described below in alphabetical order (by author):

469.   Beyer, R. von. "Le voyage de Liszt à Berlin, d'après de vieux papiers de famille," trans. J. Peyraube. *Revue musicale* "Numéro special" (1 May 1928), pp. 71-75.

      A "literary" sketch of Liszt's triumphal 1842 visit to Berlin, illustrated with several portraits of the artist and with quotations from contemporary descriptions of "Lisztomania" and its effects. Includes brief descriptions of his successful appearance before students at the University of Berlin.

      Detailed descriptions of Liszt's Berlin performances have appeared in dozens of newspapers and magazines. Zsigmond Vita's article "Erdélyi magyar naplóiró Liszt Ferenc Berlini hangversenyeiről" (*Magyar zene* 1/7-8 [August-October 1961], pp. 153-163), for example, reprints in Hungarian an eyewitness account by János Gáskar originally published in 1842. Anecdotes about Liszt and the German capitol have also appeared in a number of obscure publications; see, for example, "Franz Liszt in Berlin," *Berliner Konzertzeitung* 4/20 ("2. Februarwoche"), pp. 3-4.

470.   Irmen, Hans-Josef. "Franz Liszt in Bonn, oder: Wie die erste Beethovenhalle entstand." *Studien zur Bonner Musikgeschichte des 18. und 19. Jahrhunderts* ed. Marianne Bröcker and Günther Massenkeil. Beiträge zur rheinischen Musikgeschichte, 116. Cologne: Arno Volk, 1978; pp. 49-65.

      ML283.8B65S8   ISBN 3-872-52109-8

      A brief study of Liszt's efforts not only on behalf of musical events at the 1845 Beethoven festival at Bonn but toward constructing a temporary concert hall for the celebration concerts. No illustrations.

471.   Kaufmann, Paul. "Franz Liszt am Rhein." *Der schaffende Rhein* [Koblenz] 7 (1931), pp. 44-55.

An account of Liszt's interest in the Rheinland and contributions to the Beethoven memorial project organized in part by Kaufmann's father Leopold Kaufmann, Mayor of Bonn during the 1840s. Includes passages from the older Kaufmann's letters. Unfortunately difficult to obtain.

Not to be confused with Paul Kaufmann's more familiar article "Franz Liszt am Rhein" (*Musik* 26 [1933-1934], pp. 118-121), which deals with Liszt's visits to Bonn, Cologne, and Nonnenwerth during the early 1840s. Includes passages from Leopold Kaufmann letters omitted from the *Schaffende Rhein* study.

Two nineteenth-century publications also provide valuable information about Liszt's German concert tours:

472.   Breidenstein, H. K. *Festgabe zu der am 12ten August 1845 stattfindenden Inauguration des Beethoven-Monuments*. Bonn: Habicht, 1845. 37pp.
ML410.B4B74

The official "program" for the dedication of the Beethoven memorial statue substantially paid for by Liszt. An important source of information about Liszt's musical contributions to the August 1845 ceremonies as well as to German musical life of that decade.

Reprinted in 1983 by L. Röhrscheid of Bonn (ISBN 3-79280-471-9). Also reprinted in *Liszt saeculum* 25 (1979), together with the complete text of Breidenstein's *Zur Jahresfeier der Inauguration des Beethoven-Monuments* (Bonn: T. Habicht, 1846), which contains programs for concerts presented by Liszt and other artists at the 1845 Bonn ceremonies. The *Jahresfeier* text in English (trans. Hilary Casson) as well as the original German.

473.   Schreiber, F. J. A. *Andenken. Dr. Franz Liszt und dessen Anwesenheit in Breslau*. Breslau: G. Günther, 1843. 14pp.

Rare: the University Library, Wrocław, Poland, owns two copies of this book.

Describes Liszt's extended visit to Breslau in early 1843 and records several anecdotes about his largess. Illustrated with an otherwise unknown portrait of Liszt at the keyboard; supplemented with programs for most of his Silesian recitals. Overlooked in item 39 and other early Liszt bibliographies.

Liszt visited Bayreuth several times during the 1870s and 1880s, and he died there in 1886. Two articles deal with Liszt and this small Bavarian town:

474.   Kapp, Julius. "Franz Liszts Opfertod in Bayreuth." In item 35; pp. 13-17.
         Deals primarily with Liszt's last hours in Bayreuth. Unfortunately brief. No illustrations or extensive quotations from eyewitnesses.

475.   Waters, Edward N. "Liszt: Bayreuth's Forgotten Man." *Studia musicologica* 11 (1969), pp. 473-480.
         Describes Liszt's trips to Bayreuth to visit his daughter Cosima and son-in-law Richard Wagner and the cool reception accorded Liszt on most of those visits. Among other documents quoted by Waters is an otherwise unpublished note Liszt sent Emiglio Broglio in 1876.

Finally, two articles deal with Liszt as a "German" composer and musical master:

476.   Frenzel, Heinrich. "Der deutsche Franz Liszt." *Zeitschrift für Musik* 101 (1934), pp. 23-27.
         Argues that Liszt was German (rather than Hungarian) because: 1) he could not speak Hungarian; 2) he lived and worked extensively in Germany; 3) he claimed that he "felt at home" in Weimar (in his letter to Gille of 10 September 1863), and so on. Interesting to students of Nazi-inspired, pro-German propaganda. Useless as musicology, Liszt's Hungarian loyalties having been irrefutably established.

477.   Raabe, Peter. "Franz Liszt und das deutsche Musikleben." *Zeitschrift für Musikwissenschaft* 104 (1937), pp. 253-259.
         A brief survey of Liszt's intermittent but lifelong association with Germany, German music, and German musicians. Written after Hitler's ascent to power, this article—like item 476 (above)—deserves to be consulted by students of Nazi propaganda.
         Other Nazi-inspired, pro-German Liszt publications include Hans Engel's "Franz Liszt — Deutscher!" (published in *Deutsche Musikkultur* 1 [1936], pp. 102-103). Nor were claims to Liszt limited to pre-World pre-World War II German propagandists. See Franz Schneider, "'Génie oblige!' Rhapsodische Gedanken über Franz Liszts politischen Charakter," *Bulletin: Musikrat der DDR* (?1986), pp. 2-13, which makes Liszt out to have been a prototypical Marxist-Leninist.

<u>(Great Britain)</u>

See "England" and "Scotland."

<u>J. Holland</u>

Liszt visited the Netherlands during the 1840s, and several of his most important compositions received their premier performances in that nation. Only one study of any length, however, deals exclusively with Liszt and Holland:

478.   Scholcz, Peter. "Liszts eerste concerten in Nederland, 1842." *Piano Bulletin* [European Piano Teachers Association] No. 1 (1986), pp. 20-29.
        Describes Liszt's visit to Holland during November-December 1842 and his concerts in Amsterdam, den Haag, Leiden, etc. Illustrated with a facsimile page from the *Nederlandsch musikaal tijdschrift*, two lithographs of Liszt's reception by students in Schouwburg, several short press clippings, and—on the cover—a portrait of Liszt in old age. In Dutch.
        Other, much briefer articles by Scholcz include: "Liszts laaste bezoeken aan Nederland," *Franz Liszt Kring* 6 (1984), pp. 18-23.

<u>K. Hungary</u>

Liszt may not have lived as long in Hungary as he did in Germany, but he always considered Hungary his homeland. A number of studies describe Liszt's Hungarian visits and acquaintances, but the three described immediately below are especially important:

479.   Legány, Dezső. *Liszt Ferenc and his Country, 1869-1873*, trans. Gyula Gulyás. Budapest: Editio Musica, 1983. 325pp.
        ML410.L7L333 1983   ISBN 963-13-1541-X
        A splendid account of Liszt's sojourns in Hungary during the early 1870s. Legány describes his subject's personal and professional activities sympathetically and in great detail. Supplemented with quotations from Liszt letters, press clippings, etc. Concludes with valuable notes and bibliographic citations.
        This volume appeared originally in Hungarian with the title *Liszt Ferenc Magyarországon. 1869-1873* (Budapest: Editio Musica, 1983). NB: To a considerable extent it and its sequel, item 480 (below) incorporate the contents of other studies by Legány (e.g., items 483-484) as well as material presented in item 481. See also Chapter II.

480.   Legány, Dezső. *Liszt Ferenc Magyarországon. 1874-1886.* Budapest: Editio Musica, 1986. 301pp.
        ML410.L7L34 1986   ISBN 963-30-625-6
        Equally outstanding, this volume deals with Liszt's last visits to his homeland, his contributions to Hungarian musical life, and his activities on behalf of Hungarian composers and performers. Like its predecessor, this volume is filled with valuable quotations from Liszt's correspondence. In Hungarian; an English-language translation was scheduled to appear

shortly as the present research guide went to press. NB: The review by Mária Eckhardt, published in *Studia musicologica* 31 (1989), pp. 424-428, identifies Legány's volume by an English-language title but refers to the original Hungarian text.

481.   Prahács, Margit. "Franz Liszt und die Budapester Musikakademie." In item 30; pp. 49-94.

An important study of Liszt's contributions to the establishment of Budapest's Academy of Music between the 1840s and his death in 1886. Contains a great deal of information about Budapest concert programs and Academy repertory during the 1870s and 1880s as well as quotations from newspaper articles and the complete texts of several official letters addressed to Liszt (in his capacity as the first director of the Academy) in 1873 and 1875.

Prahács's article was originally published in Hungarian under the title "A zeneművészeti Főiskola levéltárában" in *Zenetudományi tanulmányok* 7 (1959), pp. 427-582. In Hungarian; French-language summary (pp. 692-693).

Three other important studies of Liszt's Hungarian sojourns also deserve to be consulted:

482.   Sebestyén, Ede. *Liszt Ferenc hangversenyei Budapesten. Hat évtized krónikája.* Budapest: Liszt Ferenc Társaság Kiadása, 1944. 210pp. ML410.L7S852M

Covers six decades of concerts Liszt presented in Budapest between the 1820s and the 1880s. Superseded to a considerable extent by items 479-481 but still worth consulting. In Hungarian.

483.   Legány, Dezső. "Liszt and the Budapest Musical Scene: Influences and Contacts, 1869-1886." *New Hungarian Quarterly* 27/103 (Autumn 1986), pp. 119-130.

Presents information touched on in items 479-480 and 488 as well as facts about Liszt's relationships with Ole Bull, Ferenc Korbay, and Niels Gade, and the texts of two Liszt letters written in 1886.

484.   Legány, Dezső. "Liszt's Homes in Budapest." *New Hungarian Quarterly* 24/93 (Fall 1984), pp. 1-10.

A description of several Budapest apartments inhabited by Liszt between 1871-1880, including rooms in the Academy of Music on the Sugár-út.

Reprinted in the *Journal of the American Liszt Society* 17 (1985), pp. 4-14, together with two photographs of Liszt, pictures of some of his Budapest furniture, and a floor-plan of his rooms in the Academy building.

In addition to the years he spent in Hungary during the last decades of his life, Liszt also toured his native land during the late 1830s and 1840s. The following eyewitness account of the first of those tours deserves close attention:

485.   Schober, Franz von. *Briefe über F. Liszts Aufenthalt in Ungarn.* Berlin: Schlesinger, 1843. 62pp.
        ML410.L7S36
        An account of Liszt's spectacularly successful Hungarian concerts of the late 1830s and 1840, written at Liszt's request. Includes the texts of several well-known Liszt letters, two of them also published in contemporary Pest newspapers.

Three other books and articles dealing with Liszt's Hungarian sojourns and activities are described below, in alphabetical order (by author):

486.   Csekey, István. "Franz Liszt in Pécs (Fünfkirchen)," trans. Hanna Schüler. *Musikforschung* 11 (1958), pp. 69-75.
        Describes Liszt's October 1846 visit to this southern Hungarian town. Includes quotations from contemporary newspaper reports of Liszt's activities and performances.
        Other studies dealing with similar material by Csekey include *Liszt Ferenc Baranyában* (Pécs 1956), an Hungarian-language pamphlet about Liszt in southern Hungary illustrated with black-and-white photographs, among them two facsimiles of 1846 concert programs.

487.   Eckhardt, Mária [P.]. "Liszt kapcsolata korának hazai kórusmozgalmával." *Magyar zene* 19 (1978), pp. 121-129.
        Concerned primarily (but not entirely) with Hungarian performances of Liszt's choral works as well as his interest in choral music between c. 1840 and the 1880s. Eckhardt refers frequently to Sebestyén's study (item 482), and she quotes liberally from Liszt's published correspondence. In Hungarian.

488.   Legány, Dezső. "L'arrivée de la musique française et de la musique belge à Budapest: Le rôle de Liszt," trans. Édith Weber. *Revue musicale* 405-406-407 (1987), pp. 87-93.
        Demonstrates that Liszt did much to bring French and Belgian music, especially opera, to Budapest. Legány refers to the careers of a number of

artists, including Franz Servais. Includes the text of a Liszt letter written in 1881. No musical examples.

Among other tributes to Liszt and Hungary is the following little-known study:

489.   Siklóssy, Ladisla. "Le centenaire de retour de François Liszt dans sa patrie." *Nouvelle revue de Hongrie* [Budapest] 33 (1940), pp. 115-124.
    A survey of Liszt's association with Hungary, published as a tribute to the composer on the 100th anniversary of his 1840 Pest concerts. Omitted (as were several other short Liszt-and-Hungary studies) from item 40.

L. Iberia (including Portugal and Spain)

Although he never returned to the Iberian peninsula in later life, Liszt toured Spain, Portugal, and Gibraltar during 1844-1845. The most reliable single account of that tour is:

490.   Stevenson, Robert. "Liszt in the Iberian Peninsula, 1844-1845." *Inter-American Music Review* 7/2 (Spring-Summer 1986), pp. 3-22.
    A detailed history of Liszt's visits to Madrid, Lisbon, Andalusia, Valencia, and Barcelona, supplemented with numerous quotations from contemporary newspapers and magazines. Stevenson summarizes portions of item 495 and refers to such variegated sources as the *Bayreuther Blätter*, dictionaries of important Spanish and Portugese musical figures, and José Vianna da Motta's "O centenario de Liszt," *Illustraçã portuguesa* (13 November 1911). Illustrated with two examples of Iberian folk music.

Stevenson's Inter-American Music Review *article (item 490 above) is conflated from three previous publications described individually below:*

491.   Stevenson, Robert. "Liszt at Barcelona." *Journal of the American Liszt Society* 12 (1982), pp. 6-13.
    Describes Liszt's visit to Barcelona during April 1845 and some of the musical performances he heard in that city. Stevenson quotes lengthy passages from reviews published originally in the *Diario de Barcelona*.

492.   Stevenson, Robert. "Liszt at Madrid and Lisbon, 1844-45." *Musical Quarterly* 65 (1979), pp. 493-512.
    Claims that Liszt was "both the first and the greatest virtuoso to tour the Spanish peninsula," and supports this claim by cataloging Liszt's Iberian repertory and summarizing his reception in Madrid and Lisbon during 1844-1845. This article contains numerous quotations from newspapers like the *Diario de Madrid, Revista de teatros, Revista universal*

Lisbonense, etc. Concludes with a discussion of *Le forgeron*, the only composition known to date from Liszt's visit to Lisbon and one of the sources for *Les préludes*.

An article by Stevenson concerning Liszt's concerts in Andalusia appeared as "Liszt in Andalusia" in the *Journal of the American Liszt Society* 26 (1989), pp. 33-36.

493.   Stevenson, Robert. "Liszt on the East Coast of Spain." *Journal of the American Liszt Society* 4 (1978), pp. 11-17.

In part a synthesis of Eduardo Ranch's *Centenario* pamphlet (item 494 below). Stevenson reviews Liszt's visit to Valencia and Barcelona during March-April 1845, quoting from notices and reviews published in the playbills, the newspaper *Diario marcantil de Valencia*, and other sources.

Two uncommon books devoted to Liszt's Iberian tours also deserve to be consulted:

494.   Ranch, Eduardo. *Centenario de la estancia de Franz Liszt en Valencia.* Valencia: Ranch, 1945.

ML410.L7R32 (according to a National Union Catalog entry)

Not seen but quoted extensively by Stevenson in item 493 (above) and other articles. In Spanish.

495.   Reis, Pedro Batalha. *Liszt na sua passagem por Lisboa em 1845.* Lisbon: Sassetti, 1945. 172pp.

ML410.L7B29

A patriotic description of Liszt's Portuguese sojourn, illustrated with a number of portraits, concert programs, and facsimile reproductions of ms. pages, a photograph of one of Liszt's pianos, and so on. In Portuguese.

Finally, three articles also provide valuable information about Liszt and Iberia:

496.   Bedbrook, Gerald S. "Liszt in Lisbon." *Liszt Society Journal* 6 (1981), pp. 29-30.

A description of Liszt's visit to the Portuguese capital during January-February 1845, drawn to a considerable extent from item 495 (above). Illustrated with two portraits of Liszt and a picture of the artist's "Lisbon" piano.

497.   Forinelli, Arturo. "Liszt y España." *Escorial* 9 (1943), pp. 9-42.

A little-known study of Liszt's travels in Spain, especially of his relationship with Spanish music and musicians. Apparently cited nowhere in the Liszt literature except item 40. In Spanish.

498.   Laires, Fernando. "Franz Liszt in Portugal." *Piano Quarterly* 23/89
         (Spring 1975), pp. 34-37.
              A cursory account of Liszt's 45-day visit to Portugal. Laires describes
         individual concerts as well as social events and decorations Liszt received
         in honor of his art.

M. Ireland

Only one study deals primarily with Liszt's Irish visits:

499.   Arnold, Ben, and Michael Saffle. "Liszt in Ireland (and Belgium): Reports
         from a Concert Tour." *Journal of the American Liszt Society* 26 (1989),
         pp. 3-11.
              Traces Liszt's 1840-1841 tour of Ireland by means of contemporary
         press notices and reviews. Item 440 also contains information about
         Liszt's Irish experiences.
              Among the clippings reprinted in item 499 is one dealing with an oth-
         erwise little-known Liszt performance in Dinant, Belgium. (With regard
         to Liszt and Dinant, see also item 432.)

N. Italy

*Liszt was fond of Italy; during the late 1830s and early 1860s he lived there for se-
veral years. No study has dealt comprehensively with Liszt's Italian sojourns, but at
least two experts have examined individual visits in detail. Their books and articles
are described below in alphabetical order (by author and/or title):*

*   Horvath, Emmerich Karl. *Franz Liszt in Italien: Aufenthalt mit Marie
         Gräfin d'Agoult von 1837-1839.*
              The most recent detailed description of Liszt's first extended visit to
         Italy. Described as item 13c.

500.   Segnitz, Eugen [von]. "Franz Liszt und Italien. Liszts erster Aufenthalt von
         1837 bis 1839." *Neue Musikzeitung* [Stuttgart] 25 (1903-1904), pp. 51-54
         and 102-104.
              Describes Liszt's first extended visits to Italy. No longer the only work
         on this subject, having been supplanted by Horvath (item 13c), by item
         507, and by portions of item 1a. Illustrated with a well-known portrait of
         Liszt as a young man (p. 53).

501.   Segnitz, Eugen [von]. *Franz Liszt und Rom.* Musikalische Studien, 8.
         Leipzig: Hermann Seemann, 1901. 74pp.
              ML410.L7S4

Deals with Liszt's Roman sojourns of the 1830s and 1860s. Includes more than 65 references to letters, published works of reminiscence, etc. Bibliographic citations in the form of notes. No musical examples.

Reprinted by Kraus in 1976. A similar article by Segnitz also appeared under the title "Francesco Liszt e Roma" in *Rivista musicale italiana* 13 (1906), pp. 113-134. In Italian. NB: This article evidently was intended as the first in a series, but subsequent installments were never published.

Seven other articles dealing with Liszt and Italy are described or cross-referenced below in alphabetical order (by author):

502.   Angelis, Aberto de. "Liszt à Roma." *Rivista musicale italiana* 18 (1911), pp. 308-355.

Primarily a study of Liszt's life in Rome during 1861-1865, although de Angelis also refers to Liszt's travels of the 1880s. References to several of his musical works are scattered throughout this article. In Italian.

503.   Chiti, Gian Paolo. "Montemario — Oasis for Franz Liszt for 1862-1868." *Journal of the American Liszt Society* 20 (1986), pp. 82-109.

Describes the hill called Monte Mario outside Rome, the chapel built on that hill by Giovanni de Rossi in 1628, and Liszt's life in one of the church's cells during the 1860s. Chiti quotes from several accounts of Liszt's activities during those years as well as from the published correspondence. Concludes with detailed notes, a bibliography of "essential" sources, and five photographs of the "Madonna del Rosario" today.

504.   Helbig, Nadine. "Liszt in Rome." *Liszt Society Journal* 3 (1978), pp. 37-43.

Supplements in the *Liszt Society Journal* 4 (1979), pp. 19-25; and 10 (1985), pp. 30-36.

Opens with an eyewitness account of Liszt in Rome that appeared originally in 1907 in the *Deutsche Revue* and in certain editions of item 371. Subsequent articles in this series consist of materials taken from various sources, including the diaries of Curd von Schloezer. Miscellaneous illustrations.

*   Mastroianni, Thomas. "The Italian Aspect of Franz Liszt."

Devoted more to Liszt's Italianate music and musical contacts than his visits to Italy. Described in greater detail as item 736.

505.   Rüsch, Walter. "Franz Liszt in Bellagio." *Liszt-Studien* 1 (1977), pp.
        155-162.
            Discusses Liszt's sojourn of the mid-1830s in terms of d'Agoult's
        Mémoires (item 248) and Liszt's compositions of that time. No musical
        examples.

506.   Stradal, August. "Franz Liszts Aufenthalt in Rom im Winter 1885/86."
        Neue Musikzeitung [Stuttgart] 9-10 (1926), pp. 188-192 and 213-215.
            Reminiscences of Liszt's last visit to the Eternal City, written by one
        of his pupils. Illustrated with three small photographs of the Via Bubuino
        and of memorials in Roman graveyards.

507.   Suttoni, Charles. "Franz Liszt à Milan." *Revue musicale* 405-406-407
        (1987), pp. 177-187.
            A carefully documented account of Liszt's 1838 travels in Italy, espe-
        cially Milan. Includes extensive quotations (some translated into French)
        from Milanese newspapers like *La moda*, from the *Allegmeine musikalische
        Zeitung*, and from Liszt's correspondence (including his letters to several
        periodicals).

O. Luxembourg

*Few studies of Liszt's brief visits to this small country have appeared in print. The
most easily available is:*

508.   Penning, Jim. "Liszt in Luxembourg." *Liszt Society Journal* 9 (1984), pp.
        45-53.
            Deals with Liszt's several visits this Duchy. Penning quotes articles
        originally published in 1845 and 1886 in the *Luxemburger Wort* and the
        L'Indépendance Luxembourgeoise. Illustrated with a facsimile of an adver-
        tising poster for a Liszt concert and several photographs of "Liszt
        pianos."
            A more detailed and much more extensively illustrated account of
        Liszt's visits to Luxembourg is difficult to obtain. See Guy May, "Franz
        Liszt und Luxemburg," *Nos Cahiers* 3 (1986), pp. 87-122. May's study
        (also published as a pamphlet) includes the French-language text of an
        article about Liszt that appeared in 1886 in the *Jean de Luxembourg*.
        Otherwise in German.

P. Poland

*Like his visits to Luxembourg, Liszt's Polish travels have received comparatively little
attention. One brief account of these travels may be found in:*

509.   Donath, Adolf. "Franz Liszt und Polen." *Liszt-Studien* 1 (1977), pp. 53-64.

Primarily a description of Liszt's visits to Chopin's homeland during the 1840s, although Donath also mentions Liszt's friendship with pianist and composer Juliusz Zarebski during 1854-1855 and the possibility that Liszt possessed a passive understanding of the Polish language.

Other studies of Liszt's Polish visits and colleagues, published in Polish, include István Csaplarós, "Koncerty Liszta w Polsce w 1843 R" in *Ruch muzyczny* 5/20 (1961), pp. 3-5.

Polish borders have shifted several times since the eighteenth century; part of what was Germany, or Austro-Hungary, or even Russia in Liszt's day is today Polish soil. The study cross-referenced below deserves to be mentioned under "Poland" as well as "Germany":

*   Schreiber, F. J. A. *Andenken.*

Reviews the concerts Liszt presented in and around Breslau (today, Wrocław) during 1843. Described in greater detail as item 473.

(Portugal)

(see "Iberia")

Q. Russia

Although brief, Liszt's visits to Russia in 1842-1843 and 1847 helped open that nation's ears to Western European music. Among recent summaries of Liszt's relationship with Russia and her composers is:

510.   Krauklis, G[eorgii] V[ilgelmovich]. "Ferents List i russkaia muzykal'naia kul'tura." *Studia musicologica* 29 (1987), pp. 285-294.

Describes Liszt's impact on Russian music through eyewitness accounts of his performances and reminiscences of his later years recorded by Russian critics and composers. Extensive bibliographic citations but no musical examples. In Russian throughout.

Other, briefer synopses of much of the same material also exist. See, for instance, D. Lehmann's "Bemerkungen zur Liszt-Rezeption in Russland in den vierziger und fünfziger Jahren des 19. Jahrhunderts," published in *Studia musicologica* 5 (1963), pp. 211-215. No musical examples.

Three other accounts of Liszt's Russian tours, all of them published since the 1930s, are described below in alphabetical order (by author):

511.   Gojowy, Detlef. "Liszt et la Russie." *Revue musicale* 405-406-407 (1987), pp. 95-101.

A survey of Liszt's visits to Russia and associations with or influences on contemporary Russian composers. Contains lengthy quotations from letters written by Glazounov, Shostakovich, and even Prokofieff. No musical examples.

512.   Khvostenko, V. "List v russii." *Sovetskaia muzyka* Nos. 11-12 (November-December 1936), pp. 30-48 ["1842"] and 78-92 ["1843"].

Essentially a sizeable collection of press clippings associated with Liszt's visits to Moscow and St. Petersburg and taken from *Severnaia pchela, Moskvitianin,* and other newspapers. In Russian throughout.

Omitted from several standard Liszt bibliographies. Cited by Walker but incorrectly dated from "1937" (item 1a; p. 378n).

513.   Rudakova, Je. "Liszt in Rußland." *Sowjetwissenschaftl. Kunst und Literatur* [Berlin] 3/10 (March 1962), pp. 313-322.

Deals with Liszt's Russian tours of 1842-1843, his acquaintances among Russian composers, etc. Includes quotations from Stasov's reviews of Liszt performances as well as information about Russian observations of Liszt's death, including a description of a November 1886 Liszt concert.

Rudakova's article also appeared in Russian under the title "List v russii" in *Sovetskaia muzyka* 25/11 (November 1961), pp. 68-76.

R. Scotland

Only one brief study deals exclusively with Liszt's concerts in this country:

514.   Wright, William. "Press Reviews of Liszt's Concerts in Scotland." *Liszt Society Journal* 13 (1988), pp. 65-69.

Describes concerts Liszt presented in Edinburgh and Glasgow during January 1841. Wright quotes extensively from newspapers like the Glasgow *Courier* and the Edinburgh *Evening Courant.* Illustrated with a poor nineteenth-century picture of the Edinburgh Assembly Rooms, where Liszt performed.

(Spain)

See "Iberia"

S. Switzerland

Liszt's Swiss sojourns were comparatively few and far between, but he did visit that country several times during the 1830s-1850s. No studies describe all his visits; two of the best deal with his "honeymoon" trip of 1835-1836:

515.   Bory, Robert. *Un retraite romantique en Suisse. Liszt et la Comtesse d'Agoult*, 2nd (revised) ed. [Lausanne and] Paris: Victor Attinger, 1930. 173pp.
           ML410.L7B65 1930
           A book-length account of Liszt's extended visits to Switzerland in the 1830s with the mother-to-be of his three children. Supplemented with portraits and other illustrations as well as an appendix (pp. 99-172) containing 36 letters written by Liszt, d'Agoult, Geroge Sand, and Pictet. A previous edition (1923) lacks some of this material.
           Also published in 1934 in German as *Franz Liszt and Marie d'Agoult in der Schweiz*, trans. Ludwig Überfeldt.

516.   Eckhardt, Mária [P.] "Diary of a Wayfarer: The Wanderings of Franz Liszt and Marie d'Agoult in Switzerland, June-July 1835." *Journal of the American Liszt Society* 11 (1982), pp. 10-17.
           Draws upon Liszt's pocket diary for 1835 (F-Pn N.a.fr. 14.320), in which the composer recorded details of his exploits with d'Agoult. Eckhardt concentrates on the contents of the diary rather than on its provenance and physical characteristics.

Other publications about Liszt and Switzerland include:

517.   Burdet, Jacques. "Liszt et Mendelssohn dans le Canton de Vaud." *Revue musicale de Suisse Romande* 25/2 (June 1972), pp. 6-7.
           Deals with part with concerts Liszt presented at Lausanne on 16 July and 8 October 1836. Burdet includes the programs for these concerts.

*   Pictet, Adolphe. *Une course à Chamounix*.
           An eyewitness account of Liszt's 1830s visits to Switzerland with the Comtesse d'Agoult. Described in greater detail as item 245.

518.   Szadrowsky-Burckhardt, M. "Wagner und Liszt in St. Gallen, 1856." *Schweizerische Musikzeitung* 96 (1956), pp. 476-480.
           A discussion of the joint concert presented by Wagner and Liszt in St. Gallen on 23 November 1856. Szadrowsky-Burckhardt quotes from published letters to provide information about Liszt's and Wagner's attitudes toward their unusual project.

519.   Viala, Claude. "Franz Liszt au Conservatoire (1835-1836)." *Revue musicale de Suisse Romande* 38 (1985), pp. 122-129.
  Describes Liszt's brief career at the Geneva Conservatory and refers to the keyboard manual he may have composed at that time. Illustrated with Henry (not Ary) Scheffer's 1835 portrait of Liszt, a contemporary sketch of Liszt playing a four-hands work, and facsimiles of Liszt's 1830s handwriting.

T. Turkey

Liszt visited Turkey only once, in 1847. Only one article has been devoted exclusively to that visit:

520.   Missir de Lusignan, Livio. "Liszt et l'empire Ottoman en 1847." *Revue musicale* 405-406-407 (1987), pp. 189-196.
  Deals primarily with Liszt's visits to and concert performances in Constantinople during July-August 1847. Includes quotations from the *Courrier de Constantinople* as well as several secondary sources on Turkish history. Interesting but in some respects less satisfactory than item 1a; pp. 440-442, even though Missir de Lusignan corrects Walker on several points. No facsimile reproductions or other illustrations.

INTELLECTUAL AND RELIGIOUS INTERESTS

Although ill educated by today's standards, Liszt was an avid reader and art lover; he knew many of the important painters, poets, and philosophers of his day, and he flirted with several movements—including Saint-Simonism, Freemasonry, and religious reform. He also experimented with musical programmism and developed the "symphonic poem" as one result of such experimentation.

Intellectual Interests

Most studies of Liszt's fascination with philosophy and literature deal with at most one or two facets of this intriguing topic—e.g., Freemasonry or the Franciscan tradition or Liszt's relation with literary figures. The finest of these specialized studies is:

521.   Autexier, Philippe A. *Mozart & Liszt sub rosa*. Poitiers: Philippe A. Autexier, 1984. 190pp.
  [No LC or ISBN numbers available]
  A valuable monograph, consisting of essays summarizing the Masonic activites of Mozart and Liszt (printed in both French and German) followed by hundreds of annotated texts associated with those activities.

Autexier traces Liszt's flirtation with Freemasony from its beginnings in 1840s Germany to its end with the composer's death in 1886; he reproduces letters, diplomas, Masonic lodge registers, newspaper notices, diary entries, and so on—many of them previously unknown. Illustrated with a number of facsimile reproductions. Privately printed and somewhat difficult to obtain. A "Supplement à la partie documentaire," containing corrections to the original volume, was issued by Autexier in 1986. Reviewed in item 132.

Material borrowed from this study appeared as "F. L. . . T" in item 36; pp. 172-183. NB: A two-part article based on Autexier's material appeared as: Lennart Rabes, "Franz Liszt the Freemason," in *Liszt saeculum* 32 (1983), pp. 22-57; and 33 (1984), pp. 10-22.

Another, quite different study of the same general topic by the same author also deserves attention:

522.   Autexier, Philippe A. "The Masonic Thread in Liszt." *Journal of the American Liszt Society* 22 (1987), pp. 3-18.

Summarizes Liszt's interest in Freemasonry but concentrates on his Masonic activities in Bordeaux in 1844. Illustrated with tables, two short musical examples, and a previously unpublished portrait of Liszt dating from his Bordeaux visit.

An excellent introduction to Liszt's involvement with Romanticism may be found in:

523.   Lang, Paul Henry. "Liszt and the Romantic Movement." *Musical Quarterly* 22 (1936), pp. 314-325.

A short but insightful survey of Liszt's involvement with Romantic principles, especially those of French Romanticism, and the impact those principles had on fundamental aspects of his compositional development. Lang believes that "Liszt's great innovation and achievement consisted in proving that it was possible to create a well-rounded and logically organized piece of music without forcing the ideas into the established frames of traditional [i.e., Classical] forms." Unfortunately, no illustrations or musical examples.

Liszt was involved for a time with several revolutionary movements in 1830s France. The best shorter study of one such involvement is:

524.   Locke, Ralph P. "Liszt's Saint-Simonian Adventure." *19th Century Music* 4 (1981), pp. 209-227.

Contends that Liszt "sought to distance himself from a movement whose ideas he never ceased to admire," and reviews a large body of documentary evidence about Liszt and Saint-Simon's followers to support that contention. Locke's article is valuable not only for its discussion of its subject's idealism but also for its information about Saint-Simon, his followers among early nineteenth-century musicians, and beliefs and practices attributed to of the philosopher's disciples. Illustrations include a page of Liszt's corrections for the first volume of Ramann's survey study (item 3a).

Important corrections for this article appear in *19th Century Music* 5 (1982), p. 281. The article itself is based to a considerable extent on Locke's dissertation, *Music and the Saint-Simonians: The Involvement of Félicien David and Other Musicians in a Socialist Movement* (University of Chicago, 1980).

Liszt's occasional intellectual interests extended beyond Freemasonry, Romanticism, and Saint-Simon's teachings to include international cultural currents. A useful introduction to Liszt's fascination with those currents is:

525.   Pestalozza, Luigi. "Il ruolo di Liszt nella formazione delle culture nazionali in Europa." *Studia musicologica* 28 (1986), pp. 201-212.

A survey of Liszt's lifelong, complex involvement with contemporary artistic and intellectual movements—among them, the *Gazette musicale*, publishers like Breitkopf & Härtel, composers like Wagner, Berlioz, and Grieg, and so on. In Italian.

Five other worthwhile studies of Liszt's intellectual and artistic interests—especially painting, literature, and philosophy—are described below in alphabetical order (by author):

526.   Bauer, Marion. "The Literary Liszt." *Musical Quarterly* 22 (1936), pp. 295-313.

Summarizes the contents of Liszt's principal literary works and identifies and discusses his interest in poems and plays by Dante, Hugo, Goethe, etc. Bauer completed her essay before questions were raised about the authenticity of Liszt's literary output. Consequently, Bauer generally takes Liszt "at his word," assuming that only a few of his books and articles—including his biography of Chopin (reprinted in items 165a and 171)—reflect "the collaboration of Princess Carolyne von Sayn-Wittgenstein." (With regard to that purported collaboration, see items 175ff., especially items 177-178.)

527.   Faure-Cousin, Jeanne, and France Clidat. *Aux sources littéraires de Franz Liszt*. Entire double issue of *Revue musicale* 292-293 (1973).

A book-length examination of the literary works behind such well-known compositions as *Mazeppa* (Byron and Hugo), the *Faust* symphony (Lenau), the "Petrarch Sonnets," and the *Dante* symphony. Concludes with a four-page chronological summary of Liszt's life and activities.

528.   Guichard, Léon. "Liszt et la littérature française." *Revue de musicologie*
       56 (1970), pp. 3-34.
       Describes Liszt's relationships with several important literary figures
       of 1830s-1840s France, including Lamennais, Lamartine, and Victor Hugo.
       An appendix deals with the problem of the authenticity of Liszt's literary
       works; a second appendix identifies by "author" those Liszt compositions
       inspired by works of French literature; and a third reviews the
       Lamartine/Autran problem *vis-à-vis* the symphonic poem *Les préludes*.

529.   Hankiss, Jean. "Liszt écrivain et la littérature europénne." *Revue de
       littérature comparée* 17 (1937), pp. 299-329.
       Discusses relationships between Liszt's own literary works and those
       of previous and contemporary European authors. Somewhat out of date.

530.   Salmen, Walter. "Liszt und Wagner in ihren Beziehungen zur bildenden
       Kunst." *Liszt Studien* 3 (1986), pp. 152-161.
       Summarizes Liszt's interest in painting, sculpture, etc., and his refer-
       ences to particular art-works in compositions like the *Faust* symphony, the
       Totentanz, several shorter piano pieces, and so on. No illustrations or
       musical examples.

Shorter studies of Liszt's intellectual interests include:

531.   Grabócz, Márta. "Liszt és a 'filozófiai eposzok'." *Magyar zene* 27 (1986),
       pp. 21-28.
       Examines Liszt's flirtation with philosophical movements during the
       1830s, including Saint-Simon's teachings. In Hungarian.

532.   Hill, Nancy Klenk. "Landscape, Literature, and Liszt." *Journal of the
       American Liszt Society* 8 (1980), pp. 15-24.
       Deals with Liszt's interest in painting and literature, especially with his
       characteristically Romantic convictions that 1) literature (i.e., program or
       story) must "mediate to the other arts," including music; and that 2) Liszt,
       like other Romantics, was interested in depicting landscapes in pieces like
       the *Album d'un voyageur, Ce qu'on entend sur la montagne* (the so-called
       "Mountain Symphony"), and so on. Illustrated with quotations from
       Delacroix's diaries and from poems by Goethe, Homer, Wordsworth, and
       so on. No musical examples.

533.   Révész, Imre. "Liszt és Lamennais." *Zenetudományi tanulmányok* 1
       (1953), pp. 115-123.

A brief study of Liszt's relationship with Felicité Lamennais. No illustrations or extended quotations. In Hungarian only; no foreign-language abstract.

Religious Interests

Liszt was a Roman Catholic as well as a sometime Freemason, Saint-Simonist, and avid reader. As a Catholic he was especially interested in the reform of liturgical music and in "new" kinds of religious music. The two best introductions to Liszt, Catholicism, and music are:

534. Felix, Werner. "Die Reformideen Franz Liszts." *Festschrift Richard Münnich zum 80. Geburtstag*, ed. Hans Pischner. Leipzig: Deutscher Verlag für Musik, 1957. pp. 104-115.
ML55.M62P5 1957
Describes Liszt's enthusiasm for remaking Christian music along theatrical as well as liturgical lines.
An evaluation of some of Felix's ideas, written by Zoltán Gárdonyi, appeared as "Néhány ujább Liszt-tanulmányról" in *Magyar zene* 1/3 (December 1960), pp. 238-242.

535. Heinrichs, Josef. "Franz Liszts kirchenmusikalischer Reformplan." *Musica Sacra* 76 (1956), pp. 44-49.
Discusses Liszt's "plan" for the reform of Catholic music, his relationship with the Cecilianist movement, etc. "Pläne" (i.e., "plans") would have been more appropriate, since Liszt's opinions about church-music reform changed several times during the course of his life. Illustrated with a Liszt portrait.

Four other studies of Liszt's ideas about religious issues are described below in alphabetical order (by author):

536. Bangert, Mark. "Franz Liszt's Essay on Church Music (1834) in the Light of Felicité Lamennais's System of Religious and Political Thought." *Student Musicologists at Minnesota* 5 (1972), pp. 182-219.
Describes the origins of Liszt's first article (actually published in 1835) and its significance for his lifelong interest in church-music reform. Bangert argues plausibly that Liszt's essay was probably written under the direct influence of Lamennais. Concludes with a complete translation into English of the essay itself (pp. 176-180).
Reprinted in *Church Music* [St. Louis, Missouri] "No. 2" (1973), pp. 17-25. See also items 170 and 973.

537.   Gájdoš, Vševlad [Jozef]. "War Franz Liszt Franziskaner?" *Studia musicologica* 6 (1964), pp. 299-310.

Traces the Liszt family's involvement with Franciscanism from Adam Liszt's unsuccessful novitiate through his son's honorary memberships in several Franciscan societies. Gájdoš concludes that, despite his flirtations with this order and its teachings, Liszt never became a "real" Franciscan. See also item 395.

NB: It is not clear whether this study was published as an independent volume, or merely as an offprint from *Acta Academiae Scientiarum et Artium Slovacae* 10 (?1944), pp. 482-?502.

Another article by Gájdoš about Liszt and Franciscanism appeared under the title "Bol František Liszt frantiskanom?" in *Slovenská hudba* 12 (1968), pp. 258-260. In Slovak. Not seen but identified in RILM 2 (1968); entry 2048. Also by Gájdoš is *Zu den Beziehungen Franz Liszts zur Slowakei. Der Ursprung der Franziskanertradition in der Familie Franz Liszts* (Bratislava: Slovenská Akadémia Vied a Umeni, 1944). Finally, see László Bucsi, "Liszt és a magyar ferencesek" (*Magyar zene* 28 [1987], pp. 50-52); in Hungarian.

538.   Nixon, Philipp. "Franz Liszt on Religion." *Journal of the American Liszt Society* 17 (1985), pp. 15-19.

A brief review of Liszt as a devout man; thus, in part, a refutation of attacks on Liszt's faith by Newman (in item 376) and other scholars. Quotations from several Liszt letters but no illustrations.

539.   Saffle, Michael. "Liszt and Cecilianism: The Evidence of Documents and Scores." *Der Caecilianismus: Anfänge — Grundlagen — Wirkungen*, ed. Hubert Unverricht. Eichstätter Abhandlungen zur Musikwissenschaft, 5. Tutzing: Hans Schneider, 1988; pp. 203-213.

ISBN 3-7952-0550-6   [No LC number available]

Describes Liszt's real, if less than passionate devotion to the Cecilianist movement through references to letters, newspaper clippings, and such compositions as the *Missa choralis*. No musical examples.

Poorer, shorter, or less informative articles about Liszt and Catholicism have also appeared in print. Only one example is given here:

540.   Angelis, Alberto de. "Christo in Liszt." *Rivista musicale italiana* 48 (1946), pp. 380-386.

A brief discussion of Liszt and Catholicism, including references to the composer's relationship with Pius IX (see item 580), the oratorio *Christus*, the *Dante* symphony, and so on. In Italian.

LISZT AND THE LADIES

Whether Liszt was actually a womanizer is uncertain; that he had several important love affairs during his life cannot be denied. Biographers and scholars have devoted several books to the women in Liszt's life; the most comprehensive are:

541.	Horvath, Emmerich Karl. *Frauen um Liszt. Die Sprache der Liebe.* Eisenstadt: Ernst & Georg Horvath, 1971. 124pp.
	ML410.L7H7
	A privately-printed, ill-organized survey of Liszt's adventures with the Comtesse d'Agoult, the Princess Sayn-Wittgenstein, Agnès Street-Klindworth, and other ladies—among them, Charlotte van Hagen and the infamous Lola Montez. Outfitted with some two dozen illustrations, many of them having nothing directly to do with the topic in question. Concludes with an index of names.

542.	Kapp, Julius. *Franz Liszt und die Frauen.* Leipzig: Friedrich Rothbarth, 1911. 86pp.
	ML410.L7K4
	A survey of this complex and fascinating topic. Kapp concentrates on Liszt's relationships with d'Agoult and Sayn-Wittgenstein, but he also mentions Lina Schmalhausen, George Sand, Charlotte von Hagen, etc. Illustrated with portraits of Liszt's most important female friends.

543.	La Mara. *Liszt und die Frauen.* Leipzig: Breitkopf & Härtel, 1911. 321pp.
	ML410.L7L69
	Describes Liszt's relationships with twenty-six women, including such little-known figures as Countess Louis Plater, Emilie Merian-Genast, Sofie Menter, and Nadine Helbig, as well as the obligatory Caroline de Saint-Criq, Marie d'Agoult, and Carolyne zu Sayn-Wittgenstein. Illustrated with 23 portraits. A second edition appeared in 1919.

Liszt and Marie d'Agoult

At least two studies have been devoted exclusively to Liszt's relationship with the Comtesse d'Agoult. The first is addressed to the general public; the second is somewhat more specialized:

544.	Haldane, Charlotte. *The Galley Slaves of Love: The Story of Marie d'Agoult and Franz Liszt.* London: Harvill, 1957. 243pp.
	ML410.L7H25
	A novel-like account of Liszt's stormy relationship with the Comtesse d'Agoult, prejudiced in favor of the lady. Haldane goes so far as to claim

that the Liszt/d'Agoult affair was "the most typical romance of the Romantic Age." Portraits and other illustrations.

545.   Hevesy, André de. "Liszt et Madame d'Agoult." *Revue musicale* "Numéro special" (May 1928), pp. 33-46; and 8 (June 1928), pp. 155-168.

A study of this complex topic, based to a considerable extent on letters that eventually appeared (or will appear) in items 194-195. Illustrated with Ary Scheffer's famous Liszt portrait. The significance of this article is described in greater detail in item 41.

Liszt and Christina Belgiojoso

An article about Liszt and the Princess Belgiojoso also deserves attention:

546.   Brombert, Beth Archer. "The Wanderer's Fantasy." *Liszt Society Journal* 6 (1981), pp. 24-28; and 8 (1983), pp. 7-15.

A synopsis of Liszt's extended relationship with Princess Christina Belgiojoso, with whom he corresponded and to whom he dedicated his fantasy on themes from Bellini's *I puritani*. The second installment of this article is illustrated with a reproduction of a pastel portrait of the Princess, c. 1836.

Derived from Brombert's book *Christina: Portraits of a Princess* (London: Hamish Hamilton, 1978).

Liszt and Carolyne Sayn-Wittgenstein

Three articles deal exclusively with Liszt's attempts to marry the Princess Sayn-Wittgenstein, attempts that finally came to nothing:

547.   Walker, Alan. "Liszt, Carolyne, and the Vatican: The Story of a Thwarted Marriage." *Journal of the American Liszt Society* 24 (1988), pp. 33-44.

Adapted from source materials discussed at greater length in item 1b; pp. 566-580. By referring to long-misplaced Vatican documents, Walker proves that Liszt could have married the Princess Sayn-Wittgenstein but almost certainly chose instead to defer to appeals from the Princess's daughter Marie [Hohenlohe] and her family. Includes the complete text (in Latin and English) of a lengthy document verifying the Princess's annulment.

548.   Grazia, Donna M. di. "Liszt and Carolyne Sayn-Wittgenstein: New Documents on the Wedding That Wasn't." *19th Century Music* 12/2 (Fall 1988), pp. 148-162.

Describes Liszt's thwarted attempt to marry Sayn-Wittgenstein as revealed in Vatican documents previously discovered by Alan Walker (see item 547 above). Concludes with an appendix of "Principal Characters" in the Liszt/Wittgenstein affair as well as a second appendix devoted to identifying and summarizing the contents of 45 archival sources. Illustrated with facsimile reproductions of two documents, the second a letter in Liszt's hand dated 16 October 1860 and addressed to Cardinal De Luca.

549.   Merrick, Paul. "Liszt's Transfer from Weimar to Rome: A Thwarted Marriage." *Studia musicologica* 21 (1979), pp. 219-238.

Casts doubts on the "fortuitousness" of Liszt's last-minute failure to marry the Princess Sayn-Wittgenstein on 22 October 1861. Merrick bases his concludes on evidence derived from a variety of documents, including Liszt's correspondence with Sayn-Wittgenstein and with Mgr. Hohenlohe, later his close friend. As much a study of Liszt's relationship with the Princess as with Italian authorities. Superseded by items 1b and 547-548 (above).

Liszt and Other Women

Four additional studies of "Liszt ladies" are described or cross-referenced below in alphabetical order (by author):

550.   Fabre, Michel. "Liszt et Plante: Le premier amour et le dernier concert." *Revue internationale de musique française* 16 (1985), pp. 107-114.

Deals with Liszt's 1844 visit to Pau where, between engagements as a concert artist, he visited his childhood sweetheart Caroline Saint-Circq. No illustrations.

551.   Keeling, Geraldine [Field]. "Liszt and Lina Schmalhausen." *Journal of the American Liszt Society* 5 (1979), pp. 47-53.

Discusses the warm relationship Liszt enjoyed with Schmalhausen between 1879-1886. Keeling also discusses a photograph of Liszt and Schmalhausen taken at Weimar in 1884, and she quotes extensively from published Liszt reminiscences as well as Kinsky's catalog of the long-defunct Wilhelm Heyer collection.

552.   Walker, Alan. "Liszt and Agnes Street-Klindworth: A Spy in the Court of Weimar?" *Studia musicologica* 28 (1986), pp. 47-63.

Describes Liszt's emotionally charged relationship with the "Freundin" to whom the letters in item 186c were addressed, and who functioned as a political agent in Weimar during the 1850s. Illustrated with quotations from Liszt's correspondence and with a facsimile page from a letter Liszt addressed to his inamorata in 1856. (Much of this material reappears in item 1b; pp. 209-224.)

*   Wallace, William. *Liszt, Wagner and the Princess.*
Devoted as much to Liszt's relationship with Wagner and Wagner's with the Princess. Described in greater detail as item 558.

LISZT AND HIS CONTEMPORARIES

Liszt knew thousands of his contemporaries, among them some of the most important figures in nineteenth-century art, music, poetry, publishing, religion, politics, and letters. Studies of Liszt's relationships with a variety of figures are described below. Studies of Liszt's musical indebtedness to or influence on eighteenth-, nineteenth-, and twentieth-century composers are described in Chapter XIII.

Liszt and Berlioz

Among Liszt's most cherished colleagues and friends was the French composer and journalist Hector Berlioz. Unfortunately, much of the Liszt-Berlioz correspondence appears to have been lost, and only two studies have been devoted exclusively to the Liszt-Berlioz relationship:

553.   Bailbé, Joseph-Marc. "Liszt et Berlioz: Une poétique du voyage." *Revue musicale* 405-406-407 (1987), pp. 167-176.
Describes the "voyages" of Liszt and Berlioz during the 1830s and 1840s (i.e., the thoughts and experiences as well as the actual travels of the two composers). Includes quotations from several letters as well as the *Lettres d'un bachelier* (see items 165b and 169-170), George Sand's *Consuelo*, Jules Janin's *Voyage en Italie*, and so on.

554.   Haraszti, Emile. "Berlioz, Liszt, and the Rákóczy March." *Musical Quarterly* 26 (1940), pp. 200-231.
Traces the origins of the Rákóczy tune used by Berlioz and Liszt to *Pannonia*, a collection of Hungarian songs published between 1826-1829. Haraszti concludes that Liszt was the first to use this tune (in the earliest version of his fifteenth "Hungarian Rhapsody"), but that Berlioz made better use of it in his *Damnation of Faust*. Illustrated with several short musical examples, a facsimile of the first page of Berlioz's *Marche hongroise*, and a facsimile of a poster advertising Berlioz's concert at the National Hungarian Theater (Pest) on 20 February 1846.

Liszt and Schumann

Liszt's real friendship with Schumann was short-lived, but the two musicians met on several occasions and corresponded fairly frequently. Valuable studies dealing with Liszt and Schumann include:

555.   Kapp, Julius. "Franz Liszt und Robert Schumann." *Musik* 13 (1913-1914), pp. 67-85.

Summarizes Liszt's relationship with Schumann. Kapp mentions such topics as Liszt's 1840 Leipzig concerts—presented, as it were, under Schumann's "protection"—the Leipzig premiere of Schumann's *Genoveva* and Liszt's remarks about that work, and so on. Illustrated with numerous quotations from the composers' substantial correspondence.

556.   Walker, Alan. "Schumann, Liszt, and the C Major Fantasie, Op. 17: A Declining Relationship." *Music & Letters* 60 (1979), pp. 156-166.

A study of Liszt's unsteady relationship with Schumann, inspired by the sale in 1977 of the original *Fantasie* ms. Illustrated with facsimile reproductions of three Schumann ms. pages owned by the National Széchenyi Library, Budapest.

Liszt and Wagner

None of Liszt's relationships has inspired more attention—or misunderstanding—than his admiration for, emnity toward, and familial ties with Richard Wagner. Two books have been devoted almost exclusively to Liszt and Wagner; they are described below:

557.   Kapp, Julius. *Richard Wagner und Franz Liszt. Eine Freundschaft.* Berlin: Schuster & Loeffler, 1908. 204pp.

ML410.W19K27

Describes Liszt's friendship and quarrels with Wagner over much of their lives—i.e., from the early 1840s, when they first met, through Wagner's death in 1883. Kapp devotes whole sections of his book to Liszt's support of Wagner's creative efforts; to the quarrel that separated the composers for more than a decade when Cosima, Liszt's daughter, left her first husband Hans von Bülow for Wagner; and to the last, more or less reconciled years of Liszt-Wagner friendship. Concludes with dozens of quotations from Liszt's and Wagner's letters about each other's characters and compositions, and with an index.

558.   Wallace, William. *Liszt, Wagner and the Princess.* New York: E. P. Dutton, 1927. xiv, 196pp.

ML410.L7W3

An "anti-Liszt legend" study of Liszt's relationships with Princess Sayn-Wittgenstein and his son-in-law, Richard Wagner. Wallace is especially harsh on the Princess, claiming that she was a "bigoted and opinionated woman who kill[ed] the soul in Liszt, day by day, inch by inch." Illustrated with five plates of portraits. Concludes with a bibliography.

Two shorter but equally important studies of the Liszt-Wagner musical symbiosis are cross-referenced below:

*   Bergfeld, Joachim. "Richard Wagner und Franz Liszt." In item 35; pp. 43-62.
     Deals with musical as well as biographical issues. Described in greater detail as item 697.

*   Winkler, Gerhard J. "Liszt und Wagner."
     Described as item 698.

Four more specialized studies of the Liszt-Wagner relationship also deserve attention; they are described below in alphabetical order (by author and/or title):

559.   Abert, Amalie, and Léon Guichard. "Liszt und Wagner." *Report of the Eighth Congress of the International musicological Society, New York (1961)*, ed. Jan LaRue. 2 volumes. Kassel: Bärenreiter, 1962.
     [No LC number available]
        559a. [in: Papers: Vol. 1, pp. 314-332.]
        559b. "Liszt, Wagner, and the Relationship between Music and Literature in the 19th Century": Vol. 2, pp. 140-145.
     Item 559a summarizes the Liszt-Wagner relationship and musicologists' attitudes in Germany and France toward both composers. Item 559b is a transcript of a roundtable discussion of the same topics. Comments in several languages.

560.   Ackermann, Peter. "Oper und musikalisches Drama: Franz Liszts Tannhäuser-Abhandlung." *Neue Zeitschrift für Musik* 145/11 (1984), pp. 4-7.
     Summarizes the events surrounding Liszt's early performances of Wagner's opera in Weimar. Illustrated with a photograph of the Weimar Hoftheater, a facsimile reproduction of a poster proclaiming Wagner a criminal (for his participation in the Dresden revolution of 1849), etc. No musical examples.

561.   Haraszti, Emile. "Deux agents secrets de deux causes ennemies: Wagner et Liszt." *Revue d'histoire diplomatique* 66 (1952), pp. 223-244.

Similar in contents to item 562 (below), which is much easier to obtain. See also item 552.

562.   Haraszti, Emile, and Bertita Paillard. "Franz Liszt and Richard Wagner in the Franco-Prussian War of 1870," trans. Willis Wager. *Musical Quarterly* 35 (1949), pp. 386-411.

Contends that during the 1850s and 1860s Liszt "was a source of information to the French government," although none of his purported diplomatic reports appears to have survived (386-398). Haraszti argues from such evidence as Liszt's friendship with French ministers at the Weimar court, and his attitudes toward French and Prussian royalty and political leaders. The rest of the article deals with Wagner.

Liszt and Other Contemporaries

Dozens of studies have been devoted to Liszt's relationships with other individuals, including Beethoven, Chopin, Longfellow, and Pope Pius IX. Twenty-four of those studies are described below in alphabetical order (by author and/or title):

563.   Bellas, Jacqueline. "Janin et Liszt, ou le critique et l'amitié." *Jules Janin et son temps: Un moment du Romantisme*, with a preface by Pierre-Georges Castex. Paris: PUF [Publications de l'Université de Rouen], 1974; pp. 61-84.

Describes Liszt's rather amiable relationship with Jules Janin, an important nineteenth-century French music critic. Bellas quotes extensively from Janin's articles in the *Journal des débats* and other of his publications as well as the published Liszt correspondence.

564.   Bellas, Jacqueline. "La tumultueuse amitié de Franz Liszt et de Maurice Schlesinger. Autour d'une correspondance inédite." *Littératures* [Annales de la Faculté des Lettres et Sciences humaines de Toulouse, Nouv. sér. t. 1.] 12 (1965), pp. 7-20.

Discusses Liszt's relationship during the 1830s and early 1840s with Maurice Schlesinger, editor and publisher of the *Revue et gazette musicale de Paris*. Includes the complete texts of nine letters addressed by Liszt to Schlesinger between 1827-1841 as well as quotations from the "Bachelor" essays originally published in the *Revue et gazette* (and attributed by many scholars to the Comtesse d'Agoult).

565.   Bellas, Jacqueline. "Liszt et la fille de Madame D. . . . Documents inédits." *Littératures* [Annales de la Faculté des Lettres, Université de Toulouse-Le Mirail] 2 (1980), pp. 133-140.

Describes Liszt's short-lived relationship with Euphémie Didier, a pupil of his during the early 1830s. Includes the complete text of a letter addressed to Liszt by Mlle Didier on 12 February 1831 as well as letters (or quotations from letters) addressed by Mlle Didier to Liszt at about the same time.

566.   Chantavoine, Jean. "Franz Liszt et Heinrich Heine." *Courrier musical* [Paris] 14 (1911), pp. 386-393.

A useful introduction to Liszt's relationship with Heine and to the Heine texts Liszt chose to set as songs. Illustrated with several quotations from Heine's verse, part of Kriehuber's famous painting *Une matinée chez Liszt*, and a facsimile of a letter Liszt wrote in Rome on 27 July 1869.

567.   Deaville, James [A.]. "Franz Brendel — ein Neudeutscher aus der Sicht von Wagner und Liszt." *Liszt-Studien* 3 (1986), pp. 36-47.

Describes Brendel's relationships with Liszt and Wagner and the roles he played during the 1850s as editor of the *Neue Zeitschrift für Musik* and an influential champion of the "New German School" of composition. Deaville cites a variety of source materials, including Wagner's prose works and a number of Liszt letters.

568.   Gájdoš, Vševlad [Jozef]. "Franz Liszt und Stanislaus Albach." *Burgenlänische Heimatblätter* 33 (1971), pp. 156-168.

Discusses Liszt's visits to Eisenstadt in 1840, 1846, and 1848, with special reference to Albach's diary descriptions of these visits. Also includes two Liszt letters and the dedication inscription of Liszt's *Missa quattor vocum*.

569.   Gut, Serge. "Frédéric Chopin et Franz Liszt: une amitié à sens unique." *Sur les traces de Frédéric Chopin*, ed. Daniel Pistone. Paris: Champion-Slatkine, 1984; pp. 53-68.

ML410.C54S87   ISBN 2-8520-3133-7

Not seen. Cited in the bibliography for item 18 and in other secondary sources.

570.   Hamburger, Klára. "Franz Liszt, Carl Alexander grand-duc de Weimar et Michelangelo Caetani duc de Sermoneta." *Studia musicologica* 25 (1983), pp. 145-158.

Deals with letters exchanged during the 1860s by Grand-Duke Carl Alexander of Weimar and Duke Michelangelo Caetani, especially in light of Liszt's activities in Rome during that time. Illustrated with four pages of facsimile reproductions.

What might be called "early installments" of this article appeared under the titles "Franz Liszt et Michelangelo Caetani, duc de Sermoneta" in *Studia musicologica* 21 (1979), pp. 239-265; "Liszt Ferenc ès Michelangelo Caetani, Sermoneta hercege" in *Magyar zene* 20 (1979), pp. 173-197; and "Liszt Ferenc, Carl Alexander weimari nagyherceg és Michelangelo Caetani, Sermoneta hercege" in *Magyar zene* 24 (1983), pp. 291-304. The *Studia musicologica* article contains documentary facsimiles as well as the complete texts of two Liszt letters dating from 1872 and 1878.

571.   Hamburger, Klára. "Liszt and Émile Ollivier." *Studia musicologica* 28 (1986), pp. 65-77.

Describes Liszt's relationship with his son-in-law Émile Ollivier, husband to his daughter Blandine and a important figure in nineteenth-century French culture. Concludes with the texts of six previously unpublished letters addressed by Liszt to Démosthène and Ollivier between 1858-1866. No illustrations.

Also published in Hungarian under the title "Liszt és Émile Ollivier" in *Magyar zene* 28 (1987), pp. 75-87. Illustrated in this version with eight pages of letter texts and translations into Hungarian.

572.   Hintzenstern, Michael von. "Der Kreis evangelischer Kirchenmusiker um Franz Liszt." *Musik und Kirche* 56 (1986), pp. 120-125.

Treats of Liszt's relationships with such figures as Johann Gottlob Töpfer, Alexander Wilhelm Gottschalg, Christoph Bernhard Sulze, and Karl Müller-Hartung. (With regard to Gottschalg, see also item 573 below.)

A similar article by Hintzenstern appeared under the title "Franz Liszt und der Weimarer Organistenkreis — die Geschichte einer langjährigen Zusammenarbeit," in *Musik und Gottesdienst* 20 (1986), pp. 197-203. A second article appeared under the almost identical title "Franz Liszt und die Weimarer Organistenkreis" in item 37; pp. 140-152.

573.   Hintzenstern, Michael von. "Franz Liszt und sein 'legendarischer Kantor.' Zur Zusammenarbeit mit A. W. Gottschalg." *Musik und Kirche* 56 (1986), pp. 115-120.

A useful outline of Liszt's relationship with Gottschalg, the organist-editor-friend to whom Liszt dedicated such works as the *Évocation à la Chapelle Sixtine* and the variations on Bach's "Weinen, Klagen, Sorgen, Zagen." Quotations from contemporary periodicals and the published Liszt correspondence.

574.   Jung, Hans Rudolf. "Der Liszt-Schüler Bernhard Stavenhagen (1862 bis 1914) und seine Beziehungen zu Weimar." In item 32; pp. 13-23.

Touches on Liszt's relationship with Stavenhagen, one of the most important virtuoso pianists of the early twentieth century.

Additional information about Liszt pupils may be found in many of the items described in Chapter XX; Stavenhagen, for example, is discussed in item 1051.

575.   Keeling, Geraldine. "Liszt and J. B. Streicher, a Viennese Piano Maker." *Studia musicologica* 28 (1986), pp. 35-46.

Describes Liszt's professional relationship with Streicher and his pianos, a relationship that lasted from the late 1830s to the early 1860s. Illustrated with portraits of Streicher and his wife, and with photographs of two Streicher pianos owned today by the Hungarian National Museum.

576.   Keiler, Allan. "Liszt and Beethoven: The Creation of a Personal Myth." *19th Century Music* 12/2 (Fall 1988), pp. 116-131.

Examines surviving information about Liszt's early musical training, preferences, and performances, based on archival documents as well as on some of the earliest surviving Liszt biographies (e.g., items 366-367 and 369). Much of this essay (and of item 130) is devoted to the "Weihekuss" story; Keiler considers the story part of "a complicated personal myth" constructed by Liszt by the 1840s. See also item 1a, pp. 81-85; and item 131.

577.   Marix [or Marix-Spire], Thérèse. "Histoire d'une amitié: Fr. Liszt et H. de Balzac." *Revue des études hongroises* 12 (1934), pp. 36-68; and "Appendice," pp. 323-329.

Examines the comparatively brief but complicated history of Liszt's relationships not only with Balzac but with the notorious Madame de Hanska, especially during the early 1840s. NB: Corrections to the first part of the article appear on pp. 328-329 of the "Appendice." See also item 41; entry 231.

578.   McCarthy, Margaret W[illiam]. "Amy Fay's Reunions with Franz Liszt: 1875, 1876, 1885." *Journal of the American Liszt Society* 24 (1988), pp. 23-32.

Describes trips Fay made to visit Liszt in Weimar after her musical reminiscences (item 237) had already become famous. Illustrated with passages from little-known Fay letters and with portraits of Fay and her sister.

579.   Merrick, Paul. "Liszt and Cardinal Hohenlohe." *Liszt Society Journal* 6 (1981), pp. 31-32.
       Describes the man who seems to have "encouraged" Liszt to abandon plans to marry the Princess Sayn-Wittgenstein. (On this topic, see also items 1b, 255, and 547.)

580.   Merrick, Paul. "Liszt and Pope Pius IX, 1846-1878." *Liszt Society Journal* 7 (1982), pp. 39-41.
       A mere sketch of Liszt's relationship with this extraordinarily influential church leader.
       Another, even more cursory article on this topic appeared as: Willi Reich, "Papst Pius IX. bei Franz Liszt" in the *Neue Zeitschrift für Musik* 119 (March 1958), pp. 145-146.

581.   Raabe, Peter. *Grossherzog Carl Alexander und Liszt*. Leipzig: Breitkopf & Härtel, 1918. v, 113pp.
       ML410.L7R131
       A ground-breaking account of Liszt's long, important, but difficult relationship with his principal patron in Weimar. Covers events between the early 1840s and Liszt's death in 1886. Illustrated with portraits, pictures of Weimar "Liszt places," and fold-out facsimiles on blue paper of two letters. (Additional information about Liszt and the Grand Duke appears throughout item 1b.)

582.   Rosenthal, Albi. "Franz Liszt and his Publishers." *Liszt saeculum* 38 (1986), pp. 3-40.
       Evaluates Liszt's relationships with more than a dozen publishers, including Schlesinger, Kistner, Härtel, Senff, and Schuberth. Rosenthal's conclusions are supported by the contents of letters (most of them previously unpublished) owned by Rosenthal himself. A valuable collection of documentary material, presented as a "survey" of this neglected topic. Illustrated with 13 facsimiles of letters and contracts; unfortunately, many of these illustrations are so poor as to be unreadable.
       Liszt's relationship with Ricordi, the Milan music publisher, has recently been reevaluated by András Kürthy in "L'histoire du rapport de Liszt et de la Casa Ricordi refletée par leur correspondance," *Studia musicologica* 29 (1987), pp. 325-342. Illustrated with three facsimile pages of Liszt letters.

583.   Saffle, Michael. "Adalbert von Goldschmidt: A Forgotten Lisztophile." *Journal of the American Liszt Society* 21 (1987), pp. 31-41.
       Describes Liszt's relationship with Goldschmidt and his piano transcription of passages from the Viennese composer's oratorio *Die sieben*

Todsünden. Illustrated with several musical examples as well as a facsimile reproduction of the original sheet-music cover for Liszt's arrangement.

584.   Scharnagl, August. "Franz Liszt — Franz Witt." *Musica sacra* 106 (1986), pp. 444-447.

The only published study of Liszt's somewhat shaky relationship with nineteenth-century Germany's most important Cecilianist and the founder of both *Musica sacra* and the *Fliegende Blätter für katholische Kirchen-Musik*. Illustrated with quotations from the published Liszt-Witt correspondence and a fragmentary facsimile of a letter Liszt addressed to Witt on 15 July 1874 from the Villa d'Este outside Rome.

NB: The complete text of this last letter appears in German and English translation in item 210.

585.   Silverman, Richard S. ".Longfellow, Liszt, and Sullivan." *Music Review* 36 (1975), pp. 253-260.

Reviews biographical and musical connections between Liszt and his contemporaries Henry Wadsworth Longfellow and Sir Arthur Sullivan, refering briefly to Liszt's *Die Glocken des Strassburger Münsters* and to stylistic similarities between Liszt's and Sullivan's styles. Musical examples. See also item 586 (below).

586.   Waters, Edward N. "Liszt and Longfellow." *Musical Quarterly* 41 (1955), pp. 1-25.

Describes Longfellow's admiration for Liszt's music and his visits to Liszt during the winter of 1868-1869. Waters reprints complete a number of Liszt letters from 1868-1874, and he quotes from a variety of other primary sources—some of which touch on *Die Glocken des Strassburger Münsters*, Liszt's only composition on a Longfellow text. Illustrated with musical examples, two portraits of Liszt, and two facsimiles of Liszt letters.

MISCELLANEOUS BIOGRAPHICAL STUDIES

Two studies deal with rumors that Liszt was descended from Hungarian noblemen:

587.   Mona, Ilona. "Über Franz Liszts Nobilität: Dichtung und Wahrheit." *Fontes artis musicae* 29 (1982), pp. 169-182.

Reviews published statements for and against claims made on Liszt's behalf that their hero was descended directly from Hungarian nobility. Illustrated with facsimile reproductions of several documents, among them an advertisement placed in Viennese newspapers by Liszt's "cousin"

Eduard von Liszt to obtain information about the family's ancestry. In German; abstracts in French and English (p. 182).

Based on the author's *Liszt Ferenc és a reformkor 1839-1840* (Budapest: Editio Musica, 1980). Not seen; a reference to it appears in RILM 16 (1982), p. 321. A reproduction of the coat of arms belonging to the defunct "Liszti" family of Hungary—arms once reputed to be Liszt's own—appears in Karl Semmelweis, "Das Adalwappen Franz Liszts," *Burgenländische Heimatblätter* 31/1 (1969), pp. 43-45.

588.   Walker, Alan. "'Edelwerden ist viel mehr, denn edel sein von Eltern her'," trans. Susanne Klement. In item 88; pp. 11-14.

Deals with much of the material found in item 587 (above). Revised and translated into German from item 1a.

Two studies discuss orders and patents of nobility received by Liszt during his lifetime:

589.   Keeling, Geraldine. "Liszt and the Legion of Honour." *Liszt Society Journal* 10 (1985), p. 29.

Corrects Walker's statement (in item 1a; p. 146) that Liszt was received into the French Legion of Honor only in 1860, instead of 1845. Keeling cites the *Revue et gazette musicale* 12/20 (18 May 1845), p. 159, to prove her point.

590.   Kunnert, Heinrich. "Der Ritterstand Franz Liszts." *Burgenlänische Heimatblätter* 5/2 (1936), pp. 50-51.

Describes the title and rank acquired by Liszt when he became a Knight of the Iron Crown, 3rd class, under the monarchy of Austro-Hungary in 1859. Includes quotations from the *Wiener Zeitung*, where the original announcement of Liszt's award appeared, and from Hungarian newspapers.

Ten studies devoted to miscellaneous biographical topics of various kinds are described below in alphabetical order (by author):

591.   Bellas, Jacqueline. "François Liszt et le "département des livres'." *Studia musicologica* 28 (1986), pp. 89-97.

Deals with Liszt's sojourn in Switzerland during 1835-1836 as well as documents concerning that sojourn (among them a letter Liszt sent his mother in July 1835), the authorship of one of Liszt's earliest articles, and especially Liszt's personal library.

592.   Lakatos, István. "A Kolozsvári Dalkör tiszteletbeli tagjai: Mosonyi, Erkel, Ábrányi, Ruzitska és Liszt." *Magyar zenetörténeti tanulmányok* 3 (1973), pp. 79-84.

Explains that Liszt was offered an honorary membership in the Kolozsvár Singing Circle in 1872, but his reply to the Circle's letter has been lost. In Hungarian; summaries in German and English.

593.   Legány, Dezső. "Liszt's and Erkel's Relations and Students." *Studia musicologica* 18 (1976), pp. 19-50.

Describes Liszt's students and musical activities during his years with the Academy of Music, Budapest. Legány includes a catalog of the repertory performed by Liszt's pupils at the Academy between 1878-1885 and a list of his pupils in Budapest during 1876-1886. (Much of this material also appears in items 481, 483, and especially in item 480.)

A similar article by Legány appeared under the title "Erkel és Liszt Zeneakadémiája (1876-1877)" in *Magyar zenetörténeti tanulmányok* 3 (1973), pp. 103-113. In Hungarian; summaries in English and German. Not seen; described as RILM 10 (1976); entry 2932. Still another article appeared as "Erkel és Liszt Zeneakadémiája (1875-1876)" in *Magyar zenetörténeti tanulmányok* 2 (1969), pp. 247-266. Also in Hungarian; summaries in German, English, and Russian.

594.   Lehrs, K. "Franz Liszt. Ehrendoctor der philosophischen Facultät der Universität zu Königsberg." *Wissenschaftliche Monats-Blätter* [Königsberg] 4 (1876), pp. 175-176.

Explains how Liszt came to be awarded an honorary doctorate in music by Königsberg (instead of Berlin). Behrs also describes the award ceremonies and other details of Liszt's visit to East Prussia in 1842. Material from this essay reappears in item 3 and other Liszt studies.

595.   Merrick, Paul. "Liszt in 1848: A Revolutionary Change of Heart?" *Liszt Society Journal* 4 (1979), pp. 6-8.

Treats briefly of Liszt's involvement (at a distance) with the tragic Hungarian Revolution of 1848.

596.   Möller-Weiser, Dietlind. "Franz Liszt und die Goethe-Stiftung — Chronologie eines Fehlschlages." *Festschrift Arno Forchert zum 60. Geburtstag am 29. Dezember 1985*, ed. Gerhard Allroggen and Detlef Altenburg. Kassel: Bärenreiter, 1986; pp. 252-263.

ML55.F657 1986

Describes Liszt's plans for a "Goethe Foundation" to support artistic endeavors of various kinds. (The holograph draft of Liszt's proposal for this project is described as item 167. Additional information about Liszt's plans for the foundation appears in item 1b; pp. 126-129ff. See also item 462.)

597. O'Shea, John. "Franz Liszt — A Medical History." *Liszt saeculum* 36-37 (1985-1986), pp. 60-62.

Refers to Liszt's youthful seizures as well as to his dental problems, sebaceous cysts (not moles or warts), poor vision in old age, and final, fatal illness in Bayreuth. Not entirely reliable.

598. Riehn, Rainer. "Wider die Verunglimpfung des Andenkens Verstorbener. Liszt soll Antisemit gewesen sein . . ." In item 33; pp. 100-114.

Evaluates and rejects charges that Liszt, like Wagner, was anti-Jewish. (With regard to Liszt, anti-Semitism, and the authorship of his book on Gypsy music [item 165f], see item 1b; esp. pp. 388-390.)

A shorter version of Riehn's article appeared under the title "Tentation antisémite ou calomnie?" in item 36; pp. 230-241.

599. Sietz, Reinhold. "Das Niederrheinische Musikfest 1857 under dem Dirigenten Franz Liszt." *Zeitschrift des Aachener Geschichtsvereins* 69 (1957), pp. 79-110.

Discusses and evaluates Liszt's unfortunate relationship with musicians and critics at the 1857 Aachen Music Festival, based on documents belonging to the Aachener Stadtarchiv.

NB: Richard Pohl left an eyewitness account of Liszt's participation at the Festival. See "Vom Aachener Musikfest, Pfingsten 1857" in item 227; pp. 181-198.

600. Valentin, Erich. "Eine Mozart-Initiative Franz Liszts." *Acta Mozartiana* 33 (1986), pp. 17-19.

Deals with Liszt's interest in Mozart's music, his transcriptions from Mozart's works, and especially a proposal to celebrate the centenary of Mozart's birth by establishing a "Mozart Foundation" similar to those already established on behalf of Bach and Handel. Valentin reproduces the complete text of Liszt's letter to Eduard Liszt of 9 February 1856.

Finally, any figure as important as Liszt is bound to be written about from what politely may be called eccentric points of view. Several such studies devoted to biographical details have appeared in print (among them item 406). Another, somewhat more specialized study is described below:

601.   Harrison, Vernon. "Franz Liszt: An Astrological Study." *Liszt Society Journal* 5 (1980), pp. 2-14.

Uses astrological data and methods to describe Liszt's character and to determine the precise time of his birth. Those skeptical of such investigations will not be slow to notice that Harrison's argument is circular: he uses personality traits to help fix Liszt's time of birth, then writes as if that time had something to do with Liszt's character. Illustrated with arcane charts and diagrams.

XI: MUSICAL SURVEY STUDIES

Surprisingly few survey studies of Liszt's musical output have appeared in print; these studies are described below. Studies of individual compositional techniques and devices (e.g., harmony, form, keyboard figuration, etc.) are described in Chapter XII; studies devoted to stylistic influences and Liszt's position vis-à-vis nineteenth- and twentieth-century music (especially nationalism and twentieth-century practices) are described in Chapter XIII. Studies devoted to individual compositions and genres are described in Chapters XIV-XIX.

Only two volumes claim to introduce their readers to all of Liszt's compositions, paraphrases, and transcriptions:

602.   Searle, Humphrey. *The Music of Liszt*, rev. ed. New York: Dover Books, 1966.

        ML410.L7S395 1966

        The best single-volume survey of Liszt's compositional output available. Searle begins with juvenilia and moves briskly—sometimes a bit too briskly—through an immense body of work. A composer himself, he offers penetrating observations about many Liszt pieces; unfortunately, his observations are supplemented with comparatively few musical examples. Concludes with a chronological outline of Liszt's life and an early version of Searle's *New Grove* catalog (revised as item 47).

  *   Raabe, Peter. *Liszts Schaffen*.

        Describes most of Liszt's works systematically and intelligently but in a cursory manner. Described in greater detail as item 2b.

A third study, superior in many ways to Searle's and Raabe's, deals more directly with Liszt's compositional style than with individual compositions:

603.   Gut, Serge. *Franz Liszt: Les éléments du langage musical.* Paris: Klincksieck, 1975. xvii, 504pp.

        ML410.L7G95

        Identifies and analyzes Liszt's distinctive "musical language." After considering influences on Liszt's musical and literary output, Gut turns to such "grammatical" and "syntactical" topics as melody, harmony, and rhythm. Within these broader categories he also discusses individual "words" and "phrases," including pentatonic and "twelve-tone" melodic structures, "Bel canto" writing, individual intervals as units of harmonic structure and expression, dissonance, modal writing, Hungarian and Gypsy rhythms, etc. Illustrated with 200 musical examples, identified both in the text and in a separate index (pp. 501-504). Includes a useful bibliography and a catalog of Liszt's works (pp. 473-495). A borderline study, dealing as much with compositional practices and influences as with genres and individual pieces; cross-referenced in Chapters XII-XIII.

Revised from Gut's dissertation *Franz Liszt: Les éléments du langage musical* (Dissertation: University of Poitiers, 1972; 508pp.). Summarized in DAI 41 (1981), p. 680C [entry 5/4526c].

Several early twentieth-century monographs about Liszt's musical works deserve attention even today. Among them is:

604.   Hervey, Arthur. *Franz Liszt and his Music*. London: John Lane, 1911. 160pp.
        ML410.L7H33
        A "borderline" study: contains sketches of Liszt's life (pp. 1-21), a chapter entitled "The Musician and the Man" (pp. 22-46), another about Liszt's personality and influence, descriptions of various pieces, catalogs of compositions and literary works, and a bibliography.

        Among older surveys of Liszt's music is August Stradal's *Franz Liszts Werke* (Leipzig: C. F. Kahnt, 1904), a highly condensed survey of Liszt pieces familiar to turn-of-the-century concert audiences. Illustrated with musical examples.

Five other surveys of Liszt's music concentrate on one or more "special topics" (e.g., his sketches and revisions, or the influence of revolutionary and religious ideas on his compositional style and output). These studies are identified below in alphabetical order (by author):

605.   Banowetz, Joseph. *Franz Liszt: An Introduction to the Composer and His Music*. Park Ridge, Illinois: General Words and Music, 1975. x, 61pp.
        MT247.L77   [No ISBN number available]
        Examines Liszt's music through examples—in effect, a collection of keyboard pieces (and arrangements of works originally composed for other media) identified in an introductory essay, then allowed to speak for themselves. Contains *En rêve*, the "Five Hungarian Folksongs," two early versions of "Transcendental Etudes," *Sospiri!*, and so on. No fragmentary musical examples or bibliography.

        Other introductions of this kind to Liszt's music also exist. See, for example, *Liszt* by Sir Alexander C. Mackenzie (London and Edinburgh: T. C. & E. C. Jack, 1913). Mackenzie's book includes an introductory essay (pp. 7-30) and several piano pieces: the *Liebestraum* No. 3, the third *Consolation*, and so on.

606.   Dömling, Wolfgang. *Franz Liszt und seine Zeit*. Laaber: Laaber-Verlag, 1985. 336pp.
      ML410.L7D83 1985   ISBN 3-9215-1886-5
      Devoted to both Liszt's music and to its "background" (i.e., the times, circumstances, and individuals that influenced the creation and form of individual compositions). Dömling's book is thus part biography, part purely "musical" study; yet biographical facts are treated throughout this book more as means than ends, more as keys to Liszt's creativity than to his character or personal life. Includes a chronological table (pp. 9-46) as well as portions of documents dealing with Liszt's character and musical activities and a catalog of compositions. Illustrated with 32 portraits of Liszt and his contemporaries and with numerous musical examples. Reviewed in item 132.

607.   Hansen, Bernard. *Variationen und Varianten in den musikalischen Werken Franz Liszts*. Dissertation: Universität Hamburg, 1959. 187pp.
      [No LC number available]
      A study of Liszt's compositional output and style based on ms. revisions and "alternate" passages as well as differing versions of selected vocal and instrumental compositions. Hansen refers regularly throughout his dissertation to D-WRgs Liszt mss. as well as the Breitkopf & Härtel edition of Liszt's works (item 136) and other publications. Illustrated with a large number of hand-copied musical examples, detailed corrections and additions to Raabe's catalog of Liszt's works (pp. 96-101), an excellent bibliography, and innumerable bibliographic citations in the form of endnotes. A fine study, unfortunately difficult to obtain.

608.   Merrick, Paul. *Revolution and Religion in the Music of Liszt*. London and New York: Cambridge University Press, 1987. xvi, 328pp.
      ML410.L7M4 1987   ISBN 0-521-32627-3.
      Begins by taking Liszt seriously as a man of political and religious ideas, then goes on to demonstrate how those ideas influenced much of his compositional output—not just the masses and oratorios, but the Sonata in b minor, certain symphonic works (including *Les morts*), the shorter choral pieces, etc. Merrick devotes entire chapters to the unfinished "Revolutionary" symphony (reprinted in facsimile in item 2b), Liszt's interest in Palestrina's music (see item 686) and religious symbolism in the Sonata (see items 776-777). Illustrated with 192 handsomely printed musical examples; concludes with a short chronological table of Liszt's Weimar activities (pp. 311-314) and extensive bibliographic citations in the form of endnotes.

Uneven in quality, Merrick's book has won mixed reviews from well-known Lisztians: Alexander Main, for instance, criticized it rather harshly in the *Journal of the American Liszt Society* 22 (1987), pp. 75-78. Also reviewed by Alan Walker in the *Times Literary Supplement* for 10 July 1987; and in item 132.

609.   Saffle, Michael. *Franz Liszt's Compositional Development: A Study of the Principal Published and Unpublished Instrumental Sketches and Revisions.* Dissertation: Stanford University, 1977. ix, 203pp.

ML410.L7S24 1979 [sic]

Summarizes the enormous musical legacy left by Liszt in the form of sketches, drafts, revisions, and "alternate" versions for hundreds of piano pieces, orchestral works, songs, choral works, and so on. Most of this dissertation discusses sketches and revisions for representative instrumental works, but one chapter also discusses song revisions. Musical examples and a bibliography that served as the starting-point for item 40 as well as for the present research guide.

Summarized in DAI 38/9 (March 1978), pp. 5117A-5118A. Reprinted in the *Journal of the American Liszt Society* 4 (1978), pp. 69-70.

Liszt's Revisions and the Development of his Compositional Style [working title], a much more sophisticated examination of representative sketches and revisions for representative Liszt works of virtually every kind, is currently under preparation by the present author, with support from the Fulbright Foundation and the Liszt Ferenc Memorial Museum and Research Centre, Budapest.

XII: STUDIES IN COMPOSITIONAL TECHNIQUES

Liszt's characteristic compositional style, as well as many of his technical procedures and innovations, has been described and evaluated by dozens of experts. Published studies of Liszt's overall style and individual compositional procedures are discussed below. Studies dealing with aesthetic issues, especially issues pertaining to religious and programmatic elements in Liszt's compositional output as a whole, are also described below (at the end of the present chapter). Studies devoted to compositional style and individual compositions are described below in Chapters XIV-XIX.

GENERAL STUDIES

Only two book-length discussions of Liszt's compositional methods (as opposed to his compositions per se *or his "musical language") have appeared in print:*

610.   MacIntosh, Wilson Legare, Jr. *A Study of the Technical and Stylistic Innovations of Franz Liszt as Demonstrated in an Analysis of Selected Etudes.* Dissertation: Columbia University, 1983. v, 277pp.

       [No LC number available]

       An exploration of "[Liszt's] technical and stylistic innovations" through detailed analyses of eight representative keyboard etudes drawn from the "Transcendental" and "Paganini" etudes, the *Trois études de concert* (or "Three Concert Etudes"), and the *Zwei Konzertetüden.* MacIntosh discusses in some detail Liszt's expansion of keyboard sonorities (including certain harmonic practices) as well as keyboard writing and technical aspects of piano-playing. Musical examples.

       Summarized in the *Journal of the American Liszt Society* 16 (1984), p. 187.

611.   Bellak, Richard Charles. *Compositional Technique in the Transcriptions of Franz Liszt.* Dissertation: University of Pennsylvania [Philadelphia], 1976. xxx, 142pp.

       MT145.L51134M

       Examines such techniques as harmony, phrase structure, motivic development, etc., in a variety of transcriptions Liszt prepared from compositions by Beethoven, Mozart, Verdi, and himself. Bellak asserts that "even the most literal transcriptions of Liszt go far beyond the immediate goal of transferring from one medium to another" and that works like the *Réminiscences de Don Juan* are so formidable that they assert their existence as "independent works of art." Illustrated with diagrams and musical examples.

Summarized in DAI 37/4 (October 1976), p. 1860A; reprinted in the *Journal of the American Liszt Society* 2 (1977), pp. 40-41.

General studies of Liszt's musical idiom include:

*   Bárdos, Lajos. *Liszt Ferenc a jövő zenésze.*
         Deals with many aspects of Liszt's thematic and harmonic idiom, especially with regard to twentieth-century musical practices. Described in greater detail as item 745.

*   Gut, Serge. *Franz Liszt: Les éléments du langage musical.*
         A highly detailed description of Liszt's characteristic musical gestures, devices, chord progressions, and so on, illustrated with numerous musical examples. Described in greater detail as item 603.

Another study is devoted exclusively to compositional style in Liszt's keyboard studies:

*   Schütz, Georg. "Form, Satz- und Klaviertechnik in den drei Fassungen der 'Grossen Etüden' von Franz Liszt."
         Described as item 790.

Still another study deals with Liszt's overall musical style in terms of Romantic traditions and devices:

612.   Jiránek, J[aroslav]. "Franz Liszts Beitrag zur Musiksprache der Romantiker." *Studia musicologica* 28 (1986), pp. 137-151.
        Evaluates the stylistic evolution of Liszt's music, based in part on a comparative study of two versions of *Vision* and *Wilde Jagd* ("Transcendental Etudes" Nos. 6 and 8). Jiránek concentrates on stylistic rather than documentary issues, however, and he contents that his discussion "goes beyond the realm of romantic keyboard creativity and deals comprehensively with Liszt's contribution to the language of musical Romanticism." Illustrated with ten musical examples and two tables of differences between early and late versions of the etudes in question.
        A less significant study (devoted only in part to Romanticism and Liszt) appeared as: György Kroó, "Einige Probleme des Romantischen bei Chopin und Liszt," *The Book of the First International Musicological*

Congress Devoted to The Works of Frederic Chopin: Warsaw, 16-22 February 1960, ed. Zofia Lissa (Warsaw: Polish Scientific Publishers, 1963), pp. 319-323. No musical examples.

STUDIES OF INDIVIDUAL COMPOSITIONAL PROCEDURES

Liszt employed virtually every device available to nineteenth-century composers: chromatic harmony, modal figures, motivic and melodic transformation, various kinds of structural patterns and devices, keyboard figurations of many kinds, and so on. Studies devoted to individual compositions are described in Chapters XIV-XIX. Studies devoted to compositional processes per se *are described below, in the order of the processes mentioned above:*

Harmony

Liszt's harmonic vocabulary was enormous, and his use of that vocabulary flexible and imaginative. Three book-length studies of harmony in Liszt's music summarize different phases of his development as an harmonic genius:

613.   Torkewitz, Dieter. *Harmonisches Denken im Frühwerk Franz Liszts.* Freiburger Schriften zur Musikwissenschaft, 10. Munich: Emil Katzbichler, 1978. 127pp.
          ML410.L7T25 1978   ISBN 3-8739-7057-0
          An outstanding analysis of Liszt's compositional innovations dating from 1824-1839, almost all of them for piano. Torkewitz deals with such topics as Reicha's possible influence on Liszt's sense of unconventional harmony, the influence of programmism on harmonic choices, and the probability that Liszt made concessions in his post-1835 keyboard works because of the unfavorable reception his earliest pieces received from the critics. Profusely illustrated with musical examples. Concludes with a lengthy bibliography.

614.   Damschroder, David Allen. *The Structural Foundations of 'The Music of the Future': A Schenkerian Study of Liszt's Weimar Repertoire.* Dissertation: Yale University, 1981. iv, 185pp.
          ML410.L6D189
          Proposes that "linear analytical procedures" similar to those developed by Heinrich Schenker can be used to demonstrate "creditable—and successful —extensions of compositional procedures in ten works written by Liszt during the late 1840s and 1850s, among them the Sonata in b minor, movements of the *Faust* symphony, and several piano pieces. Damschroder also deals briefly with the evolution of "Zukunftsmusik"

("Music of the Future") and with Weimar's importance in nineteenth-century musical history. Numerous musical examples.

Summarized in DAI 42/5 (November 1981), p. 1843A; reprinted in the *Journal of the American Liszt Society* 13 (1983), pp. 190-191.

615.   Lemoine, Bernard C. *Tonal Organization in Selected Late Piano Works of Franz Liszt.* Dissertation: Catholic University of America, 1976. iv, 244pp. ML410.L7L4456

Investigates "elements of tonal organization and structural coherence" in six late Liszt piano works: *Nuages gris, La lugubre gondola* Nos. 1-2, *R.W.—Venezia, Unstern,* and the *Bagatelle sans tonalité.* Includes 11 musical examples and several graphs illustrating chord progressions and overall harmonic patterns.

Summarized in DAI 37/3 (September 1976), p. 1289A. An article derived directly from this dissertation appeared under the same title in *Liszt-Studien* 2 (1981), pp. 123-131.

Sixteen other studies of Liszt's harmonic practices are described or cross-referenced below in alphabetical order (by author and/or title):

616.   Cinnamon, Howard. "Tonal Arpeggiation and Successive Equal Third Relations as Elements of Tonal Evolution in the Music of Franz Liszt." *Music Theory Spectrum* 8 (1986), pp. 1-24.

Deals with the unbalancing effects of augmented triads and other "equal third relations" in several of Liszt's characteristic works. Diagrams and 17 musical examples.

617.   Damschroder, David Allen. "Structural Levels: A Key to Liszt's Chromatic Art." *College Music Symposium* 27 (1987), pp. 46-58.

Argues that "Roman-numeral" analysis of Romantic harmony is doomed to failure and that only a Schenkerian approach to those practices can help critics understand Liszt's "chromatic practice." Illustrated with more than a dozen examples, including isolated chord progressions, Schenkerian diagrams, and excerpts from works like the Sonata in b minor and *Vallée d'Obermann.*

618.   *"Exempli gratia:* When Is an Augmented-sixth Chord not an Augmented-sixth Chord?" *In Theory Only* 1/11-12 (February-March 1976), pp. 76-79.

An unsigned analysis of the chord in measure 1 of Liszt's song *Il m'aimait tant,* explaining that in its several appearances in the song it never functions as a "German" augmented-sixth. Musical examples.

619.   Hitzlberger, Thomas. "Zwischen Tonalität und Rationalität. Anmerkungen zur Sequenz- und Figurationstechnik Liszts." In item 764; pp. 32-59.

Deals almost equally with characteristic motivic or scalar figures in Liszt's music and with the harmonic working-out of those motifs and figures. Illustrated with motivic examples and diagrams as well as with excerpts from the *Faust* symphony, various keyboard etudes, and the *Totentanz* for piano and orchestra.

*   Johnsson, Bengt. "Modernities in Liszt's Works."

A survey of radical stylistic gestures in Liszt's works, especially his later piano pieces and especially in terms of harmony. Described in greater detail as item 752.

620.   Longyear, Rey M., and Kate R. Covington. "Liszt, Mahler, and a Remote Tonal Relationship in Sonata Form." *Studien zur Instrumentalmusik. Lothar Hoffmann-Erbrecht zum 60. Geburtstag*, ed. Anke Bingmann et al. Frankfurter Beiträge zur Musikwissenschaft, 20. Tutzing: Hans Schneider, 1988; pp. 457-468.

ML460.S9 1988   ISBN 3-7952-0526-3

Describes Liszt's use of tonic-minor/mediant-major modulations, possibly "the most remote feasible key-relationship[s] for the construction of a sonata-form exposition in the nineteenth century." Illustrated with musical examples drawn from *Tasso* and the first and third movements of the *Faust* symphony as well as from Mahler's Symphony No. 2. (With regard to the topic of this essay, see item 621 [below] and item 873.)

621.   Longyear, Rey M., and Kate R. Covington. "Tonic Major, Mediant Major: A Variant Tonal Relationship in 19th-century Sonata Form." *Studies in Music* [University of Western Ontario] 10 (1985), pp. 105-139.

Deals with the specified harmonic relationship in *Les préludes* and *Orpheus* (pp. 126-130) as well as in works by Beethoven, Dvořák, Rimsky-Korsakov, and other Romantic composers. Three diagrams and numerous musical examples.

622.   Ott, Leonard [W]. "Closing Passages and Cadences in the Late Piano Music of Liszt." *Journal of the American Liszt Society* 5 (1979), pp. 64-74.

Examines final and non-final cadential patterns in more than a dozen Liszt works, including numbers from the *Weihnachtsbaum* suite, *La lugubre gondola* No. 1, the third "Mephisto Waltz," etc. Includes 25 musical examples.

*   Pisk, Paul. "Elements of Impressionism and Atonality in Liszt's Last Piano Pieces."

Deals primarily with harmonic devices insofar as they anticipate "modern" musical practices. Described in greater detail as item 756.

623.   Revitt, Paul J. "Franz Liszt's Harmonization of Linear Chromaticism." *Journal of the American Liszt Society* 13 (1983), pp. 25-52.

A comparatively detailed discussion of Liszt's harmonizations of chromatic lines, based on the assumption that such harmonizations must be understood as "part of a broader view of nineteenth-century musical style." Beginning with simpler examples, Revitt works his way through passages taken from the *Faust* symphony, portions of the *Album d'un voyageur*, the "Transcendental" and "Paganini" etudes, *Hungaria*, and so on. Includes 32 musical examples, several of them taken from full orchestral scores.

624.   Rummenhöller, Peter. "Die verfremdete Kadenz: Zur Harmonik Franz Liszts." *Zeitschrift für Musiktheorie* 9 (1978), pp. 4-16.

Describes delayed and avoided cadential patterns in such Liszt works as the Concerto in A Major, *Orpheus*, and two of the "Petrarch Sonnets" as well as works by Beethoven. Rummenhöller concludes that altered cadential patterns do more to disturb "cadential events" than do other kinds of chromaticism. Illustrated with 24 musical examples.

625.   Rummenhöller, Peter. "Zur Harmonik in Franz Liszts Liedern." *Musica* 37 (1983), pp. 232-238.

Identifies and discusses "harmonic leitmotives" in several works, among them the songs *Über allen Gipfeln ist Ruh* and *O! quand je dors*. Ten musical examples.

626.   Seidel, Elmar. "Über den Zusammenhang zwischen der sogenannten Teufelsmühle und dem 2. Modus mit begrenzter Transponierbarkeit in Liszts Harmonik." *Liszt-Studien* 2 (1981), pp. 172-206.

Identifies the so-called "Devil's Mill" harmonic progression (built upon a rising or falling chromatic bass-line and consisting entirely of dominent-seventh, diminished-seventh, and second-inversion chords). Seidel describes how Liszt uses related progressions in the "Dante" sonata, *Ce qu'on entend sur la montagne*, and *Ab irato*. Concludes with 26 musical examples, several of them representations of "Devil's Mill" patterns.

627. Sólyom, György. "Alkonszonanciák. Sajátos harmóniai jelenség Liszt kései zenéjében." *Magyar zene* 25 (1984), pp. 161-164.

    A short study of "false consonances," enharmonic chord progressions, and harmonic patterns in several Liszt works. Nine musical examples. In Hungarian.

628. Todd, R. Larry. "The 'Unwelcome Guest' Regaled: Franz Liszt and the Augmented Triad." *19th Century Music* 12/2 (Fall 1988), pp. 93-115.

    Examines Liszt's life-long use of augmented chords. In supporting his argument that "Liszt was the first composer to establish the augmented triad as a truly independent sonority," Todd compares passages from the *Harmonies poétiques et religieuses, Lyon, La lugubre gondola*, etc., with works by Wagner and Schumann and with harmonic progressions from texts by K. F. Weitzmann. Sixteen mostly multipartite musical examples.

629. Zeke, Lajos. "'Successive Polymodality' or Different Juxtaposed Modes Based on the Same Final in Liszt's Works: New Angle on the 'Successive and Simultaneous' Unity of Liszt's Musical Language." *Studia musicologica* 28 (1986), pp. 173-185.

    Describes "harmonic" variation in Liszt's music, especially the Sonata in b minor, through an examination of scales and chords that share common finals. Zeke also discusses tritone figures and the "Gypsy" scale (see item 636). A difficult article to summarize, and one that perhaps has as much to do with scalar patterns as with harmonic language and function. Illustrated with several diagrams and five musical examples.

    An Hungarian-language version of this article appeared as "Szukszcessziv polimodalitás. A hangrendszer kiépítésének egy sajátos módja Liszt műveiben" in *Magyar zene* 27 (1986), pp. 83-101.

Modality and "Exotic" Scales

Most of the unusual scales, melodic patterns, and harmonic progressions in Liszt's compositions can be divided into two categories: those generally familiar to European composers before the middle of the nineteenth century and those of "exotic" or folk origin. Patterns derived from or related to the Church modes of medieval and Renaissance music belong to the first category; they appear in a number of Liszt works. The most detailed description of these patterns appears in:

630. Bárdos, Lajos. "Modale Harmonien in den Werken von Franz Liszt," trans. Imre Ormay. In item 30; pp. 133-167.

    Identifies and describes harmonic progressions in Liszt's music derived from Catholic liturgical music as well as from such modified modes as the so-called "harmonic" major, the Indolydian scale, etc. Copiously illustrated with musical examples, many of them taken from sacred works like

Christus, the "Hungarian Coronation Mass," *St. Elizabeth*, and so on, as well as from works by Josquin, Lasso, and Palestrina.

Originally published under the title "Modális harmóniák Liszt műveiben" in *Zenetudományi tanulmányok* 3 (1955), pp. 55-81. In Hungarian; summaries in German (p. 550) and English (p. 551). Also published under the same title in *Harminc írás* (Budapest 1969).

A much more abbreviated study of the same topic also deserves attention:

631.   Gut, Serge. "Die historische Position der Modalität bei Franz Liszt." *Liszt-Studien* 1 (1977), pp. 97-103.

A brief review of selected modal melodic and harmonic patterns found in such sacred works by Liszt as the 1859 *Te deum*, the "Seven Sacraments," the 1878 *Pater noster*, and so on. Eight musical examples.

Whole-tone melodic and harmonic figures, often associated with composers like Debussy and Ravel, were also familiar to Liszt and appear throughout his compositional corpus. The only study devoted exclusively to these patterns is described below:

632.   Thompson, Harold Adams. *The Evolution of Whole-Tone Sound in Liszt's Original Piano Works.* Dissertation: Louisiana State University, 1974. xv, 316pp.

ML410.L7T5 1974

Combines "analysis with a musicological approach" to explore Liszt's use of whole-tone materials (including "rotating-mediant" constructions, a term borrowed from George Rochberg) in such pieces as the "Dante" sonata, the *Csárdás obstiné, Unstern*, and the *Bagatelle sans tonalité*. Extensively illustrated with musical examples. Concludes with a short bibliography.

Summarized in DAI 36/1 (July 1975), p. 22A.

Five other studies of scalar patterns (especially "exotic" patterns) employed by Liszt are described or cross-referenced below in alphabetical order (by author and/or title):

633.   Bárdos, Lajos. "Die volksmusikalischen Tonleitern bei Liszt," trans. Imre Ormay and Franz Winkler. In item 30; pp. 168-196.

Identifies scalar patterns in Liszt's works derived from traditional music, especially Hungarian folk tunes, and discusses their significance in works like the "Hungarian Rhapsodies," *Christus* and *St. Elizabeth*, the Sonata in b minor, etc. Illustrated with dozens of musical examples, some of them taken from the works of Bartók. Concludes with a table of the 13 principal scales Liszt borrowed from folk music—e.g., the "Hungarian" minor, modified Aeolian, Dorian, and Phrygian scales, the so-called "Kecskeméti" scale, etc.

Originally published under the title "Liszt Ferenc népi hangsorai" in *Harminc írás* (Budapest 1969). In Hungarian. Another article by Bárdos dealing with "exotic" scalar patterns in Liszt's music was published under the title "Liszt Ferenc 'népi' hangsorai" in *Magyar zenetörténeti tamulmányok* 1 (1968), pp. 177-200.

634. Gárdonyi, Zoltán. "Neue Ordnungsprinzipien der Tonhöhen in Liszts Frühwerken." In item 30; pp. 226-273.

Describes the appearance in Liszt's youthful piano pieces of such devices as whole-tone and pentatonic scalar patterns, modulations and chord progressions based on whole-tone patterns, the use of Neapolitan chords and progressions in subdominant passages, etc. Illustrated with 58 musical examples, several of them from works by Chopin and Bartók.

635. Gárdonyi, Zoltán. "Neue Tonleiter- und Sequenztypen in Liszts Frühwerken (Zur Frage der 'Lisztschen Sequenzen')." *Studia musicologica* 11 (1969), pp. 169-199.

Similar in certain respects to item 634 (above). Discusses motivic and scalar materials in youthful Liszt keyboard compositions (including whole-tone passages, the use of the tritone, diminished and augmented thirds, etc.) and their significance in works like the original version of the *Harmonies poétiques et religieuses*, the "Malédiction" concerto, the *Grand galop chromatique*, and so on. Copiously illustrated with musical examples.

Studies by Gárdonyi published in Hungarian have been incorporated into his more recent works—e.g., "Distancia-elvű jelenségek Liszt zenéjében" in *Zenetudományi tanulmányok* 3 (1955), pp. 91-100. Summarized in German and English (p. 551).

* Kovács, Sándor. "Formprinzipien und ungarische Stileigentümlichkeiten in den Spätwerken von Liszt."

Refers throughout to "exotic" (i.e., Hungarian) and whole-tone patterns in Liszt's late piano pieces. Described in greater detail as item 645.

636. Ott, Leonard [W]. "The Gypsy Scale: A Stylistic Detail." *Journal of the American Liszt Society* 2 (1977), pp. 24-31.

Describes and evaluates the role played by the so-called "Gypsy" scale (C/D/E-flat/F-sharp/G/A-flat/B/C) in a large sample of Liszt's compositions, including the fourth "Mephisto Waltz," the *Trauer-Vorspiel und Marsch*, and the *Csárdás macabre*. Several musical examples.

Motivic and Thematic Processes

A competent creator of melodies, Liszt established a reputation for himself as a "transformer" of melodic materials, whether written originally by himself or by other composers. The most fulsome study of melodic transformation in Liszt's music is:

637.   Anderson, John Lyle. *Motivic and Thematic Transformation in Selection Works of Liszt.* Dissertation: Ohio State University, 1977. xiv, 154pp.
MT92.L57A5 1977aM
Examines thematic transformation as a process common to the works of Liszt, Berlioz, and Franck, and explains how that process functions in such Liszt compositions as the Sonata in b minor, the *Faust* symphony, *Les préludes*, and the Piano Concerto No. 2. Through analysis, Anderson attempts to answer "the provocative question: what can be done to a given thematic idea?" in "free form" music of the mid-nineteenth century. He also mentions thematic-transformational processes in works by Bartók and Schönberg. Analytical diagrams and tables, musical examples, and a bibliography.
Summarized in DAI 38/5 (November 1977), p. 2400A; reprinted in the *Journal of the American Liszt Society* 8 (1980), pp. 102-103.

At least four other studies explore Liszt's characteristic use of motivic materials and processes in compositions of various kinds:

638.   Fowler, Andrew. "Franz Liszt's 'Petrarch Sonnets': The Persistent Poetic Problem." *Indiana Theory Review* 7/2 (Winter 1986), pp. 48-68.
Argues that "subsurface motivic relationships reveal a bond" between the final piano-solo version of "Sonnet 47" and the final version for baritone and piano. Illustrated with four musical examples, Petrarch's text in Italian and English, and the complete piano and (final) vocal versions of "Sonnet 47" (pp. 60-68).

639.   Fowler, Andrew. "Multilevel Motivic Projection in Selected Piano Works of Liszt." *Journal of the American Liszt Society* 16 (1984), pp. 20-34.
Describes how the simultaneous projection on several levels of motivic materials provides "structural coherence" in works like the *Funérailles* and *Pensées de mort* from the *Harmonies poétiques et religieuses* as well as the "Dante" sonata. Fowler illustrates his remarks with several diagrams and almost a dozen numbered musical examples.

*   Hitzlberger, Thomas. "Zwischen Tonalität und Rationalität . . ."
Deals to a considerable extent with scalar and motivic figures in Liszt's works. Described in greater detail as item 619.

640.   Viret, Jacques. "L'expressivité mélodique chez Franz Liszt: Etude de
         sémantique musicale." *Liszt-Studien* 2 (1981), pp. 237-244.
         A brief discussion of undulating melodic patterns in *Sposalizio* from the
         Années de pèlerinage and such Liszt songs as the "Petrarch Sonnet" No.
         123, *Freudvoll und leidvoll, Ich möchte hingehn*, and portions of *Christus*
         and the *Faust* symphony. Illustrated with 33 musical examples. (With re-
         gard to *Sposalizio*, see item 807.)

Form and Structure

*Liszt's ingenious—some would say, cavalier—use of existing musical forms and his
facility in building musical structures upon programmatic foundations, have received
comparatively little attention from scholars. Only one book-length study devoted
exclusively to this topic has ever been completed:*

641.   Backus, Joan [Pauline]. *Aspects of Form in the Music of Liszt: The Prin-
         ciple of Developing Ideas.* Dissertation: Victoria University [Toronto,
         Canada], 1985.
         [No LC number available]
         Not seen. According to the DAI abstract identified below, a detailed
         study of the "delicate balance [in Liszt's music] between the expression of
         thematic elements and the requirements of formal order." Drawing on Carl
         Dahlhaus's idea of the "history" of a theme, Backus describes thematic
         transformation (the "principle of developing ideas") in the *Harmonies
         poétiques et religieuses*, the "Dante" sonata, the *Faust* symphony, and so
         on. Illustrated with musical examples. Concludes with a bibliography.
         Summarized in DAI 47/3 (September 1986), pp. 703A-704A. See also
         items 770 and 807.

*Most studies of form in Liszt's music have dealt with traditional structural shapes,
especially large-scale shapes like the sonata-allegro form. Among these studies are
four articles, described below in alphabetical order (by author):*

642.   Angerer, Manfred. "Die Einsamkeit der meditierenden Seele. Zu Liszts
         Konzeption der musikalischen Großform." *Österreichische Musikzeit-
         schrift* 41 (1986), pp. 72-76.
         Evaluates Liszt's innovations in large-scale musical forms, with refer-
         ences to works like the symphonic poems, the Sonata in b minor,
         Christus, etc. Angerer maintains that Liszt rejected classical forms because
         they hindered the unity he sought to achieve between genuine expressive-
         ness and large-scale structure. Illustrated only with a portrait of Liszt; no
         musical examples.

643.   Kaplan, Richard. "Sonata Form in the Orchestral Works of Liszt: The Revolutionary Reconsidered." *19th Century Music* 8 (1984), pp. 142-152.

Attempts to prove that many of Liszt's larger works, including *Orpheus* and the first movement of the *Faust* symphony, can be understood in terms of sonata-allegro form. Illustrated with diagram-analyses of the *Faust* movement as well as seven short musical examples from *Les préludes, Prometheus, Orpheus,* and other symphonic poems.

Corrections to and criticisms of Kaplan's article, written by Rey M. Longyear and Kate Covington, were published in *19th Century Music* 9 (1985), pp. 158-160.

644.   Kovács, Sándor. "Formprinzipien und ungarische Stileigentümlichkeiten in den Spätwerken von Liszt." *Liszt-Studien* 2 (1981), pp. 114-122.

Describes Liszt's structural use of such devices as whole-tone and "Hungarian" scale patterns in *Nuages gris, Unstern,* parts of the "Hungarian Historical Portraits," etc. Nine musical examples.

Derived from Kovács's "Formaproblémák és magyaros stiluselemek Liszt kései zongoraműveiben," which appeared in Hungarian in *Magyar zene* 20 (1979), pp. 157-164.

645.   Kroó, György. "A romantikus szonáta néhány problémája Chopin-nél és Liszt-nél." *Magyar zene* 1/1 (September 1960), pp. 23-30.

Deals with "extensions" of traditional sonata-allegro patterns in the piano concertos and certain character pieces by Chopin and Liszt. No musical examples. In Hungarian.

Other Compositional Procedures

Other stylistic devices employed by Liszt in his compositions include instrumentalized recitatives and other vocal figures, characteristic motifs (some of them described under items 619, 635, 637, and so on), unusual sonorities, keyboard figures of various kinds, self-borrowings, and the use of repetition to reinforce musical structures and expression. Seven studies devoted exclusively to such devices are described below in alphabetical order (by author):

646.   Arnold, Ben. "Recitative in Liszt's Solo Piano Music." *Journal of the American Liszt Society* 24 (1988), pp. 3-22.

Identifies and categorizes dozens of recitative passages—some labelled as such by Liszt, some unlabelled—in pieces ranging from the Sonata in b minor to the late keyboard works. Illustrated with detailed tables and more than a half-dozen musical examples.

647.   Batta, András. "Die 'Glockenspiel-Idee' bei Liszt: Ein Problem der Lisztschen Kompositionstechnik." *Liszt-Studien* 2 (1981), pp. 25-35.
        Describes the appearance of a "Glockenspiel-motive" (e.g., G-sharp/E/C-sharp) and related motives in such works as *Les cloches de Genève*, portions of the "Transcendental Etudes," the *Weihnachtsbaum* piano pieces, etc. Nine musical examples.
        Another version of this article appeared in Hungarian under the title "A 'harangjátékelv' Liszt zenéjében" in *Magyar zene* 20 (1979), pp. 147-156.

648.   Chomiński, Jósef M. "Einige Probleme der Klangtechnik von Liszt." *Studia musicologica* 5 (1963), pp. 37-47.
        Deals with densities, timbres, accented notes and chords, rhythmic patterns, dynamics, and other aspects of sheer sound in Liszt's output as a whole. No musical examples.
        Originally published in Polish as "Głowne problemy techniki dzwiekowej Liszta" in *Muzyka* [Warsaw] 6/4 (1961), pp. 37-46. Translated into German on pp. 102-109 of the same periodical.

649.   Federhofer, Hellmut. "Die Diminution in den Klavierwerken von Chopin und Liszt." *Studia musicologica* 5 (1963), pp. 49-57.
        Devoted to such characteristic Lisztian keyboard figures as octaves, scale-like ornaments, arpeggios of several kinds, etc. Federhofer also comments on the declamatory character of certain Liszt melodies, likening them to operatic tunes. Two musical examples.
        Another,somewhat more general comparison of Chopin's and Liszt's piano writing appeared as: Yakov Mil'shtein, "Fortepiannaya faktura Shopena i Lista," *The Book of The First International Musicological Congress Devoted to The Works of Frederic Chopin: Warsaw, 16-22 February 1960*, ed. Zofia Lissa (Warsaw: Polish Scientific Publishers, 1963), pp. 341-346. No musical examples. In Russian.

650.   Seidel, Wilhelm. "Über Figurationsmotive von Chopin und Liszt." *Report on the International musicological Society Congress, 1972*, ed. Henrik Glahn et al. Copenhagen: Hansen, 1974; pp. 647-651.
        ML36.I67 1972
        Discusses the character of keyboard figuration in the Baroque, Classic, and Romantic periods and the influence of figuration on rhythm and form. Illustrated with musical examples from Chopin's and Liszt's works.

651.   Stricker, Rémy. "Liszt et l'emprunt." *Revue musicale* 405-406-407 (1987), pp. 65-72.

A brief, unsatisfactory introduction to "borrowings" in Liszt's music, including self-borrowings in *Christus*, the *Trauermarsch* for piano solo, and other works. No musical examples.

652.   Torkewitz, Dieter. "Modell, Wiederholung — Sequenz. Über Liszts Technik der Intensivierung, mit einer Anmerkung zu Wagner." *Liszt-Studien* 3 (1986), pp. 177-188.

Describes Liszt's regular "intensification" of harmonic and melodic materials through repetition and transformation; analyzes systematically the employment of such procedures in the symphonic poem *Hamlet* as well as portions of *Orpheus* and Wagner's *Siegfried*. Contains several diagrams and about a dozen short musical examples.

AESTHETICS AND "COMPOSITIONAL PRINCIPLES"

Liszt's compositional style and procedures can be understood in part through investigations of aesthetic issues associated with motivic and melodic transformation, structural articulation, and "programmism" in some of his most representative works. Studies of aesthetic issues per se *are described below, but many of the studies described in Chapters XIII-XIX deal with similar issues, albeit more peripherally.*

Aesthetics and Personality

Only one study speculates at length about possible relationships between Liszt's character and musical expression:

653.   Takács, Menyhért. *Liszt Ferenc érzelmi világa. Lélektani adalékok a romantikus zene esztétikájához/Die Gefühlswelt Franz Liszts: Eine Studie zur Kunstpsychologie der romantischen Musik.* musicologica Hungarica, 4. Budapest: National Széchényi Library, 1941. 234pp.
    ML410.L7T3

An introduction to Romantic music in general and Liszt's music in particular by way of "feelings," the roles they played in Liszt's life and character (including his religious faith), and the emotional character of certain Liszt compositions. Contains no musical examples but concludes with a bibliography. Bilingual: in Hungarian (pp. 1-206) and German (pp. 207ff.).

Religious Issues

The role played by Liszt's religious beliefs and attitudes in both sacred and secular compositions has been examined by at least four specialists:

654.   Gifford, David E. *Religious Elements Implicit and Explicit in the Solo Piano Works of Franz Liszt.* Dissertation: University of Missouri at Kansas City, 1984. viii, 75pp.

        ML410.L7G44 1985

        Discusses attitudes that may have influenced Liszt's choices of keys, melodic materials, and final Plagal cadences in piano pieces with "religious" titles. Gifford concludes that at least some of Liszt's piano pieces have "musical characteristics which set them apart from other piano compositions," characteristics that justify "referring to these particular works as religious." Musical examples and a short bibliography.

        Summarized in DAI 45/9 (March 1985), p. 2687A; reprinted in the *Journal of the American Liszt Society* 19 (1986), p. 182.

655.   Heinemann, Ernst Günter. *Franz Liszts Auseinandersetzung mit der geistlichen Musik: Zum Konflikt zwischen Kunst und Engagement.* Musikwissenschaftliche Schriften, 12. Munich and Salzburg: Emil Katzbichler, 1978. 160pp. [+ 45pp. of musical examples].

        ML410.L7H34   ISBN 3-87397-111-9

        A sophisticated, albeit somewhat disappointing discussion of "conflicting" stylistic elements in Liszt's music, especially his more important religious works—e.g., *Christus,* the *Missa choralis, Via crucis,* etc. Heinemann contends that much of Liszt's sacred music reflects compromises between its composer's imagination, performance-practice stipulations, and liturgical requirements. Short examples appear throughout the book itself, and 34 longer examples appear as an appendix (pp. 116-160). Contains an excellent bibliography and some intriguing arguments. (Many of Heinemann's arguments also appear in item 659.)

656.   Knotik, Cornelia. *Musik und Religion im Zeitalter des Historismus: Franz Liszts Wende zum Oratorienschaffen als aesthetisches Problem.* Wissenschaftliche Arbeiten aus dem Burgenland, 64. Eisenstadt: Burgenländisches Landesmuseum, 1982. 98pp.

        ISBN 3-85405-077-1   [No LC number available]

        A study of several interrelated musical and aesthetic topics, including programmism in works like the *Hunnenschlacht* and *Ce qu'on entend sur la montagne,* the influence of Beethoven on Liszt's musical development, etc. Central to Knotik's arguments is a lengthy discussion (pp. 38-80) of *Christus,* relationships between that work, Liszt's Catholicism and compositional orientation, and nineteenth-century attitudes toward religious art, the theology of "Christ" oratorios, and so on. Interspersed with musical examples of various kinds and several pictures, among them the illustration on which the *Hunnenschlacht* was based. Contains a number of portraits, pictures of Liszt "monuments" in the Austrian Burgenland, and other illustrations; also contains a useful bibliography.

657.   Niemöller, Klaus W[olfgang]. "Zur religiösen Tonsprache im Instrumentalschaffen von Franz Liszt." *Religiöse Musik in nicht-liturgischen Werken von Beethoven bis Reger*, ed. Walter Wiora et al. Studien zur Musikgeschichte des 19. Jahrhunderts, 51. Regensburg: Gustav Bosse, 1978; pp. 119-142.
         ML2900.R44   ISBN 3-76492-135-8
         Discusses the role of religious elements in Liszt's musical output as a whole, especially his instrumental works. Niemöller reaffirms the influence of Lamennais, Lamartine, and other figures on Liszt's religious thinking; he also deals with Liszt's early literary works and religious aspects of the late piano pieces. No musical examples.

Taste

Questions associated with Liszt's musical taste and output have been discussed in two uneven but intriguing articles:

658.   Benary, Peter. "Geschmack und Stil bei Franz Liszt." *Liszt Studien* 1 (1977), pp. 37-45.
         A multi-faceted essay that deals, in turn, with Liszt's character, the position of the virtuoso vis-à-vis musical life in general and nineteenth-century European musical life in particular, Carolyne Sayn-Wittgenstein's opinions of Liszt's works, and the expressive nature of the symphonic poems. No musical examples.

659.   Heinemann, Ernst Günter. "Kunstbegriff und Engagement bei Liszt." *Liszt Studien* 1 (1977), pp. 105-114.
         A sketch of Liszt's musical career; at the same time, a speculative essay dealing with Liszt's purported attempt to combine elements of high art and "kitsch" in his compositions, among them many of his best-known religious works. No musical examples. See also item 655.

Programmism and Semiotics

Many studies of Liszt's music and aesthetics have dealt with programmism and the related field of musical semiotics. Studies of programs for individual Liszt works are scattered throughout Chapters XIV-XIX, especially Chapter XVI. Nine studies de-

voted to programmism per se *are described below in alphabetical order (by author and/or title):*

660.   Ackermann, Peter. "Absolute Musik und Programmusik: Zur Theorie der Instrumentalmusik bei Liszt und Wagner." *Liszt Studien* 3 (1986), pp. 21-27.

    Concerned to a considerable extent with Wagner's theories and theoretical treatises, but Ackermann also touches on Liszt's ideas about musical programmism and the ability of instrumental works (e.g., the *Tannhäuser* overture) to "tell a story." Numerous citations from the Liszt/Wagner literature but no musical examples.

661.   Altenburg, Detlef. "Eine Theorie der Musik der Zukunft. Zur Funktion des Programms im symphonischen Werk von Franz Liszt." *Liszt Studien* 1 (1977), pp. 9-25.

    A short but systematic summary of Liszt's attitudes toward program-music and the "Music of the Future," accompanied by detailed bibliographic citations in the form of endnotes. No musical examples.

662.   Bongrain, Anne. "La figuration musicale dans les poèmes symphoniques de Liszt." *Revue musicale* 405-406-407 (1987), pp. 57-64.

    A quasi-semantic discussion of issues relating to programmism in Liszt's music and to melodic materials in various of the Symphonic Poems. No musical examples.

    Some of Bongrain's material may have been derived from her thesis *Eine Faust-Symphonie* (University of Paris-Sorbonne 1976). Not seen but cited in item 18.

663.   Felix, Werner. "Liszts Schaffen um 1848. Versuch zur Deutung seiner Programmusik." *Studia musicologica* 5 (1963), pp. 59-67.

    Reviews the programmatic compositions Liszt completed during his early "Weimar years" (i.e., c. 1848-1854) and speculates upon the influence of Hungary and the Hungarian uprisings on such works as *Hungaria*, the *Arbeiterchor, Héroïde funèbre*, and so on. Illustrated with two short musical examples and an outline of Liszt's early "Weimar" programmatic works (pp. 60-61).

664.   Grabócz, Márta. *Morphologie des oeuvres pour piano de Liszt. Influence du programme sur l'évolution des formes instrumentales.* Budapest: MTA Zenetudományi Intézet, 1986. 216pp.

    ISBN 963-01-7293-3   [No LC number available]

    Similar to items 665-666 (below) but longer, more detailed, and much less well-known. Illustrated with 75 often multipartite musical examples, numerous tables, and other analytical aids. Outfitted with an appendix containing literary quotations that appeared at the beginnings of certain Liszt keyboard pieces; concludes with a bibliography. Except for quotations, in French throughout.

665.   Grabócz, Márta. "Die Wirkung des Programms auf die Entwicklung der instrumentalen Formen in Liszts Klavierwerken." *Studia musicologica* 22 (1980), pp. 299-325.

Treats a number of interrelated topics dealing with programmism, musical form, and keyboard compositions like *Lyon*, "Vallée d'Obermann" from the *Années de pèlerinage*, settings of the "Petrarch Sonnets," etc. Among other points, Grabócz emphasizes Liszt's position as a forerunner of twentieth-century music, the presence of "bridge" structures in his programmatic works, and musical "topoi" like pastoral and "makabreske" figures. Illustrated with numerous musical examples.

A similar article by Grabócz appeared in Hungarian under the title "A programszerűség hatása a hangszeres formák fejlődésére Liszt zongoraműveiben" in *Magyar zene* 21 (1980), pp. 278-300. See also item 666 (below).

666.   Grabócz, Márta. "Renaissance de la forme énumérative, sous l'influence du modèle épique, dans les oeuvres pour piano de Liszt; facteurs de l'analyse structurale et sémantique." *Studia musicologica* 26 (1984), pp. 199-218.

Another examination of Liszt's works from a semiotic viewpoint. No musical examples.

Several articles by Grabócz (including this one) have been supplanted by item 664 (e.g., "Stratégies narratives des 'épopées philosophiques' de l'ère romantique dans l'oeuvre pianistique de F. Liszt," *Studia musicologica* 28 [1986], pp. 99-115).

667.   Kabisch, Thomas. "Außermusikalische Implikationen des musikalischen Materials: Zum Spätwerk Franz Liszts." *Musica* 39 (1985), pp. 549-556.

A discussion of programmatic elements in pieces like *Von der Wiege bis zum Grabe*, the *Réminiscences de Boccanegra*, and some of the late piano pieces. Illustrated with several musical examples and two analytical diagrams.

668.   Slomma, Horst. "Liszts Programmusik im Blick musikästhetischer Reflektionen." In item 37; pp. 89-100.

Reviews influential ideas about Liszt's musical programmism, the "world-wide" impact of those ideas and of the symphonic poem as a genre, and important ideas about programmism presented by Dahlhaus, Hanslick, Busoni, and other commentators. No musical examples.

Yet another study—this one devoted to Liszt, programmism, and musical semiotics—deserves special attention:

669.   Tarasti, Eero. "The Mythical in Liszt and Slavonic Music." *A Semiotic Approach to the Aesthetics of Myth and Music, especially that of Wagner, Sibelius and Stravinsky.* Approaches to Semiotics, 51. The Hague, Paris, and New York: Mouton, 1979; pp. 131-151.
     ML3849.T37   ISBN 9-0279-7918-9
     An insightful analysis of musical and programmatic elements in *Tasso, Les préludes,* and *Die Ideale.* Musical examples.

Issues in Nineteenth-century Music Criticism

Comparatively little has been written about aesthetic principles, nineteenth-century music criticism, and the application (in theory or historical fact) of such principles and within such criticism to Liszt's music. Survey studies incorporating discussions of these issues (especially item 1b; pp. 338-367) are described in Chapter III, while press notices and other forms of nineteenth-century criticism are identified or at least referred to throughout Chapters VIII-X. Three additional studies dealing exclusively with aesthetics and Liszt's critics are described below in alphabetical order (by author):

670.   Altenburg, Detlef. "Vom poetisch Schönen: Franz Liszts Auseinandersetzung mit der Musikästhetik Eduard Hanslicks." *Ars musica, musica scientia: Festschrift Heinrich Hüschen zum fünfundsechzigsten Geburtstag,* ed. Detlef Altenburg. Cologne: Verlag der Arbeitsgemeinschaft für Rheinische Musikgeschichte, 1980; pp. 1-9.
     ML55.H87 1980   3-8858-3002-7
     A complicated discussion of *Vom poetisch Schönen* (Hanslick's book), the "Music of the Future," Liszt's correspondence with Hanslick, Brendel, Schumann, and other figures, and so on—in effect, an essay about the conflict between "New German School" musical figures and anti-programmism as an aesthetic posture. No musical examples.

671.   Nagler, Norbert. "Die verspätete Zukunftsmusik." In item 33; pp. 4-41.
     Deals with the so-called "Zukunftsmusik" movement, Liszt, and other figures associated with that movement. No musical examples.

672.   Suppan, Wolfgang. "Franz Liszt — zwischen Friedrich von Hausegger und Eduard Hanslick: Ausdrucks- contra Formästhetik." *Studia musicologica* 24 (1982), pp. 113-131.

Discusses Wagner, Brahms, and Liszt, with references to Hausegger's *Musik als Ausdruck* (1885) and to Liszt's refusal to write a preface to Hanslick's *Vom musikalisch-Schönen*. No musical examples.

XIII: STUDIES IN STYLISTIC INFLUENCES

Liszt influenced—and was influenced by—more than a dozen important composers as well as by the national and traditional musics of France, Germany, Hungary, Italy, Russia, and so on. Studies of musical influences on Liszt and of Liszt's musical influences on others are described below. Studies of Liszt's personal and professional relationships with other composers, as well as his travels and international activities, are described in Chapter X. Studies devoted primarily to Liszt's compositional style and individual compositional techniques are described in Chapter XII.

INFLUENCES ON LISZT

No large-scale study of Liszt's musical background has appeared in print, but at least one excellent article is devoted to just that topic:

673.　Walker, Alan. "Liszt's Musical Background." In item 31; pp. 36-78.

A useful, compact summary of the most important musical influences on Liszt's compositions and compositional style. Among other figures, Walker discusses Czerny, Paganini, Chopin, and Wagner; he also mentions other piano virtuosos (including Dreyschock and Thalberg) and the evolution of Liszt's keyboard style. Includes a black-and-white reproduction of Barabás's 1847 and Lehmann's 1839 oil portraits of Liszt, a facsimile of a page from a holograph of his Polonaise in c minor, and 38 musical examples from the "Transcendental" and "Paganini" etudes, the Sonata in b minor, late works like *Am Grabe Richard Wagners*, etc.

Classical or "Antique" Influences

"Classical" influences on Liszt's music-making include Bach, Haydn, Mozart, and other pre-Romantic composers as well as such "classical" genres as grand opera. Studies devoted exclusively to links between Liszt and Bach, Beethoven, Mozart, etc., are described later in the present chapter under appropriate sub-headings.

The two studies described immediately below deal with the broader topic of classical music and Liszt's musical style:

674.   Chantavoine, Jean. "Franz Liszt et l'art classique." *Courrier musical* 9 (1906), pp. 193-198 and 231-235.

     Discusses formal and expressive influences exerted by classical composers, especially Beethoven, on Liszt's music. In the second part of this article Chantavoine deals with works like *Les préludes* and the *Faust* symphony to demonstrate that Liszt made use of, but was not pinned down by, classical models. No musical examples.

675.   Felix, Werner. "Franz Liszt a klasika/Franz Liszt und die Klassik." In item 34; pp. 21-38.

     A brief survey of eighteenth-century musical influences on Liszt—among them, Bach and Handel. No musical examples. An "appendix" to this article appeared under the title "Noch einmal: Franz Liszt und die Klassik" in item 37; pp. 64-70.

A third article examines Liszt's use of "antique" musical materials in several of his most experimental compositions:

676.   Ackermann, Peter. "Alte und neue Musik im Spätwerk Franz Liszts." *Alte Musik als ästhetische Gegenwart. Bericht über den international musikwissenschaftlichen Kongreß Stuttgart 1985.* 2 volumes. Kassel: Bärenreiter, 1987; Vol. 2, pp. 251-255.

     ML36.I629 1985   ISBN 3-7618-0767-8

     An intriguing discussion of "old" musical elements (e.g., the appearance of complete Protestant hymn tunes in unusual settings, melodic references—or possible references—to works by Hassler and Bach, use of modal harmonies, etc.) in works like the *Via crucis*. Ackermann argues that quotations from older works did not provide Liszt with "novel" musical material; instead, they suited his last years, his mood of "compositional negation." One short musical example.

Eleven studies dealing with the influence on Liszt of individual "antique" composers or brands of music are described below according to composer or musical genre, then alphabetically (by author and/or title):

A. Bach

677.   Kabisch, Thomas. "Zur Bach-Rezeption Franz Liszts." *Alte Musik als ästhetische Gegenwart. Bericht über den international musikwissenschaftlichen Kongreß Stuttgart 1985.* 2 volumes. Kassel: Bärenreiter, 1987; Vol. 1, pp. 477-484.

     ML36.I629 1985   ISBN 3-7618-0767-8

     Identifies and discussions Bach quotations or paraphrases in such Liszt works as the "Weinen, Klagen" variations and Liszt's transcription of

Bach's Prelude and Fugue in g minor, BWV 542. Five musical examples, four of them in an appendix.

B. Beethoven

678.   Loos, Helmut. "Die Beethoven-Nachfolge Franz Liszts." *Beethoven und die Nachwelt: Materialien zur Wirkungsgeschichte Beethovens*, ed. Helmut Loos. Bonn: Beethoven-Haus, 1986; pp. 41-64.
ML410.B41B4153 1986   [No ISBN number available]
A valuable introduction to Beethoven's influence on Liszt's life and music. Loos dodges the question of Beethoven's presence at Liszt's 13 April 1823 concert, but he does discuss the Beethoven works Liszt played during his virtuoso tours of 1838-1847 and Liszt's transcriptions of the Beethoven symphonies. Illustrated with several portraits as well as two facsimiles from Liszt's piano transcriptions of Beethoven's symphonies Nos. 3 and 9.

679.   Stockhammer, Robert. "Die Bedeutung Beethovens im Leben Franz Liszts." *Musica* 15 (1961), pp. 529-534.
Discusses Beethoven's influence on Liszt's activities and music. Stockhammer quotes from a variety of sources, including the famous *Konversationshefte*. Illustrated with two portraits of Beethoven. No musical examples.

680.   Tari, Lujza. "Eine instrumentale ungarische Volksmelodie und ihre Beziehungen zu Liszt und Beethoven." *Studia musicologica* 25 (1983), pp. 61-71.
Identifies a traditional Gypsy figure and discusses its appearance in Liszt's Hungarian Rhapsody No. 14 and the slow movement of Beethoven's Quartet, Op. 59, No. 2. Tari claims that Liszt probably "collected" the melodic figure in question during his 1840s concert tours. About a dozen musical examples.

681.   Wolff, Konrad. "Beethovenian Dissonances in Liszt's Piano Works." *Journal of the American Liszt Society* 1 (1977), pp. 4-8.
Contends that Liszt's concept of dissonance was influenced by Beethoven, who rammed dissonances "down the listener's ear drums" [sic]. Discusses three dissonant chords and chord progressions taken from the second *Valse oubliée*, the *Csárdás obstiné*, and Liszt's cadenza for Beethoven's C-minor Concerto. Several musical examples.

C. Gregorian Chant

682.   Sambeth, Heinrich. "Die Gregorianische Melodien in den Werken Franz Liszts, mit besonderer Berücksichtigung seiner kirchenmusikalischen Reformpläne." *Musica sacra* 55 (1925), pp. 255-265.

    A discussion of Liszt's Catholic faith, his lifelong interest in the reform of liturgical music, the appearance of Gregorian melodies in works like the *Missa choralis*, etc. No musical examples. Derived from item 683 (below). NB: The title of Sambeth's article appears in several forms throughout the Liszt literature.

683.   Sambeth, Heinrich. *Franz Liszt und die Gregorianische Melodien und ihre Bedeutung für die Entwicklung seiner Religiosität und Kunstanschauung.* Dissertation: University of Münster, 1923.

    Typescript. The Musikwissenschaftliches Seminar, University of Heidelberg, owns a copy: shelf number D1855d.

    An extensive study of Liszt's attitudes toward Catholic music, especially Gregorian chant, and his use of Gregorian melodies in works like the *Missa choralis*. Typescript copy, with numerous hand-copied musical examples.

D. Handel

684.   Rackwitz, Werner. "Liszts Verhältnis zur Musik Georg Friedrich Händels." *Studia musicologica* 5 (1963), pp. 267-275.

    Deals with such topics as Liszt's occasional performances during the 1840s of Handel keyboard works, his interest in some of Handel's oratorios—among them, *Judas Maccabeus*—and his arrangement of the Sarabande and Chaconne in 1873 from *Almira*. No musical examples.

E. Mozart

685.   Sittner, Hans. "Liszt und Mozart." *Österreichische Musikzeitschrift* 27 (1972), pp. 405-411.

    A brief survey of Liszt's attitudes toward Mozart's music and his use of Mozartian themes in operatic paraphrases. No musical examples.

    Other studies of Mozart's impact upon Liszt's music include James Paraklias, "Nineteenth-century Musical Tributes to Mozart" in *Studies in Music* [University of Western Ontario] 8 (1983), esp. pp. 54ff.

F. Palestrina

686.   Seidel, Elmar. "Ueber die Wirkung der Musik Palestrinas auf das Werk
        Liszts und Wagners." *Liszt-Studien* 3 (1986), pp. 162-176.
        Describes Liszt's contact with and fondness for Palestrina's *Stabat
        mater* and *Magnificat octo tonum*, and the influence of those and other
        works on portions of the *Missa choralis* and Wagner's *Parsifal*. Concludes
        with 12 hand-copied musical examples.

G. Protestant Church Music

687.   Sulyok, Imre. "Evangelisch-Lutherische Beziehung in den Werken von
        Franz Liszt." *Musik und Kirche* 56 (1986), pp. 125-128.
        A compact survey of Lutheran elements in Liszt's music, especially
        hymn tunes and music associated with Protestant texts. Among other
        compositions Sulyok refers to Liszt's organ transcription of *Ein fester Burg
        ist unser Gott*, his setting of *Der 137. Psalm*, and his use of the famous
        "BACH" motif in several non-liturgical works. No musical examples.

Nineteenth-century Influences

*Liszt was influenced by several composers and musical movements contemporary
with him. Certain studies of his relationship with the "Music of the Future" and other
nineteenth-century compositional currents are described below; others are described
in appropriate portions of Chapters X and XII as well as in item 1b; pp. 338-367.*

*No general study of direct musical influences on Liszt has ever been published.
Instead scholars have discussed the influences of individual nineteenth-century composers, especially Wagner. Biographical studies of other composers and Liszt are
described in Chapter X. Eighteen musical studies are described or cross-referenced
below according to composer, then—in most cases—alphabetically (by author):*

A. Berlioz

*No study devoted exclusively to Berlioz's influence on Liszt (or, for that matter, to
Liszt's influence on Berlioz) has ever appeared in print. One study, however, deserves
to be cross-referenced here:*

*   Haraszti, Emile. "Berlioz, Liszt, and the Rákóczy March."
        In part a compendium of the settings both composers made of
        Hungary's "national" tune. Described in greater detail as item 554. See also
        item 700.

B. Chopin

688.   Badura-Skoda, Paul. "Chopin und Liszt." *Österreichische Musikzeitschrift* 17 (1962), pp. 60-64.

Deals with several topics: Liszt's biography of Chopin, his use of mazurka rhythms in several piano pieces, his fondness for Chopin's music, and so on. No musical examples.

689.   Handman, Dorel. "Chopin's Influence on Two Liszt Etudes." *Musical America* 69/3 (February 1949), pp. 28, 164.

Compares Chopin's Op. 10, No. 9 and Op. 25, No. 2 etudes with Liszt's "Transcendentals" Nos. 2 and 10. Illustrated with 17 short musical examples.

690.   Pattison, F. L. M. "A Folk Tune Associated with Chopin and Liszt." *Journal of the American Liszt Society* 20 (1986), pp. 38-41.

Identifies a tune incorporated by Chopin in a recently-discovered *Allegretto* for piano and in Liszt's "Duo" sonata for piano and violin. Illustrated with a facsimile reproduction of the Chopin *Allegretto* ms.

C. Czerny

691.   Gardavský, Č. "Liszt und seine tschechischen Lehrer." *Studia musicologica* 5 (1963), pp. 69-76.

A study of Czerny's influence on Liszt, especially in terms of keyboard technique, phrasing, and concert repertory. Gardavský also touches on Liszt's relationship with Reicha and his harmonic innovations. No musical examples.

Czerny and Liszt may have influenced each other in their "Romantic" styles of keyboard composition. Studies this topic include Randall Sweets, "Carl Czerny Reconsidered: Romantic Elements in his Sonata, Op. 7," *Journal of the American Liszt Society* 16 (1984), pp. 54-71.

*   Wehmeyer, Grete. "Carl Czerny."

Deals primarily with the Liszt-Czerny relationship and related biographical issues. Described in greater detail as item 414.

D. Gounod

692.   Sobe, Gotthold. "Liszt und Gounod." In item 32; pp. 24-28.
       Describes Liszt's relationship with Gounod during the middle years of the nineteenth century. Includes the text of a letter Liszt addressed to Gounod on 24 January 1861. No musical examples.

E. Meyerbeer

693.   Kantner, Leopold. "Meyerbeersche Spuren in Werken Franz Liszts." *Liszt-Studien* 2 (1981), pp. 90-96.
       Evaluates Liszt's knowledge of Meyerbeer's works as well as similarities between certain Liszt and Meyerbeer compositions—among them willingness to use musical materials that originated in countries other than their own, "bombastic" expressive devices, a fondness for Italianate melody, and so on. Two musical examples, drawn from *Tasso* and Meyerbeer's *Le prophète*.

F. Paganini

694.   Batta, András. "Paganini és Liszt." *Liszt kiskönyvtár* 1 (1982), pp. 7-14.
       A brief survey of this interesting, often ignored topic. In Hungarian.

G. Rossini

695.   Risaliti, Riccardo. "Liszt & Rossini." *Liszt Society Journal* 4 (1979), pp. 16-19.
       A brief survey of Liszt's interest in Rossini's music and his transcriptions from and paraphrases on such works as the *Soirées musicales*, the operas *Ermione* and *Armida*, etc. Illustrated with a single musical example from the opening of Liszt's *Impromptu brillant sur des thèmes de Rossini et Spontini*.
       Translated by Adrian Williams from Risaliti's Italian-language article "Rossini e Liszt," which appeared originally in the *Bollettino del centro Rossiniano di studi* No. 3 (1972), pp. 40-46.

H. Schubert

696.   Kabisch, Thomas. *Liszt und Schubert*. Berliner musikwissenschaftliche Arbeiten, 23. Munich and Salzburg: Emil Katzbichler, 1984. 153pp.
       ML390.K12 1984   ISBN 3-87397-063-5
       An insightful discussion of Schubert's music and its influence on Liszt's performing career and compositional development. Kabisch evalu-

ates the musical style of both composers in terms of variation-writing, rhythmic figures, harmony, part-writing, motivic and structural preferences, form, etc., before analyzing in some detail works like Schubert's A-minor Sonata (Op. post.) and Liszt's *Totentanz*. Kabisch also discusses Liszt's Schubert transcriptions and eyewitness accounts of Liszt's Schubert performances. Illustrated with numerous musical examples as well as with quotations from letters, press clippings, and other documents. Concludes with an unusually useful bibliography.

A very short discussion of some of these issues appeared in Dutch as: Luc van Hassalt, "Liszt en Schubert," *Piano Bulletin* 4/1 (1986), pp. 42-44. Illustrated with two musical examples.

I. Wagner

The musical relationship shared by Liszt and Wagner during much of their lives was almost as complex as it was important. Two of the best introductions to this relationship are:

697.   Bergfeld, Joachim. "Richard Wagner und Franz Liszt." In item 35; pp. 43-62.

An outline of Liszt's complex, occasionally unfortunate relationship with Wagner and the musical interrelationships of these two composers. Bergfeld discusses in some detail such topics as Wagner's debt to Liszt, Liszt's activities on behalf of Wagner's compositions and career, etc. Illustrated with nine musical examples.

698.   Winkler, Gerhard J. "Liszt und Wagner. Notizen zu einer problematischen Beziehung." *Österreichische Musikzeitschrift* 41 (1986), pp. 83-89.

Reviews certain problems associated with Liszt's artistic influence on Wagner (and vice versa), including similarities between portions of Wagner's music-dramas and pieces by Liszt like *Unstern, Am Grabe Richard Wagners*, and *Excelsior!* (With regard to this last composition, see items 701-702.) Illustrated with several short musical examples and a reproduction of Wilhelm Backmann's painting of Wagner "at home" at Wahnfried with Liszt, Cosima, and Hans von Wolzogen.

Five somewhat more specialized discussions of Liszt's and Wagner's symbiotic musical relationship are described below in alphabetical order (by author and/or title):

699.   Eősze, László. "Liszt und Wagner. Neue Aspekte eines Künstlerbundes." *Studia musicologica* 28 (1986), pp. 195-200.

A sketch of Liszt's relationship with Wagner, followed by discussions of "Wagner-respect" as exemplified in *Am Grabe Richard Wagners*. Illustrated with two passages from the latter work.

A similar article by Eősze appeared in Hungarian as "Liszt és Wagner (Egy művészbarátság új megvilágításban)" in *Magyar zene* 28 (1987), pp. 131-140. This last article contains four musical examples, among them passages from *Orpheus*, the *Faust* symphony, and Act II of *Die Walküre*.

700.   Gut, Serge. "Berlioz, Liszt und Wagner: Die französischen Komponisten der Neudeutschen Schule." *Liszt-Studien* 3 (1986), pp. 48-55.

An intelligent attempt to define "New German" music of the 1850s in terms of an admiration for Beethoven's work, attitudes derived from French Romanticism, a fascination with "advanced" harmonic practices, instrumental writing, programmism, and so on. Copious quotations from Wagner's correspondence but no musical examples.

701.   Gut, Serge. "De Liszt à Wagner en passant par 'Parsifal'." *Revue musicale de Suisse Romande* 30 (1977), pp. 152-155.

A study of certain similarities between *Parsifal* and such Liszt works as *Excelsior* and *Am Grabe Richard Wagners*. Brief musical examples.

Shorter studies of the Liszt-Wagner relationship include Gut's own "Faust et Wotan" (in item 36; pp. 162-171); and Renzo Cresti, "Berlioz e Liszt guidano Wagner," *Richerche Musicali* 5 (March 1981), pp. 26-43. This last item not seen but cited in RILM 15 (1981); entry 627.

702.   Marget, Arthur W. "Liszt and 'Parsifal'." *Music Review* 14 (1953), pp. 107-124.

Compares the opening of Liszt's *Excelsior!* with musical moments in *Parsifal*. Marget also refers to programmatic elements in *Am Grabe Richard Wagners*. Also includes the text of a note Liszt sent Longfellow in or around 1874. Two short musical examples.

703.   Schibli, Sigfrid. "Richard Wagner/Franz Liszt: Isolde's Liebestod." *Neue Zeitschrift für Musik* 146/9 (September 1985), pp. 28-30.

Treats of Wagner's "Love-Death" music and Liszt's transcription of it. A quasi-popular article, accompanied by several illustrations.

LISZT'S INFLUENCE ON OTHER COMPOSERS

No single study of Liszt's general influence on other composers has appeared in print. Studies dealing with similarities between Liszt's compositional style and twentieth-century practices are described at the end of the present chapter. Other references to modern aspects of individual works by Liszt, especially those of his last years, are scattered through Chapters XII and XIV-XIX.

Nineteen studies of Liszt's influence on important nineteenth- and early twentieth-century composers are described or cross-referenced below by composer, then alphabetically (by author):

<u>A. Bartók</u>

704.   Falvy, Zoltán. "Franz Liszt e Béla Bartók," trans. Gudrum Stühff-Mazzoni. *Nuova rivista musicale italiana* 3 (1969), pp. 664-671.

Describes parallels in the lives and works of the two composers, as presented in Bartók's writings about Liszt. No musical examples. In Italian.

705.   Kecskeméti, István. "An Early Bartók-Liszt Encounter." *New Hungarian Quarterly* 9/29 (Spring 1968), pp. 206-210.

Discusses Bartók's early musical development, especially between 1905-1908, as well as certain similarities between his Bagatelle, Op. 6, No. 14, and Liszt's *Bagatelle sans tonalité*. No musical examples.

A similar article by Kecskeméti appeared in Hungarian under the title "Egy korai Bartók — Liszt-találkozás mefisztó jegyében" in *Magyar zene* 7/4 (1966), pp. 3-8 [also given as pp. 352-357 in some copies]. Two musical examples.

706.   Somfai, László. "Liszt's Influence on Bartók Reconsidered." *New Hungarian Quarterly* 27/102 (Summer 1986), pp. 210-219.

Summarizes Bartók's lifelong interest in Liszt, beginning in 1896 and culminating in his essays about Liszt and Hungarian music (items 111-112). NB: Somfai challenges Kecskeméti (item 705 above) and the possibility that Liszt's music influenced Bartók's directly; Somfai stresses "indirect" influences. Illustrated with a catalog of Liszt pieces performed in public by Bartók during his career (pp. 214-215) and several musical examples.

A similar Liszt-Bartók article by Somfai appeared in Hungarian under the title "Bartók és a Liszt-hatás. Adatok, időrendi összefüggések, hipotézisek" in *Magyar zene* 27 (1986), pp. 335-351. This article includes the scale-like passages found in Liszt's B-minor Sonata that Bartók used in some of his own pieces but never acknowledged as "Lisztian." A second Liszt-Bartók article appeared in Hungarian in the same issue of *Magyar zene*. See Imre Sulyok, "Bartók Béla kézírása a weimari Liszt-anyagban"; pp. 352-353.

B. Cornelius

707.   Jacob, P. Walter. *Der beschwerliche Weg des Peter Cornelius zu Liszt und Wagner.* Kleine Mainzer Bücherei, 8. Mainz: H. Krach, 1974. 90pp.
PT3807.M32K55   [No ISBN number available]
Contains a chapter (pp. 30-52) devoted to Cornelius's personal and professional relationship with Liszt. Other references to Liszt are scattered through Jacob's work, but no index to them is provided.

708.   Niemöller, Klaus W[olfgang]. "Cornelius und Franz Liszt." *Peter Cornelius als Komponist, Dichter, Kritiker und Essayist,* ed. Kurt Oehl. Studien zur Musikgeschichte des 19. Jahrhunderts, 48. Regensburg: Gustav Bosse, 1977; pp. 81-92.
ML410.C8P48   ISBN 3-7649-2125-0
Describes Liszt's relationship with Cornelius as well as his influence on Cornelius's thinking and musical style. Illustrated with quotations from Cornelius's literary works rather than with musical examples.

C. Debussy

709.   Biget, Michelle. "Étude comparée du geste pianistique chez Liszt et chez Debussy." *Revue musicale* 405-406-407 (1987), pp. 155-163.
Deals with similarities and differences between Liszt's keyboard writing and that of Debussy. Unfortunately illustrated only with excerpts from Liszt's Sonata in b minor, although Biget refers to such Debussy pieces as *Pour le piano, L'Isle joyeuse,* and the *Études.*

710.   Gut, Serge. "Liszt et Debussy: Comparaison stylistique." *Liszt-Studien* 2 (1981), pp. 63-77.
Describes whole-tone patterns, chords composed of fourths and fifths, pentatonic passages, and other "Impressionistic" effects in the works of Debussy and Liszt—among them, portions of the *Années de pèleinage, Via crucis, Unstern,* and Debussy's *Images.* As much a discussion of differences between the two composers' styles as of Liszt's influence on Debussy. About two dozen musical examples.

711.   Ujfalussy, József. "Debussy és Liszt." *Magyar zene* 28 (1987), pp. 115-118.
A brief sketch of Liszt's influence on Debussy's work. No musical examples.

D. Grieg

712.   MacDougald, Duncan. "Liszt y Edvard Grieg: Franz Liszt y la formación de la estructura musical del siglo XIX." *Revista musical Chilena* 10/50 (July 1955), pp. 17-27.

    Deals to a considerable extent in Liszt's relationship with Grieg, although MacDougald also refers vaguely to "compositional influences." No musical examples, but the author illustrates some of his observations with quotations from letters exchanged by the two composers. In Spanish.

E. Janáček

713.   Stědroň, B. "Leoš Janáček und Ferenc Liszt." *Studia musicologica* 5 (1963), pp. 295-299.

    Discusses both composers' interests in "revolutionary" politics, Janáček's interest in Liszt's music, and especially Janáček's arrangement of Liszt's *Missa pro organo*. No musical examples.

F. Mahler

714.   Williamson, John. "Liszt, Mahler and the Chorale." *Proceedings of the Royal Music Association* 108 (1981-1982), pp. 115-125.

    Treats of chorale tunes and endings in Liszt works (among them, the *Faust* and *Dante* symphonies) as well as of the influence those endings exerted upon Mahler's "Resurrection" symphony. Several short musical examples.

G. Ravel

715.   Weiss-Aigner, Günther. "Eine Sonderform der Skalenbildung in der Musik Ravels." *Musikforschung* 25 (1972), pp. 323-326.

    Demonstrates that Ravel's early works were influenced by whole- and half-step scale patterns related to the diminished-seventh chord and derived from Liszt's works.

H. Saint-Saëns

716.   Pollei, Paul. "Lisztian Piano Virtuoso Style in the Piano Concerti of Camille Saint-Saëns." *Journal of the American Liszt Society* 7 (1980), pp. 59-76.

    Reviews Lisztian borrowings and adaptations in important keyboard works by Saint-Saëns, including several of the piano concertos, the *Rhapsodie d'Auvergne*, and the Toccata, Op. 72. Pollei maintains that

Saint-Saëns (especially in his concertos) "inherited the virtuosic procedure
. . . characterized by Franz Liszt in his most expansive manner." Pollei
also classifies virtuoso passages in Saint-Saëns's music as "bravura, toccata,
cascade, filligree, and semplice." Musical examples.

I. Schumann

717.   Serauky, Walter. "Robert Schumann in seinem Verhältnis zu Ludwig van
Beethoven und Franz Liszt." *Robert Schumann: Aus Anlass seines 100.
Todestages*, ed. Eberhard Rebling. Leipzig: Breitkopf & Härtel, 1956; pp.
68-72.
    ML410.S4M68
    Contains brief remarks about Liszt's personal relationship with
Schumann as well as Schumannesque elements in the B-minor Sonata and
Liszt's two piano concertos. No musical examples.

*   Walker, Alan. "Schumann, Liszt and the C Major 'Fantasie,' Op. 17."
    Deals primarily with the Liszt/Schumann relationship as well as a re-
cently discovered ms. of the *Fantasie*, although Walker also refers to
Liszt's and Schumann's influences on each other between 1840-1856. Described in greater detail as item 556.

J. Skriabin

718.   Gárdonyi, Zsolt. "Paralipomena zum Thema 'Liszt und Skrjabin'." In
item 764; pp. 9-31.
    An examination of Liszt's influence on Skriabin, including the Russian
composer's possible derivation of his well-known 'Mystical Chord" from
the concluding measures of Liszt's *Nuages gris*. Illustrated with 23 musical
examples drawn from works by Bartók, Debussy, Ravel, and Stravinsky
as well as sonatas by Skriabin and Liszt's *Années de pèleinage* and
Prometheus.
    NB: Another study deals with closely related material, especially with
Nuages gris. See Lawrence Kramer, "The Mirror of Tonality: Transitional
Features of Nineteenth-century Harmony" in *19th Century Music* 4 (1981),
esp. pp. 203-206. Illustrated with five examples drawn from the piano piece
in question.

<u>K. Smetana</u>

719.   Hudec, Vl. "Zum Problem des 'Lisztartigen' in Smetanas symphonischen Dichtungen." *Studia musicologica* 5 (1963), pp. 131-137.

Evaluates Liszt's influence on his Czech contemporary, especially on works like *Richard III, Wallenstein's Camp*, and *Hakon Jarl*. Hudec also deals with literary influences on Liszt and Smetana, thematic transformation as a compositional device, and certain relationships between music and philosophy. Illustrated with a number of musical examples, among them quotations from *Tasso* and *Ce qu'on entend sur la montagne*.

Less important articles about Liszt and Smetana have also appeared in print. See, for instance, Otto Beyer, "Liszt und Friedrich Smetana," *Neue Musik-Zeitung* [Stuttgart] 14 (1893), pp. 238-239. Includes the text of a Liszt letter dated 12 April 1854.

720.   Jiránek, J[aroslav]. "Liszt és Smetana." *Magyar zene* 1/9 (December 1961), pp. 26-32.

A brief survey of Liszt's relationship with and influence on Smetana. Not to be confused with item 721 (below). No musical examples. In Hungarian.

721.   Jiránek, J[aroslav]. "Liszt und Smetana. (Ein Beitrag zur Genesis und eine vergleichende Betrachtung ihres Klavierstils.)" *Studia musicologica* 5 (1963), pp. 139-192.

Describes Smetana as a "creative student" of Liszt and examines in considerable detail Smetana's keyboard writing in terms of Liszt's keyboard and compositional styles. Includes dozens of musical examples, many of them taken from compositions by Smetana almost unknown to concert audiences today.

LISZT AND NATIONAL MUSICAL TRADITIONS

Liszt was fascinated by traditional or "national" musics, including Gypsy music and folk tunes from a variety of cultures. He was also influenced by musical developments in such lands as Czechoslovakia, Mexico, and Russia. Studies of national elements in his compositions or musical outlook are described below. Studies of his travels and sometime fascination with various national or folk traditions, including that of the Gypsies, are described in appropriate sections of Chapters VI and X.

General Studies

Three articles, all of them published several decades ago, describe how Liszt used national materials in some of his compositions, and how his use of these materials influenced musical movements throughout Europe:

722.   Gárdonyi, Zoltán. "Nationale Thematik in der Musik Franz Liszts bis zum Jahre 1848." *Studia musicologica* 5 (1963), pp. 77-87.
   Summarizes Liszt's youthful interest in national musical materials and discusses the appearance of such materials in works like the "Revolutionary" symphony (never completed), several settings of the "Rákóczi" march tune, the "Spanish Fantasy," etc. No musical examples. (With regard to the "Rákóczi" tune, see item 554.)

723.   Georgii, Walter. "Franz Liszt und die nationalen Besonderheiten des Musikempfinden." *Allgemeine Musik-Zeitung* 43 (1916), pp. 487-490.
   A compact, somewhat disjointed discussion of various national influences on Liszt's music, including travels, Italian and Dutch paintings, Goethe's *Faust*, etc. No musical examples.

724.   Kraft, Günther. "Franz Liszt und die nationalen Schulen in Europa." *Festschrift Richard Münnich zum 80. Geburtstag.* ed. Hans Pischner. Leipzig: Deutsche Verlag für Musik, 1957; pp. 85-103.
   ML55.M62P5 1957
   Deals with the complex issue of national motifs and references in dozens of Liszt works. Contains a catalog of "national" compositions (pp. 97-99) but no musical examples.

A fourth article, published much more recently, deals with the influence of the Lisztian symphonic poem on the development of nationalistic musical consciousness before about 1914:

725.   Altenburg, Detlef. "La notion lisztienne de poème symphonique dans son interpénétration avec la conscience nationale à fin du XIXe siècle et au début du XXe." *Revue musicale* 405-406-407 (1987), pp. 287-295.
   A discussion of the symphonic poem and its use by nationalist composers like Dvořák, Janáček, Sibelius, and the young Richard Strauss. No musical examples.

Specialized Studies

Liszt's enthusiasm for the works of nationalist composers and for the music of Hungary, his self-proclaimed native land, influenced his own musical development

*as well as the development of musical nationalism in much of nineteenth-century
Europe. In all, nineteen studies of Lisztian influences on the music-making of several
nations are described or cross-referenced below by nationality, then—in most
cases—alphabetically (by author and/or title):*

Czech Music

(see "Slovak Music")

A. French Music

726.   Timbrell, Charles. "Liszt and French Music " *Journal of the American
         Liszt Society* 6 (1979), pp. 25-33.

         Summarizes Liszt's influences on French music during the 1870s as
         well as the influences of French music on him during the 1820s and 1830s.
         Timbrell itemizes such "French" characteristics of Lisztian works as: 1) the
         use of *idée fixe* motifs; 2) the use of pure orchestral colors; 3) the in-
         terpolation of ad libitum passages and use of frequent changes in meter and
         phrase lengths; and so on. Concludes with a valuable discussion of Lisztian
         elements in compositions by Saint-Saëns, d'Indy, Franck, and Debussy.
         Illustrated with musical examples.

B. Hungarian Music

*Liszt's interaction with Hungarian music and musical figures extended across his
entire compositional career. Two book-length studies, sometimes confused with each
other, describe with unusual thoroughness Hungarian elements in Liszt's works:*

727.   Gárdonyi, Zoltán. *Die ungarischen Stileigentümlichkeiten in den
         musikalischen Werken Franz Liszts.* Ungarische Bibliothek, 1/16. Berlin:
         Walter de Gruyter, 1931. 84pp.
              ML410.L7G2 [sometimes: ML410.L7G21]
         A study of Hungarian influences on Liszt's compositions and style. Il-
         lustrated with 13 musical examples (pp. 81ff) as well as tables of thematic
         sources for the Hungarian Rhapsodies (pp. 76-79).
              Other, highly specialized investigations into Liszt's Rhapsodies and
         Hungarian music of the early nineteenth century (including the
         "Verbunkos" or recruiting dance) have also appeared in print. See, for ex-
         ample, Géza Papp, "Liszt ismeretlen verbunkos-átiratai," *Magyar zene* 28
         (1987), pp. 173-188; and "Az úgynevezett Chopiczky-nóta. Néhány
         hangszeres adalék Liszt VI. Rapszódiájának első témájához," *Magyar zene*
         28 (1987), pp. 43-48. Both articles are amply illustrated with musical ex-
         amples.

728.   Gárdonyi, Zoltán. *Liszt Ferenc magyar stilusa/La style hongrois de Franz Liszt.* musicologica Hungarica, 3. Budapest: National Széchenyi Library, 1936. 125pp.
        ML410.L7G2
        Deals more with Hungarian influences on Liszt's compositional style than specific Hungarian tunes or sources for individual compositions. Gárdonyi discusses *Zum Andenken,* the Hungarian Rhapsodies, and *Hungaria* at some length, and he refers to Hungarian aspects of late Liszt piano pieces. Concludes with twelve pages of musical examples and a useful bibliography. Bilingual in French (pp. 57-120) and Hungarian. NB: This monograph should not be confused with item 727 (above), even though both items have been assigned the same Library of Congress catalog number!

Six other studies dealing with Hungarian music and Liszt are described or cross-referenced below:

729.   Beninger, Eduard. "Franz Liszt und die ungarische Musik." *Burgenländische Heimatblätter* 5/2 (May 1936), pp. 41-50.
        A brief survey of Liszt's "Hungarian" experiences, associations, and music.

730.   Csomasz Tóth, Kálmán. "Egy népszerű dallamunk eredetéhez." *Magyar zene* 15 (1974), pp. 73-77.
        Demonstrates that "Magasan repül a daru," a tune Liszt used as the basis of his Hungarian Rhapsody No. 14, was probably borrowed from a singing exercise found in the 1740 Hungarian edition of the *Geneva Psalter.* Musical examples. In Hungarian.

731.   Gárdonyi, Zoltán. "Zoltán Kodály über Liszts Hungarismen." *Studia musicologica* 25 (1983), pp. 131-134.
        Concerned for the most part with the remarks about Liszt recorded in a letter Kodály sent Gárdonyi on 24 November 1929. No musical examples. NB: Like several other "Hungarian" Liszt articles, this one blends patriotic enthusiasm with biographical and musical information.

732.   Gergeley, Jean. "Liszt et l'école hongroise de Paris." *Revue musicale* 405-406-407 (1987), pp. 75-86.
        Deals with Liszt, Hungarian and "Turkish" musical traditions of the early nineteenth century, and Hungarian composers living in Paris during the late nineteenth and early twentieth centuries—among them, Sándor Bertha and Kornél Ábrányi. Illustrated with ten musical examples from

works like Liszt's *La notte*, Adalbert Gyrovetz's *Fête hongroise*, Bertha's *Palotás*, and so on.

*   Kovács, Sándor. "Formprinzipien und ungarische Stileigentümlichkeiten in den Spätwerken von Liszt."
          As much a study of Liszt's compositional techniques in general as of characteristic Hungarian influences. Described in greater detail as item 645.

733.   Wilheim, A[ndrás]. Liszt és a huszadik század." *Magyar zene* 27 (1986), pp. 115-125.
          Another brief survey. In Hungarian.

Finally, two articles deal specificially with Gypsy music and its influence on Liszt's musical interests and development:

734.   Mayerhofer, Claudia. "Liszt und seine Beziehung zu den Zigeunern." In item 88; pp. 76-90.
          Deals with the Gypsies as transient "citizens" of nineteenth-century Austro-Hungary, Liszt's interest in their music, and his book about Gypsy music (item 165f). Concludes with photoreproductions of two letters dealing with the latter work. Illustrated with several pictures of Gypsy music-makers dating from Liszt's lifetime but no musical examples.

735.   Sárosi, Bálint. "Liszt und die Zigeunermusikanten." In item 88; pp. 91-95.
          Brief remarks on the character of the Gypsy music Liszt knew and its influence on some of his compositions. Illustrated with a facsimile reproduction of a page from D-WRgs Liszt ms. J-9 (the first page of Hungarian Rhapsody No. 8).

C. Italian Music

736.   Mastroianni, Thomas. "The Italian Aspect of Franz Liszt." *Journal of the American Liszt Society* 16 (1984), pp. 6-19.
          Identifies and discusses four important influences on Liszt's music-making: Italian art and literature; Niccolò Paganini; the Roman Catholic Church; and Italian opera. Illustrated with a very poor reproduction of a painting by Raphael as well as with 12 musical examples drawn from portions of the *Années de pèlerinage*, the "Dante" sonata, and Liszt's paraphrase on Verdi's *Rigoletto*.

D. Mexican Music

737.   Stevenson, Robert. "Liszt in Mexico, 1840-1911." *Inter-American Music Review* 7/2 (Spring-Summer 1986), pp. 23-32.

Deals primarily with performances of Liszt's works in Mexico prior to World War I. Stevenson also includes the text of a diploma awarding Liszt honorary membership in the Mexican Philharmonic Society and a complete facsimile reproduction of the funeral march dedicated by Liszt to the memory of Mexico's Emperor Maximilian I, who died in 1867. No other musical examples.

E. Polish Music

738.   Swaryczewska, Katarzyna. "Franciszek Liszt a muzyka polska." *Muzyka* [Warsaw] 6/4 (1961), pp. 21-36.

Reviews Liszt's interest in Polish composers (among them, Chopin), Liszt's own mazurkas and other adaptations of Polish musical materials, etc. In Polish; summary in German (p. 102).

F. Russian Music

An important book has been devoted exclusively to the symbiotic relationship between Liszt's music and the musical life and style of Russian composers:

739.   László, Zsigmond. *Liszt és az orosz zene.* Budapest: Magyar-Szovjet Társaság, 1955. 120pp.

ML410.L7L26   ISBN 963-564-216-4

Identifies and discusses Russian elements in Liszt's works and Lisztian elements in Russian music, especially in pieces by nineteenth-century composers. Strongly influenced by Marxist-Leninist orthodoxy. Illustrated with plates of portraits and other pictorial materials, and with a few poorly printed musical examples. In Hungarian.

An article by László with the same title as his book appeared in *Új zenei szemle* 6/1 (January 1955), pp. 7-9. Several musical examples.

Two shorter but nevertheless important studies of the same general topic also deserve attention:

740.   Abraham, Gerald. "Liszt's Influence on the 'Mighty Handful'." *On Russian Music: Critical and Historical Studies.* New York: Charles Scribner, 1939; pp. 81-90.

[No LC number available]

An introduction to Liszt's influence on selected works by Musorgsky, Balakirev, Rimsky-Korsakov, Borodin, and Cui. Illustrated with brief excerpts from *Der nächtliche Zug* and the *Totentanz* as well as from pieces by Musorgsky and Rimsky-Korsakov. Inadvertently omitted from item 40. Reprinted in 1970 by Books for Libraries Press of Freeport, New York.

741.   Mil'shtein, Yakov [Isaakovich]. "Az orosz Liszt-kutatás kevéssé ismert lapjai." *Magyar zene* 18 (1977), pp. 354-361.
        Describes logical extensions of Lisztian compositional processes in works by Skrjabin, Rachmaninoff, Prokofieff, and so on. Mil'shtein also mentions Liszt artifacts preserved in Soviet collections. In Hungarian.

G. Slavic Music

742.   Bełza, Igor. "Liszt i kultura muzyczna narodow słowiańskich." *Muzyka* [Warsaw] 6/4 (1961), pp. 3-20.
        Summarizes Liszt's interest in the traditional and art musics of Eastern Europe, including those of Poland, Czechoslovakia, etc. No musical examples or summary. In Polish.

743.   Nováček, Z[denko]. "Der entscheidende Einfluss von Liszt auf die fortschrittliche Musikorientation in Preßburg." *Studia musicologica* 5 (1963), pp. 233-239.
        Deals with Liszt's visits to Preßburg (today, Bratislava) in 1840, 1858, 1872, etc., and more especially with Liszt's influence on local figures like Ludmilla Sámoysky, Fany Kováts, and Karl Mayrberger. No musical examples.
        NB: The title given for this article on the contents page of *Studia musicologica* and in some reference works is different from the title reproduced above from the first page of the article itself.

LISZT AND MODERN MUSIC

Liszt's relationship with twentieth-century music is difficult to evaluate. In some senses, Liszt seems to have anticipated—possibly even influenced—certain progressive tendencies characteristic of much modern composition. In other senses, Liszt seems merely to have indulged in musical experimentation for its own sake. Studies that concentrate on Lisztian experiments per se are described in relevant portions of Chapter XII, or in previous portions of the present chapter. The studies described below emphasize similarities between Liszt's music and musical movements or styles associated with the early twentieth-century musical avant-garde.

At least three detailed studies have been devoted exclusively to innovations in Liszt's music and, at least implicitly, Liszt's anticipation of certain twentieth-century musical practices:

744.   Bárdos, Lajos. "Ferenc Liszt, the Innovator." *Studia musicologica* 17 (1975), pp. 3-38.

A catalog of modernisms found throughout Liszt's works, especially those of his last years. Amply illustrated with musical examples. More familiar than item 745 (below) but similar to it.

745.   Bárdos, Lajos. *Liszt Ferenc a jövő zeneésze.* Budapest: Akadémiai Kiadó, 1976. 86pp.

ML410.L7B27   ISBN 963-05-0739-0

Describes most of Liszt's "progressive" harmonic and structural innovations. Illustrated with dozens of well-chosen musical examples. Highly useful but less widely available in Western Europe and the United States than item 744 (above). In Hungarian.

746.   Szelényi, István. "Der unbekannte Liszt." *Studia musicologica* 5 (1963), pp. 311-331.

Another catalog of Liszt's modernisms: "metabolons" (i.e., tetrachord patterns of several kinds similar to those found in writings about ancient Greek music); whole-tone scalar patterns; unusual scales like the so-called "Hungarian" minor, and so on. Illustrated with dozens of short examples drawn from the Sonata in b minor, the "Dante" sonata, *Prometheus*, the "Malédiction" concerto, etc.

Reprinted (also in German) in item 30; pp. 274-291. Also published in Hungarian under the title "Az ismeretlen Liszt" in *Magyar zene* 1/9 (December 1961), pp. 11-25. Yet another article by Szelényi dealing with related topics appeared in Hungarian under the title "Előfutár vagy valóraváltó? Stíluskritikai kísérlet Liszt alkotókorszakaival kapcsolatban" in *Magyar zene* 8 (1967), pp. 231-241.

A shorter but even more important study attempts to compare entire "modern" Liszt pieces with twentieth-century examples:

747.   Forte, Allan. "Liszt's Experimental Idiom and Music of the Early Twentieth Century." *19th Century Music* 10 (1987), pp. 209-228.

Approaches the topic of Liszt's influence on modern music with caution, and with careful attention to previous studies. Forte maintains that "When [Liszt] created what was remarkably similar . . . to the innovative music that followed the 'Jahrhundertwende,' he anticipated a siginificant historical development"—without, however, having influenced that development directly. Illustrated with 14 musical examples (many of them Schenkerian reductions) taken from or referring to both versions of *Vallée d'Obermann* and to *Hamlet, Blume und Duft,* etc.

Three shorter but nevertheless intelligent and useful surveys of stylistic innovations in Liszt's music also remain useful:

748.   Searle, Humphrey. "Liszt's Final Period (1860-1886)." *Proceedings of the Royal Music Association* 78 (1951-1952), pp. 67-81.

A "borderline" study, dealing with Liszt's overall compositional development and with several individual works as well as stylistic innovations in his late piano pieces. An influential essay, published when Liszt's last compositions were little-known. Nine musical examples. (With regard to the dissemination during the 1950s of Liszt's last keyboard works, see Chapter II.)

749.   Searle, Humphrey. "Liszt and 20th Century Music." *Studia musicologica* 5 (1963), pp. 277-281.

Not to be confused with item 748 (above). Concentrates on issues of musical form, "tone rows" in several Liszt works, and harmonic experiments of various kinds. Illustrated with four musical examples, all of them taken from the last piano pieces.

An article with the same title and virtually the same contents (but without musical examples) appeared in the *New Hungarian Quarterly* 3/6 (April-June 1962), pp. 217-220. Searle also published other articles about modernities in Liszt's music. Among them: "Liszt and the 20th Century," in *Piano Quarterly* 23/89 (Spring 1975), pp. 38-40.

750.   Walker, Alan. "Liszt and the Twentieth Century." In item 31; pp. 350-364.

Deals primarily with Impressionistic and atonal elements in such Liszt pieces as the *Csárdás macabre* the *Dante* symphony, several of the Hungarian Rhapsodies, and the *Bagatelle sans tonalité*. Twenty-four musical examples.

Finally, ten additional articles, most of them devoted to rooting out avant-garde elements in certain Liszt works, are described below. The three best of these articles are:

751.   Dahlhaus, Carl. "Franz Liszt und die Vorgeschichte der neuen Musik. Zum 150. Geburtstag des Komponisten." *Neue Zeitschrift für Musik* 122 (1961), pp. 387-391.

A penetrating look at progressive motivic, harmonic, and structural elements in the first movement of the *Dante* symphony and *Hamlet*. Dahlhaus concludes that these and other Liszt works—not just the last piano pieces, but works composed as early as the 1830s and 1840s—anticipate the "voice" ["Stimmung"] of modernism, with its world-weariness and anxiety. Illustrated with 14 musical examples.

752.   Johnsson, Bengt. "Modernities in Liszt's Works." *Svensk Tidskrift for Musikforskning* 46 (1964), pp. 83-117.
       A useful catalog, primarily of harmonic devices, illustrated with dozens of musical examples drawn from every period of Liszt's compositional career.

753.   Leibowitz, R[ené]. "Les prophéties de Franz Liszt." *L'évolution de la musique de Bach à Schoenberg.* Paris: Correa, 1951; pp. 141-153.
       ML160.L8
       One of the earliest arguments in favor of Liszt as a "modern" composer and in support of unusual musical moments in his pieces as "anticipations" of twentieth-century practice. Musical examples.

At least seven shorter—and, to put it bluntly, less innovative or enlightening—articles have also been devoted to Impressionistic or avant-garde elements in Liszt's compositions. Cited here in order of publication and with only cursory annotations, primarily because they appear in so many Liszt bibliographies (among them, item 40), and because their mere existence demonstrates changing attitudes toward Liszt's music and the development of a modern musical style:

754.   Danckert, Werner. "Liszt als Vorläufer des musikalischen Impressionismus." *Musik* 21/5 (February 1929), pp. 341-345.
       Interesting primarily because it was published sixty years ago, when Liszt's late piano pieces were almost unknown. Danckert discusses pentatonic, whole-tone, and "watery" devices associated with Debussy and Ravel. Illustrated with five short musical examples and a portrait of Liszt painted by Sally von Kügelgen in 1886.

755.   Hübsch-Pflege, Lini. "Liszts Einfluß auf die Entwicklung der neuen Musik." *Musikhandel* 12 (1961), pp. 309-310.
       An extremely cursory study.

756.   Pisk, Paul. "Elements of Impressionism and Atonality in Liszt's Last Piano Pieces." *Radford Review* 23 (1969), pp. 171-176.
       Presented as a paper at the first meeting of the American Liszt Society. No musical examples.
       Presented at the same meeting and printed in the same volume is a slightly longer article by Harriet T. Hering entitled "Liszt's Influence on Early Twentieth-century Piano Music" (pp. 135-142); illustrated with 10 musical examples.

757.   Haglund, R. "Liszt som modernist." *Musikrevy* 36 (1981), pp. 165-169.
        In Swedish.

758.   de Groot, Cor. "Niet de oude maar de jonge Liszt was een avantgardist:
        wie speelt hem nog zoals hij het wilde?" *Mens en melodie* 41 (1986), pp.
        438-450.
        Includes comments about Liszt's keyboard works of the 1830s and
        1840s as well as the late piano pieces. In Dutch.

759.   Rabes, Lennart. "Franz Liszt — en avantgardist." *Musikrevy* 41 (1986), pp.
        181-187.
        Illustrated with a photograph of Liszt as well as musical examples
        taken from the Sonata in b minor, the *Faust* symphony, *Via crucis*, and
        several late piano pieces. In Swedish.

760.   Rackwitz, Werner. "Tradition und Zukunftsmusik. Zur musikalischen
        Position Franz Liszts." *Musik und Gesellschaft* 36 (1986), pp. 338-341.
        Includes information about historical and aesthetic issues as well as
        Liszt's influence on twentieth-century practices.
        A number of articles like this one were published in 1986, the most
        recent 'Liszt-Year." Among them was Wolfgang Marggraf's "'. . . den
        Speer   in   den   unendlichen   Raum   der   Zukunft   schleudern.'
        Traditionsbezüge und Innovationen im Schaffen Franz Liszts," which ap-
        peared in the same issue of *Musik und Gesellschaft*, pp. 342-347.

XIV: ORIGINAL WORKS FOR SOLO PIANO

Liszt's original works for piano, separated here for purposes of discussion from his piano paraphrases and transcriptions, constitute by far the best-known part of his compositional output. Studies devoted to Liszt's original piano works are described below. Editions of Liszt's piano music and studies related to those editions are described in Chapter V. Studies devoted primarily to aspects of Liszt's compositional technique or development and only secondarily to the piano music per se are described for the most part in Chapter XII. A few monographs devoted to revisions of individual piano pieces are described in Chapter VIII. Finally, recorded performances of a number of keyboard works are described in the Appendix.

GENERAL STUDIES

Only one book-length survey of Liszt's piano works has appeared in print:

761.   Westerby, Herbert. *Liszt, Composer, and his Piano Works: Descriptive Guide and Critical Analysis, Written in a Popular and Concise Style.* London: William Reeves, 1936. xxii, 336pp.
MT145.L51W4
Essentially a performer's guide to Liszt's more familiar compositions for solo piano. A "borderline" work, Westerby's book also includes a sketch of Liszt's life and chapters on his compositional style and pedagogical topics. Old-fashioned in some respects but still useful in others: piano teachers, for instance, may wish to consult Westerby's descriptions of individual pieces ranked according to technical and interpretive difficulty. Portraits, musical examples, diagrams, and a bibliography.
Reprinted in 1970 by Greenwood Press.

Another, more restricted survey of Liszt's piano music may be found in a series of musical survey studies issued in a single volume:

762.   Range, Hans-Peter. *Franz Liszt: Einführung in die konzertanten Klavierwerke*. Von Beethoven bis Brahms, 6 [but published with other volumes]. Lahr/Schwarzwald: Moritz Schauenburg, 1968; pp. 167-188.
       MT140.R35 1968
       A work-by-work description of Liszt's better-known piano compositions (with and without orchestra). Includes brief synopses of the Sonata in b minor and the "Transcendental Etudes" as well as paraphrases like the *Réminiscences de Don Juan*, the two concertos, etc. Superficial. No musical examples.

Three more specialized surveys of Liszt's piano works also exist:

763.   Thiedt, Catherine Eleanor. *The Idiomatic Character of Romantic Keyboard Composition: A Comparison of Selected Piano and Organ Works of Franz Liszt and a Study of Differences in their Styles*. Dissertation: University of Rochester, 1975. ix, 218pp.
       MT145.L51T44 1975
       Evaluates Liszt's approach to keyboard writing through an examination of three organ works and piano transcriptions of two of those works.
       Summarized in DAI 36/11 (May 1976), p. 7039A.

764.   *Virtuosität und Avantgarde. Untersuchungen zum Klavierwerk Franz Liszts*, ed. Zsolt Gárdonyi and Siegfried Mauser. Mainz: Schott, 1988. 116pp.
       ISBN 3-7957-1797-3   [No LC number available]
       A collection of comparatively lengthy essays about Liszt's virtuoso and experimental keyboard writing. Contains items 619, 718, 790, and 828. Numerous musical examples; in German throughout.

765.   Hinson, Maurice. *At the Piano with Liszt*. Sherman Oaks, California: Alfred Publishing Co., 1986. 63pp.
       M22.L77H5   [No ISBN number available]
       A collection of Liszt's original piano music introduced by short essays about Liszt the pianist and teacher, Liszt's use of musical form, contemporary approaches to performing Liszt's piano works, etc. Includes 17 compositions, among them the first *Consolation*, the third "Hungarian Rhapsody," excerpts from the *Weihnachtsbaum* suite, and so on. Illustrated with several portraits of Liszt and miscellaneous musical examples. (Resembles item 605 in format but not in contents.)

*Finally, the innovations Liszt introduced through his original solo piano compositions
are described in:*

766.   Walker, Alan. "Liszt and the Keyboard." *Musical Times* 118 (1977), pp.
          717-721.
              A useful introduction to this complex topic, illustrated with seven short
          musical examples.
              Corrections by Howard Schott to some of Walker's observations were
          published in the *Musical Times* 118 (1977), p. 911. NB: Many of
          Walker's observations reappear in item 1a; pp. 285-318.

SPECIALIZED STUDIES

*Liszt wrote most of his original works for piano during the late 1830s, 1840s, and
1850s. Studies devoted to many of these works—e.g., the Sonata in b minor, the
"Transcendental" and "Paganini" etudes, and so on—are described below under
"Mature Piano Pieces." Works completed before c. 1840 are described below under
"Earlier Piano Pieces"; works composed during Liszt's late years are are described
under "Late Piano Pieces." Again, recorded performances of piano pieces are described in the Appendix.*

Earlier Piano Pieces (1827 — c. 1840)

*Only two monographs have been devoted exclusively to Liszt's earlier piano pieces,
especially those composed before c. 1840. One of these monographs deals primarily
with stylistic issues:*

767.   Kókai, Rezső. *Franz Liszt in seinem frühen Klavierwerken.* Leipzig: Franz
          Wagner, 1935. 140pp.
              ML410.L7K7 1969
              A valuable study of Liszt's musical development before the mid-1830s.
          Among other topics, Kókai deals systematically with Liszt's use of the-
          matic material and rhythmic figures, his youthful brand of keyboard writ-
          ing, and his use of musical form. Illustrated with 88 musical examples,
          some of them taken from D-WRgs Liszt sketchbooks (pp. 121-140), as
          well as with facsimile reproductions from D-WRgs Liszt mss. N6 and J44.
          Also contains a useful bibliography and a catalog of Liszt works written
          between 1822-1840 (pp. 9-18).
              Reprinted by Bärenreiter in 1969.

*   Torkewitz, Dieter. *Harmonisches Denken im Frühwerk Franz Liszts.*
      Deals almost exclusively with harmony in piano pieces Liszt completed
      before the mid-1830s. Described in greater detail as item 613.

Two articles deal primarily with early keyboard pieces:

768.   Stradal, August. "Die ersten Jugendwerke Franz Liszts." *Neue Zeitschrift
       für Musik* 80 (1913), pp. 109-115.
           Identifies Liszt's earliest compositions, including their little-used opus
       numbers. Stradal repeatedly corrects Ramann's "official" Liszt biography
       (item 2). A worthwhile study; some of its contents still do not appear
       systematically in Liszt catalogs, including item 47.

769.   Gut, Serge. "Nouvelle approche des premières oevures de Franz Liszt
       d'après la correspondance Liszt — d'Agoult." *Studia musicologica* 28
       (1986), pp. 237-248.
           Discusses a host of early Liszt works, principally "original" piano
       pieces and operatic transcriptions, in terms of references to them in item
       194. Illustrated with the (?complete) musical text of a previously unpub-
       lished piece, the *Valse à Marie* (pp. 243-244), composed in November
       1842. Numerous bibliographic citations in the form of footnotes.

*Four other studies of early Liszt piano pieces are described or cross-referenced below
in alphabetical order (by author):*

770.   Backus, Joan [Pauline]. "Liszt's 'Harmonies poétiques et religieuses': In-
       spiration and the Challenge of Form." *Journal of the American Liszt So-
       ciety* 21 (1987), pp. 3-21.
           Describes Liszt's piece in terms of musical and "rhetorical" qualities.
       Outfitted with a diagram and 10 musical examples.

771.   Main, Alexander. "Liszt's 'Lyon': Music and the Social Conscience." *19th
       Century Music* 4 (1981), pp. 228-243.
           Traces the history and explains the "revolutionary" significance of this
       early work, later incorporated into the *Album d'un voyageur.* Main pro-
       vides new dates for several early Liszt piano pieces (p. 243), and he reprints
       most or all of a letter Liszt addressed to Félicité Lamennais on 18 De-
       cember 1837. Seven musical examples.
           A shorter, Hungarian-language study of the same piece also exists:
       Gábor Darvas, "Liszt Ferenc: Lyon (Zenei dokumentum a
       munkásmozgalom történetéhez)," *Új zenei szemle* 4/1 (January 1953), pp.
       18-21. Eight musical examples.

*   Reich, Nancy B. "Liszt's Variations on the March from Rossini's 'Siège de Corinthe'."
      Deals with a composition completed by Liszt in 1830 and lost for more than a century. Described in greater detail as item 309.

*   Torkewitz, Dieter. "Die Erstfassung der 'Harmonies poétiques et religieuses' von Liszt."
      Devoted in part to the first version of the *Harmonies*. NB: This piece must not be confused with the suite of the same name, discussed below under "Mature Piano Pieces." Torkewitz's study is described in greater detail as item 341.

Mature Piano Pieces (1848 — c. 1870)

No book-length survey exists of the piano pieces Liszt composed during and for about a decade after his so-called "Weimar Years." These "mature" works may be thought to include the third book of Années de pèlerinage *pieces, the "St. Francis Legends," and other works of a less radically experimental character composed during Liszt's later years. Only his most experimental and last pieces are generally considered "late" in style; they are discussed below in a section of their own.*

One brief introduction to Liszt's "mature" piano pieces appeared in print two decades ago:

772.   Kentner, Louis. "Solo Piano Music (1827-1861)." In item 31; pp. 79-133.
       Primarily a discussion of such works as the Sonata in b minor, the "Dante" sonata, the Ballades, various versions of the *Etudes d'exécution transcendante*, and so on. Although Kentner claims in his title to discuss Liszt's early keyboard works, he concentrates almost entirely on works from the Weimar years. Illustrated with 76 musical examples as well as several plates of Liszt portraits. See also item 824.

Studies devoted exclusively to individual mature Liszt piano pieces are described below according to the titles of the pieces in question, then alphabetically (by author):

A. The Sonata in b minor (recorded in items A16-A20, A66, and A76)

No other Liszt composition has received so much attention from performers and scholars as the B-minor Sonata. Each of the studies described below has its merits, but two of the best and most wide-ranging examinations of this masterpiece deserve special attention:

773.   Longyear, Rey M. "Liszt's B Minor Sonata: Precedents for a Structural Analysis." *Music Review* 34 (1973), pp. 198-209.

A study of Liszt's masterpiece in terms of "double-function form" (see item 775) as well as the result of "several generations of experimentation" on the part of composers like Beethoven and Schubert. Illustrated with a "double function" diagram (p. 198), a second analytical diagram (p. 203), and three multipartite musical examples.

*   Winklhofer, Sharon. *Liszt's Sonata in B Minor: A Study of Autograph Sources and Documents.*

Discusses the melodic, harmonic, structural, and expressive character of the Sonata as well as source materials of various kinds. Described in greater detail as item 293. See also item 294.

At least one dissertation purports to deal with the Sonata in terms of Liszt's mature piano music as a whole:

774.   Becker, Ralf-Walter. *Formprobleme in Liszts h-moll Sonate: Untersuchungen zu Liszts Klaviermusic um 1850.* Dissertation: University of Marburg, 1979. 162pp.

Typescript. The Universitätsbibliothek, Marburg a.d.L., owns at least one copy.

Discusses at some length the compositional genesis and contents of the Sonata as well as other piano pieces composed by Liszt during the 1840s and 1850s. Dozens of musical examples, several tables, and a bibliography.

Not summarized in either DAI or the *Journal of the American Liszt Society.*

A highly influential discussion of the Sonata's structure may be found in:

775.   Newman, William S. *The Sonata Since Beethoven*, 3rd ed. History of the Sonata Principle, 3. New York: W. W. Norton, 1983.
            ML1156.N44 1983   ISBN 0-393-95290-8

A detailed survey of piano sonatas composed in the nineteenth and early twentieth centuries. Newman maintains that Liszt's Sonata must be understood in terms of "double function form"—i.e., in terms of both a one-movement and a multi-movement sonata form. Illustrated on pp. 359-378 with musical examples and a diagram of the famous "double-function" analysis (p. 375). (With regard to the "double function" question, see also item 1b; pp. 149-157, as well as item 782.)

NB: Newman also discusses the "Dante" sonata and provides an analytical diagram on p. 372 of his book.

Two studies of the Sonata and Liszt's musical symbolism are unusually provocative:

776. Szász, Tibor. *Liszt's Divine and Diabolical Symbolism: Key to the Religious Program in the Sonata in B Minor.* Dissertation: University of Michigan, 1985. ?pp.
[No LC number available]
A highly speculative yet detailed study of the Sonata in terms of melodies found elsewhere in Liszt's music (e.g., the "Crucifixion music" from the *Via crucis*), the possible presence of a program in the Sonata based on Biblical texts and Milton's *Paradise Lost*, motifs from the Sonata which recur in other of Liszt's programmatic pieces, and so on. Illustrated with quotations from Liszt's correspondence, tables of themes, reproductions of Renaissance woodcuts illustrating scenes from the Last Judgment, etc., etc.
Not seen; the description above is based on the contents of item 777 (below) and conversations with the author. Not summarized in either DAI or the *Journal of the American Liszt Society* (although item 777 itself appeared in the latter publication). A lecture presented by Szász on 26 June 1986 at the Library of Congress was published under the title "Liszt's Symbolism and Musical Structure" (Typescript: US-Wc shelf-number ML410.L7S95 1986).

777. Szász, Tibor. "Liszt's Symbols for the Divine and Diabolical: Their Revelation of a Program in the B Minor Sonata." *Journal of the American Liszt Society* 15 (1984), pp. 39-95.
Apparently a preliminary version of item 776 (above) but not to be confused with it. Also illustrated with diagrams, charts, and numerous musical examples.

Eight other articles about Liszt's Sonata are described or cross-referenced below in alphabetical order (by author):

778. Felix, Václav. "Uplatněni principu čisté tóniky v Lisztově Sonátě h moll." *Zivá hudba* (1973), pp. 5-40.
Not seen. According to RILM 10 (1976); item 2868, an analysis of the Sonata's structure, based upon principles developed by Karel Janáček. Musical examples and bibliographic citations. In Czech; summary in German.

779. Kański, Jósef. "The Problem of Form in Franz Liszt's Sonata in B Minor." *Journal of the American Liszt Society*
Subtitled "Transformations of the Sonata Form in the Romantic Period," Kańsky's article is devoted primarily to structural issues and to defending the thesis that Liszt's work is a "monothematic composition

based entirely on one, two-part theme [i.e., measures 8-17] . . . subject to harmonic, rhythmic, and agogic transformations." Also contains remarks about virtuoso keyboard writing and related issues. Seventeen musical examples.

Originally published in Polish under the title "Problem formy w Sonacie h-Moll F. Liszta" in *Studia muzykologiczne* 4 (1955), pp. 276-294.

780.   Kardos, István. *Die klassische Sonatenform in Liszt's H-moll* [sic]. Berlin: F. W. Peters, 1972. 16pp.

The National Széchényi Library, Budapest, owns a copy: shelf-number SZ Liszt 177.

A review of the most traditional elements of sonata-allegro form in Liszt's masterpiece. Illustrated with five pages of musical analysis and a detailed analytical diagram (pp. 8-9).

*   Longyear, Rey M. "The Text of Liszt's B Minor Sonata."

Described in greater detail as item 162. Longyear deals primarily in this article with the famous "Lehmann ms." and only in passing with the Sonata as music. (With regard to the ms., see also item 147.)

781.   Ott, Bertrand. "An Interpretation of Liszt's Sonata in B Minor," trans. Sida Roberts and P. Vaugelle. *Journal of the American Liszt Society* 10 (1981), pp. 30-38; and 11 (1982), pp. 40-41.

Discusses the Sonata in terms of the Faust story, Berlioz's music for the *Damnation de Faust*, and Liszt's own *Faust* symphony. Observing that "it would be a pity" to consider the Sonata a mere formal structure, Ott argues that the piano piece can be considered a "launching pad" for his largest orchestral work. The "Conclusion" discusses in programmatic terms details of the Sonata's structure verified in part by Winklhofer in her examination of previously unknown material hidden under pasteovers in the "Lehmann ms." (reproduced in item 147). Illustrated with quotations from *Faust* by Goethe and several musical examples.

A shorter version of this article appeared under the title "Pour une interprétation de la sonate de Liszt" in the *Revue musicale de Suisse Romande* 37 (1984), pp. 172-183.

782.   Saffle, Michael. "Liszt's Sonata in B Minor: Another Look at the 'Double Function' Question." *Journal of the American Liszt Society* 11 (1982), pp. 28-39.

Reviews the double-function scheme proposed for the Sonata by Newman (item 775) and explains how Liszt used melodic materials to fulfill "at one and the same time" requirements of both single- and multi-movement sonata forms. Several musical examples.

783. Sandresky, Margaret V. "Tonal Design in Liszt's Sonata in B Minor." *Journal of the American Liszt Society* 10 (1981), pp. 15-29.

    Evaluates the harmonic "ground play" of the Sonata as a "dramatic struggle between the two opposing [harmonic] forces" of the descending opening theme and the "upward thrust" of subsequent passages, esp. measures 334ff. Two tables summarize Sandresky's analytical argument. Musical examples.

784. Schibli, Sigfried. "Sonate für Klavier h-Moll." *Neue Zeitschrift für Musik* 145/11 (November 1984), pp. 29-32.

    A short survey of the Sonata's origins and character, written for a non-specialist audience. Several musical examples.

One monograph apparently devoted exclusively to the Sonata is virtually unobtainable in Western Europe and the United States:

785. Tsukkerman, V. *Sonata si-minor F. Lista.* Moscow: "Muzyka," 1984.

    [No LC number available]

    Not seen. A review of Tsukkerman's work appeared in Russian in *Sovetskaia muzyka* (November 1985), pp. 102-103.

Two studies of the Sonata consider it primarily in terms of other Liszt pieces or works by other composers:

786. Rea, John Rocco. *Franz Liszt's "New Path of Composition": The Sonata in B Minor as Cultural Paradigm.* Dissertation: Princeton University, 1978. 447pp.

    [No LC number available]

    Evaluates Liszt's accomplishments as a composer based primarily on an examination of thematic transformation and other processes in the Sonata. Rea also deals with musical and theoretical works that shaped Liszt's earlier compositional style, and he proposes a new theory of thematic transformation in the Sonata and the first movement of the *Faust* symphony. Concludes with a bibliography.

    Summarized in DAI 39/6 (December 1978), p. 3217A; reprinted in the *Journal of the American Liszt Society* 7 (1980), pp. 96-97. NB: Rea's work was identified under the author's second name in item 40.

787. Schläder, Jürgen. "Zur Funktion der Variantentechnik in den Klaviersonaten f-moll von Johannes Brahms und h-moll von Franz Liszt." *Hamburger Jahrbuch für Musikwissenschaft* ["Brahms und seine Zeit"] 7 (1984), pp. 171-197.

    ISBN 3-89007-018-3

787.   Schläder, Jürgen. "Zur Funktion der Variantentechnik in den Klaviersonaten f-moll von Johannes Brahms und h-moll von Franz Liszt." *Hamburger Jahrbuch für Musikwissenschaft* ["Brahms und seine Zeit"] 7 (1984), pp. 171-197.
        ISBN 3-89007-018-3
        Compares variations on thematic materials found in Brahms's Op. 5 Sonata and Liszt's Sonata in b minor. Schläder pays special attention to such topics as motivic extension, the harmonic implications of motivic and thematic materials and the realization of those implications in developmental passages, etc. Illustrated with a diagram and about a dozen musical examples.

Finally, one disappointing study of the Sonata's musical organization should be avoided by conscientious researchers:

788.   Egert, Paul. "Die Klavier-Sonate in h-moll von Franz Liszt." *Musik* 28-2 (1936), pp. 673-682.
        An old-fashioned study, devoted to discovering "Leitmotive" in Liszt's composition, and to linking the Sonata metaphysically with the musical grammar of the medieval German musicians. Several musical examples. (With regard to this study, see item 293; p. 118.)

<u>B. The Etudes</u> (recorded in items A5-A6, A11, A24-A26, A67, A72-A73, A76, and A101)

Although Liszt's "Transcendental Etudes" are monuments to his abilities as composer and *virtuoso performer, only one book-length study has been devoted exclusively to them:*

789.   Conway, James Bryant. *Musical Sources for the "Etudes d'exécution transcendante": A Study in The Evolution of Liszt's Compositional and Keyboard Techniques.* Dissertation: University of Arizona, 1969. 214pp.
        ML410.L7C66
        Evaluates the changes Liszt made in transforming early versions of the "Transcendentals" into the version published in 1852 and to discussing keyboard writing and style as exemplified by these works. Numerous musical examples and a bibliography. An appendix presents an English-language translation of the critical notes that accompanied the 1826 and 1852 editions of the etudes when they were reprinted in item 136. A competent musicological study written primarily from a pianist's point of view.
        Summarized in DAI 30/5 (November 1969), p. 2055A.

Two shorter studies of these pieces also exist:

*   Jiránek, J[aroslav]. "Franz Liszts Beitrag zur Musiksprache der Romantik."
     Deals to a considerable extent with two of the "Transcendentals" and their expressive significance. Described in greater detail as item 612.

790.   Schütz, Georg. "Form, Satz- und Klaviertechnik in den drei Fassungen der 'Grossen Etüden' Franz Liszts." In item 764; pp. 71-115.
       Reviews the evolution of the "Transcendentals" through three published editions: those of 1826, 1839, and 1852. Schütz discusses details of melodic development and transformation, form, and harmony as well as of Liszt's keyboard figuration. Illustrated with analytical diagrams and harmonic/motivic reductions as well as musical examples from all three versions of these pieces. See also item 906.

Only one extended study has been devoted to the so-called "Paganini Etudes":

791.   Altman, Ian Henry. *Liszt's Grand Etudes after Paganini: A Historical and Analytical Study.* Dissertation: University of Cincinnati, 1984. iii, 310pp.
       ML410.L7A68 1985
       Examines Liszt's tribute to Paganini's genius in terms of the origins of both versions of the "Paganini Etudes," the differences between the versions, and the musical character of these pieces—works, according to Altman, which lie "between the *partition* [i.e., mere transcription] and the fantasy." Musical examples and a short bibliography.
       Summarized in DAI 45/6 (December 1984), p. 1565A; reprinted in the *Journal of the American Liszt Society* 18 (1985), p. 183.

Finally, at least one study examines Liszt and the evolution of the keyboard etude as a genre:

792.   Gurk, Else. *Die Entwicklung der Klavieretüde von Mozart bis Liszt, unter besonderer Berücksichtigung der Methode des Klavierunterrichts.* Dissertation: University of Vienna, 1930. 123pp.
       Typescript. Musicological Library of the University of Vienna: shelf-number E135.
       Deals with early Romantic keyboard studies of several composers, among them Liszt (pp. 107-123)—the culmination of the "virtuose Stil." Describes in some detail keyboard figurations in the earliest version of the "Transcendental" etudes. Musical examples and bibliographic citations.

C. The "Années de pèlerinage" and Related Works (recorded in items A1, A7,
   A12, A16, A19, A21-A23, A29-A32, A68-A71, A74, A77, and A97)

*The three volumes of Liszt's "Years of Pilgrimage," as well as several sets of pieces
belonging to those volumes and several works upon which portions of those volumes
are based, have received considerable analytical and critical attention. Of three
book-length studies devoted to these volumes, however, only one is relatively recent:*

793.   Wilson, Karen Sue. *A Historical Study and Stylistic Analysis of Franz
        Liszt's "Années de pèlerinage."* Dissertation: University of North Carolina,
        1977. xiv, 313pp.
           ML410.L7W55 1977
           A two-part study: the first part examines the origins of all three *Années*
        volumes; the second discusses stylistic issues—among them, thematic ma-
        terial, harmonic progressions, structure, texture, sonority, and keyboard
        writing. Musical examples and a bibliography.
           Summarized in DAI 39/1 (July 1978), p. 20A; reprinted in the *Journal
        of the American Liszt Society* 7 (1980), p. 97.

*Two other book-length discussions of the "Pilgrimage" volumes are much more su-
perficial as well as old-fashioned:*

794.   Rüsch, Walter. *Franz Liszts Années de pèlerinage. Beiträge zur Geschichte
        seiner Persönlichkeit und seines Stiles.* Bellinzoca: Leins & Vescovi, 1934.
        62pp.
           ML410.L7R8
           Deals with all three "Years of Pilgrimage" volumes in a somewhat
        cursory manner. Numerous musical examples as well as a one-page bibli-
        ography. NB: This book was presented as a doctoral dissertation in 1934
        at the University of Zürich.

795.   Cornette, Arthur Jacob Hendrik. *Liszt en zijne "Années de pèlerinage."*
        Antwerp: Opdebeek, 1924. 60pp.
           ML410.L7C8
           Originally published in 1917, this "impressionistic" account of Liszt's
        pieces as souvenirs of happy wanderings has been reprinted several times.
        Cited throughout the literature but really not worth consulting. In Dutch.
           Other Dutch-language studies of *Années* pieces have appeared in print.
        See, for example, Martijn van den Hoek's article "'Funerailles': een
        interpretatieles" (*Piano Bulletin* 4/1 [1986], pp. 30-35), which contains nine
        musical examples.

*Eight other, mostly shorter studies of the "Pilgrimage" volumes are described or
cross-referenced below, in alphabetical order (by author):*

796.   Cinnamon, Howard. *Third-Relations as Structural Elements in Book II of Liszt's "Années de pèlerinage" and Three Later Works*. Dissertation: University of Michigan, 1984. 302pp.
[No LC number available]
Discusses characteristic harmonic practices not only in *Années* pieces but in the first movement of the *Faust* symphony, *La lugubre gondola*, and the song *Blume und Duft*. These practices include "tonic arpeggiating [i.e., I-III-V-I] progressions" of varying sophistication. Musical examples. (With regard to Cinnamon's analysis of harmonic practices in other Liszt works, see items 616, 808, and 934.)
Summarized in DAI 24/12 (June 1985), p. 3475A; reprinted in the *Journal of the American Liszt Society* 18 (1985), p. 182.

797.   Eigeldinger, Jean-Jacques. "Les Années de pèlerinage de Liszt: Notes sur la genèse et l'esthétique." *Revue musicale de Suisse Romande* 33 (1980), pp. 147-172.
Deals with such diverse topics as musical "tourism" during the late eighteenth and nineteenth centuries, the influences of the Swiss countryside and of Italian painting, sculpture, and poetry on Liszt's music, and the theory that the third *Années* volume represents an interior journey of the soul and of religious sentiment. Eigeldinger includes commentary on each movement from the three *Années* volumes and analyses some of the pieces. Musical examples and other illustrations, including facsimiles of original-edition covers.
Comparatively few studies have been devoted to Book III of the *Années* cycle. One such study, received too late to be described independently in this guide, deserves close attention. See Dolores Pesce, "Liszt's 'Années de pèlerinage,' Book 3: A 'Hungarian' Cycle?" *19th Century Music* 13/3 (Spring 1990), pp. 207-229. Illustrated with analytical diagrams, musical examples, etc.

798.   Gorczycka, Monika. "Nowatorstwo techniki dzwiekowej 'Années de pèlerinage' Liszta." *Muzyka* [Warsaw] 6/4 (1961), pp. 47-59.
Deals with Liszt's keyboard writing in many of the "Years of Pilgrimage" pieces. Musical examples. In Polish; summarized in German on pp. 109-110 of the same periodical.
Other Polish-language studies dealing with Liszt's keyboard writing are more general in character. See, for example, Jerzy Morawski, "Faktura fortepianowa Liszta" in *Muzyka* [Warsaw] 7/1 (1962), pp. 29-38. Summarized in French on p. 59.

*   Heinemann, Ernst Günther. "Liszt's 'Angelus' — Beobachtungen zum kompositorischen Entstehungsprozess."
         Described as item 331.

*   Hughes, William H., Jr. *Liszt's "Première Année de pèlerinage: Suisse."*
         For the most part a study of how certain "Years of Pilgrimage" pieces were revised for inclusion in the "Swiss" volume. Described in greater detail as item 332.

799.   Kirby, F. E. "Liszt's Pilgrimage." *Piano Quarterly* 23/89 (Spring 1975), pp. 17-21.
         Describes portions of the *Années*, especially the *Vallée d'Obermann* and the "Dante" sonata as well as illustrations accompanying those pieces in the editions of 1855 and 1858. Illustrations but no musical examples.

*   Mueller, Rena [Charnin]. "Le cahier d'esquisses du 'Tasso' et la composition des 'Harmonies poétiques et religieuses'."
         Described as item 334.

800.   Presser, Dieter. "Liszts 'Années de pèlerinage. Première Année: Suisse' als Dokument der Romantik." *Liszt-Studien* 1 (1977), pp. 137-153.
         Evaluates Liszt's pieces in terms of music by Beethoven and Schumann, polarities like "Man" vs. "Nature," elements of phrase-structure and periodicity, harmonic progressions, and so on. Illustrated with a number of interesting diagrams but no musical examples.

Several studies of the "Album d'un voyageur" and its relationship to portions of the "Pilgrimage" volumes must be considered as variations upon the ideas of a single author:

801.   Kroó, György. *Az első Zarándokév: Az Albumtól a Suite-ig.* Budapest: Zeneműkiadó, 1986. 128pp.
         ML410.L7K86 1986   ISBN 963-33-0602-7
         A detailed discussion of issues involved in the transformation of the seven *Album* pieces into seven numbers from the first *Années* volume. Illustrated with facsimiles of covers for early editions of the works in question, and with musical examples. Extensive quotations from Liszt's correspondence of the 1830s and 1840s appear in an appendix (pp. 112-128) in their original languages. Commentary and translation from quotations in Hungarian.

Summarized in an Italian-language article entitled "Ferenc Liszt: dall'Album alla Suite" (*Musica/Realtà* 19 [April 1986], pp. 117-137; and 20 [August 1986], pp. 149-169.) See also item 802 (below).

802.   Kroó, György. "'La ligne intérieure' — the Years of Transformation and the 'Album d'un voyageur'." *Studia musicologica* 28 (1986), pp. 249-260.

As interesting as item 801 (above) and much more accessible for non-Hungarian readers. Kroó describes the ideas behind and the compositional history of the *Album d'un voyageur* and the several volumes of the *Années de pèlerinage*, especially before 1842 and especially in terms of Liszt's possible attitudes toward creating collections of his own works. Unfortunately, no musical examples.

Historical studies of the "Album" include:

803.   Main, Alexander. "New Dates for the Traveller's Album." *Journal of Musicological Research* 3 (1981), pp. 411-422.

A shorter version of "Liszt and Lamartine: Two Early Letters," published in *Liszt-Studien* 2 (1981), pp. 132-142. Main devotes both articles to the histories of several early Liszt piano works, among them the *Album*. (With regard to Main's arguments about these works, see also item 711.) No musical examples.

The *Liszt-Studien* version of this article is cited in item 40 and in item 41; entry 813. The *Journal of Musicological Research* version was overlooked in item 40; because it contains no Liszt letters, it was excluded from item 41.

*   Stradal, August. "Das 'Album d'un voyageur' und 'La première année de pélerinage' (La Suisse) von Franz Liszt."

Compares the original *Album d'un voyageur* with Liszt's revisions of that work for the first book of the "Years of Pilgrimage" pieces. Described in greater detail as item 339.

Although published as part of the second volume of the "Years of Pilgrimage," the so-called "Dante" sonata is often discussed by itself. Three of these discussions are described below in alphabetical order (by author):

804.   Grew, Eva Mary. "Liszt's Dante Sonata." *The Chesterian* 21 (1940), pp. 33-40.

Deals primarily with Liszt's interest in Dante and his poems. Grew concludes that there are no important similarities between the sonata and the *Dante* symphony. No musical examples.

805.   Robert, Walter. "'Après une lecture de Dante (Fantasia quasi Sonata)' of
        Liszt." *Piano Quarterly* 23/89 (Spring 1975), pp. 22-27.
        A survey of the circumstances surrounding the composition of the
        "Dante" sonata. Illustrated with two portraits of Liszt and two musical
        examples.

806.   Winklhofer, Sharon. "Liszt, Marie, and the Dante Sonata." *19th Century
        Music* 1 (1977), pp. 15-32.

        As much a study of Liszt's wanderings with Marie d'Agoult and his early
        piano output as a description of the work itself. Several musical examples.

*Five studies dealing with other, individual "Pilgrimage" pieces are described or
cross-referenced below in alphabetical order (by author):*

807.   Backus, Joan [Pauline]. "Liszt's 'Sposalizio': A Study in Musical
        Perspective." *19th Century Music* 12/2 (Fall 1988), pp. 173-183.
        Proposes a program from Liszt's piece based on examination of two
        versions of *Lo sposalizio della Vergine* by Raphael and Perugino. Backus
        illustrates her theory with an analytical diagram and seven musical exam-
        ples as well as reproductions of the paintings mentioned above; to a con-
        siderable extent her article is couched as a reply to remarks made by Leon
        Plantinga in *Romantic Music: A History of Musical Style in Nineteenth-
        century Europe* (New York 1984), p. 188.

808.   Cinnamon, Howard. "Chromaticism and Tonal Coherence in Liszt's
        'Sonetto 104 del Petrarca'." *In Theory Only* 7/3 (1983), pp. 3-19.
        A Schenkerian examination of Liszt's "Sonnet 104," especially the pi-
        ano transcription, emphasizing certain chromatic figures and
        mediant/sub-mediant relationships as structural elements. Six diagram-
        matic representations of harmonic progressions but no musical examples.

809.   Neumeyer, David. "Liszt's 'Sonetto 104 del Petrarca': The Romantic Spirit
        and Voiceleading." *Indiana Theory Review* 2/2 (Winter 1979), pp. 2-22.
        Deals with voiceleading and its implications for musical structure in the
        "Petrarch Sonnet" No. 104, especially the piano version. Illustrated with
        four pages of Schenkerian reduction diagrams and 16 musical examples.
        An Hungarian-language pamphlet devoted to both the piano and vocal
        settings of the "Sonnets" appeared as: Kálmán d'Isoz, *Liszt három
        Petrarca szonettjeröl* (Budapest: Liszt Ferenc Zeneművészeti Főiskola,
        1941/42 [sic]; 15pp.). Rare: the Liszt Ferenc Research Centre in Budapest
        owns at least one copy.

*   Schenkmann, Walter. "The 'Venezia e Napoli' Tarantelle."
        Deals primarily with the transformation of the earlier *Tarentelle* into
        the later *Tarentella*. Described in greater detail as item 335.

810.   Stein, Richard. "Liszts 'Vallée d'Obermann'." *Musik* 13 (1913-1914), pp.
        262-269.
        Not so much a study of differences between the "Obermann" portions
        of the *Album d'un voyageur* and the first volume of the *Années de pèleinage*
        as an essay about the significance of improvisation in Romantic music.
        Illustrated with almost a dozen musical examples used by Stein to dem-
        onstrate the variety and flexibility of Liszt's keyboard figurations.

Finally, one article is devoted exclusively to Venezia e Napoli, *the 'Appendix' to*
Volume II of the "Years of Pilgrimage":

811.   Stradal, August. "Liszts Sammlung Venezia e Napoli." *Neue Musikzeitung*
        23 (1922), pp. 376-378.
        A short but useful synopsis of this delightful collection. Among other
        things, Stradal points out thematic relationships between *Tasso*, the
        Triomphe funèbre du Tasse, and the *Chant du goldolier*. Several musical
        examples.

D. The "Hungarian Rhapsodies" (recorded in items A5, A8, A15, A23-A24,
    A27-A29, A76, A98, and A101)

Surprisingly few studies of the "Hungarian Rhapsodies" have appeared in print.
Perhaps the most comprehensive is:

812.   Gárdonyi, Zoltán. "Paralipomena zu den Ungarischen Rhapsodien Franz
        Liszts." In item 30; pp. 197-225.
        A detailed study of the "Rhapsodies," especially of their origins and
        thematic materials. Six musical examples supplement a great deal of in-
        formation about mss. and other sources. (With regard to the themes of the
        "Rhapsodies" and their "Hungarian" character, see item 722 and especially
        items 727-728.)
        Most studies of the "Rhapsodies" at least mention the *Magyar dallok*
        and *Magyar rhapsodiák*, collections of shorter piano pieces on which many
        of the "Rhapsodies" were based. A very brief discussion of the *Dallok* may
        be found in August Stradal, "Zwei verschollene ungarische Rhapsodien
        von Franz Liszt," *Neue Zeitschrift für Musik* 78 (1911), pp. 229-230. Two
        short musical examples.

Another important but much older study also deserves to be consulted:

813.   Arminski, Hermann. *Die ungarischen Phantasien von Franz Liszt.* Disser-
        tation: University of Vienna, 1929. 186pp.
            Typescript. Musicological Library of the University of Vienna: shelf-
        number E122.
            Describes form, melodies, harmonic processes, and other musical as-
        pects of the "Rhapsodies"; also discusses Liszt's book about the Gypsies
        (item 165f) and selected aspects of keyboard writing and performance.
        Musical examples. A comparatively unimportant work, having been su-
        perseded almost entirely by items 727-728.

*Five more specialized studies of the "Rhapsodies" are described or cross-referenced
below in alphabetical order (by author):*

814.   Altenburg, Detlef. "Liszts Idee eines ungarischen Nationalepos in
        Tönen." *Studia musicologica* 28 (1986), pp. 213-223.
            An introduction to the history of the "Rhapsodies," especially
        Tomášek's use of "rhapsody" as a title for keyboard works and various
        ways in which Liszt's pieces embody his attitudes toward the Hungarian
        people. No musical examples.
            NB: A study by Kenneth DeLong dealing with some of the same ma-
        terial, including Tomášek's works, appeared as "The Piano Rhapsodies of
        J. V. Voříšek" in the *Journal of the American Liszt Society* 26 (1989), pp.
        12-18. Illustrated with a number of musical examples.

*   Eckhardt, Mária [P.]. "Die Handschriften des Rákóczi-Marsches von
        Franz Liszt."
            Deals with H-Bn mss. for this famous "Hungarian Rhapsody" based
        on the famous "Rákóczi" tune. Described in greater detail as item 297.

*   Gárdonyi, Zoltán. "Eine unbekannte Liszt-Rhapsodie?"
            Described in detail as item 328. See also item 313.

*   Kecskeméti, István. "Unbekannte Eigenschrift der XVIII. Rhapsodie von
        Franz Liszt."
            Described as item 305.

*   Winkler, Gerhard J. "Noch einmal: Franz Liszts 'XX. Ungarische
        Rhapsodie.' Rekonstruktion einer Unterstellung."
            Described as item 313. See also item 328.

Less useful, even confusing studies associated—at least in title—with the "Rhapsodies" should be consulted only with caution:

815. Bertha, Alexandre de. "Les 'Rhapsodies Hongroises' de Franz Liszt." *Report of the Fourth Congress of the International musicological Society (1911)*. London: Novello, 1912; pp. 210-224.
  [No LC number available]
  Sums up the compositional history and describes the musical character of the more familiar "Rhapsodies." Bertha spends much of this essay discussing the friendship between Liszt and Chopin, Liszt's patriotism as an Hungarian, etc. In French; an English-language abstract appears on p. 54.

816. Jankélévitch, Vladimir. *Les et la rhapsodie. I: Essai sur la virtuosité.* De la musique au silence, 5. Paris: Plon, 1979. 183pp.
  ML410.L7J3, vol. 1 ISBN 2-259-00427-X
  A work of aesthetic speculation and a discussion of virtuosity, *not* an historical or analytical discussion of the "Rhapsodies" themselves. Illustrated with reproductions of portraits, sheet-music covers, concert programs, and other documents as well as a few musical examples (most of them from the "Transcendentals"). Unfinished: no second volume has appeared in print.

E. The Mephisto Waltzes (recorded in items A19, A23, A25, A27, A75, A77, and A97)

Only two studies of these pieces are currently available:

817. Feofanov, Dmitry. "How to Transcribe the Mephisto Waltz for Piano." *Journal of the American Liszt Society* 11 (1982), pp. 18-27.
  Discusses the little-known evolution of the "Mephisto Waltz" No. 1 from orchestral work to piano solo. Feofanov quotes passages from Lenau's *Faust* and speculates about the virtues of a "combined" waltz based both on Liszt's keyboard arrangement and on Busoni's transcription of the original orchestral version. Several musical examples.

818. Hunt, Mary Angela. *Franz Liszt: The "Mephisto Waltzes."* Dissertation: University of Wisconsin, 1979. ii, 169pp.
  ML410.L7H94 1985
  A survey study of these four fascinating pieces as well as the *Bagatelle sans tonalité*. Hunt also considers differences between keyboard and orchestral versions of the first "Mephisto." Musical examples.
  Summarized in DAI 40/6 (December 1978), p. 2971A; reprinted in the *Journal of the American Liszt Society* 10 (1981), p. 126.

<u>F. Other Mature Piano Pieces</u> (recorded in items A3, A17-A18, A22-A23, A34, A66, A71, A76-A77, A96-A97, and A101)

Seven studies of other mature Liszt piano works are described or cross-referenced below in alphabetical order (by author):

819.   Block, Joseph. "Liszt's 'Die Zelle in Nonnenwerth'." *Piano Quarterly* 81 (1973), pp. 4-11.
        Traces the history of *Die Zelle in Nonnenwerth* as piano piece and song. Block also reprints one of the two 1843 versions of the piece and suggests how the piece should be performed.

820.   Cook, Nicholas. "Liszt's Second Thoughts: 'Liebestraum' No. 2 and Its Relatives." *19th Century Music* 12/2 (Fall 1988), pp. 163-172.
        Discusses the so-called "Cross" motif in several Liszt works, among them the second *Liebestraum*, the first of the *Fünf kleine Klavierstücke* (sometimes called the "Vier [or four] kleine Klavierstücke," because only four appeared in item 136), an untitled piece in E Major, and the song *Gestorben war ich*. Five musical examples and several quotations from the text of *Gestorben*. (With reference to the "cross" motif, see also item 776.)

821.   Diercks, John. "'The Consolations': Delightful Things Hidden Away." *Journal of the American Liszt Society* 3 (1978), pp. 19-24.
        Examines Liszt's *Consolations* as a "six-unit group" of piano pieces. Diercks several times remarks on the Mendelssohn-like quality of these works, adding that they "represent a master composer in his creative prime." Musical examples.

*   Helm, Everett. "A Newly Discovered Liszt Manuscript."
          Evaluates an early version of *Consolation* No. 5. Described in greater detail as item 299.

822.   Szelényi, László. "Franz Liszt: 'Wiegenlied — Chant de Berceau'." *Musikerziehung* 34 (1980-1981), pp. 19-24.
        A brief discussion of this charming piece, illustrated with a few musical examples.

823.   Wagner, Günther. "Die Klavierballaden von Liszt." *Die Klavierballade um die Mitte des 19. Jahrhunderts* by Günther Wagner. Berliner musikwissenschaftliche Arbeiten, 9. Munich and Salzburg: Emil Katzbichler, 1976; pp. 49-70.
        ML747.W33
        An analytical discussion of both Liszt ballades, especially the Ballade in b minor. Wagner compares Liszt's musical structures to sonata-allegro conventions. Musical examples and useful analytical diagrams.

*   Wuellner, Guy. "Franz Liszt's 'Liebestraum' No. 3: A Study of 'O lieb' and its Piano Transcription."
        Described as item 344.

Later Piano Pieces (c. 1870 — 1886)

Liszt's last piano pieces were forgotten for decades. Since the 1950s, however, they have become famous for their unusual textures and harmonic vocabulary. The best as well as the most widely available introduction to these pieces is:

824.   Ogden, John. "Solo Piano Music (1861-1886)." In item 31; pp. 134-167.
        Compares Liszt's earlier and later compositional styles, then describes such works as the "St. Francis Legends," the "Spanish Rhapsody," the variations on "Weinen, Klagen, Sorgen, Zagen," the third volume of the *Années de pèlerinage*, the "Christmas Tree" suite, and so on. Illustrated with more than 50 musical examples.
        NB: The third *Années* volume and associated pieces is discussed above under "Mature Piano Pieces.")

Two book-length studies of these pieces are also worth consulting:

825.   Lee, Robert Charles. *Some Little-known Late Piano Works of Liszt (1869-1886): A Miscellany.* Dissertation: University of Washington, 1970. viii, 264pp.
        ML410.L7L44x 1970b
        Essentially a study of some two dozen works, little known to pianists as late as the 1960s but much more familiar today. The compositions in question include the famous *Bagatelle sans tonalité* and several of the works associated with motifs from the life and music of Wagner. Outfitted with a useful bibliography as well as facsimile reproductions and musical examples.
        Summarized in DAI 31/7 (January 1971), p. 3584.
        Some of the pieces Lee describes were edited by him and published as *Drei späte Klavierstücke* (Kassel: Bärenreiter, 1969). Lee also published an

edition (Seattle 1963) of three other late Liszt pieces: *Sospiri!, Toccata,* and the *Carousel de Madame Pelet-Narbonne.* NB: All of these pieces have also been published in item 137.

826.   Shipwright, Edward Ralph. *A Stylistic and Interpretive Analysis of Selected Compositions from the Late Piano Works of Franz Liszt.* Dissertation: Columbia University, 1977. iii, 332pp.
    MT145.L51S44 1976
    Analyses selected compositions from Liszt's last years, including the *Csárdás macabre, Réminiscences de Boccanegra, Aux cyprès de la Villa d'Este, En rêve,* and so on. Shipwright also deals briefly with programmism as a possible analytical paradigm in pieces like *Unstern* and with Liszt's harmonic vocabulary and its relationship with Hungarian music and musical impressionism.
    Summarized in DAI 37/8 (February 1977), p. 4949A; reprinted in the *Journal of the American Liszt Society* 5 (1979), pp. 91-92.

Four additional surveys of these pieces also deserve attention:

827.   Goode, William M[yrick]. *The Late Piano Works of Franz Liszt and Their Influence on some Aspects of Modern Piano Composition.* Dissertation: Indiana University, 1965. vii, 107pp.
    ML410.L7G5M
    A rather disappointing study of this topic, replete with hand and photocopied musical examples. Concludes with a bibliography. (With regard to more recent discussions of much of the same material, see items 744ff.)
    Summarized in DAI 24/11 (May 1964), p. 6761.

828.   Mauser, Siegfried. "Demontage und Verklärung: Zur Form und Dramatugie in den späten Klavierstücken Franz Liszts." In item 764; pp. 60-70.
    Discusses the thorny problem of programmism and expressive devices or references in pieces like *R.W.—Venezia* and *La lugubre gondola.* Mauser several times refers to Karl-Heinz Stockhausen's theory of "Moment-form." Illustrated with three musical examples, among them the whole of *Resignazione* and *In festo transfigurationis.*

829.   Redepenning, Dorothea. "Erinnerung und Vergessen: Bemerkungen zu einigen Spätwerken Franz Liszts." *Liszt-Studien* 3 (1986), pp. 119-127.
    Deals with remembrance, lamentation, and sorrow as emotional themes in such late Liszt piano pieces as the *Romance oubliée, Am Grabe Richard Wagners,* and *Sospiri!* as well as the song *Pourquoi donc.* Redepenning concludes that these pieces employ characteristic composi-

tional devices, including extremely slow tempi, repetition, and the development of thematic material through variation. Two musical examples.

830.   Yeomans, William. "The Late Piano Works of Liszt." *Monthly Musical Record* 79 (1949), pp. 31-37.

A pioneering introduction to such pieces as *Nuages gris, Unstern, Sursum corda,* and so on. Illustrated with seven musical examples.

Studies of individual late Liszt piano works are described or cross-referenced below according to titles, then in alphabetical order (by author and/or title):

A. "Csárdás macabre" (recorded in items A34 and A74)

831.   Szelényi, István. "Liszt Ferenc 'Csárdás macabre'-ja." *Új zenei szemle* 4/10 (October 1953), pp. 6-8.

One of the earliest descriptions of this fascinating piece, published for the first time during the early 1950s. Musical examples. In Hungarian.

Another article by Szelényi about this piece (or, rather, about a two-piano arrangement of it) appeared in Hungarian as "A 'Csárdás macabre' hiteles szövege" in *Új zenei szemle* 6/1 (January 1955), pp. 7-9. See also Ervin Major, "A 'Csárdás macabre' története," *Új zenei szemle* 4/10 (October 1953), pp. 9-11. Also in Hungarian.

832.   Wellings, Joy. "The 'Csárdás macabre': A Study of Motivic Unity." *Liszt Society Journal* 7 (1982), pp. 2-6.

Describes Liszt's piece primarily in terms of motivic processes; illustrated with 14 musical examples. NB: Wellings' article is apparently based on an unpublished University of Melbourne thesis dealing with Liszt's piano music.

B. "Unstern"

833.   Kabisch, Thomas. "Struktur und Form im Spätwerk Franz Liszts: Das Klavierstück 'Unstern' (1886)." *Archiv für Musikwissenschaft* 42 (1985), pp. 178-199.

Examines motivic and rhythmic patterns in one of Liszt's best-known late works. Illustrated with a diagram of underlying rhythmic patterns in *Unstern* as well as six musical examples.

834.   Rexroth, Dieter. "Zum Spätwerk Franz Liszts — Material und Form in dem Klavierstück 'Unstern'." *Bericht über den international musikwissenschaftlichen Kongreß Bonn 1970*. Kassel: Bärenreiter, 1971; pp. 544-547.

Demonstrates that the scale pattern used in *Unstern* is related to "material-pitch constellations, key relationships, and formal and structural organization" (RILM 7 [1973]; item 3673).

Another article about *Unstern* has appeared recently in an Italian-language publication. See Maria Francesca Agresta, "'Unstern' come chiave di lettura dell'ultimo Liszt," *Civiltà musicale* 2/2 (June 1988), pp. 9-25. Among other things, this article reproduces the entire composition in question on pp. 22-25.

C. The "Wagner" Pieces, including *La lugubre gondola* Nos. 1-2 (recorded in items A17, A33, and A66)

835.   Stenzl, Jürg. "L'énigme Franz Liszt: Prophéties et conventions dans les oeuvres tardives: 'R.W.—Venezia' (1883)." *Revue musicale* 405-406-407 (1987), pp. 127-135.

Describes the form and musical contents of Liszt's late tribute to Wagner, including "innovations" (i.e., unusual harmonies, motivic "cells," and so on) and a few Hungarian or Gypsy elements. Illustrated with the complete text of *R.W.—Venezia* amd two facsimile reproductions of fragments from a ms. of the piece in a private Swiss collection.

836.   Winkler, Gerhard J. "Liszt contra Wagner. Wagnerkritik in den späten Klavierstücken Franz Liszts." *Liszt-Studien* 3 (1986), pp. 189-210.

Deals with Liszt's transcriptions of Wagner's *Parsifal* as well as short piano pieces like *R.W.—Venezia, Am Grabe Richard Wagners*, and *Excelsior*. Winkler analyzes keyboard passagework and compositional details; he also maintains that these works reflect back at the world musical elements that originated with them and were made much of by Wagner; hence "Wagner-criticism" in this article's title. Illustrated with quotations from Liszt letters, Göllerich's diary entries (item 1047), and poems by Lenau as well as 13 musical examples.

D. The "Hungarian Historical Portraits"

*   Claus, Linda. "An Aspect of Liszt's Late Style: The Composer's Revisions for 'Historische, Ungarische Portraits'."
         Described as item 324.

837.   Kroó, György. "Franz Liszts 'Ungarische Bildnisse'." *Musik und
        Gesellschaft* 11 (1961), pp. 599-603.
        A short introduction to these pieces, illustrated with more than a dozen
        very short thematic examples and a reproduction of the Liszt portrait
        painted by Bernhard Blockhorst.
        Another article by Kroó about these pieces appeared in Hungarian
        under the title "Liszt Ferenc: Magyar arcképek" in *Új zenei szemle* 7/1
        (January 1956), pp. 9-17. Six musical examples.

838.   Legány, Dezső. "Hungarian Historical Portraits." *Studia musicologica* 28
        (1986), pp. 79-88.
        Discusses issues related to three letters Liszt addressed to Olga von
        Meyendorff (26 February 1885) and to the publisher Táborszky (8 June
        and 30 July 1885). Six musical examples taken from "Széchenyi,"
        "Teleki," and other of the "Portraits" are also discussed in some detail.

839.   Wellings, Joy. "Liszt's 'Hungarian Historical Portraits'." *Liszt Society
        Journal* 11 (1986), pp. 88-92; and 12 (1987), pp. 48-53.
        Examines each of the "Portraits" in turn, describing them in terms of
        thematic material, harmonic progressions, keyboard writing, etc., as well
        as in terms of their namesakes. Twenty musical examples.

E. Other Late Piano Pieces (some recorded in items A31, A33-A34, and A74-A75)

*   Kecskeméti, István. "[Liszt] Discoveries: An Unknown Piano Piece."
        Identifies and discusses the *Siegesmarsch* Liszt composed around 1870.
        Described in greater detail as item 304a.

840.   Pugliatti, Salvatore. "Espressioni musicali francescane: "La predica agli
        uccelli' di Liszt." *La rassegna musicale* 14 (May 1941), pp. 208-217.
        A measure-by-measure programmatic analysis of "St. Francis Preach-
        ing to the Birds," the first of the two "Legends" for piano. Musical ex-
        amples. NB: The *Rassegna musicale* is scarce in the United States; the
        Performing Arts Division of The New York Public Library owns a copy.

*   Schnapp, Friedrich. "Liszt: a Forgotten Romance."
        Deals with a previously unknown early version of the *Romance
        oubliée*. Described in greater detail as item 310.

841.   Szelényi, István. "Liszt Ferenc: Hangnemnélküli bagatell." *Új zenei szemle*
        7/9 (September 1956), pp. 3-7.
            Describes the "Bagatelle Without Tonality" in stylistic terms. Szelényi
        mentions that the figure E/F/B, which opens the *Bagatelle*, appears in *De
        Profundis*, the unfinished oratorio *St. Stanislaus*, and so on. Seven musical
        examples.
            Two facsimiles of the original ms. of the *Bagatelle* were published in
        Szelényi's article "Adalékok Liszt 'Hangnamnélküli bagatell' cimű
        művéhez" *Magyar zene* 6 (1965), pp. 399-404. In Hungarian.

842.   Szelényi, István. "Liszt: Negyedík elfelejtett keringő." *Új zenei szemle* 6/7-8
        (July-August 1955), pp. 8-10.
            Devoted to the fourth *Valse oubliée*, composed c. 1885. NB: The
        complete "Valse" is printed as an eight-page insert to this article.

843.   Torkewitz, Dieter. "Anmerkungen zu Liszts Spätstil. Das Klavierstück
        'Preludio funèbre (1885)'." *Archiv für Musikwissenschaft* 35 (1978), pp.
        231-236.
            Deals with technical deails of the composition in question as well as
        with programmism and dramatic effect. Only one musical example.

844.   Wellings, Joy. "Liszt's Christmas Tree." *Liszt Society Journal* 13 (1988),
        pp. 4-28.
            Traces the origins of this still little-known keyboard suite, then de-
        scribes each of its twelve parts in terms of melodic and harmonic material,
        form, keyboard writing, etc. Illustrated with several analytical tables and
        24 musical examples.

845.   Wuellner, Guy S. "Franz Liszt's 'Prelude on Chopsticks'." *Journal of the
        American Liszt Society* 4 (1978), pp. 37-44.
            Describes the origins and musical character of Liszt's contribution to
        a volume of *Paraphrases* on the so-called "Chopsticks" theme. Wuellner
        quotes from Liszt's correspondence with Alexander Borodin, who sent a
        copy of the *Paraphrases* to Liszt in 1877 and who evidently saw to it that
        Stassov published Liszt's letter of acknowledgment in a Russian magazine.
        One musical example.

XV: ORIGINAL WORKS FOR ORGAN

Comparatively little known even today, Liszt's compositions for organ include some of the finest works for that instrument written during the nineteenth century. Most of the books and articles described in this chapter fall into two categories: general studies of Liszt's organ music and activities or specialized studies of individual compositions. A new complete edition of Liszt's organ music is described in Chapter V (item 142). Studies devoted to Liszt's arrangements and transcriptions for the organ are described in Chapter XIX, while instrument and performance-practice studies are described in Chapter XX. Recorded performances are described in the Appendix.

GENERAL STUDIES

Only two book-length surveys of Liszt's organ music exist. These are:

846. Schwarz, Peter. *Studien zur Orgelmusik Franz Liszts. Ein Beitrag zur Geschichte der Orgelkomposition im 19. Jahrhundert.* Berliner musikwissenschaftliche Arbeiten, 3. Munich: Emil Katzbichler, 1973. 139pp.
ML410.L7S39   ISBN 3-8739-7031-7
An uneven discussion of Liszt's organ works and the compositional principles employed in them. Schwarz deals competently with some of the pieces he analyzes; in attempting to describe other works in terms of twentieth-century practices, however, he overlooks or ignores conflicting ms. evidence as well as the "climate" of nineteenth-century musical style. Numerous musical examples and a short bibliography.
Summarized (in English) in the *Journal of the American Liszt Society* 5 (1979), p. 91.

847. Kielniarz, Marilyn Torrison. *The Organ Works of Franz Liszt.* Dissertation: Northwestern University, 1984. v, 250pp.
ML410.L7K5 1984a
Traces "the major developments in Liszt's process of organ composition," especially thematic transformation, chromaticism, and other

devices. Numerous musical examples. Concludes with an annotated bibliography of source materials and performance editions.
Summarized in *DAI* 46/2 (August 1985), p. 296A.

*A number of articles have also dealt with Liszt's organ works. Eleven of these articles
are described or cross-referenced below, in alphabetical order (by author and/or title):*

848.   Brafield, Mark. "The Organ Works of Liszt." *Liszt Society Journal* 4
        (1979), pp. 9-12.
        Describes basic features of the *Phantasie und Fuge über den Choral
        "Ad nos, ad salutarem undam"* and the *Praeludium und Fuge über BACH*
        (also referred to, respectively, as "Ad nos" and "BACH") as well as the
        variations on "Weinen, Klagen." Brafield also mentions some of the
        shorter pieces and the character of the Merseburg Cathedral organ for
        which Liszt wrote several of his larger organ pieces. Concludes with
        translations of letters Liszt addressed to Breitkopf & Härtel on 1 December
        1851, and to Louis Köhler on 24 May 1853. Several short musical exam-
        ples.

849.   Busch, Hermann J. "Franz Liszts Orgelmusik für die kirchenmusikalische
        Praxis." *Musica sacra* 106 (1986), pp. 435-443.
        One of the few studies devoted to shorter works like the *Missa pro
        organo* and the *Requiem für die Orgel* as well as some of the larger works.
        Busch traces Liszt's interest in religious music to his earliest literary works
        and considers the suitability of various compositions for liturgical use and
        for performance on particular instruments.

*   Collet, Robert. "Choral and Organ Works."
        A study of Liszt's vocal music which also mentions the "Ad nos" and
        "BACH." Described in greater detail as item 946.

850.   Gárdonyi, Zoltán. "The Organ Works of Franz Liszt." *New Hungarian
        Quarterly* 26/100 (Winter 1985), pp. 243-252.
        A summary of Liszt's accomplishments as an organist and organ
        composer. No musical examples.
        Published originally in Hungarian under the title "Liszt Ferenc
        orgonamuzsikája" in *Magyar zene* 25 (1984), pp. 333-345.

Bernhard Sulze, and Alexander Wilhelm Gottschalg may have had on them. Illustrated with a musical example from the first version of Liszt's "BACH" (reputed to have been influenced by Töpfer's Fantasia in c minor).

860.   Todd, R. Larry. "Liszt, Fantasy and Fugue for Organ on 'Ad nos, ad salutarem undam'." *19th Century Music* 4 (1981), pp. 250-261.

An analysis of "Ad nos" based on the premises that the work is written in one-movement, monothematic sonata-allegro form with a two-part development separated by an "Adagio," and with the fugue serving as recapitulation. Todd also mentions such devices in "Ad nos" as whole-tone scale-patterns, diminished-seventh harmonies, and augmented triads. Several musical examples.

861.   Zacher, Gerd. "Eine Fuge ist eine Fuge ist eine Fuge. (Liszts B-A-C-H Komposition für Orgel.)" *Musik und Kirche* 47 (1977), pp. 15-23.

Explains that Liszt solved certain subtle problems in fugal practice and chromaticism in the "BACH" Prelude and Fugue by use of variation and sonata-allegro form. Zacher also identifies five fugal expositions, identifies the structural center of the fugue itself (measures 170-174), and compares the work as a whole with Bach's G-minor Fugue, BWV 542. Musical examples and diagrams.

Reprinted in item 33; pp. 88-99.

XVI: ORIGINAL WORKS FOR ORCHESTRA AND OTHER INSTRUMENTAL ENSEMBLES
(including concertos and chamber works)

ORCHESTRAL WORKS

Liszt's compositions for orchestra rank among his most important and controversial works. Source and document studies for some of these works are described in Chapter VIII. Recordings of most of them—symphonies, symphonic poems, and so on—are described in the Appendix.

General Studies

No recent study deals with all of Liszt's orchestral compositions, but two books published almost a century ago describe most of them in some detail:

862. Chop, Max. *Franz Liszts symphonische Werke, geschichtlich und musikalisch analysiert.* 2 volumes. Reclams Universal-Bibliothek, 6519 and 6548. Leipzig: Phillip Reclam, 1924-1925.
MT130.L7C4
Introduces Liszt's better-known orchestral works. Volume I is devoted to the *Faust* and *Dante* symphonies as well as the works associated with Lenau's *Faust.* Volume II deals solely with the first 12 symphonic poems. Scattered musical examples.

863. Heuß, Alfred. *Erläuterungen zu Franz Liszts Sinfonien und sinfonischen Dichtungen.* Leipzig: Breitkopf & Härtel, 1912. 195pp.
MT130.L7H5
A short guide to Liszt's principal symphonic works: the two symphonies, the first 12 symphonic poems, etc. Like other studies of its kind and vintage (e.g., items 886, 889, etc.), it ignores *Von der Wiege bis zur Grabe,* the *Trois odes funèbres,* the concertos, etc. Numerous musical examples.
NB: Heuß served as the editor for this volume, part of Breitkopf & Härtel's "Kleiner Konzertführer" series. The authors themselves include Hermann Kretschmar, Richard Pohl, and Georg Münzer.

A third, much shorter survey also deserves to be consulted:

864.   Searle, Humphrey. "The Orchestral Works." In item 31; pp. 279-317.
        An informative survey of Liszt's orchestral output, illustrated with oc-
casional musical examples. More an introduction to the works themselves
than to Liszt's brand of orchestration, the origin of some of his orchestral
pieces in keyboard works, the role programs of various kinds played in his
development as a composer, etc.

*Older studies of Liszt's orchestral works sometimes provide information about the
receptions those works received as well as about musical issues. Two of these studies
are:*

865.   Boutarel, Amédée. *L'oeuvre symphonique de Franz Liszt et l'esthétique
        moderne.* Paris: Henri Heugel, 1886. 61pp.
            ML410.L7B67
        A pamphlet-sized survey of Liszt's symphonic works and the
"modern tendencies" present in their formal and expressive properties.
Includes more detailed comments on the *Faust* and *Dante* symphonies.
Supplemented with a short Liszt biography (pp. 59-61).
        Originally published in installments in *Le ménéstrel.*

866.   Brendel, Franz. *Franz Liszt als Symphoniker.* Leipzig: C. Merseburg, 1859.
        55pp.
            ML410.L7B7
        An historically significant introduction to Liszt's orchestral compos-
itions and especially to his musical programmism and thematic techniques.
No musical examples.
        Reprinted from the *Neue Zeitschrift für Musik* 49/8-14 (20 August —
1 October 1858), pp. 73ff.

One article deals with important aesthetic issues:

867.   Dahlhaus, Carl. "Liszts Idee des Symphonischen." *Liszt-Studien* 2 (1981),
        pp. 36-42.
        An influential article by one of this century's most influential
musicologists. Dahlhaus uses Newman's idea of "double" structural function (see item 775) to explain how Liszt could adapt sonata-allegro form
to programmatic works. Dahlhaus's theory has been "adapted" by a
number of scholars. No musical examples. (With regard to other Liszt
studies by Dahlhaus, see items 869, 896, 910, etc.)

Finally, three studies concerned principally with issues of orchestral scoring are described or cross-referenced below:

868.　Pistone, Danièle. "Liszt et l'orchestre: Tradition et avenir." *Liszt-Studien* 2 (1981), pp. 143-152.

Describes Liszt's changing attitude toward symphonic music and the orchestra by examining the instrumentation called for in *Don Sanche, Tasso, Les préludes*, the *Faust* and *Dante* symphonies, the two piano concertos, *Christus*, etc. Illustrated with four instrumentation tables (pp. 146-149) and supplemented with a few quotations from secondary sources.

*　　Haraszti, Emile. "Les origines de l'orchestration de Franz Liszt." Described as item 296.

*　　Raabe, Peter. *Die Entstehungsgeschichte der Orchesterwerke Franz Liszts.* Described as item 295.

Studies of Individual Works

1. The Symphonies

Studies concerned with each of the two Liszt symphonies are described below according to composition, then alphabetically (by author):

A. The "Faust" Symphony (recorded in items A38-39 and A79)

869.　Dahlhaus, Carl. "Liszts 'Faust-Symphonie' und die Krise der symphonischen Form." *Über Symphonien. Beiträge zu einer musikalischen Gattung: Festschrift Walter Wiora zum 70. Geburtstag.* Tutzing: Hans Schneider, 1979; pp. 129-139.

Evaluates structural "irregularities" in the first movement of Liszt's symphony in terms of sonata-allegro form rather than musical programmism. No musical examples.

870.　Floros, Constantin. "Die Faust-Symphonie von Franz Liszt. Eine semantische Analyse." In item 33; pp. 42-87.

Demonstrates that Liszt's symphony alludes musically to Goethe's play, that the five themes of the symphony refer to five aspects of Faust's character, that the augmented-triad and major-third relation are Faustian symbols, and that the curse is the basic idea behind the "Mephistopheles" movement. Musical examples.

871.   Gruber, Gernot. "Zum Formproblem in Liszts Orchesterwerken —
        exemplifiziert am ersten Satz der Faust-Symphonie." *Liszt-Studien* 1
        (1977), pp. 81-95.
            Deals with sonata-allegro vs. programmatic (i.e., "rhetorical") elements
        in the opening movement of the *Faust* symphony. Gruber argues that
        sonata form plays an important role in Liszt's work, although he identifies
        a number of "abnormal" gestures and structural relationships. Illustrated
        with five short musical examples.

872.   Harrison, Vernon. "Liszt's Faust Symphony: A Psychological
        Interpretation." *Liszt Society Journal* 4 (1979), pp. 2-5.
            Describes a program for Liszt's symphony based on Goethe's Faust
        story and Jungian concepts like "ego," "autonomous complex," "anima,"
        and so on. Forced and unconvincing, this study—like others by Harrison
        (e.g., item 601)—has little to do with actual historical evidence or musical
        processes. Quotations from Goethe and T. S. Eliot, and six short musical
        examples.

873.   Longyear, Rey M., and Kate R. Covington. "Tonal and Harmonic Struc-
        tures in Liszt's Faust Symphony." *Studia musicologica* 28 (1986), pp.
        153-171.
            Counters attacks against the "formlessness" and "lack of coherence"
        of the *Faust* symphony since the nineteenth century by describing the
        composition's overall formal structure, fundamental motivic materials,
        certain harmonic details (e.g., parallel structures in the symphony's outer
        movements), etc. Longyear and Covington illustrate their discussion with
        outlines (pp. 156-158) and more than a dozen musical examples, many of
        them concerned with motifs and functional harmony.

874.   Niemöller, Klaus Wolfgang. "Zur nicht-tonalen Thema-Struktur von
        Liszts 'Faust-Symphonie'." *Musikforschung* 22 (1969), pp. 69-72.
            A "reply" to Ritzel's 1967 *Musikforschung* article (item 876). Niemöller
        demonstrates that the "dodecaphonic" theme for the *Faust* symphony was
        derived by Liszt from gypsy scale patterns and the augmented triads that
        can be derived from them. He also argues that the principal melody of the
        symphony's first movement may be interpreted programmatically as "a
        self-portrait of the Hungarian Liszt." Diagrams and two musical examples.

875.   Ott, Leonard [W]. "The Orchestration of the 'Faust Symphony'." *Journal
        of the American Liszt Society* 12 (1982), pp. 28-37.
            Evaluates Liszt's brand of orchestration in light of Berlioz's treatise,
        aspects of the *Symphonie fantastique*, and Ott's four-fold schema of
        "timbral flow" (e.g., alternation and exchange, overlapping, expansion and

contraction, and stability). A strikingly perceptive study, illustrated with eight musical examples and quotations from several secondary sources.

876.   Pohl, Richard. "Liszts Faust Symphonie." In item 227; pp. 247-320.
An intelligent, influential analysis of Liszt's symphony, illustrated with numerous musical examples. Originally published in the *Neue Zeitschrift für Musik* 57/1-21 (4 July-21 November 1862), pp. 1ff.
Like other early studies of Liszt's symphonic works (e.g., items 886 and 889), Brendel's article constitutes a reply to anti-Liszt reviews published in magazines and newspapers. An especially interesting defense of the *Faust* symphony, and one little-known to many scholars, appeared a few years after Brendel's article. See Eugen von Blum, *Beleuchtung des durch Franz Liszt's 'Faust-Sinfonie' in Breslau hervorgerufenen Zeitungsstreites* (Breslau: W. Jakobsohn, 1964). The Library of Congress owns a copy of this rare pamphlet (ML410.L7B6).

877.   Ritzel, Fred. "Materialdenken bei Liszt: Eine Untersuchung des 'Zwölftonthemas' der Faust-Symphonie." *Musikforschung* 20 (1967), pp. 289-294.
Argues that the opening theme of the *Faust* symphony is derived from the augmented triad, itself self-sufficient in tone image and function, an hypothesis contradicted two years later by Niemöller (item 874). Ritzel's article is illustrated with diagrams and six musical examples.

*   Somfai, László. "Metamorphoses of Liszt's Faust Symphony" and other studies.
Drawing on archival materials, Somfai explains in these studies how Liszt put together the three "portraits" that constitute this work. Described in greater detail as items 336-338.

B. The "Dante" Symphony (recorded as items A40 and A80)

878.   Barricelli, Jean-Pierre. "Liszt's Journey through Dante's Hereafter." *Journal of the American Liszt Society* 14 (1983), pp. 3-15.
A musico-programmatic analysis of the *Dante* symphony, based on the premise that "When Liszt spoke of a 'transposition of art' . . . he implied a strong measure of interpretation by one art of the other, accessible to analysis and not merely suggesting a 'reaction to' the original subject." Illustrated with lengthy quotations (in Italian) from Dante's *Commedia* and more than a dozen short musical examples.
Reprinted from the *Bucknell Review* 26 (1982), pp. 149-166.

     Franz Liszt: A Guide to Research

879.   Fitz-James, B. de Miramonde. "Liszt et la Divine Comédie." *Revue de musicologie* 22 (1938), pp. 81-93.
    Traces Liszt's idea of a symphony based on Dante's poem to a meeting with Autran in 1845. Fitz-James includes the texts of letters Liszt addressed to Autran in 1845.
    Other, older articles about Liszt's settings of the *Commedia* also exist—e.g., André Pirro, "Franz Liszt et la 'Divine Comédie'" in *Dante, mélanges de critique et d'érudition françaises* (Paris 1921), pp. 165-184. Not seen but cited in item 18.

880.   Harrison, Vernon. "The Dante Symphony." *Liszt Society Journal* 11 (1986), pp. 56-69.
    A lengthy prolegomena to Liszt's work, dealing primarily with the *Commedia* and its medieval Christian philosophy. Only at the end of his article does Harrison turn to the symphony itself (a "glorious failure" Harrison nevertheless wishes he himself had written) in order to describe its overall organization and principal melodies. Fourteen brief musical examples.

881.   Knight, Ellen. "The Harmonic Foundation of Liszt's Dante Symphony." *Journal of the American Liszt Society* 10 (1981), pp. 56-63.
    Examines interrelationships between a sectional scheme of organization and certain motifs and harmonic progressions in the *Dante* symphony. Knight contends that, despite its episodic character and comparatively weak sense of musical coherence, Liszt's symphony is a carefully constructed work. Musical examples.

882.   Pohl, Richard. "Liszts Symphonie zu Dantes 'Divina Comedia'." In item 227; pp. 238-246.
    A synopsis of the symphony by one of Liszt's most faithful apologists. Unfortunately no musical examples.

883.   Williamson, John. "Liszt and Form — Some Thoughts on the First Movement of the Dante Symphony." *New Hungarian Quarterly* 27/104 (Winter 1986), pp. 213-220.
    Considers traditional and radical elements in the *Dante* symphony. Williamson asserts that "The really remarkable aspects of [Liszt's 'Inferno' movement] are those which negate the symphonic tradition, often in pure antithesis." Seven musical examples.

2. The Symphonic Poems

Although only a handful of specialists have discussed all of these thirteen works, two book-length introductions to them do exist. These are:

884.   Krauklis, G[eorgii] V[ilgelmovich]. *Simfoncheskie poemy F. Lista.* Moscow: "Muzyka," 1974. 138pp.
        ML410.L7K83 1974
        A somewhat cursory description of Liszt's first twelve symphonic poems, accompanied by a summary of programmism and its principles and brief analyses of each work. Musical examples. In Russian.

885.   Johns, Keith [T.]. *A Structural Analysis of the Relationship Between Programme, Harmony and Form in the Symphonic Poems of Franz Liszt.* Dissertation: University of Wollongong [Australia], 1986. 359pp.
        [No LC number available]
        More detailed than item 884 (above) but difficult to obtain. (The present author owns a photocopy.) Johns concerns himself in this dissertation with virtually every aspect of these pieces: harmony, form, orchestral writing, programmism, how the pieces were received by nineteenth-century critics and audiences, etc. Numerous analytical charts and diagrams, more than 50 musical examples, and a substantial bibliography (pp. 351-359).
        A revised version of this dissertation is scheduled to appear in the "American Liszt Society Studies Series" published in cooperation with Pendragon Press.

Five older studies dealing with issues affecting most or all of the symphonic poems are described below in alphabetical order (by author):

886.   Draeseke, Felix. "Franz Liszts neun symphonische Dichtungen." *Anregungen für Kunst, Leben und Wissenschaft* 2 (1857), pp. 261ff; 3 (1858), pp. 10ff.; and 4 (1859), pp. 171ff.
        An early apology for *Les préludes, Orpheus, Festklänge, Prometheus, Tasso, Mazeppa, Hungaria, Héroïde funèbre,* and *Ce qu'on entend sur la montagne,* describing their character and merits. To a considerable extent Draeseke's monograph consists of answers to Liszt's detractors in the press. No musical examples.
        Other studies dealing with the reception of Liszt's orchestral music also appeared during the 1850s and 1860s; see Eugen Blum's pamphlet mentioned under item 876. Recent studies have also dealt with these issues. A two-part article by Keith Johns about the controversial Liszt concert held at the Leipzig Gewandhaus in February 1857, for example, is mentioned in Chapter I.

887.   Hahn, Arthur. *Franz Liszts symphonische Dichtungen. Erläuterung mit
        einer Einleitung: Das Leben Franz Liszts.* Berlin: Schlesinger, 1910. 216pp.
        MT130.L699H3
        Consists for the most part of rather pedestrian discussions of program
        and thematic materials in the first twelve poems. Musical examples.
        Reprinted separately as pamphlets in the series "Der Musikführer"
        published c. 1898 at Frankfurt a.M. by H. Bechheld. Also reprinted in
        Arthur Hahn et al., *Franz Liszt, sein Leben und seine Werke* (Frankfurt
        a.M.: H. Bechheld, n.d.). This last volume also contains a sketch of
        Liszt's life as well as analyses of the poems, the *Faust* and *Dante* sym-
        phonies (also by Hahn), and the oratorio *St. Elisabeth* (Fritz Volbach).

888.   Pohl, Richard. "Liszts symphonische Dichtungen. Ihre Entstehung,
        Wirkung und Gegnerschaft." In item 227; pp. 199-228.
        A vigorous defense of these compositions and their value, together with
        discussions of structural issues, programism and music, the reception se-
        veral of the works received in Leipzig and other cities, etc. Unfortunately
        no musical examples. Concludes with an abbreviated catalog of Liszt's
        instrumental works (pp. 220-228).

889.   Wagner, Richard. *Ein Brief von Richard Wagner über Franz Liszt's
        Symphonischen Dichtungen.* Leipzig: C.F. Kahnt, 1857. 32pp.
        Wagner's only substantial polemic written on Liszt's behalf. Published
        originally in 1857 in the *Neue Zeitschrift für Musik.*

890.   Weber, Josef. *Die sinfonischen Dichtungen Franz Liszts.*   Dissertation:
        University of Vienna, 1929. 153pp.
        Typescript. Musicological Library of the University of Vienna: shelf-
        number E116.
        Evaluates Liszt's poems in terms of their harmonic processes, melodies,
        contrapuntal writing, rhythmic figures, instrumentation, and structural or-
        ganization. Weber also provides a synopsis of each work's compositional
        history (pp. 118-149). Musical examples and a bibliography.

*Finally, seven somewhat more studies have addressed issues involving programmism,
nationalism, and the dissemination of the symphonic poem as a genre between the
1850s and World War I. These studies are identified or cross-referenced below,
again in alphabetical order (by author):*

*   Altenburg, Detlef. "La notion lisztienne de poème symphonique dans son
        interpénétration avec la conscience nationale à la fin du XIXe siècle et au
        début du XXe."
        Described as item 725.

891.   Bergfeld, Joachim. *Die formale Struktur der symphonischen Dichtungen Franz Liszts, dargestellt auf Grund allgemeiner Untersuchungen über Inhalt und Form der Musik.* Eisenach: P. Kühner, 1931. 113pp.
        [No LC number available]
        An introduction to the symphonic poem as a genre and to musical programmism, followed by structural analyses of the first twelve poems (pp. 47-107) based entirely on phrase, period, and "bar" forms. Numerous diagrams but no musical examples.

*   Bongrain, Anne. "La figuration musicale dans les poèmes symphoniques de Liszt."
        Discusses issues relating to thematic materials in the Symphonic Poems and programmism in general. Described in greater detail as item 662.

892.   Dyson, Vernon. "Liszt's Symphonic Poems: An Aspect of the Development of Programme Music." *Liszt Society Journal* 3 (1978), pp. 8-13.
        Another discussion of programmism and the symphonic poem as a "new" musical genre. Unfortunately, Dyson's article is less valuable than many others (e.g., item 894).
        Another superficial discussion of the same topics appeared as: Valerie Dyson, "Liszts Symphonic Poems: An Aspect of the Development of Programme Music," *Liszt Society Journal* 3 (1978), pp. 8-13. No musical examples.

893.   Heinrichs, Josef. *Über den Sinn der Lisztschen Programmmusik.* Kempen: Thomas Druckerei- und Buchhandlung. 1929. 111pp.
        ML410.L7H35
        Concerned with most of Liszt's symphonic works as well as the Sonata in b minor and such topics as the relationship between programmism and non-musical arts. Musical examples and a bibliography.

894.   Marggraf, Wolfgang. "Die Idee der Sinfonischen Dichtung." In item 37; pp. 5-18.
        Reviews Liszt's contributions to the creation of this form, with special attention to arguments about the character and significance of symphonic poems promulgated by Carl Dahlhaus in item 896 (below) and elsewhere. No musical examples.

895.   Miller, Norbert. "Musik als Sprache. Zur Vorgeschichte von Liszts Symphonischen Dichtungen." *Beiträge zur musikalischen Hermeneutik.* Studien zur Musikgeschichte des 19. Jahrhunderts, 43. Regensburg: Gustav Bosse, 1975; pp. 223-287.

      ML3797.1.B45   ISBN 3-7649-2102-1

Examines and evaluates issues concerned with programmism and Liszt's orchestral works. NB: Item 897 is described by Miller as an "appendix" to this article.

Most published studies of the symphonic poems concern individual compositions and their characteristics. Studies of this kind are described or cross-referenced below in alphabetical order (by title of symphonic poem, then by author). NB: Recordings of all thirteen symphonic poems are described as items A41 and A81 in the Appendix:

A. "Ce qu'on entend sur la montagne"

896.   Dahlhaus, Carl. "Liszts Bergsymphonie und die Idee der Symphonischen Dichtung." *Jahrbuch des Staatlichen Instituts für Musikforschung Preußischer Kulturbesitz 1975* (Berlin 1976), pp. 96-130.

      ML5.S74   ISBN 3-87537-142-9

A highly intriguing investigation of one of Liszt's most problematic symphonic poems. Dahlhaus discusses the symphonic poem as a genre, evaluates *Ce qu'on entend* in terms of sonata-allegro form (see especially p. 114), and reprints Hugo's poem in French (pp. 129-130). Illustrated with scattered short musical examples.

897.   Heuß, Alfred. "Eine motivisch-thematische Studie über Liszts symphonsiche Dichtung 'Ce qu'on entend sur la montagne.' Zur 100. Wiederkehr von Franz Liszts Geburtstag am 22. Oktober 1911." *Zeitschrift der Internationalen Musikgesellschaft* 13 (1911-1912), pp. 10-21.

An early study of programmism and its musical expression in Liszt's longest symphonic poem. Musical examples.

898.   Kelkel, Manfred. "Wege zur 'Berg-Symphonie' Liszts." *Liszt-Studien* 3 (1986), pp. 71-89.

Evaluates conflicting opinions concerning *Ce qu'on entend sur la montagne* and its formal organization and semantic (i.e., programmatic and expressive) character. Kelkel quotes dozens of authorities, including Ramann (item 3), Floros (item 897), and so on; he also includes dozens of musical examples and intriguing outlines of harmonic and motivic relationships (pp. 84-89).

899. Miller, Norbert. "Elévation bei Victor Hugo und Franz Liszt: Über die Schwierigkeiten einer Verwandlung von lyrischen in symphonische Dichtungen." *Jahrbuch des Staatlichen Instituts für Musikforschung Preußischer Kulturbesitz 1975* (Berlin 1976), pp. 131-159.
   ML5.S74   ISBN 3-87537-142-9
   A discussion of the so-called "Mountain Symphony" that concentrates on difficulties for listeners in the work and the composition's failure during its initial performances. No musical examples.

900. Raffalt, Reinhard. *Ueber die Problematik der Programm-Musik: Ein Versuch ihres Aufweises an der Pastoral-Symphonie von Beethoven, der Berg-Symphonie von Liszt und der Alpensinfonie von Strauss.* Passau: Ablassmayer & Penninger, 1949. 91pp.
   ML3855.R3
   Devoted in part to explaining how Liszt contributed to the evolution of programmism in nineteenth-century orchestral music. Musical examples and a bibliography.

B. "Hamlet"

901. Wehnert, Martin. "Imagination und thematisches Verständnis bei Liszt — dargestellt an 'Hamlet'." In item 37; pp. 30-46.
   Deals with implications of Shakespeare's play and aesthetic issues as well as Liszt's transformation of literary material into programmatic music. No illustrations or musical examples.
   A programmatic analysis of *Hamlet*, written by Edward Murphy, is scheduled to appear in Volume 29 of the *Journal of the American Liszt Society.*

C. "Héroïde funèbre"

902. Riedel, Friedrich W. "À propos de l'Héroïde funèbre: Quelques caractéristiques stylistiques des musiques funèbres de Liszt, de ses prédécesseurs et de ses contemporains." *Revue musicale* 405-406-407 (1987), pp. 29-35.
   Discusses stylistic elements in *Héroïde funèbre* from the vantage point of funeral pieces by Beethoven, Chopin, Spohr, etc., as well as in terms of the internal organization of musical materials in the symphonic poem itself. Diagrams and lists of representative nineteenth-century funeral compositions but no musical examples.

<u>D. "Hunnenschlacht"</u> (also recorded in item A44)

903.   Kaiser, Manfred. "Anmerkungen zur Kompositionstechnik Franz Liszts: Am Beispiel der 'Hunnenschlacht'." *Liszt-Studien* 1 (1977), pp. 125-129.
        An attempt to grapple with formal organization in the "Battle of the Huns," one of Liszt's less well-known symphonic poems. Kaiser proposes that this work is written in what he calls "open form" (instead of sonata-allegro form), defending himself by likening some of Liszt's motivic and harmonic materials—and, by extension, his sense of musical order—to those of avant-garde composers. Illustrated with a few musical examples.

*   Knotik, Cornelia. *Musik und Religion im Zeitalter des Historismus.*
        Deals in part with programmism in *Hunnenschlacht.* Described in greater detail as item 656.

<u>E. "Die Ideale"</u>

904.   Batta, András. "Liszt's Hommage à Weimar: Die Ideale (Die Apotheose der Apotheose)." In item 37; pp. 47-56.
        Reviews remarks by Raabe (in item 4) about *Die Ideale,* important points about the character of Liszt's symphonic poems, the place of *Ideale* in Liszt's output, etc. No musical examples.

<u>F. "Mazeppa"</u> (also recorded in items A44 and A82)

905.   Stradal, August. "Liszts Mazeppa-Werke." *Neue Zeitschrift für Musik* 78 (1911), pp. 577-583 and 597-601.
        Describes how Liszt's etude evolved through several keyboard versions and into the symphonic poem of the same name. Illustrated with a number of musical examples.
        Other, much shorter studies of this symphonic poem include: Albert Brussee, "De Mazeppa-musiek van Franz Liszt," *Franz Liszt Kring* 8 (1986), pp. 5-32. Also deals with the piano etude of the same name. Illustrated with four facsimiles of mss. as well as 32 musical examples. In Dutch.

<u>G. "Orpheus"</u> (also recorded in items A38 and A44)

906.   Motman, Tim van. "Liszts 'Orpheus II': Een andere interpretatie." *Mens en melodie* 36 (1981), pp. 274-277.
        Argues against Jos van der Zanden's programmatic interpretation of Liszt's composition (see item 908). No musical examples. In Dutch.

907. Schibli, Sigfrid. "Franz Liszt: 'Orpheus'." *Neue Zeitschrift für Musik* 147/7-8 (July-August 1986), pp. 54-56.

An introduction to the history and musical contents of this symphonic poem. Like other essays by Schibli (e.g., items 703 and 784), this one is intended as much for musical amateurs as for performers and scholars.

908. Zanden, Jos van der. "Liszts 'Orpheus.' Relaties tussen musiek en programma." *Mens en melodie* 35 (1980), pp. 607-615.

Analyses the structure and fundamental harmonic patterns in Liszt's symphonic poem and attempts to relate them to the story of Orpheus as told in Ovid's *Metamorphoses*. Musical examples and other illustrations. In Dutch.

H. "Les préludes" (also recorded in items A14, A42, and A82)

909. Main, Alexander. "Liszt after Lamartine: 'Les préludes'." *Music & Letters* 60 (1979), pp. 133-148.

Asserts that this symphonic poem did not simply grow "out of the Autran choruses [*Les quatres éléments*] in some way that cannot be traced in detail." Instead, Main attempts to prove that a Lamartine-like program can be assigned to the structure and thematic transformations of Liszt's symphonic poem. Six musical examples as well as two tables (pp. 142-143) outlining that program in literary and thematic form. (With regard to the theories Main argues against, see items 323, 329, and 345 [all of them cross-referenced below] as well as items 256, 295-296, and 909.)

*   Bonner, Andrew. "Liszt's 'Les préludes' and 'Les quatre élémens'."
Described as item 323.

*   Chailley, Jacques. "Quel fut l'inspirateur des 'Préludes' de Liszt?"
Described as item 345.

*   Haraszti, Emile. "Genèse des Préludes de Liszt qui n'ont aucun rapport avec Lamartine."
Deals with materials Liszt used in composing *Les préludes*. Described in greater detail as item 329.

<u>I. "Prometheus"</u>

910.   Dahlhaus, Carl. "Zur Kritik des ästhetischen Urteils. Über Liszts
        'Prometheus'." *Musikforschung* 23 (1970), pp. 411-419.
        Describes *Prometheus* as a "document" rather than a living masterpiece
        because of what Dahlhaus considers its outmoded "musical poeticism." In
        terms of the anti-aesthetics of the avant-garde, however, the composition
        can be understood to anticipate "compositional features of new music"
        (RILM 5 [1971]; entry 3812). No musical examples.

911.   Torkewitz, Dieter. "Innovation und Tradition. Zur Genesis eines
        Quartenakkords. Über Liszts 'Prometheus'-Akkord." *Musikforschung* 33
        (1980), pp. 291-302.
        Traces the unusual chords in the opening measures of *Prometheus* to
        works from Liszt's early years as a composer (see item 613). Musical ex-
        amples.

*   Williamson, John. "The Revision of Liszt's 'Prometheus'."
        Described as item 343.

<u>J. "Tasso: Lamento e trionfo"</u> (also recorded in items A43 and A82)

*   Johns, Keith [T.]. "More on 'Tasso' . . ."
        As much about Liszt's symphonic poem as about the arrangement of
        that work he prepared for piano duet. Described in greater detail as item
        301.

<u>K. "Von der Wiege bis zum Grabe"</u>

912.   Schläder, Jürgen. "Der schöne Traum vom Ideal. Die künstlerische
        Konzeption in Franz Liszts letzter Symphonischen Dichtung." *Hamburger
        Jahrbuch für Musikwissenschaft* ["Programmusik"] 6 (1983), pp. 47-62.
        ISBN 3-9215-1899-7
        Evaluates *Von der Wiege bis zum Grabe* in terms of its programmatic
        design. Illustrated with analytical diagrams, a reproduction of the painting
        by Count Zichy used by Liszt as the inspiration for this work, and short
        musical examples.

WORKS FOR OTHER INSTRUMENTAL ENSEMBLES

Liszt's enormous output includes several concertos for piano and orchestra (as well as the three "Funeral Odes" and several incidental orchestral pieces), concertos for piano and orchestra, a few chamber pieces, and a few miscellaneous works that call for instrumental ensembles. Document and source studies dealing with the concertos—and, to a more limited extent, with the smaller orchestral works—are described in Chapters VIII, XIV, and XIX. Recordings of them are identified and discussed in the Appendix.

Concertos

Only two studies—the first a volume difficult to obtain in the United States, the second quite cursory—have dealt with Liszt's works for piano and orchestra as a genre:

913.   Khokhlov, Iu. *Fortep'iannie kontserty F. Lista.* Moscow: "Gos. Muz. Izd.," 1953. 71pp.
       [No LC number available]
       Not seen but cited in several standard music bibliographies. In Russian.

914.   Collet, Robert. "Works for Piano and Orchestra." In item 31; pp. 248-278.
       A short, rather disappointing survey of this fascinating topic. Illustrated with excerpts from the Concertos for piano and orchestra as well as Liszt's *Totentanz*, fantasies on Berlioz's *Lélio* and Beethoven's *Ruin of Athens*, etc.

Two dissertations also deal with Liszt's most important piano/orchestra pieces:

915.   Engel, Hans. *Die Entwicklung des deutschen Klavierkonzertes von Mozart bis Liszt.* Leipzig: Breitkopf & Härtel, 1927. 271pp.
       ML1263.E56
       A survey study, dealing only in part with Liszt. Illustrated with scattered musical examples, especially on pp. 258-260. Similar in design to item 916 (below).

916.   Stengel, Theophil. *Die Entwicklung des Klavierkonzertes von Liszt bis zur Gegenwart.* Heidelberg: Reiher & Kurt, 1931. 146pp.
       ML706.S75 1931
       Describes the evolution of the post-Romantic piano concerto, with special reference to Liszt (pp. 9-26) and his followers among composers of the so-called "Weimar School" (pp. 26-50). Illustrated with four pages

of musical examples. Supplemented with numerous quotations from secondary sources and a bibliography.

In a review of Stengel's work published in the *Zeitschrift für Musikwissenschaft* 15 (1932-1933), pp. 181-183, Hans Engel corrects many of Stengel's statements but calls the author's remarks about Liszt "the most solidly based in the book."

Six more specialized studies of Liszt's piano/orchestra pieces are described or cross-referenced below in alphabetical order (by author and/or title). NB: Performances of individual concertos are described in items A11, A45-A47, A82-A83, and A99:

*   Hinson, Maurice. "Long Lost Liszt Concerto?"

Described as item 346. See also item 347 (cross-referenced after item 919).

917.   Johns, Keith [T.]. "'De Profundis. Psaume instrumental': An Abandoned Concerto for Piano and Orchestra by Franz Liszt." *Journal of the American Liszt Society* 15 (1984), pp. 96-104.

Describes this fragmentary early work with the help of analytical diagrams and several musical examples. Johns includes quotations from Liszt letters and other documentation.

918.   Johns, Keith [T.]. "'Malédiction': The Concerto's History, Programme, and Some Notes on Harmonic Organization." *Journal of the American Liszt Society* 18 (1985), pp. 29-35..

Examines another early Liszt concerto, this one published in item 136. Several analytical diagrams and two musical examples.

Another article about the "Malédiction" concerto exists. See István Szelényi, "Liszt e-Moll zongoraversenye," published in *Új zenei szemle* 6/7-8 (July-August 1955), pp. 19-23. Includes eight musical examples, among them passages from the symphonic poem *Prometheus* and other works. In Hungarian. 920.)

919.   Kroó, György. "Gemeinsame Formprobleme in den Klavierkonzenten von Schumann und Liszt." *Robert Schumann: Aus Anlaß seines 100. Todestages*, ed. Hans Joachim Moser et al. Leipzig: Breitkopf & Härtel, 1956; pp. 136-143.

ML410.S4M68

Compares both of Liszt's concertos with the Schumann A-minor concerto. Kroó is especially interested in details of sonata-allegro form. Illustrated with about a dozen musical examples.

*   Prahács, Margit. "Liszts letztes Klavierkonzert."
      Described as item 347.

920.   Rosenblatt, Jay. "A Recently Recovered Liszt Concerto." *Journal of the
       American Liszt Society* 26 (1989), pp. 64-66.
       Describes an early work first mentioned in item 81 but put together
       by Rosenblatt from D-WRgs and Soviet ms. fragments and performed by
       several major American orchestras during the 1989-1990 concert season.
       Rosenblatt will almost certainly publish additional descriptions of this
       work; Editio Musica of Budapest is preparing to publish a full score.

Chamber Works

*Liszt's chamber-music output was restricted to a single sonata (also known as the
"Duo") which may date from the mid-1830s, and to arrangements for his own works
for small ensembles. Studies dealing with several of these arrangements are described
in Chapter XIX. The four studies described below deal almost exclusively with the
sonata; they are presented in alphabetical order (by author). Performances of
lesser-known chamber works are described in item A48:*

921.   Gergely, Jean. "Reconstitution et première audition de la Sonate pour
       violon et piano de Liszt." *Revue de musicologie* 45 (1960), pp. 91-92.
       A brief account of the discovery and first performance of the "Duo"
       for violin and piano. Cited here primarily because so little has been pub-
       lished about this work. See also item 923.

922.   Sebestyén, Albert. "Franz Liszts Originalkompositionen für Violine und
       Klavier." *Liszt-Studien* 1 (1977), pp. 163-178.
       Describes the discovery and contents of the "Duo," which was based
       on themes taken from Chopin's Mazurka, Op. 6, No. 2. Sebestyén also
       mentions arrangements by Liszt for violin and piano, among them settings
       of the *Romance oubliée* and movements from *Christus*. Illustrated with five
       extended musical examples.

923.   Serly, Tibor. "De vioolsonate van Franz Liszt." *Mens en melodie* 15
       (1960), pp. 348-350.
       A brief account of the "Duo" by its discoverer. Item 921 covers most
       of the same material. In Dutch.

924.   Walker, Alan. "Liszt's Duo Sonata." *Musical Times* 116 (1975), pp. 620-621.
        Traces the history and describes the contents of this early work. Based on internal evidence, Walker declares that the "Duo" was written in 1851-1852. Two musical examples.

Ensemble Works with Wind Instruments

A single short article deals with miscellaneous Liszt pieces utilizing wind instruments. NB: Recordings of Liszt works arranged for band are described as item A100:

925.   Whitwell, David. "Liszt: His Music for Winds." *Instrumentalist* 21/5 (December 1966), pp. 65-67.
        Deals with Liszt's brass and wind parts in 15 works, including settings of the *Soldatenlied* and *Weimars Volkslied*, an arrangement of the tune "Nun danket alle Gott," etc. No musical examples.

XVII: ORIGINAL WORKS FOR SOLO VOICE

*No comparable portion of Liszt's compositional output has received less attention
from scholars than his songs and recitations for solo voice, some of which rank
among the finest works of their kind. The studies described below include virtually
everything ever published about these pieces. Studies of revisions for some of Liszt's
songs are described in Chapter VIII, while stylistic studies which draw upon portions
of these and other songs are described in Chapters XII-XIV. Recorded performances
are described in the Appendix.*

GENERAL STUDIES

*Only one modern, book-length study has been devoted exclusively to Liszt's solo vo-
cal works:*

926.　Montu-Berthon, Suzanne. *Un Liszt méconnu. Mélodies et Lieder. Revue
　　　musicale* 342-343-344 (1981): entire triple issue.

　　　A piece-by-piece analysis of Liszt's songs and recitations, illustrated
with 138 musical examples. Montu-Berthon's observations are accurate
but somewhat commonplace (e.g., she spends a great deal of time discussing Liszt's melodies but overlooks or ignores such fascinating topics
as his numerous revisions or versions of songs still unpublished in the early
1980s). Especially valuable for observations about French prosody and
those songs set to French-language texts. Unfortunately, the hand-copied
musical examples are often difficult to read.

Two older book-length studies of Liszt's works for solo voice also deserve attention:

927.　Reuss, Eduard. *Liszts Lieder.* Leipzig: Max Brockhaus, 1907. viii, 96pp.
　　　ML410.L7R5

　　　A survey of Liszt's more familiar songs and recitations, describing
many of their more obviously musical and expressive characteristics. Illustrated with numerous musical examples.

　　　This volume is virtually identical with the series of articles Reuss published under the same title in the *Bayreuther Blätter* 7/9 (1906), pp.
165-197; and 10/12 (1906), pp. 250-312.

928.   Wenz, Joseph. *Franz Liszt als Liederkomponist.* Dissertation: University
         of Frankfurt a.M., 1921. The Stadt- und Universitätsbibliothek, Frank-
         furt, owns a typescript copy.

         A survey study of Liszt's songs, especially those with German-language
         texts. Wenz's work included at least one then-unpublished piece: a version
         of *Nonnenwerth* (?later published as item 151). Illustrated with other mus-
         ical examples.
         NB: This dissertation may no longer exist. Several years ago the present
         author examined the D-F copy mentioned above. Since then this copy has
         apparently been stolen or misplaced by library officials.

*Several valuable shorter studies provide basic information about Liszt's songs and
revisions. Five of these studies are described below in alphabetical order (by author):*

929.   Cooper, Martin. "Liszt as a Song Writer." *Music & Letters* 19 (1938), pp.
         171-181.
         An introduction to Liszt's songs, with special emphasis on their ex-
         pressive character and "fantastically unequal [musical] quality." Illustrated
         with five musical examples.

930.   Douglas, John. "Franz Liszt as a Song Composer." *NATS Journal* [Na-
         tional Association of Teachers of Singing]. 43/4 (March-April 1987), pp.
         4-15.
         A comparatively detailed survey of Liszt's songs, beginning with
         Angiolin, dal biondo crin and early versions of the "Petrarch Sonnets."
         Douglas also discusses some of Liszt's song transcriptions. Illustrated with
         18 musical examples and tables of pedagogical information.

931.   Headington, Christopher. "The Songs." In item 31; pp. 221-247.
         A survey of Liszt's solo-vocal works, concentrating on such topics as
         the relationship between words and music, the languages of Liszt's texts,
         melodic line and musical texture, national elements in certain songs,
         tonality, musical structure, and interpretation through performance. Illus-
         trated with numerous musical examples, facsimile reproductions of two
         mss., and a table ("Example 14") of fifteen cadential formulae taken from
         almost as many compositions.

932.   Hughes, Edwin. "Liszt as Lieder Composer." *Musical Quarterly* 3 (1917),
         pp. 390-409.
         A competent survey article. Hughes deals not only with some of
         Liszt's better-known German-language songs, but he discusses the unfa-
         vorable reception those songs received in late nineteenth-century

Germany. Illustrated with more than a dozen short examples from such works as *Vergiftet sind meine Lieder, Die Vätergruft, Ich möchte hingehn,* etc.

933.   Werba, Eric. "Franz Liszt und das Lied." *Österreichische Musikzeitschrift* 16 (1961), pp. 412-415.

A very brief discussion of Liszt's German-language songs, including *Der du von dem Himmel bist, Die Vätergruft, Es muß ein Wunderbares sein,* etc. No musical examples.

STUDIES OF INDIVIDUAL SONGS

Only a handful of studies devoted to individual Liszt songs and recitations (or groups of songs and recitations) have ever appeared in print. Three of these studies deal almost entirely with stylistic issues:

934.   Cinnamon, Howard. "Tonal Structure and Voice-Leading in Liszt's 'Blume und Duft'." *In Theory Only* 6/3 (April 1982), pp. 12-24.

Demonstrates how familiar voice-leading procedures establish unusual harmonic relationships based on thirds, relationships characteristic of the structure of Liszt's song. Illustrated with detailed voice-leading graphs and musical examples.

*   "*Exempli gratia*: When Is an Augmented-sixth Chord not an Augmented-sixth Chord?"

Deals only with the first measure of *Il m'aimait tant.* Described in greater detail as item 618.

935.   Hantz, Edwin. "Motivic and Structural Unity in Liszt's 'Blume und Duft'." *In Theory Only* 6/3 (April 1982), pp. 3-11.

Explains how tonal ambiguities (e.g., diminished-seventh chords, augmented triads) reflect the imagery of the text Liszt set to music in 1860. Musical examples.

Two other studies deal with Liszt settings of poems by Goethe:

936.   Dalmonte, Rossana. "Liszts und Wagners Lieder nach Gedichten Goethes." *Liszt-Studien* 3 (1986), pp. 28-35.

Describes Liszt's work as a song composer in terms of tone-painting, melodic inflections and accentuation, harmonic devices, etc. Dalmonte pays special attention to songs by Wagner, Schubert, and Liszt's setting of Goethe's *Über allen Gipfeln*. Illustrated with three musical examples, only one of them by Liszt. (With respect to *Über allen Gipfeln*, see also item 937 below.)

937.   Watson, Derek. "Liszt and Goethe: The Songs." *Liszt Society Journal* 10 (1985), pp. 2-5.
        An introduction to Liszt's several settings of Goethe texts, including *Über allen Gipfeln*. Illustrated with a portrait of Goethe but no musical examples.

Thirteen additional studies describe the origins and musical character of "miscellaneous" Liszt songs. These studies are described or cross-referenced below in alphabetical order (by author and/or title). Some of these songs are recorded in items A49-A50 and A84-A85:

*   Dart, William. "Revisions and Reworkings in the Lieder of Franz Liszt."
        A cursory introduction to this extremely complex copy. Described in greater detail as item 325.

*   Fowler, Andrew. "Franz Liszt's 'Petrarch Sonnets."
        Deals with keyboard and vocal versions of these well-known compositions. Described in greater detail as item 638.

*   Friedheim, Philip. "First Version, Second Version, Alternative Version: Some Remarks on the Music of Liszt."
        A rather superficial review of Liszt's songs revisions, including *Im Rhein, im schönen Strome*. Described in greater detail as item 327.

938.   Goebel, Albrecht. "Franz Liszt: 'Die drei Zigeuner' (Ein Beitrag zum Balladenschaffen im 19. Jahrhundert)." *Musica* 35 (1981), pp. 241-245.
        Discusses the ballad as a vocal-instrumental genre in nineteenth-century music as well as Liszt's "Three Gypsies" as a composition. Illustrated with four short musical examples and the text of Lenau's poem (p. 245).

939.   Hansen, Bernard. "'Nonnenwerth': Ein Beitrag zu Franz Liszts Liederkomposition." *Neue Zeitschrift für Musik* 122 (1961), pp. 391-394.
        An introduction to the origins, character, and various versions of *Nonnenwerth*, based on Liszt's setting of *Die Zelle in Nonnenwerth*, a poem by Felix Lichnowsky. Illustrated with several musical examples, most of them used to demonstrate similarities and differences among the various

piano-vocal, solo piano, and chamber-ensemble versions of this pleasant piece. Also illustrated with a view of the Rhenish island of Nonnenwerth, c. 1840.

*   Kecskeméti, István. "[Liszt] Discoveries: An Unknown Song."
Discusses *Quand du chants* (1852) and its ms. source. Described in greater detail as item 304b.

*   Lozza, Giuseppe. "La doppia versione del Lied di Liszt 'Der Fichtenbaum'."
Described as item 333.

*   Mueller, Rena [Charnin]. "Reevaluating the Liszt Chronology: The Case of 'Anfangs wollt ich fast verzagen'."
Examines the contents and significance of a Liszt ms. recently discovered in Bayreuth collections. Described in greater detail as item 306.

*   Tagliavini, L. "La prima versione d'un lied di Liszt."
Discusses an early version of *Dichter, was Liebe sei*. Described in greater detail as item 340.

*   Szitha, Tünde. "Liszt's 'Unknown' French Songs."
Identifies a previously unknown version of *Le juif errant* and mentions other works. Described in greater detail as item 311.

*   Turner, Ronald. "A Comparison of Two Sets of Liszt-Hugo Songs."
Deals with revisions Liszt made for the six songs written on texts by Victor Hugo and originally published in the *Poesies lyriques* volume. Described in greater detail as item 342.

940.   Winkler, Gerhard J. "'Der traurige Mönch' (1860). Considérations archéologiques sur les oeuvres tardives de Liszt." *Revue musicale* 405-406-407 (1987), pp. 107-118.
The only study devoted exclusively to one of Liszt's recitations (or "mélodrames"). Winkler describes *Der traurige Mönch* in terms both of sonata-allegro and variation forms and explains how the music illuminates Lenau's text; he also compares this work with other late Liszt compositions, including *Unstern, R.W.—Venezia*, etc. The text of Lenau's poem appears in French and German on pp. 106-108; a five-page appendix contains the complete text of Liszt's composition.

941.   Winkler, Gerhard J. "'Heil mir! Ich bin es wert!' Zu Liszts Vertonung der 'Vätergruft'." *Neue Zeitschrift für Musik* 147/7-8 (July-August 1986), pp. 10-15.

Traces the history and describes the character of *Der Vätergruft*, one of Liszt's less well-known songs. Illustrated with an oil painting of Liszt made by Miklós Barabás in 1846 and with several musical examples.

XVIII: ORIGINAL WORKS FOR VOCAL ENSEMBLES

Liszt's compositions for vocal ensembles, most particularly his large-scale sacred choral works, have been subjected to increasingly intense scrutiny since World War II and especially since the early 1960s. Studies of works like Christus, Die Legende von der heiligen Elisabeth, *and the* Missa choralis *have, to a considerable extent, been completed by doctoral candidates in Germany and America; other studies have appeared in specialized journals, festival programs, and conference proceedings. These studies are described below. A few studies dealing with mss. or revisions for individual choral compositions are described in Chapter VIII. Recordings of selected choral performances are described in the Appendix.*

OPERA

Lost for many years, the score of Don Sanche—*Liszt's only opera—was rediscovered near the beginning of this century. Since then it has received a number of performances and has even been recorded (see item A86). Two articles about* Don Sanche *appeared in conjunction with an important British production of the 1970s:*

942.   Searle, Humphrey. "Liszt's 'Don Sanche'." *Musical Times* 118 (1977), pp. 815-817.
    Describes the history, rediscovery, libretto, and musical character of Liszt's composition. No musical examples.

Two other articles about Don Sanche *also deserve attention:*

943.   Chantavoine, Jean. "Die Operette *Don Sanche.* Ein verloren geglaubtes Werk Franz Liszts." *Musik* 3/11 (1903-1904), pp. 286-307.
    Explains that a full score of Liszt's only stage work survived in the archives of the Paris Opéra, then describes the libretto and music in some detail. Chantavoine illustrates his observations with a number of musical examples, among them a transcription for piano of Liszt's overture and piano-vocal transcriptions of several other numbers.
    Both the overture and Don Sanche's aria ("Repose en paix"), published as a supplement to Chantavoine's study, were reprinted in *Liszt*

saeculum 34 (1984), pp. 58-72. The "Page's Aria" from *Don Sanche* was published as a supplement to *Le Courrier musical* (June 1911).

944.   Saffle, Michael. "'Youthful Sins': Liszt's 'Don Sanche' and Wagner's 'Liebesverbot'." *Bayreuther Festspielprogramm* 5 (1986), pp. 13-25 [English]; pp. 56-72 [German]; and pp. 82-92 [French].
        Compares elements in Liszt's opera with early nineteenth-century opera as a whole, and with Wagner's *Das Liebesverbot* in particular. Illustrated with several musical examples, including passages from Liszt's and Wagner's piano music.
        NB: The *Bayreuther Programmhefte* contain other articles about Liszt's life and music. See Matthias Theodor Vogt, "Index der Bayreuther Programmhefte 1951-1986," *Bayreuther Festspielprogramme* 3-6 (1986).

Liszt planned, sketched, but never completed several other operas, among them a work in Italianate style known as Sardanapole. *Several studies of Liszt's sketches are described in Chapter VIII, but one other article deals with music Liszt wrote in conjunction with a libretto on Nerval's Faust story:*

945.   Jensen, Eric Frederic. "Liszt, Nerval, and 'Faust'." *19th Century Music* 6 (1982), pp. 151-158.
        A sketch of Liszt's relationship with Gérard de Nerval during the early 1850s, Liszt's plan to write an opera on Nerval's Faust libretto, and the influence this plan may have had on the creation of the *Faust* symphony. No musical examples.

*   Szelényi, László. "Liszts Opernpläne."
        Touches on Liszt's plans for a Faust opera as well as his sketches for *Sardanapole* and other unfinished stage works. Described in greater detail as item 320. See also item 321.

CHORAL WORKS

General Studies

Only two comparatively short surveys of Liszt's choral music as a whole have appeared in print:

946.   Collet, Robert. "Choral and Organ Music." In item 31; pp. 318-349.
        An introduction to Liszt's compositions for vocal ensembles, especially *Christus* and *Die Legende von der heiligen Elisabeth*, the "Gran" Mass, *Psalm XIII*, and so on. Unfortunately, Collet scarcely mentions Liszt's

secular choral output, although he does describe a few organ works. Illustrated with 36 musical examples and a facsimile of an autograph page from *Christus.*

947.   Merrick, Paul. "The Choral Works of Liszt." *Liszt Society Journal* 3 (1978), pp. 35-36.
        A very brief introduction to Liszt's vocal-ensemble music. No musical examples.

Specialized Studies

1. Works for Male Voices (mostly secular works)

Compositions for male chorus occupy a special place in nineteenth-century musical literature. Liszt wrote a considerable amount of music for Männerchöre; *some of it was sacred, some secular in character. Several short studies of* Männerchöre *pieces have appeared in print, but one book-length study deals with this music as a whole:*

948.   Fudge, James Thompson. *The Male Chorus Music of Franz Liszt.* Dissertation: University of Iowa, 1972. xvi, 413pp.
        ML410.L7F84 1979
        Identifies and describes in some detail most of the 70-odd male-chorus compositions completed by Liszt and identified in Searle's 1954 *Grove* catalog (see item 54). Among other topics, Fudge discusses the possibilities that Liszt wrote secular male-chorus music during the 1840s and 1850s, some of it as "warm-up" exercises for his Weimar works, and that many of the later, sacred male-chorus pieces owe their very existence to the exclusion of women from celebrations of the Roman rite. Works discussed by Fudge at some length include *An die Künstler, Ossa arida,* and *Der 129. Psalm.* Illustrated with musical examples.
        Summarized in DAI 33/12 (June 1973), p. 6951A; reprinted in the *Journal of the American Liszt Society* 7 (1980), pp. 94-95.

A shorter introduction to Liszt's male-chorus music appeared around the turn of this century:

949.   Richard, August. "Franz Liszt als Männerchorkomponist." *Neue Musikzeitung* [Stuttgart] 33 (1912), pp. 176-177.
        A useful survey of Liszt's male-chorus works, including the choral conclusion of the *Faust* symphony and such works as *An die Künstler* and the choruses for Herder's *Entfesseltem Prometheus.* No musical examples.
        According to Koch (item 39; p. 90), an article by August Göllerich entitled "Franz Liszt als Männerchor-Komponist" appeared in the *Festblätter zum 6. deutschen Sängerbundesfeste* [Graz] in 1902. Because

Göllerich was a pupil and confidante of Liszt's, this article may be of value. Unfortunately, the *Sängerbund* is extremely rare; the present author has never been able to locate a copy.

Finally, seven short studies deal with some of the small-scale, secular male-chorus pieces Liszt completed comparatively early in his career. These studies are described or cross-referenced below in alphabetical order (by author):

*   Eckhardt, Mária [P.]. "Ein Spätwerk von Liszt: der 129. Psalm."
       Primarily a manuscript study. Described in greater detail as item 298.

950.   Eckhardt, Mária [P.]. "Von 'Les quatre élémens' bis zu 'Les préludes'—ein in der Weimarperiode umgestaltetes großes Projekt Franz Liszts." In item 37; pp. 19-29.
       Deals with the history and compositional character of four unfinished choruses entitled *Les quatre élémens*, on poems by Joseph Autran. Like Haraszti's studies (e.g., items 296 and 329), Eckhardt's essay discusses how materials from these choruses were transformed into the symphonic poem *Les préludes* during the 1840s. Unlike other scholars, however, Eckhardt also describes in detail the D-WRgs mss. containing Liszt's unpublished choral music. Illustrations (in the form of an appendix to item 37) include the texts of Autran's poems and several dozen hand-copied musical examples.

*   Jung, Hans Rudolf. "Zum Autograph des 'Arbeiterchors' von Franz Liszt."
       Described as item 302.

*   Murányi, Robert [Árpád]. "Neue Liszt-Handschriften in der Széchenyi-Nationalbibliothek."
       Deals with mss. of *Ungarns Gott* and the *Rheinweinlied*. Described in greater detail as item 307.

951.   Refardt, Edgar. "Die Basler Männerchöre von Franz Liszt." *Schweizerische Musikzeitung* 82 (1942), pp. 289-291.
       Describes the history and expressive character of the *Geharnischte Lieder* composed by Liszt during the 1840s. No musical examples.
       Reprinted under the same title in *Musik in der Schweiz: Ausgewählte Aufsätze zum 75. Geburtstag Edgar Refardts* (Bern 1952), pp. 99-102.

959. Wagner, Manfred. "Liszt und Bruckner—oder ein Weg zur Restauration sakraler Musik." *Liszt-Studien* 1 (1977), pp. 225-233.
Discusses nineteenth-century movements devoted to reforming musical practice in the Roman liturgy, including Cecilianism, and the attitudes Liszt and Bruckner held vis-à-vis such movements. Wagner also describes portions of the "Gran" Mass, reviews the rejection by the Cecilianists of the *Missa choralis* (see item 977), and refers to passages found in several Papal encyclicals. No musical examples.

Twenty-one studies of individual sacred compositions by Liszt are described below according to composition, then by category and/or in alphabetical order (by author):

A. "Christus" (recorded as items A51 and A87)

Liszt's oratorio Christus *must be considered one of his finest and most influential compositions. Among other studies devoted exclusively to this work, the two described below remain among the most detailed:*

960. Orr, N[athaniel] Leon. *Liszt's "Christus" and its Significance for Nineteenth-Century Oratorio.* Dissertation: University of North Carolina, 1979. xi, 387pp.
ML410.L77O6
Discusses Liszt's most familiar oratorio in terms of its compositional history and expressive character. Musical examples.
Summarized in DAI 40/5 (November 1979), pp. 2343A-2344A; reprinted in the *Journal of the American Liszt Society* 6 (1979), pp. 62-63. NB: Orr's name is given in DAI as "Leon," not "Lee." See item 964.

961. Ramann, Lina. *Franz Liszt's Oratorium Christus. Eine Studie als Beitrag zur zeit- und musikgeschichtlichen Stellung desselben, mit Notenbeispielen und dem Text des Werkes.* 3rd ed. Leipzig: C. F. Kahnt, 1880. 134pp.
ML410.L7R3
An introduction to Liszt's oratorio, complete with information about the composition's general character (pp. 5-67) and a measure-by-measure analysis (pp. 68-126) of much of its music. Although old-fashioned, Ramann's work is nevertheless valuable for historians. Illustrated with numerous musical examples. Concludes with the complete text of *Christus*, printed as an appendix.

Seven additional Christus *studies, most of them short, also deserve attention; they are described or cross-referenced below in alphabetical order (by author):*

962.   Grunsky, Karl. "Liszts Oratorium 'Christus'." *Neue Musik-Zeitung* [Stuttgart] 23 (1902), pp. 220 and 234-235.
         Praises Liszt's oratorio and its blend of musical and religious elements, which Grunsky feels has long been unjustly neglected by scholars and concert-goers alike. Grunsky also deals briefly with early *Christus* performances and with expressive similarities between Liszt's and Beethoven's religious works. Published shortly after Liszt's death and intended as a tribute to his sacred works. No musical examples.

*   Knotik, Cornelia. *Musik und Religion im Zeitalter des Historismus.*
         Contains lengthy discussions of *Christus*, Liszt's Catholic faith, etc. Described in greater detail as item 656.

963.   Niemöller, Klaus W[olfgang]. "Das Oratorium 'Christus' von Franz Liszt: Ein Beitrag zu seinen konzeptionellen Grundlagen." *Beträge zur Geschichte des Oratoriums seit Händel: Festschrift Günther Massenkiel zum 60. Geburtstag*, ed. Rainer Cadenbach and Helmut Loos. Bonn-Bad Godesberg: Voggenreiter, 1986; pp. 329-343.
         ML55.M3 1986   ISBN 3-8024-0146-8
         Deals with Liszt's oratorio in terms of its compositional history, structural organization, use of Gregorian motives, and so on. Several musical examples.

964.   Orr, N[athaniel] Lee. "Liszt, 'Christus,' and the Transformation of the Oratorio." *Journal of the American Liszt Society* 9 (1981), pp. 4-18.
         Contends that, "in the final analysis, Liszt appears to have played a seminal role in the transformation of the nineteenth-century oratorio . . . from an essentially vocal work to a symphonic composition" of virtually Wagnerian proportions and character. Orr compares Liszt's oratorio with works composed in England, France, and Germany by composers like Parry, Berlioz, and Spohr. No musical examples. See also item 960.

965.   Pohl, Richard. "Liszts Oratorium 'Christus'." In item 227; pp. 349-357.
         A brief, enthusiastic description of *Christus* in non-technical language, published originally in 1875. No musical examples.

966.   Riedel, Friedrich W. "Die Bedeutung des 'Christus' von Franz Liszt in der Geschichte des Messias-Oratoriums." *Liszt-Studien* 2 (1981), pp. 153-162.
     Compares *Christus* with other "Messiah" oratorios by Händel, Carl Loewe, Mendelssohn, Anton Rubinstein, etc. Riedel also discusses liturgical and stylistic issues, among them the use of "Leitmotifs" as unifying devices throughout Liszt's oratorio. No musical examples; illustrated instead with several tables, including one comparing the contents of Liszt's composition with related works in terms of Jesus' life.

967.   Wagner, Gottfried. "L'éthique Lisztienne. La notion de 'caritas' dans 'Les béatitudes' du 'Christus' (1862-66)." *Revue musicale* 405-406-407 (1987), pp. 119-125.
     Evaluates the "Béatitudes" movement from *Christus* in light of Liszt's remarks about faith and religious music in his letters and literary works. No musical examples.

B. "Die Legende von der heiligen Elisabeth" (recorded as items A52 and A88)

Liszt's Elisabeth, *the only other oratorio he completed during his lifetime, is not nearly so well known as* Christus. *As a consequence, perhaps, only four important studies have been devoted exclusively to* Elisabeth *and to its relationship with other important works. The first three of these are:*

968.   Palotai, Michael. *Liszt's Concept of Oratorio as Reflected in his Writings and in "Die Legende von der heiligen Elisabeth."* Dissertation: University of Southern California, 1977. 251pp.
     ML410.L7P34 1977a
     A detailed analysis of *Elisabeth*, based on the hypothesis that Liszt broke with tradition in this work by replacing the "recitative-aria-ensemble elements" of earlier oratorios with "uninterrupted tone-painting tableaux." Palotai also analyses the text and music of *Elisabeth*, pointing out that "Liszt achieved thematic unity by using characteristic themes and their transformations demanded by dramatic actions and situations." Concludes with remarks about the compositional history of the unfinished oratorio *St. Stanislaus* and about twentieth-century oratorio writing. (With regard to *St. Stanislaus*, see also item 980.) Musical examples and a bibliography.
     Summarized in DAI 38/1 (July 1977), pp. 19A-20A; reprinted in the *Journal of the American Liszt Society* 3 (1978), pp. 39-40.

969.   Reinisch, Frank. "Liszts Oratorium *Die Legende von der Heiligen Elisabeth*—ein Gegenentwurf zu *Tannhäuser* und *Lohengrin*." *Liszt-Studien* 3 (1986), pp. 128-151.

Likens *Elisabeth* to Wagnerian stage-works, in terms both of story-telling and such musical techniques as "Leitmotifs" and thematic trans-formation. Illustrated with more than a dozen musical examples and with facsimile reproductions of two advertisements for early *Elisabeth* perform-ances.

970.   Yourji, A. *Franz Liszts Oratorium "Die Legende v. d. heiligen Elisabeth" und die neue Musikdichtung im Allgemeinen*. Leipzig: Rhode, 1868. 75pp.

[No LC number available]

Not seen; cited by Koch (item 39; p. 87). Although obscure, Yourji's study may be important to students of Liszt's sacred music as well as of nineteenth-century "Rezeptionsgeschichte."

The fourth study is actually a review of an early Elisabeth *performance:*

971.   Pohl, Richard. "'Die Legende der heiligen Elisabeth.' [Review of a concert presented by Hans von Bülow in Karlsruhe on 8 April 1873]. In item 227; pp. 331-348.

Polemical journalism that also presents valuable observations about Liszt's work and its reception on one important occasion. No musical ex-amples.

C. The Masses (recorded in items A53-54 and A89-A90)

Liszt's oratorios may be the most familiar of his sacred works, but his masses—especially the Missa choralis *and "Gran" Mass—are usually mentioned in discussions of his most successful musical creations. The best single introduction to these pieces is:*

972.   White, Charles. *The Masses of Franz Liszt*. Dissertation: Bryn Mawr University, 1973. 457pp.

[No LC number available]

A detailed survey of the five masses Liszt composed between 1848-1868, including the "Mass for Male Voices," the "Gran" Mass, the "Hungarian Coronation Mass," the *Missa choralis*, and the *Requiem* for male chorus and organ. White maintains that "Liszt's role in nineteenth-century music reform is clearly reflected in his Masses," especially in his treatment of text and his sensitivity toward the "dramaturgy" of the Roman liturgy. Illustrated with numerous musical examples. Concludes with a bibliography of secondary sources. Extensive quotations in Latin as well as the text of Liszt's essay on church music in both the original

French and English translation (pp. 414-417). (With regard to other English-language translations of this essay, see items 170 and 536.)

Summarized in DAI 34/10 (April 1974), p. 6694A; reprinted in the *Journal of the American Liszt Society* 10 (1981), pp. 127-128.

Liszt's Mass in c minor for male voices and organ was his first important liturgical work. The only published study devoted exclusively to this composition remains:

973.   Heinrichs, Josef. "Ein vergessenes Kleinod liturgischer Music — Franz Liszts Missa c-moll für Männerchor und Orgel." *Musica sacra* 82 (1962), pp. 114-119.

A brief and rather vague discussion of the so-called "Mass for Male Voices." Illustrated with a full-figure silhouette of Liszt rather than with musical examples.

Several studies of the mass Liszt composed to celebrate the dedication of the cathedral at Gran [Esztergom] in Hungary have appeared in print. The first was published immediately after the premiere of the Mass itself in 1856; the second appeared only a few years ago:

974.   Zellner, L[eopold] A[lexander]. *Ueber Franz Liszts Graner Festmesse und ihre Stellung zur geschichtlichen Entwicklung der Kirchenmusik.* Vienna: F. Manz, 1858. 81pp.

ML410.L7Z35

A discussion of liturgical and musical topics pertinent to the "Gran" Mass, followed by a movement-by-movement analysis of the work's harmony, counterpoint, text-setting, etc. Each chapter except the first is amply illustrated with musical examples, some of them drawn from Gregorian chant.

Like other of his studies, Zellner's work appeared first in his own *Blätter für Musik, Theater und Kunst* [Vienna]. NB: Zellner's study was not, however, the very first "analysis" of Liszt's mass to appear in print. A rare pamphlet, in the form of a "Musikalisch-humorischtischer Toast" written by one M. G. Brand (Pest 1856), was presented to Liszt at a banquet following the first performance of his composition. See Ilona Mona, "Erste musikalische Analyse der 'Graner Messe' von Ferenc Liszt" in *Studia musicologica* 29 (1987), pp. 343-351. Includes a complete facsimile of the pamphlet as well as a transcription of its contents.

975.   Loos, Helmut. "Franz Liszts Graner Festmesse." *Kirchenmusikalisches Jahrbuch* 67 (1983), pp. 45-59.

Deals with this work in terms of its history, thematic material, "tone-painting," etc. Loos provides two tables of themes and their various transformations, a brief catalog of devices Liszt uses in the mass to illuminate the meaning of textual passages in measures 14-351 of the Credo, and several musical examples.

The only study devoted exclusively to Liszt's "Hungarian Coronation Mass" remains:

976.   Ábrányi, Karl. *Franz Liszt's ungarische Krönungsmesse. Eine musikalische Studie*, trans. H. Gobbl. Leipzig: J. Schuberth, n.d. 24pp.
        ML410.L7A2
        Celebrates one of Liszt's most important sacred works. Among other Hungarian "finds" made by Ábrányi is a Rákóczy-like tune in the Gloria movement. Illustrated with short melodic and harmonic examples.

Two important studies of Liszt's Missa choralis *reflect the change in attitude toward this masterpiece on behalf of Cecilianist-movement authorities*

977.   Haberl, Franz Xaver. "Ueber Liszts 'Missa choralis' und principielle Fragen." *Musica sacra* 23 (1890), pp. 98-101.
        Refutes the praise lavished on this work under entry 79 in the 1870s Cecilianist catalog. In his 1890 study, Haberl denies both the liturgical and musical worth of Liszt's mass and "expells" it from the Cecilianist canon. Contains quotations from religious authorities, including one Bishop Joseph Schildknecht, who spoke against Liszt's work at a conference held at Basel on 4-5 May 1890. No musical examples. See also item 978 (below).

978.   Widmann, Wilhelm. "Die Missa choralis von Franz Liszt." *Musica sacra* 57 (1927), pp. 33-41, 84-87, 102-109, 212-219, and 252-255 ["Schlußbetrachtung"].
        An introduction to the *Missa choralis* and a detailed description of its musical-liturgical character, including its relationship to Gregorian melodies. Widmann rejects Haberl's criticism of this work (presented in item 977 above), substituting for it a better-balanced assessment of the composer's sensitivity to musical, textual, and liturgical issues. Numerous musical examples.
        The shift in Cecilianist attitudes toward the *Missa choralis* is exemplified not only in Widmann's observations but in a highly "reverential" poem by one Anton Schultheiß entitled "Missa choralis von Liszt" and published on p. 109 of Widmann's article.

Finally, Liszt's activity and effectiveness as a composer of masses have been compared with that of Bruckner:

979.   Kurthen, Wilhelm. "Liszt und Bruckner als Messenkomponisten." *Musica sacra* 55 (1925), pp. 265-271.

Discusses Liszt's masses (including the *Missa choralis*) as well as shorter works like the *Tantum ergo* apparently composed for publication by the Regensburg Cecilianists during the late 1860s, aspects of *Christus* and *Elisabeth*, and Bruckner's Masses in d minor and e minor. A single musical example identifies a two-note motif found throughout the movements of the "Gran" Mass.

According to item 39; p. 83, this article also appeared in the *Gregoriusbote* [Aachen] No. 41 (1925); and in *Musica divina* [Vienna] No. 44 (1925).

D. Other Sacred Works (recorded in items A55-A57)

In addition to oratorios and masses, Liszt also completed dozens of other, generally shorter sacred pieces. Many of these compositions remain obscure, several have never been published, and one of the most interesting of them was never completed. This last work, an oratorio based on the life of St. Stanislaus, apparently is discussed at length only in the following study:

980.   La Mara. "Franz Liszt und sein unvollendetes Stanislaus-Oratorium." *Österreichisches Rundschau* (15 October 1911), pp. 150-157.

The Liszt Research Centre, Budapest, owns a copy: shelf-number LGY 489(k).

More a sketch of Liszt's intentions concerning the oratorio than a description of its musical characteristics. La Mara quotes from about a dozen Liszt letters, but she provides no musical examples.

Several somewhat obscure but much more recent articles have also discussed *St. Stanislaus*. See, for example, Gerhard J. Winkler's "Franz Liszt und der Stumme Büßer von Ossiach," which appeared in *Der Brücke* 12 (Summer 1986), pp. 13-16. See also portions of item 298.

Liszt completed a number of psalm-settings, several of them of considerable beauty. Only one study, however, deals with all of these settings in any detail:

981.   Ramann, Lina. *Franz Liszt als Psalmensänger und die früheren Meister.
        Zu einer musikalischen Psalmenkunde. Mit Notenbeispielen.* Leipzig:
        Breitkopf & Härtel, 1886. 72pp.
            ML410.L7R31
        An enthusiastic survey of Liszt's psalms, illustrated with musical ex-
        amples. Old-fashioned but still worth consulting.

Liszt's Via crucis *was published only in the first "complete" edition of the
composer's works (item 136). This important, highly experimental work has been
dealt with in two recent articles:*

982.   Hill, Cecil. "Liszt's 'Via crucis'." *Music Review* 25 (1964), pp. 202-208.
        Describes this small-scale masterpiece, completed during 1878-1879 but
        rejected for publication by Pustet's Regensburg firm. Hill discusses Liszt's
        themes (liturgical as well as musical), the implications of performing the
        organ accompaniment on different instruments, harmonic relationships
        between the various sections of the work, and so on. Illustrated with se-
        veral short musical examples and a table of key changes between and
        during individual movements.

983.   Kaufmann, Ferdinand. "Eine Passionsmusik von Liszt." *Musica sacra* 86
        (1966), pp. 72-78.
        A short description of the liturgical significance and harmonic charac-
        teristics of *Via crucis*, illustrated with about a dozen musical examples.

*Other, generally much shorter sacred choral works by Liszt are treated in four
studies described or cross-referenced below in alphabetical order (by author):*

*   Eckhardt, Mária [P.]. "Ein Spätwerk von Liszt: der 129. Psalm."
        Deals in part with *De profundis* and other works. Described in greater
        detail as item 298.

984.   Kraus, Eberhard. "Miscellanea zur Kirchenmusik Franz Liszts." *Musica
        sacra* 106 (1986), pp. 354-363.
        Deals with a variety of works, including *Der 13. Psalm*. Like other
        scholars, Kraus maintains that Liszt's Catholicism was reflected "in works
        written throughout his life" as well as in his letters and literary creations.
        Several musical examples.

985.   Merrick, Paul. "Responses and Antiphons: Liszt in 1860." *Studia musicologica* 28 (1986), pp. 187-194.
     Describes the harmonizations of Gregorian melodies found in the *Liber usualis* completed by Liszt during the mid-nineteenth century but published only in item 136. Merrick discusses the responses themselves—there are no antiphons!—in light of Liszt's testament (see item 1b; pp. 557-563, and items 222-223), the first of the three orchestral funeral odes, and other "last" things. Illustrated with almost two full pages of examples from the responses themselves.

986.   Redepenning, Dorothea. "Meditative Musik. Bemerkungen zu einigen späten geistlichen Kompositionen Franz Liszts." *Hamburger Jahrbuch für Musik* 8 (1985), pp. 185-201.
     ISBN 0-89007-049-3   [No LC number available]
     Discusses the mood of and various compositional devices employed in *Ossa arida, Qui Marian absolvisti, Der 129. Psalm*, and other late choral works. Two musical examples.

XIX: ARRANGEMENTS, PARAPHRASES, AND TRANSCRIPTIONS

Liszt prepared at least as many arrangements and transcriptions as he did original compositions. A few studies dealing with source materials for individual paraphrases and transcriptions are described in Chapter XIII, while recordings of selected operatic fantasies and other arrangements are described in the Appendix. (A few studies described in Chapters XII-XVIII also mention paraphrases and transcriptions.) All other arrangement and transcription materials are described below.

GENERAL STUDIES

No single study deals with all Liszt's arrangements and transcriptions, but several monographs identify and discuss many of these works, whatever their performing forces or relationship with "original" compositions. Perhaps the best of these studies is:

987.   Wilde, David. "Transcriptions for Piano." In item 31; pp. 168-201.

      A discussion of selected Liszt keyboard paraphrases and arrangements, including versions of Beethoven symphonies, Bach organ works, Schubert songs, Wagner's *Tannhäuser*, Bellini's *Norma*, and so on. Wilde's exemplary discussion of Liszt's "orchestral" piano writing is illustrated with numerous musical examples.

Four other surveys are described below in alphabetical order (by author):

988.   Castelain, Marc. *Franz Liszt et la transcription d'oeuvres instrumentales.* Dissertation: University of Brussels, 1975. 184pp.

      The National Széchényi Library, Budapest, owns a copy: shelf-number SZ Liszt 181.

      Devoted exclusively to transcriptions (rather than to operatic paraphrases, arrangements of Liszt's own works, and so on). Illustrated with dozens of short, hand- and photocopied musical examples. Castelain's observations about many works are limited to "critical notes" (i.e., measure-by-measure summaries of differences between transcriptions and the originals they were derived from). Contains a bibliography and a catalog of transcriptions (pp. 25-32).

989. Drillon, Jacques. *Liszt transcripteur, ou La charité bien ordonnée*. Arles: Actes Sud, 1986. 98pp.
      ML410.L7D7 1986   ISBN 2-8686-9099-8
      Praised by Suttoni (in item 46) as a "stimulating discussion" of its topic but sometimes disappointing. Drillon deals with the kinds of transcriptions Liszt made and the implications of the transcription as an art form. Concludes with an incomplete catalog of works (pp. 83-98) and a brief bibliography. Unfortunately, Drillon's musical examples are too brief and too poorly reproduced to serve their purposes.

990. Friedheim, Paul. "The Piano Transcriptions of Franz Liszt." *Studies in Romanticism* 1 (1961), pp. 83-96.
      Describes some of Liszt's best-known keyboard adaptations, among them arrangements of Berlioz's *Symphonie fantastique*, Saint-Saëns's *Danse macabre*, the Schubert song transcriptions, etc. Friedheim makes a number of striking statements, among them the claim that Liszt's "exploitation of a full keyboard texture frequently introduces a richness and nobility into the transcriptions that is not apparent in the original versions." Nine musical examples.

991. Molnár, A. "Über Transkriptionen und Paraphrasen von Liszt." *Studia musicologica* 5 (1963), pp. 227-232.
      A brief survey of Liszt's enormous body of arrangements, transcriptions, and operatic paraphrases. No musical examples.

A fifth study deals with Liszt's transcriptions as relics of his admiration for some of his fellow composers:

992. Barbag-Drexler, Irena. "Liszts Klavierbearbeitungen: Ein Beitrag zum Thema 'Der vergessene Liszt'." *Liszt-Studien* 1 (1977), pp. 27-35.
      Evaluates Liszt's arrangements and paraphrases of works by other composers in light of his devotion to the works of Bach, Beethoven, Schubert, etc. Consequently, Barbag-Drexler discusses "original" compositions like the BACH Prelude and Fugue as well as Schubert song transcriptions and the *Rigoletto* paraphrase. No musical examples.

Two studies deal exclusively with Liszt's transcriptions for organ:

993.   Hestford, B. "Franz Liszt — The Organ Transcriptions." *Musical Opinion* 100 (1977), pp. 178-179.
         A brief survey article; of little value to researchers. No musical examples.

994.   Stevens, Gerd-Heinz. "Die Orgeltranskriptionen von Franz Liszt." *Musica sacra* 106 (1986), pp. 365-371.
         Discusses Liszt's arrangements for the organ as well as his piano arrangements of organ works, including piano versions of six Bach preludes and fugues.

Finally, one study is devoted primarily to the compositional techniques employed by Liszt in his paraphrases and transcriptions:

*   Bellak, Richard Charles. *Compositional Technique in the Transcriptions of Franz Liszt.*
         Examines harmonic and motivic devices, structural organization, cadenza-like passages, and other details of such diverse works as Liszt's arrangement of Beethoven's *Adelaïde*, the *Réminiscences de Simon Boccanegra*, and versions of what eventually became *Pensées de morts* from the rewritten *Harmonies poétiques et religieuses*. Described in greater detail as item 611.

LISZT'S TRANSCRIPTIONS OF HIS OWN WORKS

The most important published discussion of Liszt's transcriptions is devoted almost exclusively to works completed during the composer's last years:

995.   Redepenning, Dorothea. *Das Spätwerk Franz Liszts: Bearbeitungen eigener Kompositionen.* Hamburger Beiträge zur Musikwissenschaft, 27. Hamburg: Karl Dieter Wagner, 1984. 311pp.
         ML410.L7R342 1984   ISBN 3-88979-004-6
         A detailed evaluation of Liszt's later arrangements of his own compositions, inclduing the "Petrarch Sonnets," several religious works, *Nonnenwerth*, etc. Illustrated with numerous short musical examples; longer examples, including the complete text of an arrangement of *Nonnenwerth*, appear in an appendix. Concludes with an extensive bibliography. Reviewed in item 132.

Two shorter studies deal with self-transcriptions from various periods of Liszt's life:

996.   Kirsch, Winfried. "Franz Liszt als Bearbeiter eigener Werke." *Liszt-Studien* 2 (1981), pp. 97-113.

A deceptive title: Kirsch's article deals as much with Liszt's revisions of his own works as with his piano and vocal arrangements, especially those he made of his songs. Illustrated with six pages of musical examples from *Freudvoll und leidvoll, Es rauschen der Winde,* etc., and with a two-page table of original, revised, and arranged versions of 26 solo vocal works.

997.   Stewart, Arthur Franklin. "'La notte' and 'Les morts': Investigations into Progressive Aspects of Franz Liszt's Style." *Journal of the American Liszt Society* 18 (1985), pp. 67-106.

Evaluates technical features—especially "progressive" details of form and harmony—found in two Liszt self-transcriptions published for the first time in item 137. Stewart refers several times to what he calls "the aesthetics of the unexpected" in Liszt's music and attempts to associate that brand of aesthetics with aspects of Charles Sanders Peirce's thought. Illustrated with several diagrams, the original texts of Lammenais's poems (from which Liszt took the titles of and inspiration for these "Funeral Odes"). Twenty musical examples.

One additional study deals with an unusual Liszt self-transcription for chamber ensemble:

998.   Marggraf, Wolfgang. "Eine Klaviertrio-Bearbeitung des 'Vallée d'Obermann' aus Liszts Spätzeit." *Studia musicologica* 28 (1986), pp. 295-302.

Describes an unpublished arrangement made by Liszt during the latter years of his life and preserved in D-WRgs Liszt mss. X 3a-b. Marggraf deals in passing with such topics as changes Liszt made in arranging one of his best-known piano pieces for violin, cello, and piano, the musical character of the original and "revised" versions of that piece, and stylistic similarities between the arrangement and such other late works as *Unstern* and *R.W.—Venezia.* Five musical examples.

LISZT'S TRANSCRIPTIONS OF OTHER COMPOSERS' WORKS

Transcriptions of Instrumental Works

Liszt arranged or transcribed pieces by dozens of composers. The twelve studies described below are devoted to Liszt's arrangements of instrumental works by other composers. (Studies of Liszt's vocal transcriptions are described later in the present chapter.) The studies in question are described or cross-referenced according to composer, then alphabetically (by author):

A. Bach (see also item A95)

999.   Dalmonte, Rossana. "Scrittura e riscrittura: Liszt e Busoni di fronte a Bach." *La trascrizione Bach e Busoni. Atti del convegno internazionale (Empoli-Firenze 23-26 ottobre 1985)*, ed. Talia Pecker Berio. Florence: Leo S. Olschki, 1987; pp. 145-158.

    [No LC or ISBN numbers available]

    Examines Liszt's piano transcriptions of six Bach preludes and fugues as well as Busoni's arrangements of such works as the "Chromatic" Fantasy and Fugue and the Toccata in C Major. Supplemented by 10 musical examples, several of them illustrating relationships between Liszt's Bach arrangements and those Busoni made decades later. In Italian.

1000.   Eigeldinger, Jean-Jacques. "Liszt trascrittore e interprete di Bach." *L'organo* [Bologna] 11 (1973), pp. 171-181.

    Deals with Liszt's piano transcriptions of Bach organ works, especially his arrangement of Bach's Prelude and Fugue in a minor (BWV 543), as well as with documents pertaining to Liszt's interpretation of Bach works: one written by Jules Laurens (1844), the other by Karl von Lachmund (1882-1884). No musical examples. In Italian; summaries in French, German, and English (pp. 182-183).

    A shorter article about Liszt and Bach by the same author appeared as "L'interprète de Bach" in item 36; pp. 222-229.

1001.   Schloemann, Burghard. "Liszts Bach-Bearbeitungen." *Musik und Kirche* 56 (1986), pp. 128-137.

    Examines the five organ transcriptions Liszt made of Bach's instrumental and vocal works. Schloemann supplements his discussion with quotations from nineteenth-century Bach commentators; he also describes alterations Liszt made to several of Bach's musical texts. Illustrated with a tabular summary of the Liszt-Bach transcriptions (pp. 136-137), musical examples, and two plates reproducing black-and-white photographs of "Liszt organs" in Weimar and Buchheim.

B. <u>Beethoven</u> (see also items A58, A91, A95, and A101)

1002.   Cory, William Michael. *Franz Liszt's "Symphonies de Beethoven: Partitions de Piano" (Volumes I and II)*. Dissertation: University of Texas, 1981. 178pp.
ML410.L7C6 1981a
An introduction to Liszt's Beethoven transcriptions and a comparison of those works with arrangements by other composers, including Hummel, Kalkbrenner, August Horn, and Percy Goetschius. Cory also examines the 1837 and 1865 versions of the Liszt-Beethoven "Pastoral" symphony, pointing out that Liszt made extensive use in these transcriptions of "octave doubling, inventive register selection, and newly-composed patterns." Illustrated with musical examples.
Summarized in DAI 42/3 (October 1981), p. 907A; reprinted in the *Journal of the American Liszt Society* 13 (1983), p. 189.

1003.   Fittler, Katalin. "Beethoven-szimfóniák Liszt átiratában." *Magyar zene* 27 (1986), pp. 12-20.
Traces the history and briefly describes Liszt's piano transcriptions of Beethoven's symphonies. Illustrated with seven musical examples. In Hungarian.

1004.   Tollefson, Arthur. "The Liszt 'Pianoforte Scores' of the Beethoven Symphonies." *Piano Quarterly* 23/89 (Spring 1975), pp. 46-49
Describes Liszt's transcriptions of the Beethoven symphonies and assesses their historical significance and fidelity to the original orchestral versions. Pictorial illustrations but no musical examples.

1005.   Walker, Alan. "Liszt and the Beethoven Symphonies." *Music Review* 31 (1970), pp. 302-314.
Summarizes the origins and character of Liszt's best-known Beethoven transcriptions. More than a dozen musical examples.

C. <u>Schubert</u> (see also items A4, A10, A94-A95, and A101)

1006.   Eckhardt, Mária [P.]. "Liszts Bearbeitungen von Schuberts Märschen: Formale Analyse." *Studia musicologica* 26 (1984), pp. 133-146.
Describes piano transcriptions Liszt made of Schubert marches. Illustrated with facsimiles of early Schubert and Liszt editions, diagrams of the organization of Liszt's transcriptions, and musical examples.

*   Kabisch, Thomas. *Liszt und Schubert.*
         Devoted in part to Liszt transcriptions of Schubert works, among them
         the so-called "Wanderer" fantasy for piano and orchestra. Described in
         greater detail as item 696.

*   Waters, Edward N. "Liszt's 'Soirées de Vienne'."
         Described as item 312.

D. Other Composers (see item A101 for recordings of Liszt transcriptions from
   Berlioz and Chopin)

1007.   Hamburger, Klára. "Liszt Ferenc: revive Szegedin!" *Magyar zenetörténeti
         tanulmányok* (1977), pp. 317-319.
         Identifies and describes Liszt's transcription for piano of the *Marche
         turque-hongroise* by one Ignác Szabadi Frank, prepared as a means of
         raising money to help rebuild the flood-damaged city of Szeged in 1879.
         In Hungarian; summaries in English and German. A facsimile reprod-
         uction of Liszt's score is described as item 153.

1008.   Szelényi, László. "Liszt's Last Piano Transcription," trans. Adrian
         Williams. *Liszt Society Journal* 2 (1977), pp. 11-13.
         Describes the transcription Liszt prepared in 1885 of Cui's *Tarantelle*,
         Op. 12—a transcription noteworthy in part because it is more than twice
         the length of the piece it is based upon. Nine musical examples.
         Originally published in Hungarian under the title "Liszt utolsó átirata
         'Kjui-Liszt: Tarantella, 1885'" in *Uj zenei szemle* 5/11 (1954), pp. 38-40.
         A related article by Szelényi appeared under the title "Liszt's letzte
         Klavierbearbeitung in the *Liszt Information: Communication des European
         Liszt-Centre* 11 (1982), pp. 5-7.

Transcriptions of Vocal Works

1. General Studies

*About half a dozen book-length studies devoted exclusively or primarily to Liszt's
paraphrases and transcriptions of vocal music have appeared in print since World
War II. Perhaps the most intriguing of these monographs is:*

1009.   Hamilton, Kenneth Lawrie. *The Opera Fantasias and Transcriptions of Franz Liszt: A Critical Study*. Dissertation: Oxford University [Balliol College], 1989. xxi, 326pp.

      [No LC number available]

      An impressive if somewhat uneven survey of this enormous topic. Hamilton's dissertation opens with a catalog of operatic transcriptions and fantasies (pp. x-xii) which corrects or enlarges upon entries published in item 47; then follows a survey of previous Liszt opera-transcription studies and a discussion of each transcription and fantasy in turn, arranged chronologically in terms of Liszt's enormous output. Hamilton concludes his survey with four hand-copied appendices consisting of scores of unpublished paraphrases on themes from Rossini's *Siège de Corinth* (see item 309), Weber's *Freischütz* (see item 1032), and Mozart's *Nozze di Figaro* and *Don Juan* (the last not to be confused with the familiar *Réminiscences de Don Juan* discussed in item 1020). Additional musical examples and a highly useful bibliography.

Four dissertations devoted to the vocal-music paraphrases and transcriptions are described below, in alphabetical order (by author):

1010.   Crockett, Barbara Allen. *Liszt's Opera Transcriptions for Piano*. Dissertation: University of Illinois, 1968. iv, 117pp.

      [No LC number available]

      Devoted to Liszt's operatic paraphrases and arrangements, including the Wagner transcriptions and three fantasies singled out by Crockett as especially fine: Liszt's "Reminiscences" of Bellini's *Norma* and *Somnambula* and of Mozart's *Don Giovanni*. Illustrated throughout with musical examples.

      Summarized in DAI 29/7 (January 1969), p. 2292A; reprinted in the *Journal of the American Liszt Society* 9 (1981), p. 137.

1011.   Edwards, Robert Lynn. *A Study of Selected Song Transcriptions by Franz Liszt*. Dissertation: University of Oregon, 1972. 96pp.

      [No LC number available]

      Deals with Liszt's song transcriptions, including some of his self-transcriptions, as "nineteenth-century manifestations of the time-honored practice of transcribing vocal music for keyboard performance, a practice dating back to the Reina and Faenza Codices of the early fifteenth century." Edwards describes the social, economic, and artistic milieu that encouraged transcriptions like those Liszt made, and he examines a few individual transcriptions in detail.

      Summarized in DAI 33/5 (November 1972), p. 2409A; reprinted in the *Journal of the American Liszt Society* 10 (1981), p. 124.

1012. Gibbs, Dan Paul. *A Background and Analysis of Selected Lieder and Opera Transcriptions of Franz Liszt.* Lecture-recital document: North Texas State University, 1980. 56pp. and accompanying reels of magnetic recording tape.

[No LC number available]

Examines Liszt's piano transcriptions of songs and operatic music, especially his arrangements of Schubert's *Gretchen am Spinnrade* and *Auf dem Wasser zu singen*, Chopin's *Moja pieszczotka*, the "Love-Death" from Wagner's *Tristan und Isolde*, and the quartet from the final act of Verdi's *Rigoletto*. Illustrated with musical examples.

Summarized in DAI 41/7 (January 1981), pp. 2820A-2821A; reprinted in the *Journal of the American Liszt Society* 18 (1985), p. 183.

1013. Presser, Dieter. *Studien zu den Opern- und Liedbearbeitungen Franz Liszts.* Dissertation: University of Cologne, 1955. vi, 215pp.

[No LC number available; according to OCLC information, Duke University owns a photocopy of the original typescript]

Seen only once, in 1975. A survey of Liszt's opera and song paraphrases and transcriptions, copiously illustrated with musical examples. Concludes with an extensive bibliography.

NB: Some of Presser's observations in this dissertation reappear in his article "Die Opernbearbeitungen des 19. Jahrhunderts," *Archiv für Musikwissenschaft* 12 (1955), pp. 228-238.

Five shorter studies deal exclusively with Liszt's operatic transcriptions and paraphrases. These studies are described below in alphabetical order (by author):

1014. Batta, András. "'Programopera' zongorán: Sajátos stílusjegyek Liszt operaparafrázisaiban." *Magyar zene* 27 (1986), pp. 3-11.

An introduction to the opera paraphrases and a discussion of how those works recreate operatic experiences. No musical examples. In Hungarian.

A shorter version of this article appeared under the title "Les paraphrases d'opéra" in item 36; pp. 44-53.

1015. Döhring, Sieghart. "'Réminiscences': Liszts Konzeption der Klavierparaphrase." *Festschrift Heinz Becker zum 60. Geburtstag,* ed. Jürgen Schläder and Reinhold Quandt. Laaber: Laaber-Verlag, 1982; pp. 131-151.

ISBN 3-9215-1870-9   [No LC number available]

Another introduction to this topic, supplemented by a detailed examination of "great" paraphrases like those of Bellini's *Norma*, Meyerbeer's *Robert le diable*, and especially Mozart's *Don Giovanni*. A few musical examples.

1016. Hering, Hans. "Franz Liszt und die Paraphrase." *Musica* 28 (1974), pp. 231-234.

Describes some of the ways Liszt used the operatic paraphrase (e.g., as a model for improvisation, a sop to enthusiastic audiences clamoring for encores, etc.). Hering also observes that Liszt adapted declamatory operatic effects in his own compositions. (With regard to this last topic, see item 646.) No musical examples.

1017. Schaeffner, André. "Liszt transcripteur d'opéras italiens." *Revue musicale* "Numéro special" (1 May 1928), pp. 89-100.

Examines Liszt's arrangements of and paraphrases on such operas as Bellini's *Norma* and Donizetti's *Lucia di Lammermoor*. Schaeffner also mentions some of Liszt's piano pieces and draws comparisons between those pieces, the operatic transcriptions, and pieces by twentieth-century composers like Stravinsky and Poulenc. Illustrated with 8 musical examples.

1018. Suttoni, Charles. "Liszt's Operatic Fantasies and Transcriptions." *Journal of the American Liszt Society* 8 (1980), pp. 3-14.

Also published as an introduction to items 139-140. Suttoni provides brief "synopses" of each Liszt transcription or paraphrase as well as observations on Liszt's attitudes toward operatic paraphrases. No musical examples.

Some of Suttoni's remarks are adapted from his dissertation *Piano and Opera: A Study of the Piano Fantasies Written on Opera Themes in the Romantic Era* (Dissertation: New York University, 1973).

2. Specialized Studies

Sixteen studies dealing exclusively with Lisztian versions of vocal works by other composers are described or cross-referenced below according to composer, then alphabetically (by author):

A. <u>Bellini</u> (see also items A64 and A101)

1019. Schenkman, Walter. "Liszt's Reminiscences of Bellini's 'Norma'." *Journal of the American Liszt Society* 9 (1981), pp. 55-64.

Summarizes the plot of *Norma* and discusses the historical significance of Liszt's paraphrase, the musical contents and structural organization of that latter work, the function of operatic arrangements and transcriptions in nineteenth-century musical culture, etc. Schenkman also speculates about the possible influence of Bellini's "Piange" aria on the "Liebestod" from Wagner's *Tristan und Isolde*; he even suggests that Liszt's paraphrase may have inspired certain details in Wagner's music (i.e. choice of key and "subtle changes in . . . melody"). No musical examples.

B. Mozart (see also items A62 and A64)

1020.   Riethmüller, Albrecht. "Franz Liszts 'Réminiscences de Don Juan'." *Analysen. Beiträge zu einer Problemgeschichte des Komponierens. Festschrift für Hans Heinrich Eggebrecht zum 65. Geburtstag*, ed. Weiner Breig et al. [*Archiv für Musikwissenschaft*, Beiheft 23.] Wiesbaden: Franz Steiner, 1984; pp. 276-291.
    ISBN 3-515-3662-8   [No LC number available]
    Describes Liszt''s paraphrase in terms of its musical contents, the significance of those contents within Mozart's opera (and for other nineteenth-century composers, among them Schumann), the overall formal organization of Liszt's work, and so on. Outfitted with an analytical diagram and two short musical examples.

C. Rossini (see also items A94 and A101)

1021.   Howard, Walther. *Liszts Bearbeitung des Cujus Animum aus dem "Stabat Mater" von Rossini. Ein Kapitel über thematische Arbeit.* [Der kleine Hauskonzert-Führer, 3.] Berlin: Verlag für Kultur und Kunst, 1935. 48pp.
    ML410.L7Z4458M
    A somewhat ponderous comparison of Liszt's arrangement with Rossini's original. No musical examples, which makes Howard's arguments more difficult to follow.
    Another analytical pamphlet by Howard, this one devoted to the "Hungarian Rhapsody" No. 5, appeared as the first "Kleine Hauskonzert-Führer" series. Cited in item 39; p. 80. Illustrated with very short, hand-copied musical examples.

D. Schubert (see also items A61, A92, A95, and A101)

1022.   George, James Modica, Jr. *Franz Liszt's Transcriptions of Schubert's Songs for Solo Pianoforte: A Study of Transcribing and Keyboard Techniques.* Dissertation: University of Iowa, 1976. xviii, 213pp.
    ML410.L7G46 1979
    Evalutes melodic, harmonic, textural, and rhythmic devices Liszt employed in his piano transcriptions of Schubert's songs as well as in works like the Beethoven's symphonies and the Paganini violin caprices. Illustrated with 144 musical examples. Concludes with three appendices devoted to identifying Liszt's 55 Schubert song transcriptions, to differences in time signatures and tempo markings between Schubert's songs and Liszt's transcriptions, and to establishing parallel texts of *Das Sterbe-*

Glöcklein in the Schubert and Schubert-Liszt versions. Concludes with a bibliography.

Summarized in DAI 37/8 (February 1977), pp. 4684A-4685A; reprinted in the *Journal of the American Liszt Society* 3 (1978), p. 39.

*   Hilmar, Ernst. "Kritische Betrachtungen zu Liszts Transkriptionen von Liedern von Franz Schubert."

Deals primarily with Liszt mss. of Schubert song transcriptions owned by the Vienna Stadtbibliothek. Described in greater detail as item 300.

*   Kabisch, Thomas. *Liszt und Schubert.*

Deals in part with Liszt transcriptions of Schubert songs. Described in greater detail as item 696.

1023.   Ku, Hsiao-Hung. *Liszt's Schubert Lieder Transcriptions: A Study of Liszt Pianistic Idiom* [sic] *in the Transcriptive Procedure.* Lecture-recital document: North Texas State University, 1983. x, 40pp.

[No LC number available]

Identifies "conventional piano techniques" utilized by Liszt in his Schubert song transcriptions, especially in "Hark, Hark, the Lark" and *Der Lindenbaum.* Musical examples.

Summarized in DAI 44/8 (February 1984), p. 2287A; reprinted in the *Journal of the American Liszt Society* 18 (1985), p. 184.

1024.   Norris, David Owen. "Liszt's 'Winterreise'." *Musical Times* 126 (1985), pp. 521-525.

Evaluates Liszt's solo-piano transcriptions of the *Winterreise* songs in terms of their "musical felicities"—e.g., the canonic treatment in Liszt's transcription of the last verse of *Ständchen.* Illustrated with a diagram of the order and keys of the individual Liszt-Schubert *Winterreise* items, and with five musical examples.

A reply to Norris's article refers to existing editions of Liszt's Schubert song transcriptions, among them item 138. See Richard Davis, [Letter], in the *Musical Times* 126 (1985), p. 712.

1025.   Walker, Alan. "Liszt and the Schubert Song Transcriptions." *Musical Quarterly* 67 (1981), pp. 50-63.

Discusses the origins of the fifty-odd Schubert song transcriptions performed and published by Liszt during 1838-1840. Walker believes these transcriptions served at least three functions: they 1) advanced Schubert's reputation outside Vienna; 2) introduced sophistications in piano technique; and 3) enlarged Liszt's own concert repertory. Musical examples.

E. Tchaikovsky

1026.   Jones, Barrie. "Liszt and 'Eugene Onegin': Some Reflections on a Transcription." *Liszt Society Journal* 11 (1986), pp. 81-85.

Analyzes the arrangement of the "Polonaise" from Tchaikovsky's opera Liszt made for piano around 1879. Jones also mentions some of Liszt's other keyboard transcriptions and operatic paraphrases and provides diagrams of the harmonic and structural organization of the "Polonaise" itself. Illustrated with more than a dozen short musical examples.

F. Verdi (see also items A59, A93, A95, and A101)

1027.   Dorgan, Peter Paul. *Franz Liszt and his Verdi Opera Transcriptions.* Dissertation: Ohio State University, 1982. vi, 125pp.

ML410.L7D6 1982a

Examines eight transcriptions Liszt made from portions of Verdi's operas, including the *Réminiscences de Boccanegra.* Among other things Dorgan deals with "arrangements, [transcriptions, and paraphrases] individually, comparing each to its operatic original." Concludes with a catalog of Liszt's transcriptions for solo piano. Musical examples and a bibliography.

Summarized in DAI 43/5 (November 1982), p. 1339A; reprinted in the *Journal of the American Liszt Society* 19 (1986), p. 183.

G. Wagner (see also items A60, A95, and A101)

1028.   Friedlaender, Erich. *Wagner, Liszt und die Kunst der Klavier-Bearbeitung. Eine historisch-kritische Studie.* Detmold: Meyer, 1922. 55pp.

ML700.F42

Apparently the first book-length study of its kind, and a pretty poor one. Friedlaender devotes himself almost entirely with Wagner transcriptions by Tausig, Rubinstein, von Bülow, and so on, and not with Liszt's works. Contains a catalog of Wagner works in keyboard arrangements (pp. 48-51) but no musical examples.

1029.   Hirschmann, Ursula. "Die Wagner-Bearbeitungen Franz Liszts." *Richard Wagner und die Musikhochschule München . . .* Schriften der Hochschule für Musik München, 4. Regensburg: Gustav Bosse, 1983; pp. 103-121.

ML410.W13R5 1983   ISBN 3-7649-2268-0

A survey of Liszt's Wagner paraphrases and transcriptions as well as of harmonic, melodic, and rhythmic elements found in those works. Illustrated with four tables dividing published Liszt-Wagner compositions into various categories. No musical examples.

1030. Loos, Helmut. "Liszts Klavierübertragungen von Werken Richard Wagners. Versuch einer Deutung." *Liszt-Studien* 3 (1986), pp. 103-118.

A brief description of Liszt's Wagner paraphrases and transcriptions, followed by observations on individual works and by discussions of several extended quotations from Liszt's correspondence and miscellaneous documents like Pictet's description of Liszt's 1835 organ improvisation at the Fribourg cathedral (see also item 245). Loos supplements his observations with a chronological table of the most important Liszt-Wagner transcriptions (p. 111) and with extensive bibliographic citations in the form of endnotes.

1031. Redepenning, Dorothea. "'Zu eig'nem Wort und eig'ner Weis . . .' Liszts Wagner-Transkriptionen." *Musikforschung* 39 (1986), pp. 305-317.

Primarily a comparison of representative passages from *Tannhäuser, Meistersinger*, and *Parsifal* with Liszt's versions of those passages. Illustrated with 3 musical examples and a table comparing bar-form organization in *Am stillen Herd* from *Die Meistersinger* with the somewhat looser structure of Liszt's paraphrase.

<u>H. Weber</u> (see also items A93 and A95)

1032. Huschke, Wolfram. "Anmerkungen zu Franz Liszts 'Freischütz-Fantasie'." *Studia musicologica* 28 (1986), pp. 261-271.

Treats of Liszt's unpublished fantasy on themes from Weber's opera. Huschke's article is part documentary study (D-WRgs Liszt ms. I-46), part analysis of musical form, motivic materials, and textual references. No musical examples, but Huschke does outline the structural organization of the Fantasy in tabular form (p. 266).

TRANSCRIPTIONS OF LISZT'S WORKS BY OTHER COMPOSERS

Little has been published about Liszt transcriptions prepared by other composers. (Among such arrangements is one of the B-minor Sonata for wind band!) Three studies devoted to this topic are described or cross-referenced below. NB: A recording of marches by Liszt is described as item A100:

1033. Sievers, Gerd. "Franz Liszts Legende 'Der heilige Franziskus von Paula auf den Wogen schreitend' für Klavier in Max Regers Bearbeitung für die Orgel." *Hamburger Jahrbuch für Musikwissenschaft* ["Zur Musikgeschichte des 19. Jahrhunderts"] 2 (1977), pp. 125-146.

ISBN 3-921029-53-8   [No LC number available]

Compares Liszt's piano piece with Reger's organ transcription. Sievers points out that Reger, who criticized Liszt sharply for his Bach transcriptions, was unable to transcribe Liszt's music without taking enormous liberties of his own. Illustrated with diagrams and comparative musical examples.

*   Sonneck, O. G. "Liszt's Huldigungsmarsch and Weimar's Volkslied."
     Deals in part with an arrangement by Joachim Raff for military band of Liszt's march. Described in greater detail as item 349.

*   Suppan, Wolfgang. "Blasorchesterbearbeitungen Liszt'scher Werke."
     A catalog of Liszt pieces transcribed for concert and marching bands by various composers. Described in greater detail as item 56.

XX: PEDAGOGY, PERFORMANCE PRACTICE, AND INSTRUMENTS

In addition to his accomplishments as pianist, author, and composer, Liszt was the foremost piano pedagogue of his day; he also influenced keyboard performance practice and the development of the piano (and other musical instruments) during the middle decades of the nineteenth century. Studies dealing exclusively or primarily with Liszt pedagogy, performance, and instruments are described below. Certain reminiscences and related works that also deal with these topics are described in Chapter VIII.

PEDAGOGY

General Studies

Several experts have devoted themselves to analyzing Liszt's philosophy as a music teacher as well as identifying his teaching materials and techniques. Perhaps the most authoritative of these experts has produced two studies of considerable importance:

1034. Ott, Bertrand. *Liszt et la pedagogie du piano. Éssai sur l'art du clavier selon Liszt*, with an introduction by Norbert Dufourcq. Philosophie et pédagogie de la musique, 2. Issy-le-Moulineaux: Editions Scientifiques et Psychologiques, 1978. 313pp.

     ML410.L77O89   [No ISBN number available]

     A detailed discussion of Liszt's method of playing the piano, drawing heavily on iconographical evidence as well as eyewitness reports. Some of Ott's conclusions may be forced, but his work deserves examination if only for the body of material it brings together. Musical examples as well as diagrams, portraits, and other illustrations. Concludes with an extensive bibliography.

1035. Ott, Bertrand. "La pianisme lisztien *ou* le dépassement créatif: Une réalité singuilière à revivifier, une pianistique universelle à expliciter." *Revue musicale* 405-406-407 (1987), pp. 139-153.

     A synopsis of some of the topics covered in item 1034 (above), including details of actual Liszt performances. Illustrated with several useful diagrams and outlines but no musical examples.

Two other book-length studies of Lisztian pedagogy (and of that closely related topic, Lisztian keyboard technique) also deserve attention:

1036.   Machnek, Elsie Jane. *The Pedagogy of Franz Liszt*. Dissertation: Northwestern University, 1965. 231pp.
ML410.L7M2 1974M
In part a study of Liszt's attitude toward and methods of teaching piano playing. In part a comparative investigation of Liszt's methods vs. those of other nineteenth-century pedagogues, including Czerny (Liszt's own teacher), Clementi, and Hummel. Musical examples and a bibliography.
Summarized in DAI 27/6 (December 1966), pp. 1852A-1853A. NB: A second volume of this study, *Technical Studies for the Pianoforte by Franz Liszt*, is available only in typescript at the Northwestern University Library.

1037.   Ramann, Lina. *Liszt-Pädagogium. Klavier-Kompositionen Franz Liszts nebst nach unedirten Veränderungen, Zusatzen und Kadenzen nach des Meisters Lehren pädagogisch glossiert*, with a foreword by Alfred Brendel. Wiesbaden: Breitkopf & Härtel, 1986.
ISBN 3-7651-0223-7   [No LC number available]
A famous anthology of keyboard music and musical excerpts, published as a pedagogical tool. Ramann supplements Liszt's music with performance instructions and comments by a number of virtuoso Liszt pupils (August Stradal, August Göllerich, Heinrich Porges, etc.). Covers the Sonata in b minor; "Hungarian Rhapsodies" Nos. 2, 3, and 5; the *Funérailles* from *Harmonies poétiques et religieuses*, etc., as well as Smetana's Polka, Op. 7, and a Waltz in A-flat Major by Raff. Concludes (in this edition) with a concordance of *Liszt-Pädagogium* contents and the contents of items 136-137.
Originally published in five volumes by Breitkopf & Härtel of Leipzig, c. 1901 (Plate Nos. 23481-23485).

Nine somewhat more limited or superficial studies of Liszt as teacher are described below in alphabetical order (by author and/or title):

1038.   Clouzot, Marie-Rose. "Liszt pédagogue." *Revue musicale* "Numéro special" (1 May 1928), p. 128.
A one-page synopsis of Valerie Boissier's remarks (in item 232) about Liszt's keyboard instruction.

1039.   Dumm, Robert W. "Liszt's Piano Teaching: 1884-1886." *Journal of the American Liszt Society* 4 (1978), pp. 23-36.
Reviews Liszt's pedagogical activities as well as Göllerich's reminiscences and pedagogical observations (see item 1047). Dumm quotes liberally from Fay's *Music-Study in Germany* (item 237), *Life and Liszt* by Arthur Friedheim (item 238), William Mason's *Memories of a Musical Life*, and so on. No musical examples.

1040.   Gervers, Hilda. "Franz Liszt as Pedagogue." *Journal of Research in Music Education* 18 (1970), pp. 385-391.
Covers such topics as Liszt's interest in his students' analytical skills and technical development, his belief in the fusion of music and poetry as the basis of interpretation, and his role in the development of master classes.

1041.   Hedley, Arthur. "Liszt the Pianist and Teacher." In item 31; pp. 22-35.
A cursory description of Liszt's abilities as performer and pedagogue. Hedley quotes several contemporary descriptions of Liszt's playing and teaching, including those of Amy Fay (see item 237).

1042.   Mach, Elyse. "Liszt the Teacher." *Liszt Society Journal* 8 (1983), pp. 11-18.
A survey of Liszt's pedagogical methods and attitudes, including repertory suggestions, attitudes toward practicing and technical exercises, instructions on phrasing, etc. Mach quotes passages from item 232 as well as other reminiscences identified in Chapter VIII. Copiously illustrated with musical examples, including two pages of excerpts from Liszt's own technical exercises.

1043.   Michel, Paul. "Franz Liszt als Lehrer und Erzieher." *Studia musicologica* 5 (1963), pp. 217-226.
Argues that Liszt's activities as a pedagogue "brought together all his philosophical, political, artistic, and social convictions and united them in the form of practical activity [i.e., advice]." Includes quotations from works by Lamennais and Liszt as well as from a number of Liszt reminiscences.

1044.   Michel, Paul. "Franz Liszts pädagogisches Vermächtnis." In item 32; pp. 3-12.
Discusses Liszt's pedagogical activites, especially those of his later years. Includes German-language translations from several late nineteenth-century Hungarian periodicals.

1045.   Stradal, August. "Liszt as Teacher and Educator," trans. Adrian Williams.
        Liszt Society Journal 11 (1986), pp. 86-88.
        Recollections by one of Liszt's pupils on his teacher's attitudes toward
        music and music teaching. (With regard to Stradal's reminiscences of Liszt,
        see item   250.)

1046.   Ullyot, Marianne. "Chopin and Liszt: A Legacy of Teaching." *Journal of
        the American Liszt Society* 10 (1981), pp. 39-42.
        Summarizes *Chopin and Liszt: A Study of the Pianist/Composers as
        Teachers*, Ullyot's master's thesis (University of Minnesota 1974). In the
        present article she contends that both Chopin and Liszt "stood apart from
        the teaching traditions of their time" because they encouraged instrumental
        proficiency as a means of creating "a musical event." No musical exam-
        ples.

Liszt Pupils

*Liszt numbered dozens of composers and keyboard virtuosos among the men and
women who studied with him throughout his life, especially after the late 1840s.
Reminiscences of Liszt written by some of those students are described in Chapter
VIII, and specialized biographical studies mentioning a few of them are described
in Chapter X.*

No single study describes the lives and careers of all *Liszt's pupils, but the two
volumes described below tell us a great deal about many of them:*

1047.   Jerger, Wilhelm. *Franz Liszts Klavierunterricht von 1884-1886, dargestellt
        an den Tagebuchaufzeichungen von August Göllerich.* Studien zur
        Musikgeschichte des 19. Jahrhunderts, 39. Regensburg: Gustav Bosse,
        1975. 160pp.
        ML410.L7G66   ISBN 3-7649-2091-2
        A detailed account of Göllerich's life, career, and relationship with
        Liszt, followed by the text of Göllerich's diaries for 31 May-6 July 1884,
        16 June-9 September 1885, 11 November 1885—12 January 1886, and so
        on. Virtually every entry deals with Liszt's observations about music,
        keyboard technique, and performances by his students and other articles.
        For each entry Jerger provides copious annotations. Scattered, short mus-
        ical examples; supplemented by a fine, short bibliography (pp. 9-10).
        A shorter study by Jerger appeared several years ago as: "August
        Göllerich, Schüler und Interpret von Franz Liszt," *Oberösterreichische
        Heimatblätter* 26 (1972), pp. 23-32. A second article by Jerger appeared
        under the title "August Göllerichs Wirken für Franz Liszt in Linz" in the
        Burgenländische Heimatblätter 23 (1961), pp. 233-236.

1048.   Goodman, Alfred. *Die amerikanischen Schüler Franz Liszts.*
        Veröffentlichungen zur Musikforschung, 1. Wilhelmshaven: Heinrichsho-
        fen, 1972. 172pp.
          ML390.G65 1972   ISBN 3-7959-0132-6
          A reliable if incomplete survey of the lives, reminiscences, and experi-
        ences of Liszt's American pupils. Goodman provides the names of many
        pupils but overlooks several of them, including Hugo Mansfeldt (see item
        1050); he also discusses only a few pupils at length (e.g., William Mason,
        Arthur Bird, Edward MacDowell, and so on). Finally, Goodman com-
        pares the compositions of these and other pupils with works by Liszt,
        demonstrating in the process how derivative some of the American works
        were. Illustrated with musical examples from a number of works; con-
        cludes with a bibliography.

*Six studies devoted exclusively to individual Liszt pupils or to pupils who studied
with Liszt at particular institutions are described or cross-referenced below, in alphabetical order (by author):*

*   Jung, Hans Rudolf. "Der Liszt-Schüler Berhard Stavenhagen (1862 bis
        1914) und seine Beziehungen zu Weimar."
          Described as item 574.

*   Legány, Desző. "Liszt's and Erkel's Relations and Students."
          Described as item 593.

1049.   Mueller von Asow, E. H. "Hermann Cohen, ein Lieblingsschüler Franz
        Liszts." *Österreichische Musikzeitschrift* 16 (1961), pp. 443-452.
          Deals with one of Liszt's earliest and most colorful pupils, an unreliable
        character who accompanied his teacher and the Comtesse d'Agoult to
        Switzerland during the 1830s and later cheated Liszt out of 3,000 francs.
        Illustrated with quotations from Liszt's letters as well as with a portrait of
        the pupil himself. See also item 1a; pp. 221ff.

1050.   Stevenson, Robert. "Liszt's 'Favorite' California Pupil: Hugo Mansfeldt
        (1844-1932)." *Inter-American Music Review* 7/2 (Spring-Summer 1986),
        pp. 33-78.
          A lavishly documented sketch of Mansfeldt's life and musical activities,
        illustrated with facsimile reproductions of several concert programs, news-
        paper clippings, compositions, etc.
          Reprinted with alterations in the *Journal of the American Liszt Society*
        21 (1987), pp. 42-58; and 22 (1987), pp. 27-46.

1051.   Strub-Ronanye, Elgin. "Bernhard Stavenhagen: Pupil of Liszt." *Liszt Society Journal* 11 (1986), pp. 93-101.

An intriguing survey of Stavenhagen's life and career. Strub-Ronanye includes quotations from a number of sources, including a letter Stavenhagen addressed to the Italian pianist Giuseppe Buonamici on 12 August 1886, on the occasion of Liszt's death. Illustrated with several portraits (among them, a dual photograph of Liszt and Stavenhagen taken in London in April 1886) and four full-page facsimile reproductions of programs or posters for concerts Stavenhagen gave on behalf of the Liszt-Stiftung in Weimar between 1890-1894.

An article virtually identical with this one (but without illustrations) appeared as "Bernhard Stavenhagen: Pianist, Conductor, Composer and Liszt's Last Pupil" in the *New Hungarian Quarterly* 28/107 (Autumn 1987), pp. 222-228.

*   Viala, Claude. "Franz Liszt au Conservatoire (1835-1836)."

Discusses Liszt's brief career as a faculty member at the Geneva Conservatory during the mid-1830s. Described in greater detail as item 519.

PERFORMANCE PRACTICE STUDIES

Liszt performance practice is a complex topic that touches on ms. studies, studies of musical editions, accounts of actual performances, critical replies to Liszt's interpretations of works by himself and other composers, performances and publications by Liszt pupils, and a host of other topics. Studies of manuscripts and documents associated in certain instances with performance-practice issues are described in Chapter VIII, as are reminiscences by certain Liszt pupils. NB: Items A1-A15 identify and describe recorded performances by other pupils of Liszt.

General Studies

At least one comparatively recent dissertation has been devoted exclusively to Lisztian technique and interpretation:

1052.   Steinberg, Arne Jo. *Franz Liszt's Approach to Piano Playing*. Dissertation: University of Maryland, 1971. 255pp.

ML410.L7S84 1971a

A detailed study of Liszt's attitudes toward and methods of handling accentuation, dynamics, phrasing, and other piano performance practices as well as a survey of Lisztian keyboard styles and Liszt's emphasis on sight-reading skill. Numerous musical examples and a bibliography.

Summarized in DAI 32/4 (October 1971), p. 2124A; reprinted in the *Journal of the American Liszt Society* 10 (1981), pp. 125-126.

Keyboard Technique

Three book-length studies devoted exclusively to keyboard technique are described below in alphabetical order (by author):

1053.   Dobiey, Herbert. *Die Klaviertechnik des jungen Franz Liszt*. Berlin: Paul Funk, 1932. 47pp.
      ML410.L7D8
      A rather disappointing survey study, apparently identical with the author's 1931 University of Berlin dissertation. Refers (among other topics) to the keyboard compositions Liszt completed in Paris during the 1830s and to aspects of keyboard technique: octaves, leaps, passagework, etc. No musical examples.

1054.   Landau, Hela. *Die Neuerungen der Klavier-Technik bei Franz Liszt*. Dissertation: University of Vienna, 1933. 86pp.
      Typescript. Musicological Library of the University of Vienna: shelf-number E177.
      A survey of Lisztian keyboard writing and associated subjects (i.e., scales, arpeggios, passage-work of other kinds, and so on). Also describes Liszt's fingering indications, pedalling, etc. Musical examples and a bibliography.

1055.   Philipp, Isidor. *La technique de Franz Liszt*. 2 volumes. Paris: Salambert, 1932.
      MT225.P5T4
      A rare publication, missing from (or misplaced in) several collections, including those of the Library of Congress. Cited in item 39 and elsewhere throughout the Liszt literature.

Four other books describe Liszt's influence on keyboard technique and pedagogy during the late nineteenth and early twentieth centuries:

1056.   Fleischmann, Tilly. *Aspects of the Liszt Tradition*, ed. Michael O'Neill. Cork: Adore Press, 1986. viii, 132pp.
      MT140.F6 1986   [No ISBN number available]
      Discusses the "Liszt tradition" passed on by pianists like Stavenhagen and Kellermann. Fleischmann also deals with performance problems in Liszt's Ballade No. 2, the "Legends," the *Valse impromptu*, etc., as well as works by Chopin. Written years ago, Fleischmann's work appears here for the first time but in an abbreviated version. Numerous musical examples, among them passages from Liszt works selected to illustrated discussions of keyboard mechanics, practice methods, technical problems,

and so on. Also illustrated with five photographs, including one of Liszt and Stavenhagen together.

1057. *Il pianoforte e Liszt*, ed. Gian Paolo Minardi. Parma: Orchestra Sinfonica dell'Emilia-Romagna "Arturo Toscanini," 1986. 70pp.
         [No LC or ISBN numbers available]
         Deals with the piano as an instrument and with some of Liszt's accomplishments as keyboard composer, performer, and teacher. Includes "Franz Liszt" by Alfred Cortot (pp. 33-47) as well as excerpts from articles by Schumann and Heine, and from Liszt's own *F. Chopin* (items 165a and 171). Several illustrations, including caricatures of Liszt's appearances in Berlin, 1841-1842. In Italian.

1058. Matuschka, Mathias. *Die Erneuerung der Klaviertechnik nach Liszt.* Berliner musikwissenschaftliche Arbeiten, 31. Munich and Salzburg: Emil Katzbichler, 1987. 130pp.
         MT220.M46 1987   ISBN 3-8739-7071-6
         To a considerable extent an evaluation of Liszt's influence on late nineteenth- and twentieth-century piano teachers—among them Ludwig Deppe, Gustav Stöwe, Rudolf Maria Breithaupt, and so on. Diagrams, musical examples, and a bibliography.

1059. Roës, Paul. *Music, the Mystery and the Reality*, trans. Edna Dean McGray. Chevy Chase, Maryland: E. & M. Publishing, 1978. xxvii, 147pp.
         ML410.L7R673   ISBN 0-960-1832-1-3
         A "philosophical" study of musical expression and an attempt to rediscover the principles behind Liszt's keyboard artistry. Roës draws heavily on Busoni's books and articles, perhaps because Roës himself worked with Busoni. Illustrated with musical examples, photographs of Roës and casts made of Liszt's hands, musical examples, etc.; concludes with a short bibliography. A strange, unevenly organized, highly opinionated work.
         Originally published as *La musique, mystère et réalité* (Paris: Henry Lemoine, 1955).

One shorter study summarizes material presented in item 1059 (above):

1060. Beattie, Donald. "Roës' Key to the Palace of Liszt." *Journal of the American Liszt Society* 20 (1986), pp. 109-124.
         A detailed summary of the basic principles expressed by Roës in *Music: The Mystery and the Reality*. Topics addressed by Beattie include the philosophy of musical performance, the art of performance in general, and Liszt's personal attitudes toward pedagogy and keyboard technique. Illus-

trated with extensive quotations from Roës, including excerpts from Liszt's letters quoted secondhand.

Yet another study should be used only with caution:

1061.   Lee, Sang Hie. *A Psychophysiological Approach to the Technical Problems Found in the Piano Etudes of Chopin and Liszt and a Compendium of the Solutions.* Dissertation: University of Georgia, 1977. v, 145pp.
         [No LC number available]
         A disappointing attempt to catalog problems common to nineteenth-century virtuoso music "in terms of the physiological mechanics involved in piano playing." Lee discusses in detail certain passages from the "Transcendental" and "Paganini" etudes, the *Trois etudes de concert*, and the two Liszt concert studies. Concludes with a short bibliography.
         Summarized in DAI 38/8 (February 1978), pp. 4439A-4440A; reprinted in the *Journal of the American Liszt Society* 3 (1978), pp. 40-41. Michael Saffle's objections to this dissertation appeared in the *Bulletin of the Council for Research in Music Education* No. 68 (Fall 1981), pp. 51-54; and No. 79 (Summer 1984), pp. 6-10.

Five articles about Liszt's keyboard writing and performing skills are described or cross-referenced below in alphabetical order (by author):

*   Biget, Michelle. "Étude comparée du geste pianistique chez Liszt et chez Debussy."
         Deals more with Liszt's writing for the piano than with performance practices. Described in greater detail as item 709.

1062.   Esteban, Julio. "On Liszt's Technical Exercises." *Journal of the American Liszt Society* 1 (1977), pp. 17-19.
         Describes the technical exercises written by Liszt late in life and published after his death as item 143. Esteban also touches briefly on Liszt's lifelong interest in keyboard technique. No musical examples.

1063.   Gerig, Reginald. "Observations on Franz Liszt's Piano Technique." *Journal of the American Liszt Society* 18 (1985), pp. 3-28.
         Summarizes Liszt's observations on technical issues as well as certain opinions expressed by other nineteenth-century figures, including Charles Hallé, Amy Fay, Bettina Walker, etc. Concludes with a bibliography and outlines of keyboard techniques and methods of developing greater pianistic proficiency. One musical example.

Much of this article was adapted by Gerig from his own "Liszt and Virtuoso Technique," *Famous Pianists and their Technique* (Bridgeport, Connecticut: Robert B. Luce, 1974), pp. 171-195.

1064.   Gil-Marchex, Henri. "A propos de la technique de piano de Liszt." *Revue musicale* "Numéro special" (1 May 1928), pp. 76-88.
        Describes some of Liszt's contributions to keyboard writing. Gil-Marchex draws most of his examples from compositions of the 1830s and 1840s, including versions of the "Transcendental" etudes and several of operatic paraphrases. A "borderline" study, dealing both with how Liszt wrote for the piano and how he played what he wrote.

1065.   Wolff, Konrad. "Liszt's Approach to Piano Technique." *Journal of the American Liszt Society* 4 (1978), pp. 45-51.
        A discussion of certain Lisztian attitudes toward performance and technique. Wolff examines "the place which piano technique occupies within Liszt's aesthetic credo." Includes references to and quotations from a variety of publications, including item 1059. No musical examples.

Studies in Interpretation

Liszt's own approach to keyboard interpretation is summarized neatly in the following article:

1066.   Kentner, Louis. "The Interpretation of Liszt's Piano Music." In item 31; pp. 202-220.
        A short, somewhat disappointing introduction to this important topic by a justly famous pianist. More an analysis of keyboard writing than a discussion of transforming written music into sound. Illustrated with passages from some of the "Hungarian Rhapsodies," the *Années de pèlerinage*, the Sonata in b minor, and so on.

Six other articles discuss how Liszt himself may have played certain works, or how others may have played them:

1067.   Florán, Juan. "Liszt the Player of Chamber Music." *Liszt Society Journal* 11 (1986), pp. 35-38.
        A collection of quotations from French newspapers and encyclopedia articles about Liszt, Chrétien Urhan, Alexandre Batta, and chamber performances they gave together in Paris during the 1830s. Concludes with the French-language text of Florán's review published in *Le monde* on 5 February 1837.

1068.   Saffle, Michael. "New Light on Playing Liszt's 'Prelude and Fugue on BACH'." *American Organist* 16 (1982), pp. 44-49.

Discusses performance directions and registration specifications recorded in D-WRgs Liszt mss. and their implications for performances of the "BACH" prelude and fugue. Illustrated with several musical examples and facsimile pages from early editions of Liszt's organ works.

1069.   Sutter, Milton. "Liszt and the Performance of Bach's Organ Music." *Liszt-Studien* 2 (1981), pp. 207-219.

An outstanding introduction to Liszt and performance-practice problems in Bach's music (e.g., voicing in fugues, trills and other ornaments, articulation and phrasing, etc.). Sutter's evidence *vis-à-vis* Bach's organ works is indirect; there is no direct evidence that Liszt ever performed even the organ pieces he transcribed for piano. Quotations from a variety of sources, and 7 musical examples.

1070.   Newman, William S. "Liszt's Interpretation of Beethoven's Piano Sonatas." *Musical Quarterly* 58 (1972), pp. 185-209.

Discusses documented Liszt performances of individual sonatas as well as topics like Beethoven's influence on Liszt's life and artistic development, Liszt editions of works by Beethoven, and so on. Illustrated with the familiar Kriehuber picture of Liszt at the piano. Contains quotations from nineteenth-century newspapers and other documents but no musical examples.

1071.   Raessler, Daniel M. "Ferruccio Busoni as Interpreter of Liszt." *Journal of the American Liszt Society* 9 (1981), pp. 31-41.

Describes Busoni's attitudes toward Liszt and his music through three stages: misunderstanding, adoration, and admiration. Raessler also examines Busoni's "Liszt repertory" and quotes extensively from several Busoni articles. No musical examples.

1072.   Calza, Edvige. *Interpretazione letteraria dei preludi di Chopin attribuita a Liszt*. Bologna: Editrice Compositori, 1968. 42pp.
ML410.C54I49

Reproduces in facsimile a letter attributed to Liszt dealing with the correct interpretation and performance of Chopin's Preludes for piano. In Italian throughout. NB: This publication also contains a facsimile reproduction of a ms. attributed to Chopin dealing with piano methodology and technique.

INSTRUMENTS

Among the musical instruments associated most closely with Liszt are a number of pianos, organs, harmoniums, and other devices. No one study discusses all these instruments, but the two articles described below provide excellent introductions to the topic of Liszt pianos:

1073.   Keeling, Geraldine. "Liszt Pianos: Années de pèlerinage." *Liszt Society Journal* 10 (1985), pp. 12-20.

        An entertaining and informative account of the author's researches into Liszt's performances and performance-practices at the Deutsche Staatsbibliothek (Berlin), the Zentralbibliothek (Weimar), the German National Museum (Nürnberg), etc. Illustrated with snapshots of such monuments as the home of Baron Anton Augusz in Szekszárd, Hungary, and with a facsimile reproduction of a Liszt letter written on 26 December 1867 in the *American Art Journal* of 1868. See also item 1074 (below).

1074.   Keeling, Geraldine. "The Liszt Pianos — Some Aspects of Preference and Technology." *New Hungarian Quarterly* 27/104 (Winter 1986), pp. 220-232.

        An excellent survey of Liszt pianos—not merely instruments he owned, but the kinds and characteristics of the instruments he performed on and wrote for. Keeling discusses range, action, framing, stringing, and pedals as they relate to pianos built by Erard, Steinway, Graf, Pleyel, etc. Illustrated by numerous quotations from reviews originally published in the *Wiener allgemeine Musik-Zeitung, Le moniteur universal, Der Humorist,* and other nineteenth-century periodicals. No photographs or musical examples.

Individual keyboard instruments and the uses Liszt put them to are the subjects of the nine articles described below in alphabetical order (by author and/or title):

1075.   Clark, J. Bunker. "Liszt Piano at the University of Kansas." *Journal of the American Liszt Society* 4 (1978), pp. 52-56.

        Describes a Bechstein piano acquired by Liszt during his final visit to England in 1886, and currently owned by the Helen Foresman Spencer Museum of Art at the University of Kansas, Lawrence. Illustrated with a photograph evidently taken by Clark, who discusses among other topics the distinctive sound of the instrument's *una corda* pedal. No musical examples.

1. Liszt, c. 1830 (artist unknown)

2. Liszt in 1838 (lithograph by Joseph Kriehuber)

3. Liszt in the 1850s (engraving by H. Roemer)

4. Liszt in 1885 (photograph by Louis Held)

Heute, den 17. März 1840.

CONCERT

im Saale des Gewandhauses

gegeben von

FRANZ LISZT.

Erster Theil.

Ouverture zu: Der Beherrscher der Geister, von C. M. v. Weber.

Cavatine der Isabella aus der Oper: Robert der Teufel, von G. Meyerbeer, gesungen von Fräulein Schlegel.

Concertstück v. C. M. v. Weber, (Op. 79.) für Pianoforte, vorgetragen vom Concertgeber mit Begleitung des Orchesters.

Zweiter Theil.

Ouverture zu: Prometheus, von L. v. Beethoven.

Reminiscenses de la Juive. Fantaisie brillante pour Pianoforte, componirt und vorgetragen vom Concertgeber.

Duett ans: Turco in Italia, von Rossini, gesungen von Fräulein Schlegel und Herrn Pögner.

Ave Maria und *das Ständchen.* Zwei Lieder von Franz Schubert, für das Pianoforte übertragen und gespielt vom Concertgeber.

Subscriptionsbillets zu dem ersten heutigen Concerte sind von Morgens 10 Uhr bis Mittags 2 Uhr bei Herrn Friedrich Hofmeister abzuholen, an der Casse ist der Preis 2 Thaler. Sperrsitze kosten ausserdem 12 Groschen.

Der Saal wird nicht früher, als um 6 Uhr geöffnet.
Anfang um 7 Uhr.

5. Program for Liszt's concert in Liepzig, 17 March 1840

CRAVEN HILL HOUSE,

CRAVEN HILL GARDENS, W.

(BY KIND PERMISSION OF MISS EMERSON.)

WEDNESDAY EVENING, JANUARY 20TH 1886,

At HALF-PAST EIGHT o'clock.

In Aid of a Fund to Commemorate the Visit to England in
April, 1886, of

DR. FRANZ LISZT,

By Establishment of a LISZT-SCHOLARSHIP, at the Royal
Academy of Music.

CONCERT.

Pianoforte, - **M. VLADIMIR DE PACHMANN.**

Violin, - - Herr **PEINIGER.**

Violoncello, - **Mr. EDWARD HOWELL.**

Vocalist, - **Mr. WILLIAM SHAKESPEARE.**

Tickets, - Half-a-Guinea.

MAY BE OBTAINED OF

Mr. WALTER BACHE, 17, Eastbourne Terrace, Hyde Park, W.

AND

Messrs. STANLEY LUCAS, WEBER & CO., 84, New Bond Street, W.

London:—Printed by J. MILES & Co., 195, Wardour Street, Oxford Street, W.

6. Program for a concert given in London in Liszt's honor, 20 January 1886

7. "The Most Recent Messiah of the Jews," a satirical cartoon published in *Der Floh*, a Vienna newspaper, c. 1870 (Wagner is caricatured on the right, von Bülow on the left)

Crux
ut
a Nautis dubium quam mare scinditur
Anime
e-ri-gi-tur cito malus ab ipsis
Cornu veli-terum dat Domini

8. Autograph manuscript of *Crux*, a hymn composed by Liszt in 1865 (Paris: Bibliothèque Nationale)

APPENDIX: THREE LISZT DISCOGRAPHIES

The following annotated discographical citations include Liszt recordings from the early years of cylinder and 78-rpm phonodisks through long-playing records and CDs. Information about the very few published Liszt discographies may be found in Chapter IV. Cross-references to the recordings below are scattered through Chapters XIV-XIX. NB: Unless otherwise indicated, the compositions referred to below were written by Liszt. Cross-referencing by item numbers and standardizing of some titles done by Michael Saffle, who also added item A101 to the end of these discographies.

Each recording was selected by the relevant contributor for its excellence and/or historical interest.

EARLY RECORDINGS: THE LISZT PUPILS

By Artis Wodehouse

Each of fifteen recordings by a Liszt pupil—pianist or conductor—is described below, in alphabetical order (by performer, then by title:

A1.   d'Albert, Eugène (1862-1932): *Au bord d'une source* from the *Années de pèlerinage: Suisse.* Polydor 65577. Recorded 1916.

Recordings by this important Liszt pupil leave us with many unanswered questions. Despite a major career as a pianist, conductor and composer, making recordings when he should have been only slightly past physical prime, d'Albert shows very little evidence either technically or interpretively of what we might term "artistic importance." The puzzling dichotomy between his well-documented fine reputation and his recordings is a subject yet to be examined by scholars. In any case, when compared to any available version, d'Albert's rendition of the only Liszt work he is known to have recorded is flurried and technically insecure.

A2.   Ansorge, Conrad (1862-1930): Chopin-Liszt, *Glanes de Woronince* No. 2: *Mélodies polonaises.* Parlophone E 10973. Recorded 1928.

Glanes de Woronince presents a somewhat embarrassing problem for the performance-practice scholar: the work has almost always been recorded only by artists of marginal reputation; thus, no performance standard has been set for it. On the basis of this and several other recordings, it would appear that Ansorge did not have a very developed technique (certainly not by today's standards). Nevertheless, his technique compares favorably with that of Rosenthal, Lamond, Sauer, and da Motta, especially in the skill with which small-scale expressive devices are used. If nothing else, Ansorge's recordings corroborate the evidence which suggests that the language of expressive detail was an across-the-board feature in the playing of other recorded Liszt pupils, Weingartner excepted.

A3.   de Greef, Arthur (1862-1942): Polonaise No. 2 in E Major. HMV D 1364. Recorded 1927.

    See also item A101 (perf. Busoni).

    One of the relatively few larger-scaled Liszt solo piano works on record performed by a Liszt pupil. Recorded when de Greef was 65. Certain technical flaws in the playing make it unacceptable by today's standards, but there is much to admire in its grandeur, sense of long line, and strong projection of complete, uninhibited involvement. From this recording we can imagine why de Greef was the great popularizer of the Grieg Piano Concerto, which he unfortunately did not record.

A4.   de Greef, Arthur (1862-1942): Schubert-Liszt, *Soirées de Vienne* No. 6. Gramophone D 1412. Recorded 10 November 1927.

    In the case of the Liszt pupils, repertoire overlap is infrequent, the *Soirées* being an exception. Both de Greef and Rosenthal are represented on disk by excellent and quite characteristic renditions. Extrapolating common ground between the two interpretations is tricky; de Greef's grand, solidly grounded, musicianly approach (not without its own quirks, though) appears to be worlds away from the mellifluous sorcery of Rosenthal.

    Related works recorded by de Greef: the Piano Concerto No. 2, the "Hungarian Fantasy," and the "Hungarian Rhapsody" No. 12.

A5.   Friedheim, Arthur (1860-1932): *Feux Follets* from the *Études d'exécution transcendantes* (No. 5). Columbia 517. Recorded 1911.

    Other Friedheim recordings include:

        La campanella from the *Grandes études de Paganini.*
          Columbia 517. Recorded 1913.
            See also item A101 (perf. Busoni).
          "Hungarian Rhapsody" No. 2. Emerson 7235. Recorded 1920.
          "Hungarian Rhapsody" No. 6. Columbia 482. Recorded
            Part 1: 28 January 1912; Part 2: 24 February 1913.
            See also item A101 (perf. Carreno).

    Friedheim's recordings are even more disappointing than d'Albert's but for a different reason. In the case of d'Albert, we cannot understand how an artist with his reputation could possibly have played so poorly. With Friedheim (who, it should be noted, had a less prestigious career), we ask how it is that a pianist with such a lengthy, well-documented professional and personal attachment to Liszt could play not only so poorly but teach us so little. While none of the recorded Liszt pupils (Rosenthal excepted) were equal to Rachmaninoff or Hofmann, their recordings can often be moving and thought-provoking, and modern players can learn a great deal from them. Unfortunately, this cannot be said of Friedheim's disks. The problematic nature of his recordings is another subject awaiting scholarly examination.

A6. Lamond, Frederic: "Petrarch Sonnet" No. 104 from the *Années de pèlerinage: Italie.* HMV 1666. Recorded 4 February 1929.

Perhaps Lamond's most satisfying performance of a work by Liszt on record. In complete technical command of the materials, Lamond imparts to the whole a welter of small-scale expressive details so characteristic of early recorded piano performance.

A related work recorded by Lamond: *Liebestraum* No. 3.

A7. Lamond, Frederic (1868-1948): *Zwei Konzertetüden: Waldesrauschen* and *Gnomenreigen.* HMV EH 968. Both recorded 6 May 1936.

In any discussion of the performance of Liszt's music, technique is a central issue. It appears likely that none of the recorded Liszt pupils (with the possible exception of Rosenthal in his prime) either possessed as developed a technique as Liszt or equalled the abilities of their greatest colleagues: Ferruccio Busoni (1866-1924), Sergei Rachmaninoff (1873-1942) or Josef Hofmann (1876-1957). Among the recorded Liszt pupils, Lamond was overall the most plentifully and satisfactorily recorded. In good physical condition throughout his recorded career, he also had by virtue of his many recordings considerable studio experience. His performance of *Gnomenreigen* is quite satisfying musically, his technique adequate to support his interpretive ideas, but it is Rachmaninoff's rendition (recorded 1925) which astonishes us with its speed, power, tonal variety, and boldness of conception. On the other hand, Hofmann performs *Waldesrauchen* (recorded 1923) at a tempo which Lamond very likely could not sustain.

Related works recorded by Lamond: *Etude de concert* No. 3, *Un sospiro, Der Erlkönig,* and the Auber-Liszt *Tarantelle di bravura* from *Venezia e Napoli* (No. 3).

A8.   Nikisch, Arthur (1855-1922): "Hungarian Rhapsody" No. 1, arr. Doppler (?). With the Berlin Philharmonic Orchestra. Deutsch Grammophon 65906-7. Recorded 1920.

Nikisch was the most highly esteemed conductor of his era and the first great conductor to attempt to record serious classical music. However, primitive pre-1925 acoustic recording technology was especially hard on conductors and orchestras. Limited frequency response made it impossible to accurately suggest the sound of a live orchestra, the string section suffering particularly in this regard. Furthermore, the requirements of acoustic recording forced orchestras to huddle together in occasionally bizarre, always uncomfortable groupings around the recording horn. This created serious problems for ensemble playing. While the precise set-up of his recording sessions is yet to be documented, we can assume that these factors took their toll on the artistic production of Nikisch's recordings (which by today's standards have some unacceptable technical flaws). Nevertheless, his recording of "Hungarian Rhapsody" No. 2 has considerable interest; his out-of-fashion tempo modification is so pronounced that it must surely have been integral to the ensemble's live performance of the work.

A9.   Rosenthal, Moriz (1862-1946): Chopin-Liszt, *Chant polonais* No. 5 ("My Joys"). Odeon 171107. Recorded 22 May 1936. Ampico roll, L'Oiseau Lyre 414098-1. Recorded 26 October 1926.

See also item A101 (perf. Stavenhagen).

A classic of early-recorded piano performance, as perfect a document of Rosenthal's finely-wrought cantilena as exists on record. Rosenthal expands the detailed approach evidenced in the recordings of da Motta, especially, von Sauer, Lamond, and de Greef to thought-provoking luxuriance. Irrespective of whether Rosenthal's performance style reflects Liszt's practice, modern performers have much to gain from studying this recording, since Rosenthal's imaginative performance practice enhances the music in ways lost to modern performance. His intricate manner of rolling and voicing chords, improvising embellishments and interpolating cadenzas, also to be found in his rendition of *Soirées de Vienne*, add an expressive dimension which enriches the music embodied in the score.

Of particular interest is Rosenthal's Ampico roll of the same work made ten years prior to his disk recording (but omitted from item A101). L'Oiseau Lyre has made a fine recording of this roll played on a well-set-up reproducing piano.

Related works recorded by Rosenthal: *Liebestraum* No. 3, and *Chant polonais* No. 1 ("The Maiden's Wish").

A10.   Rosenthal, Moriz: Schubert-Liszt, *Soirées de Vienne* No. 6. Victor 854-A-B. Recorded 25 May 1936.

Rosenthal was undoubtedly the greatest of the Liszt pupils on record: indeed, by virtue of his technical command and unique expressivity, he was one of the greatest pianist of his era. Unfortunately, he recorded only in his declining years, so we can never properly assess his technical prowess during his prime. Nevertheless, his recorded performances reveal a continuously evolving interpretive art, and in some lucky instances, rise to the virtuosity of his peak years. Such is the case with Rosenthal's *Soirées*, one of the finest Liszt recordings ever made, it is to be numbered among his most successful and characteristic recordings.

A related work recorded by Rosenthal: "Hungarian Rhapsody" No. 2.

A11.   Sauer, Emil von (1862-1942): Piano Concerto No. 1, with the Paris Conservatoire Orchestra conducted by Felix Weingartner. Columbia LX 789-91. Recorded 1 December 1938.

No excuses need be made for this fine collaboration by two of Liszt's most prominent pupils, then 74 (Sauer) and 75 (Weingartner) years old. Sauer's pianism, at least at this point in his career had neither the power nor the speed of most modern virtuosos, yet once again, his affecting way with interpretive detail raises the rendition to a very high rank.

A related work recorded by von Sauer: Piano Concerto No. 2, with Weingartner and the Paris Conservatoire Orchestra. See also item A14.

A12.   Sauer, Emil von: *Ricordanza* from the "Transcendental Etudes." Columbia LWX 353. Recorded 1940.

See also item A101 (perf. Scharwenka).

Ricordanza demands much from performers: command of a tonal palate capable of delineating finely contrasted and evolving moods, the ability to project large-scale architectonic design through successive, long-breathed phrases, and reliable virtuoso finger-work. Sauer's recording, made when he was 76, falls somewhat short in each of these categories, yet there is much to learn from his performance. Most noteworthy is the way he creates tonal balances—lost to modern performance—which project a limpid melodic line. Another unusual feature is that his performance is faster and consequently lighter in affect than most modern performances. Whether this was Sauer's response to the time restriction of 78-rpm disks or a normal feature of his live performance is yet to be determined.

Related works recorded by von Sauer: *Liebestraum* No. 3; *Valse oubliée* No. 3; and *Consolation* No. 3.

A13.   Vianna da Motta, Jose (1868-1948): *Eglogue* from the *Années de pèlerinage: Suisse*. Pathe X 5451. Recorded 1928.

Among the recordings made by the Liszt pupils, da Motta's *Eglogue* is one of the finest. Compared with other recordings available to this reviewer, the freshness, inventiveness, and exuberance of his interpretation is strikingly apparent. His unusually varied approach (by modern standards) to rolling and voicing chords makes this recording an important study resource for pianists performing the work. Da Motta's complex and refined way of playing chords, a lost art luckily preserved on early recordings, gives the music a human, whimsical dimension similar to the function provided by ornamentation in baroque music.

A14.   Weingartner, Felix (1863-1942): *Les préludes,* with the London Symphony Orchestra. Columbia X 198. Recorded 28 February 1940.

Although Weingartner was a Liszt pupil, he was one of the first important conductors at the turn-of-the-century to initiate the ascendant modern approach to performance: adherence to the printed score and a more restrained application of tempo change and nuance. Weingartner broke early with romantic performance traditions to the extent that his interpretations were initially considered scandalous. His streamlined, restrained rendition of *Les préludes* is a case in point. To hear an interpretation more in tune with the sensibilities of the other recorded Liszt pupils (but not necessarily Liszt's own sensibilities, a matter yet to be studied) one must turn to the historic Mengelberg/Amsterdam Concertgebouw recording of the same work.

Another Liszt work recorded by Weingartner: the "Mephisto Waltz" (No. 1), with the London Symphony Orchestra.

A15.   Weiss, Joseph (1864-?): "Hungarian Rhapsody" No. 12. Parlophone E 10161. Recorded c. 1912.

See also item A101 (perf. Stavenhagen).

Weiss's playing is not equal to performances by Rosenthal, da Motta, de Greef, or Lamond. His over-tight pacing may be explained as a "flight" response to the time limitation imposed by a single disk side (a response not limited to lesser talents, Busoni being a good case in point). Weiss made very few recordings, so it is reasonable to speculate that due to lack of studio experience, we are not hearing him as he would have sounded in live performance.

LISZT RECORDINGS ON LONG-PLAYING PHONORECORDS

By Ben Arnold

The recordings discussed below are described roughly in the order of compositions discussed in Chapters XIV-XIX:

A. Original Works for Piano (see Chapter XIV)

A16.   Sonata in b minor; and *Funérailles* from the *Harmonies poétiques et religieuses*. Schumann: *Toccata*; *Arabesque*; *Traumeswirren*; and *Presto passionato*. Vladimir Horowitz, piano. Seraphim 60114.

        Selecting the most rewarding recording of the Sonata in b minor is nearly impossible, especially when one considers the number of noteworthy recordings that have been released since the advent of recorded sound. Of more than seventy Sonata recordings I have heard over the past eighteen years, however, the 1932 recording of Horowitz comes to the forefront more than any other. Now over half a century old, this performance continues to suspend belief for nearly an half hour. Horowitz's playing is exhilarating, simultaneously brash and gentle, and remains among the most stupendous on record—certainly better than his disappointing 1977 release (RCA ARL1 2548). His performance of *Funérailles* is explosive and foreboding, possibly challenged only by Barere's historical performance on Turnabout THS 65001.

A17.   Sonata in b minor; *Légendes* Nos. 1 and 2; and *La lugubre gondola* Nos. 1 and 2. Alfred Brendel, piano. Philips 6514 147.

        Brendel paces himself beautifully in this controlled and well-thought-out performance which, at over thirty minutes, is the longest playing time for any of the recommended Sonata recordings. Perhaps too "intellectual" for some, Brendel's subtle wash of evocative pianistic colors and dramatic architectonic structure combine to make this an intensely moving experience. The two *Lugubre gondola* performances are haunting, and the *Légendes* receive their best recording since that of Wilhelm Kempff (Turnabout TVS 34385).

A18.   Sonata in b minor; *Valse impromptu*; *Liebesträume* Nos. 1-3; and the *Grande galop chromatique*. Jorge Bolet, piano. London 410 115-1.

        This version of the Sonata is far superior to Bolet's earlier Everest recording (SDBR 3064) and presents an extraordinarily suave and stately performance. The *Valse impromptu* and *Liebesträume* are treated expressively, and the seldom performed *Grand galop chromatique* has the energy and humor necessary for a delightful performance.

A19.   Sonata in b minor; "Mephisto Waltz" No. 1; and *Venezia e Napoli* [complete] from the *Années de pèlerinage: Italie.* Lazar Berman, piano. Columbia/Melodiya M33927.

   Many people think of Berman as merely a technician because his "Transcendental Etudes" are so remarkable. This distinguished recording of the Sonata, however, shows how strongly his virtuosity is controlled by musical and interpretative considerations. If anything, his Sonata performance lacks the radiating brilliance found in *Venezia e Napoli* and the "Mephisto Waltz."

A20.   Sonata in b minor; and the six "Paganini Etudes." André Watts, piano. Columbia M30488.

   While Watts's first recording of the Sonata is tempestuous and dramatic (and more convincing than his later release on EMI-Angel DS-37355), the "Paganini Etudes" are even better. Watts need not have re-recorded these etudes recently (EMI Angel DS-37354), since he got them right the first time—so right, in fact, that no one else has done them better, not even himself. This early version is a perfect blend of incredible virtuosity and tasteful musicianship. Ousset's recent recording (EMI Angel DS-38259) illustrates that she is technically as gifted as Watts but not as musically convincing. Both of these recordings outclass the complete etudes of Brendel (Vox PL 10800), Farnadi (Westminster XWN 18017), Graffman (Victor LM2443), and Kentner (Vox SVBX 5453).

A21.   *Années de pèlerinage* [complete]. Lazar Berman, piano. DG 2709 076 or 2740 174.

   Berman's consistent high quality throughout these works makes this still the most engaging complete performance. His playing is straightforward, extremely tasteful and exciting, even though at times one wishes for a richer tone palette. Bolet's recent releases of the "Swiss" (Decca 410 160-1DH) and "Italian" (410 161-1DH) volumes are also admirable, especially because of their finesse, subdued virtuosity, and slower tempi which give the works a more serene character. His interpretations of the three *Sonetti del Petrarca* are the most enchanting I have heard. Brendel's second year of the *Années* is also highly recommended (Philips 6500 420), and the "Dante" sonata is served exceptionally well by Arrau (Philips 6514 273), Barenboim (DG 2531 271), and Ranki (Denon OX-7029-ND). Dinu Lipati's "Petrarch Sonnet" No. 104 (Columbia ML 2216 or EMI-Odeon HQM 1163) is a glorious and classic performance.

A22.   Ballade No. 2 in b minor; "Petrarch Sonnets" Nos. 104 and 123; *Vallée d'Obermann; Valse oubliée* No. 1; and *Les jeux d'eau à la Villa d'Este* from the *Années de pèlerinage: troisieme année.* Claudio Arrau, piano. Philips 802 906.

This record is the most satisfying Arrau recording of original Liszt compositions. The B-minor Ballade surges with great intensity, and the seeking, searching quality of *Vallée d'Obermann* is most admirably treated. All these selections demonstrate pianistic maturity and excellence. For Arrau admirers, there is a seven-disk set of Liszt's piano music available on Philips 676 8355. Horowitz's performance of the B-minor Ballade on RCA ATC1 4260 is also memorable.

A23.   *Funérailles*; *Valse Impromptu in A-flat*; "Mephisto Waltz" No. 1; *Liebestraum* No. 3; "Hungarian Rhapsodies" No. 10 and 12; and *Consolation* No. 3. Artur Rubinstein, piano. RCA LM 1905.

Rubinstein does not immediately come to mind when one thinks of the great Liszt pianists. Nonetheless, this 1955 release is a marvelous recording, highly different from other Lisztians in the era but a strangely satisfying approach all the same. Rubinstein's tempi are nearly always slower and controlled, passion is subdued, and liberties are few. While not as exciting as many other Liszt pianists, Rubinstein concentrates on inner voicings and tone quality to create some of the most refined and "polite" recorded performances of Liszt. When he comes to the octaves in *Funérailles* or the brilliant closing sections of the "Rhapsodies," he erupts into a surprising furor of speed and sound. The *Liebestraum* and *Consolation* are breathtaking in their simplicity. Rubinstein is also the only one who can play the B-minor Sonata with virtually no trace of passion and still make it somehow convincing (RCA LSC 2871).

A24.   "The Legendary Lazar Berman Plays Liszt." "Transcendental Etudes" [complete]; "Hungarian Rhapsody" No. 3; and the "Spanish Rhapsody." Lazar Berman, piano. Columbia/Melodiya M2 33928. Reissued on Musical Heritage Society MHS 3971/72.

Of the rapidly growing number of complete "Transcendentals," Berman's continues to stand out for the virtuosic ease with which he tackles these enormously difficult works. No other pianist takes the risks in tempo and expression to create such a "transcendental" recording. His "Hungarian Rhapsody" No. 3 and "Spanish Rhapsody" are also first-rate. Arrau's performance of the complete set (Philips 6747 412 [2 disks]) is outstanding and also has the best recorded sound available. Richter's *Harmonies du soir* and *Feux follets* (Columbia ML 5396) are examples of magnificent piano playing.

A25.   "Transcendental Etudes" Nos. 1-3, 5, 8, 10-11; "Mephisto Waltz" No. 1; and Impromptu. Vladimir Ashkenazy, piano. London CS 6719.

Ashkenazy has recorded little of Liszt's music, but his "Transcendentals" are brilliantly performed and on par with the Berman set. Ashkenazy is particularly successful in the quicker works (e.g., the *Wilde Jagd, Feux follets*, and *Allegro agitato molto*.)

A26.   "3 Concert Etudes": *Il lamento, La leggierezza*, and *Un sospiro*; "2 Concert Studies": *Waldesrauschen* and *Gnomenreigen*; and *Réminiscences de Don Juan*. Jorge Bolet, piano. Oiseau-Lyre DSLO 41.

Bolet reaches a higher level in the five concert etudes than he does in the more challenging "Paganini Etudes" or "Transcendentals." His playing is excellent throughout, and his "Don Juan" is remarkable for its mixture of poetry and technique, even if some of the tempos are slower than other pianists. (See items A58-A65, A91-A95, and A100 for descriptions of other performances of Liszt paraphrases, arrangements, and transcriptions.) Compared with other performances of "Don Juan" by Ogdon (Seraphim S60088), Vásáry (DG Privilege 2535 270), and Kentner (Turnabout TV 34163S), Bolet comes out well ahead. Arrau's *Waldesrauschen* and *Gnomenreigen* are also worthy alternatives (Philips 6500 043), and Barere's *Gnomenreigen* is a frenetic, breathless tour de force (Turnabout THS 65001).

A27.   "Kapell—In Memoriam." "Mephisto Waltz" No. 1; and "Hungarian Rhapsody" No. 11. Bach: Partita No. 4 in D Major (final Gigue omitted). Schubert: Ländler Nos. 1-2, 5-8, 14, and 16; and Impromptu in B-flat Major. William Kapell, piano. RCA Victor LM 1791.

Compared with twenty other performances of the famous "Mephisto," Kapell's interpretation is the most individual and fascinating. The sparkling clarity, gracefulness, and lightness are intoxicating. It may not be as "demonic" as some, but it is quintessential piano playing.

A28.   "Hungarian Rhapsodies" Nos. 1-16 and 19. György Cziffra, piano. Connoisseur Society (Nos. 1-6: CS 2097); (Nos. 7-12: CS 2098) (Nos. 13-16, 19: CS 2009). Also: "Hungarian Rhapsodies" [complete]. Michele Campanella, piano. Philips 6747 108.

Liszt's "Rhapsodies" are served well by performers, and both of these sets, though different in approach, are excellent. The most striking and unique is Cziffra, but the Campanella performances are imaginative and well-recorded. Szidon's three-disk set on DG 2709 044 is commendable but not as enthusiastically as those of Cziffra and Campanella. Cziffra has also given bravura performances of Nos. 2, 6, 12, and 15 on an earlier recording (Angel 35429) that may indeed be the finest single recording of the "Rhapsodies." Brendel provides exciting playing of Nos. 2, 3, 8, 13, 15, 17 and the *Csárdás obstinée* (Vanguard VCS 10035), and Arrau's 1951-1952 monophonic performances of Nos. 8-11 and 13 are also enjoyable (Desmar DSM 1003 or CBS M3 37866). Johansen made two disks of the *Magyar rhapsodiák* which shed considerable insight on the later "Rhapsodies" (Artist Direct 18-19).

A29. *Au bord d'une source* from the *Années de pèlerinage: Suisse*; *Funérailles*; "Petrarch Sonnet" No. 104; *Valse oubliée*; and "Hungarian Rhapsodies" No. 2 (arr. Horowitz), 6, and the "Rákóczy March" ["Hungarian Rhapsody" No. 15] (arr. Horowitz). Vladimir Horowitz, piano. RCA Victor LM 2584.

It is essential to include Horowitz in the list of great "Rhapsody" performers. From a pianist's point of view (particularly from a technical perspective), Horowitz's "Rhapsodies" provide an adventure into another realm of piano playing. His arrangements and additions to No. 2 and the "Rákóczy March" are outrageous but explosive and unforgettable. His relatively "straight" No. 6 is a tour de force, and his arrangement of No. 19 (Columbia KS 6731) is equally fascinating.

A30. Variations on "Weinen, Klagen, Zorgen, Sagen"; *Pensée des mortes* and *Bénédiction de Dieu dans la solitude* from the *Harmonies poétiques et religieuses*; and the "BACH" Prelude and Fugue. Alfred Brendel, piano. Philips 9500 286.

Brendel gives one of the strongest recorded performances of the Variations and "BACH" (piano version), although José Echániz has splendid versions as well on Musical Heritage Society OR 365. Brendel's *Bénédiction* is also outstanding, as is that of Arrau (Philips 6500 043) and Kentner (Turnabout TV 34310S).

A31. *Apparitions* No. 1; *Harmonies poétiques et religieuses* [separate piece]; *Bénédiction de Dieu dans la solitude*; "Five Hungarian Folk Songs"; *Vier kleine Klavierstücke*; *En rêve*; and *Valse capriccio sur deux motifs de Lucia et Parisina*. Louis Kentner, piano. Turnabout TV 34310S.

Among Kentner's numerous Liszt recordings, this is the most convincing. The *Bénédiction* is given a noble, communicative performance, and the shorter works are played with considerable insight and charm. Especially delightful are the *Vier kleine Klavierstücke* and the *Valse capriccio*, which is seldom performed or recorded.

A32. *Au lac du Wallenstadt, Au bord d'une source, Eglogue, Il pensieroso, Canzonetta del Salvator Rosa*, and *Gondoliera* from the *Années de pèlerinage: Italie*; and the *Légendes*. Wilhelm Kempff, piano. London LLP315. [Also Turnabout TV-S 34385, with the *Tre Sonetti del Petrarca*].

Kempff's playing is subdued and elegant in these performances of some of Liszt's most unpretentious music. His "St. François d'Assise" (the second *Legende*), with its exceptional programmatic characterizations, may still be the best recorded version.

A33. "Late Piano Music." *Dem Andenken Petőfis*; *Elegie* No 2; *Vier kleine Klavierstücke*; *La lugubre gondola* No. 1; *Nuages gris*; *R. W. Venezia*; *Schlaflos, Frage und Antwort*; and *Unstern.* Sergio Fiorentino, piano. Dover HCR 5258.

One of the first recordings of Liszt's late piano music and one of the best. Fiorentino's playing is complemented by the recent release of István Lantos containing *Urbi et orbi, Resignazione, Sancta Dorothea,* the Berceuse (2nd version), *Vexilla regis prodeunt, Stabat Mater, Wiegenlied, Recueillement,* and *Impromptu* (Hungaroton SLPD 12634). Several other pianists have distinguished recordings of late music on their albums, most notably Brendel (Philips 9500 775), Rudy (Calliope CAL. 1685), and Watts (EMI Angel DS-37355).

A34. "Elegy on themes by Louis Ferdinand of Prussia" (2nd version); *Festvorspiel Preludio pomposo*; "Albumblatt"; *Ave Maria* (1862); *Csárdás macabre*; the Sarabande and Chaconne on Handel's *Almira; Elegie* No. 2; Galop in a minor; and the *Grand galop chromatique.* Gunnar Johansen, piano. Artist Direct 25.

Gunnar Johansen was the first person to record the complete output of Liszt's piano music (save for a number of transcriptions). His set of fifty Liszt recordings is a major achievement of vast historical importance. Although the sound quality of the recordings is not to the standards of the major producers, the performances are frequently stimulating and provocative. His playing descends from Busoni's, and his recordings are certainly worth hearing for their bold, romantic, and at times, unorthodox interpretations. His set consists of many works that still have not been recorded by other pianists.

B. Original Works for Organ (see Chapter XV)

A35. "Liszt: The Complete Organ Works." Fantasy and Fugue on "Ad nos, ad salutarem undam"; Variations on "Weinen, Klagen, Sorgen, Zagen"; "BACH" Prelude and Fugue; *Introitus; Trauerode (Les Morts); Ave Maria* I, II, IV; *Ave maris stella,* etc., etc. Martin Haselböck, organ; Rudolf Josel, trombone; Ernst Kovacic, violin; Rosa Mohrenberger, alto; Women of the Arnold Schönberg Choir; Erwin Ortner, chorus master. Orfeo S 125 846 G [6 disks].

Haselböck's performances on these records surpass complete sets of Sebestyén (Vox SVBX 5328-5329 [6 disks]), Ellsasser (MGM E3576-80 [5 disks]), and Margittay, Lehotka, and Kovács (Hungaroton SLPX 11540-44 [5 disks]). (The Hungaroton and MGM sets can still be highly recommended, however.) Haselböck bases his performance on his own ten-volume Universal edition of Liszt's organ music (not yet complete; see item 142).

A36.	"BACH" Prelude and Fugue; *Trauerode; Evocation à la Chapelle Sixtine*; and *Tu es Petrus*. Daniel Chorzempa, organ. Philips 6500 376.

Chorzempa gives spectacular, overpowering performances on the Flentrop organ in the De Doelen Concert Hall, Rotterdam; the recording quality is as excellent as the performance. Anthony Newman's "BACH" is also electrifying on Columbia M31127.

A37.	Fantasia and Fugue on "Ad nos, ad salutarem undam"; and Variations on "Weinen, Klagen, Sorgen, Zagen." Daniel Chorzempa, organ. Philips 6500 215.

Chorzempa also gives first-rate performances of these two masterpieces. Equally fascinating is Simon Preston's "Ad nos" coupled with Reubke's Sonata in c minor on Psalm 94 (DG 415 139-1GH). Zsuzsa Elekes (Hungaroton SLPD 12749) and Demessieux (London LLP697) also give stunning performances of "Ad nos."

C. Original Works for Orchestra and other Instrumental Ensembles (see Chapter XVI)

A38.	A *Faust* symphony; and *Orpheus*. Alexander Young (tenor), with the Royal Philharmonic Orchestra and the Beecham Choral Society; Sir Thomas Beecham, conductor. Seraphim S-6017.

Despite its age, this remains one of the best recordings of Liszt orchestral music. The *Faust* symphony receives masterful treatment from the orchestra and great understanding from Beecham. The tempos are immensely satisfying and hold the work together incredibly well. The first and last movements are dramatic, tender, and heroic. The subtle nuances of color and tender lyricism make the "Gretchen" movement—and *Orpheus*, as well—sheer poetry.

A39.	A *Faust* symphony. Kenneth Riegel (tenor), with the Tanglewood Festival Chorus and Boston Symphony Orchestra; Leonard Bernstein, conductor. DG 2707 100 or DG 415 009-1 GX2. [2 disks]

After the Beecham performance, the second Bernstein interpretation of the *Faust* symphony with the Boston Symphony Orchestra stands out, although it is surrounded by other fine performances: Bernstein's earlier recording with Bressler, the New York Philharmonic and Choral Art Society (2-Columbia MG 699); János Ferencsik conducting the Hungarian State Symphony Orchestra (Hungaroton SLPX 12022/3); Jascha

Horenstein and the Southwest German Radio Orchestra, Baden-Baden (Turnabout TV-S 34491); and Solti with the Chicago Symphony Orchestra (London 417 399 1LH). Bernstein and the BSO open dramatically with one of the slowest first themes on record. They also compete with Solti and the LSO for the slowest and most expressive "Gretchen" movement. Bernstein's "Mephistofeles" is as energetic as it is diabolical, the strongest of the three movements.

A40.   A *Dante* symphony. Chorus of Concert de Helmond, Roland de Kroon (choir-master), with the Rotterdam Philharmonic Orchestra; James Conlon, conductor. Erato 88162.

Although the *Dante* symphony has still not received a definitive performance, those of Conlon, Lehel, and Masur (EMI ED 2907331) serve us well. György Lehel recorded the symphony on Westminster XWN 18917, then on Hungaroton SLPX 11918, but his Westminster release remains one of the most convincing interpretations available. Conlon's more recent disk, however, has a superior orchestra and better recorded sound; these make it my first choice. Conlon's "Inferno" is ominous without being pompous, spirited without being too controlled. The closing "Magnificat" opens magically with the poignant alto voices and throughout is spellbinding in its serenity.[1] See also item A80.

A41.   "Complete Symphonic poems." The London Philharmonic Orchestra; Bernard Haitink, conductor. Philips 6709 005. Also available separately: *Hamlet, Mazeppa,* and *Hungaria* (Philips 6500 046); *Von der Wiege bis zum Grabe, Hunnenschlacht* and *Ce qu'on entend sur la montagne* (Philips 6500 189); *Héroïde funèbre, Prometheus,* and the "Mephisto Waltz" No. 1 (Philips 6500 190); *Festklänge* and *Die Ideal* (Philips 6500 191); and *Les préludes, Orpheus,* and *Tasso, Lamento e trionfo* (Philips 839 788).

While the performances are inconsistent, this is still the most intriguing available set of symphonic poems, and the recorded sound is second to none. The best of Haitink's interpretations are *Hamlet, Von der Wiege bis zum Grabe, Festklänge, Die Ideal,* and especially *Héroïde funèbre.* For those who prefer a warmer, less brilliant approach, Masur and the Leipzig Gewandhaus Orchestra have two four-disk sets available of the major orchestral works including the two symphonies and all the symphonic poems (HMV SLS 5235 and 5236). See also item A81.

---

[1]   One lengthy review of Conlon's Liszt performances deserves close attention. See Patrick Rucker, "James Conlon's Liszt," *Journal of the American Liszt Society* 23 (1988), pp. 62-98. This review also includes a catalog of Liszt performances by the New York Philharmonic between 1858-1988 (pp. 96-98).

A42. *Les préludes.* Tchaikovsky: *Romeo and Juliet.* Concertgebouw Orchestra; William Mengelberg, conductor. Columbia Entré RL 3039 or Odeon 5C 047 01297.

One of the oldest performances of *Les préludes* reissued on LP and one of the most fascinating. The sound is somewhat hollow compared to today's recording technology, but the performance is so noble and angelic that it makes up for it. Mengelberg achieves fascinating shades of orchestral color in this controlled, majestic, and highly expressive performance—a style that may be too "expressive" for some. Monteux leading the Boston Symphony Orchestra in *Les préludes* is also highly recommended (RCA Victor LM1775), as is Solti with the London Philharmonic (London 7084) and Bernstein with the New York Philharmonic (Columbia 60159).

A43. *Tasso, lamento e trionfo*; *Von der Wiege bis zum Grabe*; and "Mephisto Waltz" No. 1. Orchestre de Paris; Sir George Solti, conductor. London 6925.

Solti gives three strong performances that makes this disk highly desirable. All three works are brilliantly, though tastefully controlled. Silvestri's interpretation of *Tasso* with the Philharmonia Orchestra may be more persuasive (Angel 35636), but *Les préludes* on side two makes it difficult to recommend the disk as a whole. Ormandy leading the Philadelphia Orchestra in a performance of the "Mephisto" should not be overlooked (Columbia 60159).

A44. *Hunnenschlacht*; *Mazeppa*; and *Orpheus.* The Los Angeles Philharmonic Orchestra; Zubin Mehta, conductor. Decca SXL 5535.

Mehta's *Hunnenschlacht* and *Mazeppa* are excellent; his *Orpheus* is good, but Beecham's and the Royal Philharmonic's retain the highest honors. Dean Dixon leads a ferocious and somewhat bombastic performance of *Hunnenschlacht* with the Philharmonic Symphony Orchestra of London that is also noteworthy (Westminster WL 5269 or SXN 18280).

A45. Piano Concertos Nos. 1 and 2. Sviatoslav Richter, piano; the London Symphony Orchestra; Kyril Kondrashin, conductor. Philips 835 474.

More excellent recordings of these concertos have been produced than any of Liszt's others works. Still unsurpassed, however, is the Richter-Kondrashin performance recorded more than twenty years ago. The beautiful symbiosis of the bold, energetic passion and the tender serenity is truly remarkable. The tremendous excitement in the fast, climatic parts pushes to the outer edge of intensity without ever falling over. The orchestra sounds superb, especially the solo playing of the winds and the cello, and Richter quite possibly gives his best recorded performance of any work. Other excellent recordings of both concertos include those of Brendel with the London Philharmonic Orchestra under Haitink (Philips

6500 374), and Berman with the Vienna Symphony Orchestra under Giulini (DG 2530 770). The first concerto in particular received a splendid performance by Argerich and the London Symphony Orchestra conducted by Abbado (DG 139 383).

A46.   *Totentanz*; and "Fantasy on Hungarian Folk Tunes." Saint-Saëns: Piano Concerto No. 4 in c minor, Op. 44. Michele Campanella, piano; the Monte Carlo Opera Orchestra; Aldo Ceccato, conductor. Philips 6500 095.

   While several excellent recordings of the *Totentanz* exist, this Philips release stands far above the others in overall performance and sound recording. The demonic energy of Campanella and the Monte Carlo Opera Orchestra is ferocious and hair-raising. Shura Cherkassky with Karajan and the Berlin Philharmonic Orchestra (DG 2535 175 or DG SLPM 138 692) also give an inspirited historic performance of the "Hungarian Fantasy."

A47.   Fantasia on themes from Beethoven's *Ruins of Athens*; "Grande fantaisie symphonique" on themes from Berlioz's *Lélio*; *Malédiction*; *Totentanz*; and Piano Concertos Nos. 1 and 2. Weber: *Polonaise brillante*. Schubert: "Wanderer" fantasy. Michel Béroff, piano; the Gewandhaus Orchestra, Leipzig; Kurt Masur, conductor. Angel Pantheon 2143 [3 disks].

   An excellent recording of eight piano and orchestral works of Liszt, some of which are only occasionally performed and recorded. Béroff's playing is brilliant and exhilarating throughout, and the LGO sounds terrific under Masur. Jerome Rose also has a noteworthy recording of the Liszt-Beethoven Fantasy and Weber's *Polonaise brillante* on Turnabout 34708. The "Spanish Rhapsody" (arr. Busoni), performed by Egon Petri, with Dmitri Mitropoulos conducting the Minneapolis Symphony Orchestra, is an historical recording of special merit that should also be acknowledged (Columbia Entré RL 3040).

A48.   "The Unknown Liszt Chamber Music" ["De onbekende Liszt kamermuziek"]. Fantasy and Fugue on "Ad nos, ad salutarem undam" for piano four-hands; *La lugubre gondola* for cello and piano; *Am Grabe Richard Wagners* for string quartet and harp; and *Angélus! Prière aux Agnès gardiens* [sic] for string quartet. Toos Onderdenwigngaard and Martijn van den Hoek, pianos; Hans Woudenberg, cello; and the Laran ensemble: Wim de Jong and Janneke van der Meer, violins; Just Gerretsen, viola; and Wim Mertens, cello. Editio Laran ST 5054.

   The "Ad nos" fantasy succeeds as well in the four-hand version as in the original organ version. The second side of this record consists of late chamber compositions. These works, which also are found in solo piano versions, are striking in their ability to capture the austere and haunting vision of Liszt's late years. All of the instrumentalists give superb performances in this unique Liszt recording.

D. Original Works for Solo Voice (see also Chapter XVII)

A49. *O lieb, so lang du lieben kannst, Es muß ein Wunderbares sein, Die Loreley, Angiolin dal biondo crin*, etc., etc. Dietrich Fischer-Dieskau, baritone; and Daniel Barenboim, piano. DG 2740 254 [4 disks].

In the last decade Liszt's songs have come into their own, and several stunning recordings are now available that depict him as one of the major song writers of the nineteenth century. In addition to this set, Fischer-Dieskau's most impressive single disk (with Jörg Demus, piano) of twelve selected songs (DG LPM 18793) has generated renewed interest in Liszt as a songwriter. Fischer-Dieskau gives magnificent performances of these works and is always sensitive to the text. Hermann Prey and Alexis Weissenberg present outstanding interpretations of sixteen popular Liszt songs (EMI 29 0736 1), and Gérard Souzay and Dalton Baldwin give stellar performance of *Oh! Quand je dors, Nimm einen Strahl der Sonne*, and *Ihr Glocken von Marling* on RCA (LSC 3082).

A50. *Jugendglück, Die Loreley, Ihr Glocken von Marling, Es war ein König in Thule, Freudvoll und leidvoll* (2 settings); *Ich liebe dich*, etc., etc. Hildegard Behrens, soprano; and Cord Garben, piano. DG 419 240-1GH.

Also described as item A84.

The most impressive disk devoted to Liszt's songs performed by a soprano. Behrens and Garben give sublimely moving performances of these well-chosen pieces, culminating with *Es muß ein Wunderbares sein* and *O lieb, so lang du lieben kannst*. The album "Janet Baker sings Liszt Songs" is also recommended (EMI ASD 3906).

E. Original Works for Vocal Ensembles (see also Chapter XVIII)

A51. *Christus.* Veronika Kincses, soprano; Klára Takács, mezzo-soprano; János Nagy, tenor; Sándor Sólyom-Nagy, baritone; László Polgár, bass; the Hungarian Radio and Television Chorus; the Nyiregyhaza Children's Chorus; and the Hungarian State Orchestra; Antal Dorati, conductor. Hungaroton SLPD 12831-34 [4 disks].

Also described as item A87.

Liszt's choral music is still primarily recorded on the Hungaroton label, since other companies have shown little interest in this extensive body of music. With regard to *Christus*, Liszt's largest work, Forrai (Hungaroton SLPX 11506-08 9) and Conlon (Erato NUM 75289) also lead fine performances, but Dorati's is the most satisfying and brilliant.

A52.   *Die Legende von der heiligen Elisabeth.* Kolos Kovács [also given some-
        times as "Kováts"], bass; Erzsébet Komlóssy, mezzo-soprano; Sándor
        Sólyom Nagy, baritone; Éva Andor, soprano; Józef Gregor, bass; Lajos
        Miller, baritone; György Bordás, baritone; together with Turinič Dušan;
        Eugenia Kraicírova; the Slovak Philharmonic Orchestra; the Czechoslovak
        Radio Children's Choir at Bratislava; and the Slovak Philharmonic Choir;
        János Ferencsik, conductor. Hungaroton SLPX 11650-52 [3 disks].
            Also described as item A88.
            Ferencsik leads an impressive performance of this large-scale work. Éva
        Andor is a moving Elisabeth, particularly attractive in her prayer that
        opens Scene V. The chorus of angels at the end of this scene is beautifully
        conceived and among the best moments of the oratorio.

A53.   "Hungarian Coronation Mass." Veronika Kincses, soprano; Klára Tákacs,
        mezzo-soprano; Dénes Gulyás, tenor; László Polgár, bass; the Hungarian
        Radio and Television Chorus; and the Budapest Symphony Orchestra;
        György Lehel, conductor. Hungaroton SLPX 12148.
            Also described as item A90.
            Lehel's mature leadership is apparent in this mass. The Gloria and
        Gradual have all the necessary power and intensity; and the Benediction,
        the climax of the work, is exceptionally expressive. The other available
        recording, with Szecsédy, soprano; Tiszay, contralto; Simóndy, tenor;
        Faragó, bass; and the Choir and Orchestra of Budapest Coronation
        Cathedral, conducted by Ferencsik, is also commendable (DG 254 3802).

A54.   *Missa choralis.* Margit Lászlo, soprano; Zsuzsa Barlay, mezzo-soprano;
        Alfonz Bartha, tenor; Sándor Palcsó, tenor; Zsolt Bende, baritone; Tibor
        Nádas, bass; Sándor Margittay, organ; and the Budapest Choir; Miklós
        Forrai, conductor. Hungaroton SLPX 1141.
            Although no definitive performance of the *Missa choralis* exists, Forrai
        and the Budapest Choir present an intense, gripping interpretation. The
        recording by Guest and the St. John's College Choir may have more pol-
        ished performers (Argo ZRG 760) but lacks Forrai's insight into the
        composition.

A55.   *Via crucis.* Netherlands Chamber Choir; Reinbert de Leeuw, piano and
        conductor. Philips 416 649 1.
            This great choral work, perhaps Liszt's greatest, is given an authori-
        tative performance on this Philips release with piano accompaniment.
        Dietrich Fischer-Dieskau, baritone, and Aribert Riemann, piano, also give
        a good performance with the RIAS Chamber Choir conducted by Uwe
        Gronostay (Schwann Musica Sacra Ams 3553). For those who prefer a
        performance with organ, Chantal de Zeeuw's recording is rewarding (Pierre
        Verany PV.8292).

A56.   "Choral Works V: Cantatas and Hymns." "The Bells of Strassburg Cathedral"; *Sainte Cécile*; *Cantico del Sol*; *Cantantibus Organis*; and *Psalm CXVI*. Lívia Budai, mezzo-soprano; Klára Takács, contralto; Sándor Sólyom-Nagy, baritone; György Melis, baritone; Sándor Margittay, organ; the Chorus of the Hungarian Radio and Television; and the Budapest Symphony Orchestra; János Ferencsik, conductor. Hungaroton SLPX 11797.

    This disk represents a high point in the Hungaroton series of Liszt's choral works for chorus and orchestra. The soloists are excellent and, under Ferencsik's direction, the combined forces give an exceptionally earnest performance. "The Bells of Strassburg Cathedral" and *Psalm CXVI* are the highlights on this disk that is performed with insight and sensitivity.

A57.   "Choral Works VII." *Salve regina*; *O salutaris hostia*; *Ave verum corpus*; *Ave Maria* (1852); *Ave Maria* (1869); *Pater noster* (1860); *Pater noster* (1869); *Die Seligkeiten*; *Ave maris stella*; *O Roma nobilis*; and *Nun danket alle Gott*. Sándor Sólyom-Nagy, baritone; Gábor Lehotka, organ; the Chorus "Jeunesses Musicales"; Pál Petz and Zoltán Szücs, trumpets; Tivadar Sztán, István Bazsinka, and György Kriska, trombones; László Szabó, tuba; Ferenc Pusztai, timpani; and Gábor Ugrin, conductor. Hungaroton SLPX 12234.

    This inspired recording of eleven of the shorter choral works is essential to those unfamiliar with Liszt's intense piety. The majority of these works are unaccompanied or accompanied only by organ and possess a warmth and simplicity missing from a significant portion of Liszt's large-scale works for chorus and orchestra. This record serves as one of the best introductions to Liszt's choral music; it is enthusiastically recommended.

<u>F. Arrangements, Paraphrases, and Transcriptions</u> (see also Chapters XIV and XIX)

A58.   Beethoven-Liszt: Symphony No. 5. Glenn Gould, piano. Columbia MS7095.

    At one time this recording was the only recording of Liszt transcriptions of Beethoven symphonies. Now, with numerous performances of these transcriptions available, especially on the Telefunken label, Gould's performance remains the best. The rich orchestral palette of piano colors and the life he brings to this transcription create a towering performance. Simply put, no one else has done for these symphonies what Gould has done for the Fifth. The first movement of the Sixth Symphony that Gould recorded for his "Silver Jubilee Album" (Columbia 2-CBS M2X 35914) only makes us wish he had recorded the entire work, as well as the remaining seven symphonies. See also item A91.

A59.   "Liszt: Complete Concert Paraphrases on Operas by Verdi." Fantasies on
         Rigoletto, Ernani, Il trovatore, I lombardi, Aida, Don Carlo, and *Simone
         Boccanegra.* Claudio Arrau, piano. Philips 6500 368.
         Arrau presents a scintillating performance of these transcriptions, cap-
         turing the drama inherent within Verdi's scenes. The "Miserere" from *Il
         trovatore* and the "Danza sacra" from *Aida* soar in their poignancy.
         Rigoletto is given a noble and immensely beautiful portrayal.
         Barenboim's (DG 2531 271) and Bolet's (Decca 410 257-2) performances
         of the *Rigoletto* paraphrase are also of special importance.

A60.   [Wagner Concert Paraphrases.] The "Spinning Song" from *Der fliegende
         Holländer*; the "Bridal March" from *Lohengrin*; "Feierlicher Marsch" from
         Parsifal, etc., etc. Michele Campanella, piano. Pye PCNH 2.
         Campanella gives bravura performances of these transcriptions; he is
         particularly effective in the "Spinning Song" and the "Liebestod" from
         Tristan. Bolet also has recorded a majestic *Tannhäuser* Overture, among
         the best available (RCA ARL2 0512). Kocsis (Philips 9500 970),
         Barenboim (DG 2532 100), and Johansen (Artists Direct 38) also have
         excellent single disks devoted to transcriptions of Wagner's music dramas.

A61.   "Concert Paraphrases of Schubert Lieder." *Auf dem Wasser zu singen*;
         Aufenthalt; *Der Erlkönig*; *Die Forelle*; *Horch, horch! die Lerch*; etc., etc.
         Jorge Bolet, piano. Decca SXDL 7569.
         Bolet has long been known for his Liszt transcriptions. His 1973 RCA
         release (LSC 3259) proved that. He is simply superb in this recording of
         selected Schubert songs, creating warm, singing lines throughout. Berman
         also has a splendid selection of six transcriptions on Everest 3407 (or
         Quintessence 7155); for those who can not get too much of Schubert via
         Liszt, Johansen's five-record set of sixty songs should prove enjoyable
         (Artist Direct 41-45).

A62.   "The Daemonic Liszt." *Réminiscences de Don Juan*; *Réminiscences de
         Robert le diable* (Valse infernale); the Waltz from Gounod's *Faust*; and
         selected original Liszt piano works. Earl Wild, piano. Vanguard VCS
         10041.
         Wild's best Liszt performance. His "Robert" displays phenomenal
         octave playing, and the "Mephisto Polka" is absolutely delightful. Barere
         also presents an explosive version of the Waltz from Gounod's *Faust* on
         Turnabout (THS 65001). Petri also gives a fascinating account of the
         Waltz, as well as of the "Wedding March" and "Elfin Chorus" from
         Mendelssohn's *Midsummer Night's Dream* (Westminster MCA 1414).

A63.   Berlioz-Liszt: *Symphonie fantastique*, Op. 14. Idil Biret, piano. Finnadar SR 9023.

It is hard to believe this piano transcription is so successful when one thinks of the marvelous orchestral effects Berlioz created in this symphony. Biret gives an heroic performance of this immensely difficult work. Aldo Bennici, viola, and Daniel Rivera, piano, also present a strong performance of Liszt's transcription of Berlioz's *Harold in Italy* (Musical Heritage Society MHS 4606).

A64.   "Operatic Fantasies for Piano Four Hands and Two Pianos." *Réminiscences de Don Juan*; *Réminiscences de Norma*; *Fantaisie des motifs favoris de l'opera La Somnambula*; and "Tscherkessenmarsch" from *Ruslan and Ludmilla*. Richard and John Contiguglia, pianos. Connoisseur Society CS 2039.

The Contiguglia brothers have a great deal of fun with these transcriptions, especially "Don Juan." Their playing is energetic, expressive, and technically secure. The Labeque sisters also give an excellent performance of "Don Juan" and an absolutely stunning rendition of the "Two Episodes from Lenau's *Faust*" (Angel DS 38059).

A65.   "Hungarian Rhapsodies" Nos. 1-6, transcribed by F. Doppler. The London Symphony Orchestra; Antal Dorati, conductor. Philips Festivo 6570 140. Also: Mercury 75018 and 75089.

This release contains a fine set of "Rhapsodies." Dorati captures the ethnic flavor and flamboyance necessary for these works to succeed. Bernstein's "Hungarian Rhapsody" No. 1 and Ormandy's No. 2 are extremely extroverted performances (Columbia 60159), and Karajan and the Berlin Philharmonic Orchestra are also exciting, if less flamboyant, in Nos. 4-5 (DG 2530 698).

LISZT RECORDINGS ON COMPACT DISKS

By Keith Fagan

The Liszt literature available on compact disks (or CDs) is growing rapidly. At the present time there are already more outstanding recordings available than can be described below. The recordings below are discussed roughly according to the order of compositions described in Chapters XIV-XIX. Several supplementary recent CD issues are described at the end of the present chapter:

<u>A. Original Works for Piano</u> (see also Chapter XIV)

A66.   Sonata in b minor; *Légendes*; and *La lugubre gondola* Nos. 1 and 2. Alfred Brendel, piano. Philips 410 040-2.
        See also item A17.
        There are many ways of playing Liszt's great Sonata, and there are many interesting recordings revealing different facets of it. General consensus, however, agrees that Brendel's towering, magisterial yet also sensitively lyrical performance penetrates to the heart of the music. The same is true of the two "St. Francis Legends" and the two brooding late pieces.

A67.   *Etudes d'exécution transcendante* [complete]. Claudio Arrau, piano. Philips 416 458-2.
        Maestro Arrau brings his incomparable wealth of experience and musical wisdom to this recording of Liszt's awesome etudes. There are other recorded versions, but Arrau's overwhelming authority and radiant pianism put the Philips disk in a class by itself.

A68.   "Dante" sonata; and "Polish Songs of Frédéric Chopin" [complete]. Claudio Arrau, piano. Philips 411 055-2.
        The same comments apply made in connection with Arrau's etudes (item A67) apply to this recording. Any fears that this performer's approach may be too heavy for the charming Chopin transcriptions can be laid aside. One aspect of deeply serious musicianship is, after all, the recognition that some music of a lighter nature requires charm and elegance for its performance; these are the qualities that inform Arrau's recording of the Chopin-Liszt Polish songs.

A69.   *Années de pèlerinage: Suisse* [complete]. Jorge Bolet, piano. Decca 410 160-2.

Emanating from a different school of piano playing than Arrau and Brendel, yet equally valid and stimulating in his interpretations, Bolet has put his long experience with Liszt's music at Decca's disposal for a masterly, probably historic series of Liszt recordings. This CD of the *Années*, Book I, is a glowing example. See also item A70 (below) and item A21.

A70.   *Années de pèlerinage: Italie* [complete]. Jorge Bolet, piano. Decca 410 161-2.

Liszt's genius was such that the second book of the *Années* generates a completely different musical atmosphere from the first book (see item A69 above). Bolet's performances, as serene as they are transcendental, highlight this aspect of Liszt's astonishing creativity. See also item A21.

A71.   *Venezia e Napoli* [Gondoliera, Canzone, Tarantella]; *Les jeux d'eau à la Villa d'Este*; *Bénédiction de Dieu dans la solitude*; and Ballade No. 2 in b minor. Jorge Bolet, piano. Decca 411 803-2.

This beautiful recital brings together the sunny supplement to the second book of the *Années*, the best-known piece from the more esoteric third book, the most serene masterpiece from the *Harmonies poétiques et religieuses* (arguably the most sublimely lovely composition for piano solo in Liszt's entire output), and the great second Ballade. A recital of very great music played by a master and marvellously recorded, on no account to be missed.

A72.   "Paganini Etudes" [complete]. Brahms: *Variations on a Theme of Paganini*, Books I and II. Michael Ponti, piano. Meridian CDE 84101.

Made some time ago, Michael Ponti's many recordings of almost everything by everybody (largely in Vox Box collections) may have created the unfortunate and inaccurate impression that he is a vacile pianist who fails to penetrate to the core of the music he plays. This excellently engineered recent CD disproves these rumors. A convenient collection on a single disk of the most famous and distinguished of the piano solo compositions based on Paganini's violin works.

A73.   "Paganini Etudes" [complete; 1838 version]. Chopin: *Souvenir de Paganini*. Schumann: *Sechs Concert-Etuden nach Capricen von Paganini*, Op. 10. Nikolai Petrov, piano. Olympia QCD 144.

One of the most enterprising piano CDs in the catalog, this stunningly performed and splendidly recorded issue brings together the fascinating early version of Liszt's "Paganini Etudes"—in which *La Campanella* in particular is an almost totally different composition from the later and better-known version—and the very rarely heard but unjustly neglected Op. 10 Paganini studies by Schumann. The Chopin piece has been recorded before and is no more than a pretty trifle, but it does make a charming introduction here to the bigger and better pieces.

A74.   Three "Petrarch Sonnets" [1837-1839 version]; *La lugubre gondola* Nos. 1 and 2; *En rêve*; *Nuages gris*; Bagatelle sans tonalité; "Five Hungarian Folk Songs"; *Mosonyis Grabgeleit*; *Dem Andenken Petöfis*; and *Csárdás macabre*. Robert Sherlaw Johnson, piano. Proudsound PROU CD 120 02.

   Another enterprising issue devoted to very early and very late Liszt. Listening here to the uninhibited opulence and exuberance of the original versions of the "Petrarch Sonnets," one may wonder whether the later versions are better or merely different. Johnson is an excellent pianist who plays with great authority and conviction (to my ears rather in the Petri mould); he finishes the recital with one of the most impressive performances of the *Csárdás macabre* on record.

A75.   Complete Waltzes; and *Bagatelle sans tonalité*. Leslie Howard, piano. Hyperion CDA 66201.

   In addition to his forward-looking serious works, Liszt was also a purveyor of light music which, in many cases, was equally progressive. Most of these waltzes qualify as light music; the brilliant Leslie Howard approaches them with the right mixture of exuberance, virtuosity, and sheer charm. Howard also plays Liszt's additions to the first Mephisto Waltz.

In addition to these fine recordings of Liszt's piano pieces, three CDs deserve special attention:

A76.   "Liszt the Virtuoso." CD1: Sonata in b minor; Polonaise No. 2 (with coda by Busoni); *La leggierezza*; *Un sospiro*; *Gnomenreigen*; and *Waldesrauschen*. CD2: "Transcendental Etudes" Nos. 2, 7, 9-10, and 3; "Hungarian Rhapsodies" Nos. 4, 12 and 2. Earl Wild, piano. Etcetera KTC 2010.

   During the Liszt centenary year Earl Wild performed three well-constructed recitals which he called "Liszt the Virtuoso," "Liszt the Transcriber," and "Liszt the Poet." Fortunately Etcetera recorded all of them; these three splendid recitals will not be lost in the mists of time. See also items A77-A78 (below).

*   "Liszt the Transcriber."
          See item A95.

A77.   "Liszt the Poet." CD1: *Les jeux d'eau à la Villa d'Este*; *Consolation* No.
         3 in D-flat Major; "Dante" sonata; "Petrarch Sonnets"; *Mephisto Polka*.
         CD2: Ballade No. 2 in b minor; *Liebestraum* No. 3; *Valse oubliée* No. 1;
         Funérailles; *Liebestraum* No. 2; and "Mephisto Waltz" No. 1. Earl Wild,
         piano. Etcetera KTC 2012.
              Wild has very much his own way with some of this music. For exam-
         ple, he invents an exquisite melody of his own at the top of the keyboard
         to which the final page of 'Petrarch Sonnet" No. 123 serves as an
         accompaniment; and he plays a thrilling—and very Lisztian—ending of his
         own to the first "Mephisto Waltz." Purists will deplore this sort of thing;
         Wild is only following Liszt, who would often improvise passages he had
         not actually written in the score. It is certainly not a practice to be re-
         commended to every present-day pianist, but Wild is steeped in Liszt's
         music and style, one of just a handful of pianists to whom licence of this
         kind may be readily permitted.

B. Original Works for Organ (see also Chapter XV)

A78.   [Various organ works.] CD1: "BACH" Prelude and Fugue; *Consolations*
         in D-flat Major and E Major; *Zur Trauung*; *Gebet (Ave Maria)*; *Missa pro
         organo* [complete]; *Tu es Petrus*; *Ora pro nobis*; *Ave Maria (nach
         Arcadelt)*. CD2: Fantasy and Fugue on "Ad nos, ad salutarem undam";
         Evocation à la Chapelle Sixtine; *Praeludium*; *Ave maris stella*; *Salve
         Regina*; *Trauerode*. Zsigmond Szathmáry, organist, playing the Seifert or-
         gan in the Kevelaer Basilica. EMI CDS 7 47533 8.
              A useful, well-performed and -recorded compendium of organ works
         by Liszt which can be thoroughly recommended.

C. Original Works for Orchestra and other Instrumental Ensembles (see also
   Chapter XVI)

A79.   A *Faust* symphony. Siegfried Jerusalem. tenor; the Chicago Symphony
         Orchestra and Chorus (Chorus mistress: Margaret Hillis); Sir Georg Solti,
         conductor. Decca 417 399-2(DH).
              Of many fine recordings of the *Faust* symphony, this one with Solti
         would be difficult to surpass. The performance is an exultant one by a
         great orchestra displaying notable musicianship and virtuosity in every
         department, and the recording quality is warm, rich, and sumptuous. See
         also items A38-A39.

A80.   *Dante* Symphony. Veronika Kincses, soprano; Ladies of the Hungarian
        Radio and Television Chorus (Chorus master: Ferenc Sapszon); and the
        Budapest Symphony Orchestra; György Lehel, conductor. Hungaroton
        HCD 11918-2.

        Another Hungaroton reissue to commemorate the hundredth anniver-
        sary of Liszt's death; the original recording dates from about a decade ago.
        It was always one of the most distinguished performances of the *Dante*
        symphony in an excellent recording and now takes on a new and deserved
        lease on life as a CD. See also item A40.

A81.   Symphonic Poems. CD1: *Ce qu'on entend sur la montagne, Tasso, Les
        préludes.* CD2: *Orpheus, Prometheus, Mazeppa, Festklänge.* CD3: *Héroïde
        funébre, Hungaria, Hamlet.* CD4: *Hunnenschlacht, Die Ideale, Von der
        Wiege bis zum Grabe.* CD5: *Zwei Episoden aus Lenaus Faust; Zweiter
        Mephisto-Walzer; Szózat und Hymnus.* The Budapest Symphony Orches-
        tra; Árpád Joó, conductor. Hungaroton HCD 12677-81-2.

        There have been other distinguished recordings of the complete Sym-
        phonic Poems, but this is the first to appear on CD. The sound quality is
        superb and the performances thoroughly idiomatic and convincing. The
        fifth disk contains the rarely heard *Nächtliche Zug*, the "Mephisto Waltz"
        No. 2, and *Szózat und Hymnus*—an added bonus. See also item A41.

A82.   "Karajan Collection." CD1: *Mephisto-Walzer, Les Préludes, Ungarische
        Fantasie* (Shura Cherkassky, piano); "Hungarian Rhapsody" No. 5. CD2:
        Mazeppa; "Hungarian Rhapsody" No. 2; *Tasso*; "Hungarian Rhapsody"
        No. 4. The Berlin Philharmonic Orchestra; Herbert von Karajan, con-
        ductor. Deutsche Grammophon 415 967-2 (GH2).

        The earliest of these performances dates from 1961, the latest from
        1976. They have never been absent from the catalog and are already es-
        tablished gramophone classics. With CD remastering and complete free-
        dom from extraneous noises, these splendid, exuberant performances now
        sound as good as new.

A83.   Piano Concertos Nos. 1 and 2; "3 Concert Etudes." Claudio Arrau, piano;
        the London Symphony Orchestra; Sir Colin Davis, conductor. Philips 416
        461-2.

        Recordings of the Liszt concertos, even on CD, are legion, so selecting
        the best is an almost impossible task. One of the reasons for choosing this
        version is that the two Concertos alone are rather brief for a CD, and
        Philips has remedied this by including Arrau's fine recording of the 1848
        "Concert Etudes" (played with additions to *Un sospiro* made by Liszt later
        in life). The performances of the Concertos are among the most magisterial
        and powerful ever committed to record and demonstrate Liszt's greatness

as a composer far better than many other recorded versions. See also items A45-A47.

<u>D. Original Works for Solo Voice</u> (see also Chapter XVII)

A84.   [Songs.] Hildegard Behrens, soprano; and Cord Garben, piano. Deutsche Grammophon 419 240-2.
>   Also described as item A50.
>   A most distinguished and beautifully recorded recital of Liszt's songs with the magnificent *Jeanne d'Arc au Bûcher* as its centrepiece, surrounded by a well chosen group of familiar and less familiar songs.

A85.   "Petrarch Sonnets" Nos. 47, 104, and 123 (Philippe Huttenlocher, baritone); *Angiolin dal biondo crin, Du bist wie eine Blume, Vergiftet sind meine Lieder* (Ernst Haefliger, tenor); *Wie singt die Lerche schön, Die tote Nachtigall, Wo weilt Er?* (Donna Brown, soprano); *Ich möchte hingeh'n* (Ernst Haefliger); *Wer nie sein Brot mit Tränen aß, Die Vätergruft* (Philippe Huttenlocher); *Über allen Gipfeln ist Ruh, Es rauschen die Winde, Die Loreley* (Magali Damonte, mezzo-soprano). Cyril Huvé, piano. Cluny LU C31-HM 85.
>   This recital is as enterprising as it is well performed and recorded. The use of the 1850 Erard piano adds a touch of period authenticity; this disk may enshrine the kind of sound Liszt had in mind when he wrote these songs. The "Petrarch Sonnets" are here given in the late version.

<u>E. Original Works for Vocal Ensembles</u> (see also Chapter XVIII)

A86.   *Don Sanche.* Gérard Garino (Don Sanche); Júlia Hamari (Elzire); and István Gáti (Alidor and A Knight); the Hungarian Radio and Television Chorus (Chorus Master: Ferenc Sapszon) and the Hungarian State Opera Orchestra; Tamás Pál, conductor. Hungaroton HCD 12744-45-2.
>   A rarity unlikely to be repeated on record, this enchanting performance of Liszt's only opera is a sheer delight. Liszt was little more than a child when he wrote this opera; the style is obviously derivative of contemporary composers such as Donizetti, but Liszt shows a winsome melodic gift and a lightness of touch in the composition.

A87.   *Christus.* The Hungarian State Orchestra and soloists, with Antal Doráti. Hungaroton HCD 12831-33-2.
>   Also described as item A51.
>   Not the only recording of *Christus*, even on CD, but a fine performance and an excellent recording. One of the most important issues from

Hungaroton in their very distinguished series of Liszt recordings made available at or about the time of the 1986 centenary celebrations.

A88.   *Die Legende von der heiligen Elisabeth*. The Hungarian State Orchestra and soloists, with Arpád Joó. Hungaroton HCD 12694-96-2.
Also described as item A52.
Like *Christus*, not the only recording of *St. Elizabeth* but, so far, the only one on CD. A splendid performance and recording with the great Éva Marton using her big, rich, opulent vocal equipment to superb advantage in Liszt's service and demonstrating a versatility that shows her as much at home with Liszt's tender Elizabeth as she is with Puccini's terrifying Turandot.

A89.   "Gran" Mass. Veronika Kincses, soprano; Klára Takács, contralto; György Korondy, tenor; József Gregor, bass; the Hungarian Radio and Television Chorus (Chorus master: Ferenc Sapszon); and the Budapest Symphony Orchestra, with Sándor Margittay, organ; János Ferencsik, conductor. Hungaroton HCD 11861-2.
Another Hungaroton issue commemorating the hundredth anniversary of Liszt's death, this excellent performance was first issued in 1977. The CD transfer is impeccable and makes what was originally a good recording sound even better.

A90.   "Hungarian Coronation Mass." The Budapest Symphony Orchestra and soloists, with György Lehel. Hungaroton HCD 12148-2.
Also described as item A53.
Another CD reissue, this one from a 1980 LP. Like the Gran Mass, so far the only performance on record. Once again an excellent performance and recording.

<u>F. Transcriptions, Arrangements, and Paraphrases</u> (see also Chapter XIX)

A91.   Beethoven-Liszt: Symphonies Nos. 4 and 8. Alain Planès, piano. Harmonia Mundi HMC 901194.
Perhaps the most important and ingenious of Liszt's transcriptions were his arrangements of the Beethoven symphonies. All nine have been recorded, but this sparkling CD of two of the most uninhibited of them is at once exciting and convincing. See also item A58.

A92.   "The Virtuoso Piano Paraphrases." Schubert: *Die Forelle, Horch! Horch! Die Lerch.* Chopin: *Meine Freuden, Mädchens Wunsch.* Schumann:

Widmung, etc., etc., as well as Liszt's *Consolations* and *Liebestraum* No. 3. Jorge Bolet, piano. enSayo 3406.

Some of the most tuneful and popular of Liszt's transcriptions are played here by Bolet as they should be played: with charm, elegance, and the virtuosity that disguises virtuosity.

A93.   World Première Recordings: Fantasy on *Der Freischütz* (Weber); Concert Paraphrase on *Ernani* (Verdi) [1847 version]; *Spanisches Ständchen*; "Fantasy on Italian Operatic Melodies"; Romance in e minor; "Schwanengesang und Marsch" from *Hunyadi László* (Erkel). Andreas Pistorius, piano. Capriccion 10 076.

The interest of this disk is revealed in its title. (In fact the Romance in e minor, an early version of the *Romance oubliée*, was recorded earlier.) Of the "Fantasy on Italian Operatic Melodies" the accompanying booklet confesses that neither the date of composition nor the sources of the original tunes are known. Not that it matters: the "Fantasy" is a rousing, tuneful piece and, like the other works on this disk, excellently performed and recorded.

A94.   Schubert-Liszt: *Soirées de Vienne* No. 2. Rossini-Liszt: *Soirées musicales* (Part 1: La Promessa, Il rimprovero, La partenza, L'orgia, L'invito, La pastorella dell'Alpi; La gita in gondola, La danza). Schubert-Liszt: *Soirées de Vienne* No. 7. Rossini-Liszt: *Soirées musicales* (Part 2: La regatta Veneziana, La pesca, La serenata, Li marinari). Schubert-Liszt: *Soirées de Vienne* No. 8. Jenö Jandó piano. Hungaroton HCD 12916-2.

These charming, unpretentious pieces are very rarely played; for a comprehensive conspectus of Liszt's art as a whole, however, it is necessary to consider his light music as well as his more profound works. This desirable disk is as enchanting as it is unusual.

A95.   "Liszt the Transcriber." CD1: Beethoven-Liszt: Symphony No. 1. Liszt-Liszt: *Die Loreley*. Schumann-Liszt: *Frühlingsnacht* and *Widmung*. Chopin-Liszt: *Mes joies*. Schubert-Liszt: *Du bist die Ruh*. Wagner-Liszt: "Spinning Song" from *Der fliegende Holländer*. CD2: Weber-Liszt: Overture to *Der Freischütz*. Paganini-Liszt: Etudes Nos. 2, 5 (La Chasse), and 3 (La Campanella). Bach-Liszt: Fantasia and Fugue in g minor. Schubert-Liszt: *Soirées de Vienne* No. 7. Verdi-Liszt: *Rigoletto* paraphrase. Earl Wild, piano. Etcetera KTC 2011.

Wild can perhaps be equalled in this sort of thing by a master like Bolet, but he can scarcely be surpassed. Rarities in this recital include the Beethoven-Liszt Symphony No. 1 and the Bach-Liszt Fantasy.

G. Supplementary entries

Since this discography was drafted (November 1988), many more CD issues of Liszt's music have appeared on the market. This supplement deals with a few of the most notable of them:

A96.   [Ballades, Legends, and Polonaises.] Also includes the Impromptu in F-sharp and the *Klavierstück* in A-flat Major [world premiere recording]. Leslie Howard, piano. Hyperion CDA 66301.

        Leslie Howard has announced that he intends to record the complete original works of Liszt for solo piano. If he does, and if all the disks are as good as this one and the Liszt Waltzes (item A75), his will indeed be a notable accomplishment. Even if this disk were not part of a series, it would constitute a most beautifully and intelligently planned recital in its own right. Howard is an ideal Liszt pianist, combining profound scholarship with transcendental virtuosity, and his recordings (even when they are not exclusively of Liszt's music—e.g., "Rare Piano Encores" on Hyperion CDA 66090) are always important additions to the recorded repertory of piano music.

A97.   "Mephisto Waltz" No. 1; *Tarantelle* from *Venezia e Napoli*; *Rhapsodie espagnole; Pensée des mortes*; and the *Légendes*. Stephen Hough, piano. Virgin Classics VC 7 90700-2.

        Born in 1961, Stephen Hough has already made his mark as a virtuoso of the first rank with his much-praised recording of the Hummel A-minor and B-minor concertos on Chandos CHAN 8507. Now, on this CD, he turns in a collection of Liszt performances second to none and demonstrates in the second part of the recital that he understands the deeper workings of Liszt's mind. He is completely in command of the brilliance and exuberance required for the *Tarantella* and the "Spanish Rhapsody."

A98.   "Hungarian Rhapsodies"; and *Magyar dallok*. Setrak, piano. Le Chant du Monde LDC 278.801/3.

        Neither the most immediately obvious recommendation for a set of the "Rhapsodies," nor the most blatantly virtuosic, but unquestionably one of the most interesting and scholarly recordings available. The first CD interposes the *Elégie héroique*, No. 12 of the *Magyar rhapsodiák*, between "Hungarian Rhapsodies" Nos. 4-5, giving us an opportunity to compare "Rhapsody" No. 5 with its earlier version. Also included on the third CD are the "Roumanian" rhapsody and *Magyar dallok* Nos. 1-3, 6, and 8-10. Setrak has supplied his own cadenzas for the "Hungarian Rhapsody" No. 2 and for *Magyar dallok* No. 6. By any standards, therefore, this is a most interesting issue, presented to us by a virtuoso who can overcome with consummate ease the mechanical difficulties presented by these pieces, and who always plays with great clarity and conviction. NB: Some of the tempi

Setrak adopts in this recording and his general style of playing suggest that he wants much more to interpret the music as he wishes rather than to "play to the gallery."

A99. Piano Concertos Nos. 1 and 2; and *Totentanz*. Krystian Zimerman, piano; the Boston Symphony Orchestra; Seiji Ozawa, conductor. Deutsche Grammophon 423 571-2.

Although the superb Arrau version of the two Concertos already appears in this chapter (item A83), the recording here referred to includes the *Totentanz*. Krystian Zimerman is among the finest master pianists of the younger generation, and the orchestral parts are performed with more than usual commitment and virtuosity. This is a magnificent, authoritative, and splendidly recorded version of these works that might well become a recording classic.

A100. "Marches." March from *Mazeppa*; "Hungarian Quick March"; "March Paying Homage"; "Rákóczy March," etc., etc. Brass Band of the Hungarian People's Army; László Dohos and László Marosni, conductors. Hungaroton HCD 16722.

The English titles are taken verbatim from the back cover of the CD itself; no catalog numbers are given, and identification is not as easy as it might be. However, this is of no great importance; all the tracks are transcriptions, prepared for the most part by the conductors themselves and performed with panache and temperament. This may not be one of the more serious, scholarly recordings of Liszt's music, but it is certainly one of the most exuberant and entertaining, and it is included here for that reason.

§

In addition to these discographical entries the following item is included because of the large number of compositions it contains and the intrinsic interest of many of them:

A101. "The Compositions of Franz Liszt as Performed by the Legendary Masters of the Piano." Produced by Walter S. Heebner and Recorded Treasures, Inc., of Studio City, California. No catalog number available.

A set of seven phonorecords containing dozens of pieces, many performed by Liszt pupils or early twentieth-century pianists associated by reputation with Liszt's music. Uneven but fascinating. NB: Some performances may have been "doctored": see Kent Holliday's lengthy review of this set of records in the *Journal of the American Liszt Society* 22 (1987), pp. 46-61. Holliday's article also contains a complete list of contents.

INDEX OF AUTHORS AND EDITORS

All entries refer to item numbers. Editors are indicated by "ed." (in parentheses).
Numbers in parentheses refer to studies discussed under—not as—individual items.
Page numbers are given only for items mentioned outside bibliographic citations;
only titles and page-number citations are *italicized*. Titles are given only when no
author's or editor's name is available.

SUBJECT INDEX

All entries refer to item numbers. Only subjects—not authors or editors—are indexed, and all subjects relate to Liszt. Titles of compositions, whether *italicized* or placed inside quotation marks, are indexed only when entire items are devoted to them.

Portugal: 498. *See also* "Iberia"
Postage stamps: 291-292
Prague: 434
Prelude on "Chopsticks": 845
Préludes, Les: 323, 329, 345, 909, 950
Preludio funèbre: 843
Preßburg: *See* "Bratislava"
Previously unpublished documents:
   211, 254-268, 516, 1072
Printed music: 346-349
Programmism and semiotics:
   660-669
Prometheus: 343, 910-911
Protestant music and musicians:
   572-573, 687, 859
Provence: 449
Psalm 129: 298
Psalm settings: 981
Psychology: *See* "Character studies"
Pupils: 574, 593, 1047-1051

Quand du chants: 304b
Quatre élémens, Les: 950

Raff, Joachim: 212
Raiding: 72-73. 87, 398, 408-409
Ravel, Maurice: 715
Recordings: A1-A101.
Reger, Max: 1033
Religion [and religious music]:
   534-540, 608, 654-657, 946ff.
Reminiscences: 226-252, 366, 1047
Research reports: 105-129, 384
Reviews [and related studies]: 29,
   130-135
   Of musical editions: 154-164
Revisions: 322-345, 471, 607, 609,
   612, 638, 789-790, 905, 939
Revive Szégedin!: 153
Rheinweinlied: 307
Rhineland [Germany]: 471
Romance: 310
Romantic movement: 523
Rome: 76-78, 501-502, 504, 506
Rossini, Giacchomo: 695, 1021
Rouen: 451
Rumania: *See* "Balkans"

Russia [and Russian music]: 510-513,
   739-741
R.W.—Venezia: 835

Saint-Circq, Caroline: 550
Saint-Saëns, Camille: 716
Saint-Simonism: 524
Sand, George: 170, 422
Sayn-Wittgenstein, Carolyne: 186d-g,
   202, 547-549
Schlesinger, Maurice: 564
Schmalhausen, Lina: 551
Schubert, Franz: 300, 312, 696, 1006,
   1022-1025
Schumann, Robert: 555-556, 717
Scotland: 514
Semiotics: *See* "Programmism and
   semiotics"
Siegesmarsch: 304a
Sketch studies: 301, 315-321
Skriabin, Alexander: 718
Slavic music: 742-743
Smetana, Bedřich: 719-721
Sonata form: *See* "Form and
   structure"
Sonata in b minor: 147, 162,
   293-294, 773-788
Sondershausen: 464
Songs: 145f, 151, 325, 926-941
Sopron: 101
Spain: *See* "Iberia"
Sposalizio: 807
Stavenhagen, Bernhard: 574
Steiermark [Austria]: 427
"St. Francis Legends": 840, 1033
St. Gallen [Switzerland]: 518
Stockholm: 92
St. Stanislaus: 980
Street-Klindworth, Agnès: 186c, 201,
   552
Streicher, J.B.: 575
Studia musicologica: 44
Survey studies:
   Articles: 23-29
   Books: 1-23, 479-481, 608, 761
Switzerland: 245, 515-519, 591
Symphonic poems: 662, 725, 884-912